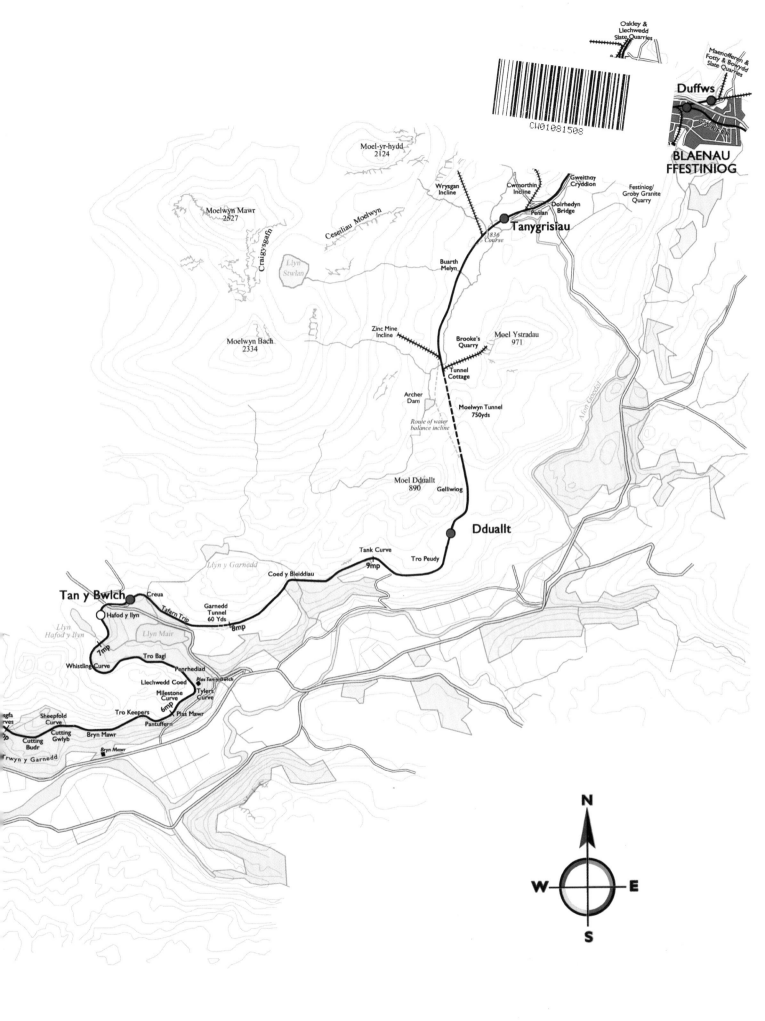

Moel-yr-hydd
2124

Oakley &
Llechwedd
Slate Quarries

Maenofferen &
Fotty & Bowydd
Slate Quarries

Duffws

**BLAENAU
FFESTINIOG**

Moelwyn Mawr
2527

Craigysgafn

Ceseiliau Moelwyn

Llyn
Stwlan

Wrysgan
Incline

Cwmorthin
Incline

Gweithay
Cryddion

Penlan

Doirhedyn
Bridge

Festiniog/
Groby Granite
Quarry

*1836
Course*

Tanygrisiau

Buarth
Melyn

Moelwyn Bach
2334

Zinc Mine
Incline

Brooke's
Quarry

Moel Ystradau
971

Tunnel
Cottage

Archer
Dam

Moelwyn Tunnel
750yds

*Route of water
balance incline*

Moel Dduallt
890

Gelliwiog

Dduallt

Tank Curve

Tro Peudy

Llyn y Garnedd

Coed y Bleiddiau

9mp

Tan y Bwlch

Creua

Tafarn Trip

Garnedd
Tunnel
60 Yds

8mp

Hafod y llyn

Llyn
Hafod y llyn

Llyn Mair

7mp

Tro Bagl

Whistling
Curve

Penrhediad

Llechwedd Coed

Milestone
Curve

Plas Tan-y-Bwlch

Tyler's
Curve

6mp

Plas Mawr

sgfa
ves

Sheepfold
Curve

Tro Keepers

Pantuffern

Cutting
Budr

Cutting
Gwlyb

Bryn Mawr

Bryn Mawr

rwyn y Garnedd

N

W E

S

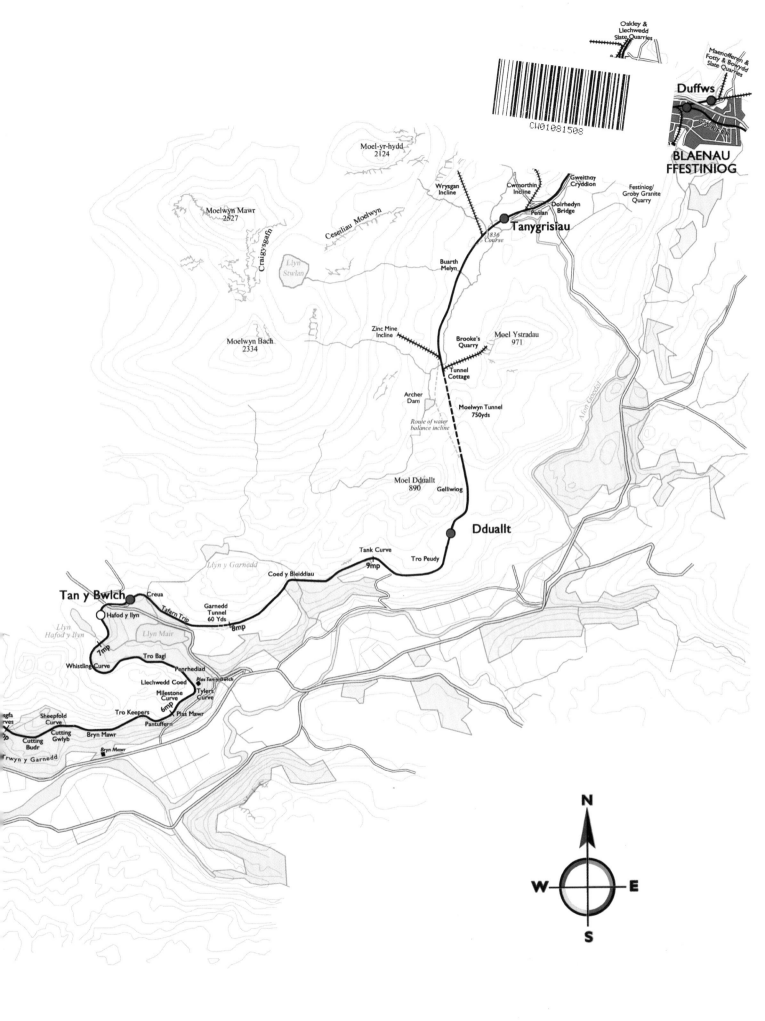

at the same time.

© Gordon Rushton 2016 : Main reference source OS Maps of 19th Century and Michael Seymour's definitive FR Map.

FESTINIOG RAILWAY

FROM SLATE RAILWAY TO HERITAGE OPERATION 1921 - 2014

FESTINIOG RAILWAY

FROM SLATE RAILWAY TO HERITAGE OPERATION 1921 - 2014

Peter Johnson

PEN & SWORD
TRANSPORT

First published in Great Britain in 2017 by
Pen & Sword Transport

An imprint of Pen & Sword Books Ltd
47 Church Street, Barnsley, South Yorkshire S70 2AS

ISBN 978 1 47389 625 3

Pen & Sword Books Ltd incorporates the imprints of Pen & Sword
Archaeology, Atlas, Aviation, Battleground, Discovery, Family History,
History, Maritime, Military, Naval, Politics, Railways, Select, Social History,
Transport, True Crime, and Claymore Press, Frontline Books, Leo Cooper,
Praetorian Press, Remember When, Seaforth Publishing and Wharncliffe.

For a complete list of Pen & Sword titles please contact:
Pen & Sword Books Limited
47 Church Street, Barnsley, South Yorkshire S70 2AS, England
E-mail: enquiries@pen-and-sword.co.uk
Website: www.pen-and-sword.co.uk

Design and typesetting
by Juliet Arthur, www.stimula.co.uk

Printed and bound in India by Replika Press Pvt. Ltd

CONTENTS

PLACE NAMES

Since the 1970s English versions of Welsh place names
have been taken out of use, but they still exist, of course, in
historic documents. Most notably, the railway company
was named Festiniog in its Act of Parliament. Whilst this is
retained for legal purposes, it has become practice to use
the form 'Ffestiniog Railway' in public documents. Here,
the archaic version has been used when relevant.
Porthmadog was originally Port Madock or Port Madoc
and then Portmadoc. Caernarfon was known as
Carnarvon until the 1930s, when it became Caernarvon.
Ffestiniog the place has been standardised as such.

ACKNOWLEDGEMENTS AND SOURCES

The first 90 years of the Ffestiniog Railway's history is covered in *Festiniog Railway The Spooner Era and Afterwards 1830-1920*, also published by Pen & Sword Transport. This book continues the story up to the end of 2014.

Whilst the last sixty years or so is still within memory for many, attempts have been made to apply the same rigour, of referring to original sources, as in the earlier book. Assistance towards this objective has been provided by the company's directors, who kindly gave access to their minutes recording their thoughts and decisions up to 2014, the directors' voices thereby providing a common thread through both books.

Another source of the directors' activities is the reports to shareholders, produced from 1844. Copies of most of these are contained in the company's archive, others at the National Archives, Kew. From

Many thousands of volunteers have given their time and money to the successful revival and operation of the Ffestiniog Railway. Here, member of the society's London area group work on the embankment in December 1966. Soon, the Hafod y Llan wharf, on the left, will be developed and the slate sheds, with red ends, and the Britannia Foundry, right, will be demolished. The white house on the hillside is Morfa Lodge, where James Spooner lived and worked. The wagons are two of the fifteen four-wheeled Hudson wagons obtained from RAF Lichfield in 1963.

Peter Waylett

1970 until 1986 the reports, which then comprised only the accounts, were published in the *Ffestiniog Railway Magazine*. Following the 1986 share issue more-detailed reports have been issued to the expanded pool of shareholders.

I am grateful, too, to the trustees of the Ffestiniog & Welsh Highland Railways Trust, who also allowed me access to their minutes, a great privilege.

The company's archive is a remarkable survival, quite unlike any other from any railway company, containing material about the railway's operations from its earliest days. Whilst it not complete and unable, therefore, to provide all the answers to questions a researcher might raise, it does contain a vast amount of material covering the railway's operations. Access to it, at Gwynedd Council's archives section at Caernarfon, has been greatly facilitated by Patricia Layzell-Ward's catalogue, which often permits documents to be referenced without viewing.

In re-telling the railway's story, the records of the Board of Trade and the Ministry of Transport, both held held at the National Archives, Kew, have been revisited. The Lands Tribunal files dealing with the company's claim for compensation from the Central Electricity Generating Board were also viewed at Kew. Containing much correspondence between the parties, they enabled the dates of incidents or exchanges, previously recorded anecdotally, to be determined.

Deposited plans and other documents were seen at the Parliamentary Archives in the House of Lords.

Copies of some Ministry of Transport inspection reports and the 1968 and 1975 Light Railway Oder plans not deposited in the National Archives were obtained from the Department of Transport in response to Freedom of Information requests.

Accessed online, the *Gazette*, formerly *The London Gazette*, remains the default site for Parliamentary and other public notices.

Noel Walley's chronology of material published in the *Ffestiniog Railway Magazine* between 1958 and 1999 published in 2000 was a most useful aid for dealing with the revival era. Other material was obtained from the *Ffestiniog Railway Magazine*, the British Newspaoer Archive, the *Daily Post* website, the digital archives of *The Times* and *The Guardian*, and my own contributions to *Steam Railway* magazine.
Some use has been made of census and other data available on the Ancestry genealogical website.

Except where noted photographs are from my collection, created over many years. Sadly, some of these have come from the estates of deceased enthusiasts whose identity is unknown. Uncredited photographs in Chapters 11-14 are mine. Many thanks are due to John Hunt, who gave me some of his FR material, and to the late Joe Lloyd, who lent me his 1950s FR negatives to copy.

I wish to extend by sincere thanks to these friends and colleagues for their ongoing support and encouragement and/or assistance with this book: John Alexander, Michael Bishop, Clare Britton, Colin Burtt, Tim Edmonds, Martin Farebrother, Adrian Gray, Alan Heywood, Paul Ingham, Peter Jarvis, Richard Kirk, Paul Lewin, Roderick Low, Stephen Murfitt, Gordon Rushton, Mark Stephenson, Andrew Stephen Thomas, Geoff and Patricia Ward, Michael Whitehouse and John Wooden.

Even for someone familiar with the Ffestiniog Railway's story, compiling this book has been quite an adventure, leading me down many unexpected avenues and widened my view of the railway. There is a great deal of material available, especially covering the past 50 years or so.

My involvement with the *Ffestiniog Railway Magazine* from 1974, as its editor from 1990 until 2003, and as a director of the Ffestiniog Railway Society from 1992 until 2003, provided many insights into the railway's operation and management at critical times, permitting some input from personal knowledge. Dealing with recent events it has become clear that contemporary records often present a nuanced view of events. Hopefully a balance has been struck on what is significant.

Unless stated otherwise, all opinions are mine; they do not represent the views of the Festiniog Railway Company, the Ffestiniog & Welsh Highland Railways Trust or any of the associated bodies. I accept responsibility for any errors.

Peter Johnson
Leicester
March 2017

INTRODUCTION

In the nineteenth century, under the influence and leadership of father and son James and Charles Easton Spooner, the Ffestiniog Railway (FR) set the scene for the use of narrow-gauge railways around the world. Its low capital cost, high dividends and technical innovations attracted attention from rulers, engineers and would-be competitors. When competition arrived a decline set in and the effects of the First World War seriously weakened the company.

The events of the 1920s and 1930s unwittingly started the railway on the road that led to the position in which it finds itself today, making the transition from being a common carrier aligned to the slate industry to become a leading Welsh tourist attraction of international renown.

By the time the Government relinquished its war-time control of the railways in 1921, the FR was well past its best, in debt, and its directors uncertain about the future. The Welsh Highland Railway promoters, who took over that year, could do nothing to reverse the reduction in traffic that had started when the London & North Western Railway had opened its branch to Blaenau Ffestiniog in 1881. Reductions in signalling and shunting costs were to no avail, and an increase in tourist traffic did little to help. Neither did operating the WHR for three years from 1934.

An atmospheric view of a short train passing the ex-Glan y Pwll trident signal post as it heads for Boston Lodge in 1955.

Passenger services, for tourists only since 1930, ended completely on the outbreak of war in 1939, followed by the goods service in 1946. Legal issues left the directors in a quandary, unable to sell the railway for scrap as they had anticipated, and the railway was abandoned. After eight years, railway enthusiast Alan Pegler and friends acquired control of the company and settled the overdraft, planning to restore services with volunteer support from the newly-formed Festiniog Railway Society.

They faced many challenges; the track was overgrown, buildings and rolling stock were in a state of disrepair. The state-owned electricity authority had decided to appropriate a part of the railway's property to construct a reservoir and power station near Tanygrisiau.

Despite legal setbacks over the claim for compensation, which took a record-breaking thirteen years to bring to a satisfactory conclusion, services were resumed and buildings and rolling stock restored. In the 1960s, a substantial boost in passengers encouraged the start of work to build the 2½-mile deviation to bypass the power station and its reservoir.

During the 1970s, local authorities and public bodies came to realise that what were then called preserved railways could make a vital contribution to a locality's economic viability and were therefore worthy of financial support. The FR benefited, and continues to benefit, from this change in attitude, unthinkable in the 1950s.

From the 1970s, the facilities at Boston Lodge were developed to enable the railway to become more self-sufficient in the provision of new carriages and locomotives. After a period of innovation for its own sake, the railway came to appreciate that its key asset was its heritage, albeit that most of its passengers preferred to avoid its heritage rolling stock, favouring modern comforts when they travelled, leading to the construction of carriages with central heating, double glazing and corridor connections that, externally at least, might have been built during the later years of the nineteenth century. At the front of the train, the angular lines of *Earl of Merioneth* (1979) developed into the Spooner-esque *David Lloyd George* (1992), followed by the recreation of *Taliesin* (1999).

Whilst efforts were made to improve the appearance of the railway from the 1980s onwards, there were concerns also about the possible impact if the Welsh Highland Railway came under the control of someone determined to develop it as a competitor. Whilst the news in 1990 that the FR Company had made a secret bid to acquire the WHR trackbed was controversial, the company held its nerve and proceeded to reinstate the 25-mile railway between Caernarfon and Porthmadog between 1997 and 2011.

The WHR development was not without its problems, especially as the railway went through a period of managerial and financial turmoil in the midst of it, but support from the Millennium Commission, the Welsh Government and benefactors, and contributors to a remarkably successful appeal, saw that project completed without incurring debt. The boost in revenues that accompanied the WHR's expansion towards Porthmadog also placed the company in a position where it could redeem its own structural debt.

Enlargement of the station at Porthmadog to provide the accommodation required to operate both the FR and WHR efficiently, enabled by continued support from donors and the Welsh Government, was completed in 2014, a significant point at which to bring this book to a close. Overcoming many obstacles since the 1920s, the railway is now in a sound position where it can plan for the future with confidence, be effective and sustainable, continuing to make its mark in the world, just as it did in the nineteenth century.

CHAPTER 1

1921-1924: THE ARRIVAL OF THE WELSH HIGHLAND RAILWAY

When the motion to remove the Ffestiniog Railway Company from the Railway Bill, which brought about the grouping of railway companies, was put to the House of Lords on 17 August 1921, the reasons given were that the Ffestiniog Railway and two other narrow gauge railways would benefit by being under unified control, that negotiations had been under way for some time and that arrangements had been made to secure this objective. If the FR were to be included in the Western group, as proposed, the unification would be impossible; the three lines should all go in together or go out together. The proposal was accepted on the basis that it was in accordance with the grouping principle of the Bill.

Apart from the FR, the other railways in this narrow-gauge grouping were the Welsh Highland Railway and the Snowdon Mountain Tramroad. When news of the FR's removal from the Western group reached the Commons, J.H. Thomas, MP for Derby, was most vociferous in his objection, alleging that it was an attempt by the North Wales Power & Traction Company to monopolise North Wales. Replying, the minister said that the FR had been the only light railway included in the Bill so it was right to exclude it.

If he meant the only independent narrow-gauge railway then he was right; for the narrow-gauge Leek & Manifold and Welshpool & Llanfair Light Railways, whilst independent, were operated by larger companies and included as subsidiary companies. The independent standard-gauge railways had been excluded from the Bill as a result of pressure applied by lobbying organisations.

The Welsh Highland Railway was the initiative of Evan R. Davies and Henry Joseph Jack. Both were

members of the Carnarvonshire County Council, Davies, a solicitor from Pwllheli, who had been had been involved in some capacity or other in various Caernarfonshire railway schemes since 1897, and Jack the managing director of the Aluminium Corporation at Dolgarrog. Davies was a friend of the Prime Minister, David Lloyd George, and had worked in his private office during the war. He and Jack brought in

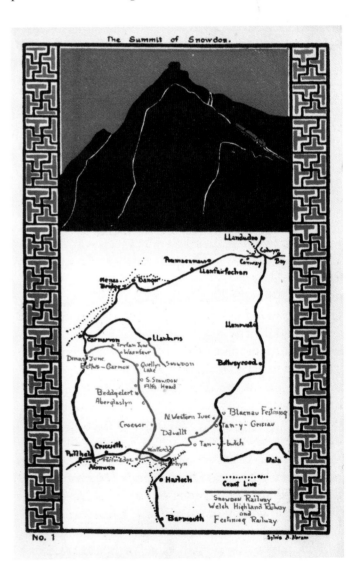

A picture postcard published by the Snowdon Mountain Tramroad in 1923, showing that it and the Welsh Highland and Ffestiniog Railways were in common ownership. (SMTH)

Evan Robert Davies (1871-1934) was a solicitor, local politician and friend of David Lloyd George. He played a key part in the development of the Welsh Highland Railway and in running the FR until his untimely death. He was also keen to promote tourism in Carnarvonshire.

Sir John Henderson Stewart Bt, a Scottish distillery owner, to supply funds and gravitas.

Stewart's involvement is something of a mystery as he had no obvious connection with Wales or Welsh affairs; he may not even have visited Wales. It is quite likely though, that his baronetcy, conferred in the King's birthday honours list announced on 5 June 1920, involved a donation to a political party. In July 1920, he had attended a charity concert at 10 Downing Street and maybe he was then asked to give his support to a project being promoted by a friend of the Prime Minister, that would benefit a relatively remote area of North Wales in which the Prime Minister was interested, as quid pro quo. However, it happened: by the end of the year he was involved in Welsh narrow-gauge railways.

In November 1914, a committee of local authorities had applied for a light railway order that would consolidate the existing powers of the North Wales Narrow Gauge Railways (NWNGR), then moribund, and the Portmadoc, Beddgelert & South Snowdon Railway (PBSSR), a subsidiary of the North Wales

Power Company, with assets including partially constructed earthworks around Beddgelert and the horse-worked Croesor Tramway, with the intention of completing the connection between the NWNGR and the Croesor Tramway to create a 25-mile long 2ft gauge railway from Portmadoc to Caernarfon.

The war had put the application into limbo, allowing Davies and Jack to reactivate it with the declared intention of creating jobs and facilitating tourism to a remote area as well as improving the transport infrastructure. The Aluminium Corporation held the key to the development with its acquisition of a controlling interest in the North Wales Power Company, and therefore the PBSSR assets, in 1918.

Seeking to obtain loans from the Ministry of Transport and the local authorities to fund what they came to call the Welsh Highland Railway (WHR), Davies and Jack needed additional funds to acquire the NWNGR and PBSSR assets, which seems to be the initial reason for Stewart's involvement. They also appear to have realised that their scheme would benefit from the involvement of the Ffestiniog Railway, which had rolling stock that could be beneficial on the new railway, and a functioning workshop.

Keeping the FR out of the proposed railway grouping was therefore essential to getting the WHR off the ground, and was achieved, as already noted, by saying that there was already in existence a grouping of narrow-gauge railways, secure in the knowledge that the Great Western Railway would not want to take on the Welsh Highland.

Stewart had become active in the railways from 1 January 1921, when he acquired the NWNGR and PBSSR assets, and paid £1,500 to keep the NWNGR going. On 21 March, he acquired the majority shareholding of the Snowdon Mountain Tramroad & Hotels Company, which was, fortuitously, on the market, and on 29 March he purchased F. P. Robjent's FR holdings, except for £1,000 ordinary stock to enable Davies and Jack to qualify as directors. Robjent, a stockbroker, had been a director since 1908.

By the end of June, Stewart held £42,999 ordinary stock, £3,660 4½ per cent preference shares and £23,340 5 per cent preference shares, not quite a majority in all classes, but enough to take control. Later in the year, Jack was to tell the Minister of Transport that it had cost £40,000 to take over the FR. Given that in December 1920 ordinary stock had been trading at 15 per cent and 5 per cent preference shares at 80 per cent, it was unlikely to have been that much.

On 15 July, £28,000 ordinary stock, £2,660 4½ per cent preference shares and £15,340 5 per cent preference shares were transferred to Jack, and £14,000 ordinary stock, £1,000 4½ per cent preference shares and £8,000 5 per cent preference shares to Davies, leaving Stewart with just £999 ordinary stock.

News that there was a takeover in the offing had obviously been the subject of gossip and speculation, for on 1 June, the *Lancashire Evening Post* had reported that the LNWR had bought the railway and would start to work it in August!

Jack and Davies formally took control on 16 July. R.M. Greaves, the retiring chairman, had not attended the two directors' meeting held since March and had sold £714 10s 7d ordinary stock and £1,000 4½ per cent preference shares to Robjent on 24 June. The other directors also resigned, with Frederick Vaughan, the managing director, resigning resigning as a director and being appointed as general manager with a salary of £225. Jack was appointed chairman on 30 July. Stewart only attended directors' meetings held in London and ceased to attend them after mid-1922.

Government control of railways ended with the enactment of the Railways Act on 19 August 1921. During 1920, a Major G.C. Spring had been commissioned to report on the condition and prospects of the NWNGR, PBSSR (including the Croesor Tramway) and the FR. Writing to Vaughan on 12 September 1921, he concluded, 'I am afraid that I have discovered nothing that was not fully known before.' His report ended, 'It is fairly obvious that before further extensions are considered the Ffestiniog Railway must first be placed in a paying condition.' It is not known who commissioned and paid for the report.

Comparing the years 1913 and 1920, Spring noted that loco mileage had increased despite a decline in traffic, attributing the difference to a reduction in the number of gravity trains run. Working expenses, 74 per cent of receipts in 1913, had risen to 160 per cent. Staff employed on the track and in Boston Lodge did not seem excessive, except for 'the large number [five] of apprentices employed'. There were too many clerks at Minffordd. Any savings made by replacing the gates at Minffordd and Penrhyn crossings with cattle guards would be minimal as one of the keepers was a pensioner, the other a woman. The mileage of the two shunting engines

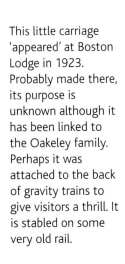

This little carriage 'appeared' at Boston Lodge in 1923. Probably made there, its purpose is unknown although it has been linked to the Oakeley family. Perhaps it was attached to the back of gravity trains to give visitors a thrill. It is stabled on some very old rail.

An assortment of wagons, including the six-wheeled Cleminson, and a quarrymen's carriage at Boston Lodge.

was largely unproductive, especially as the top shunter was based at Boston Lodge during the winter, but its cost had to be borne by the business.

Concerning the slate wagons, he noted that the railway had given up trying to charge demurrage on wagons that overstayed in the quarries or wharves. On the basis that the fleet was about 1,200, he allowed 12½ per cent to be unavailable for maintenance, giving 1,050 available for traffic. With a daily demand for 425 wagons, therefore, and knowing that the quarry managers complained about shortages, he concluded that they were either kept under load for disproportionate periods, that they remained in the quarries or that they were blocked in sidings by new arrivals. He had noticed that two loaded wagons descending an incline required four empties to balance them.

The maintenance of the works was 'an expenditure out of all proportion to the mileage and stock of the railway'; either the workshops must do more outside work or be run as a separate undertaking. Time was wasted because there was no crane capable of lifting carriages off their bogies, there was no hand crane to lift wheels into the wheel lathe, there was no planing machine for the carpenters and, when heavy loco

repairs were done in the loco shed and machining in the works, there was too much 'unnecessary walking to and fro'.

Amongst Spring's recommendations were proposals reducing the number of loco turns of more than eight hours, working on a one-engine-in-steam basis, at the expense of dislocating the service, and closing the stations with tickets sold by the guard; he also recommended terminating passenger trains at the GW station in Blaenau Ffestiniog instead of at Duffws. Whilst the FR met the criteria regarding speed and axle weight for being treated as a light railway, he thought 'it would appear that an order to treat the Ffestiniog Railway as a light railway would not have the effect of cheapening operation'.

Vaughan had his own ideas for economies, on 26 September 1921 suggesting to E.R. Davies that stations should be closed and converted to halts. Writing from 10 Downing Street, Davies supported the idea, saying that he did not see why the proposal should be affected by the nature of the railway's carriages and that in winter the guard could issue tickets. The idea was not pursued.

The new directors appointed C.E. Hemmings, secretary of the Aluminium Corporation in 1922-3, as assistant secretary to A.G. Crick, a clerk at Portmadoc, and the share register was transferred to his office at 4 Broad Street Place, London EC, in August. Legal work was deputed to Davies' Pwllheli office.

James Williamson, the Cambrian Railways' assistant engineer, was appointed engineer in succession to Rowland Jones, who had died on 13 May 1921, aged fifty-nine. He had been well regarded by the old directors, who awarded him gratuities on several occasions and minuted his passing. His son Robert was the railway's foreman platelayer. Williamson's salary was £130.

Stewart seems to have used his Ffestiniog stock as security for loans. In September 1921, preference shares totalling £27, 000 were transferred by Davies and Jack to the National Bank's nominee company; they were transferred back to Stewart in November. In June 1922 Stewart transferred £7,000 preference shares and £12,000 ordinary stock to the Royal Bank of Scotland's Dundee branch, where they stayed until December 1923.

Just what the proposals for reorganisation of the Ffestiniog and neighbouring railways were that prompted the Great Western Railway to offer the company the services of a manager, S.C. Tyrwhitt, on a temporary basis in 1921, are not known.

However, on 28 December, the directors resolved to appoint him as assistant general manager, charged with the task of negotiating with the GWR over the use of its Blaenau Ffestiniog Station as a joint station, to allow passenger services to be withdrawn from Duffws. At the same meeting, Vaughan's submission of three months' notice was accepted.

It turned out that Vaughan was ill; he seems to have finished work during February and died of heart failure on 6 April 1922, aged seventy; Crick was instructed to write to his widow expressing the board's condolences. His £6,853 0s 9d (£326,500 in 2014) estate indicates that he had been well served by his railway career.

Newspaper reports during 1921 give an indication of the poor state of affairs on the railway. In April and May, bad coal was blamed for prolonged journeys, the *Manchester Guardian* saying that on one occasion the train stopped in a wood and passengers gathered sticks to enable it to continue. The quarrymen's train was affected on the another occasion, the *Lancashire Evening Post* noting that it took two and a half hours to cover the 10 miles from Penrhyn, an average speed of 4mph.

More seriously, in February a gravity train had collided with other slate wagons at Minffordd,

Palmerston prepares to leave Duffws shortly before passenger services were withdrawn.

damaging the track and destroying a brake van. Some wagons 'were hurled over the Cambrian Railway embankment', the *Lancashire Evening Post* reported. Fortunately, no one was injured.

Traffic during the year must also have been affected by a drought that closed the quarries for two weeks in July. In 1922, they were closed by a flu epidemic in February and by snow in March.

Despite Spring's scepticism that operating the railway as a light railway would be accompanied by savings, on 6 February 1922 the directors resolved to make an application for that purpose, adding to it powers to make a physical junction with the Portmadoc, Beddgelert & South Snowdon Railway, the Welsh Highland, and for a new, joint, station in substitution for the Festiniog Railway's existing Portmadoc Station. In their planning for the WHR, they had failed to notice that although they had acquired the PBSSR's powers to run trains to/from Portmadoc, they did not have a direct connection with the FR, or a station in the town. As the WHR's limited financial position gave no scope to secure additional funding, they decided to use the resources available to the FR to secure their objectives.

Williamson obviously did not impress the directors when he produced the plans required for a siding required by the Moelwyn Granite Company in the early part of 1922, for they were accompanied with a request for a fee of 5 per cent for producing them and another 10 per cent when the work was completed. On 28 February, they decided that his fee would be 5 per cent. A few weeks later, he resigned his position with the Cambrian Railways, which may explain his attempt to obtain more from the Ffestiniog Railway. On 1 December, the directors decided to terminate his appointment with effect from 31 March 1923.

In February 1922, Tyrwhitt had produced a report regarding the use of the GWR station as a joint station in Blaenau Ffestiniog. Unspecified works were estimated to cost £300, set against annual savings of £600. He was appointed general manager of both railways with effect from 1 April 1922.

Perhaps inspired by the publicity surrounding the forthcoming grouping, Blaenau Festiniog Urban District Council had made noises about connecting the town's standard-gauge railways. The MP for Merioneth, Henry Haydn Jones, put down a written Parliamentary question for the Minister of Transport on the subject, saying that the termini were only 150 yards apart, yet anything sent to one intended for the other entailed a journey of around 100 miles to get to the right place. On 27 March 1922, he had been told that the companies concerned could not justify the expenditure. All parties seemed to overlook the presence of another railway that would have an opinion on the matter. Jones was the owner of the Bryn Eglwys slate quarries and the Talyllyn Railway.

The slate quarry owners continued with their long-standing campaign for reduced rates, the Diphwys Slate Quarry Company writing on 15 May 1922 concerning its account and asking for the rates to be reconsidered, adding that the company might 'start an agitation' against the railway and get the other quarries to join in. The directors took exception to the letter's terms and asked Tyrwhitt for background information.

Hemmings was replaced as secretary by William Richard Huson and the London office removed from Broad Street Place to 7 Victoria Street, E.R. Davies' London office, in June 1922. Huson's salary was £100.

On the railway, there were problems with passengers misbehaving. Two Llanfrothen men who alighted from what was described as an 'express train' at Penrhyn in July 1922 appeared before Penrhyndeudraeth magistrates to face charges brought by W.C. Davies, E.R. Davies' brother. With the chairman saying that the train should not have slowed down to place temptation in the way of workmen, they were fined 15s each.

At the same time the application to operate as a light railway caused some confusion in the locality, with letters and editorial in a Welsh newspaper demonstrating a lack of understanding of what a light railway was and expressing concern about the safety of the railway's future operations if the order was made.

Davies met members of Portmadoc UDC to discuss the application on 4 September 1922. He pointed out that the PBSSR/Croesor Tramway already had powers to operate trains across the road, which was vested in the Tremadoc estate not the council.

The council wanted the railway to take a shorter route across the road. It was not explained that this would have required the additional expense of rebuilding the bridge, instead of widening it using the original piers.

Taliesin pulls away from Tan y Bwlch not long before the signalling was taken out of use.

The situation was unusual, in that the road was vested in the Tremadoc estate, not the council. For reasons of economy – transhipment of coal was cited – it was also intended to transfer the locomotive works to the site of the new station. The promoters hoped that the new station would encourage the Great Western Railway to expand its own facilities in the town, and wished to obtain a strip of land from the council to provide a footpath between the new station and the GWR station. The council decided to reserve its position until it had obtained an independent engineering report on the proposed route.

The light railway commissioners held their inquiry into the application on 8 September. The main object, Davies explained, was to effect economies; since 1914, receipts had risen 105 per cent whilst wages alone had increased by 135 per cent. At the peak, there were about 250,000 visitors to the North Wales coast, compared with 60,000 on the Cambrian coast. The junction railways at Portmadoc

would encourage visitors from the North Wales coast to make the through journey from Blaenau Ffestiniog to Dinas, and hopefully, before long, to Caernarfon, without interruption.

There were still misconceptions about the order and its purpose. Portmadoc UDC thought it was appropriate to ask for the embankment tolls to be abolished, whilst Ffestiniog UDC wanted to make sure that the quarrymen would still arrive at work on time if the company ran more trains, and thought that the track was to be relaid with lighter materials, whilst Penrhyndeudraeth Parish Council, also concerned about the quarrymen reaching work on time, thought the trains would be slower.

Portmadoc UDC pushed for a shorter route across the road, passing through the former Gorseddau Railway wharf and the back garden of Ynys y Tywyn house, not understanding the reason the company resisted this alternative.

The Railway Clerks Association asked for clauses to protect the interests of its members; Davies

Duffws in 1920. Passenger trains would soon cease to call and the signalling would be removed. (FR Archives)

promised that if anyone was made redundant they would receive priority when appointments were made by the Welsh Highland Railway. The inquiry lasted half a day.

Heavy rain in September 1922 caused the Afon Barlwyd to breach its banks and flood the railway near Glan y Pwll. The same storm washed gravel and rock onto the track near the tunnel mouth to a depth of about 2ft; the morning train ran into it and got stuck. The *Dundee Evening Telegraph* reported that the carriages were flooded as well, and that after some effort, the driver managed to reverse the train back to Tan y Bwlch, whence all the passengers returned home.

Further assistance from the Great Western Railway came in the form of a visit from a headquarters traffic officer, E.A. Haynes, to assess the possibility of increasing efficiency and making savings. After a week in Portmadoc, he reported, on 15 September 1922, that there was little scope for further economy

except by curtailing the passenger service as already proposed. Operation of seven passenger trains on weekdays and an additional late train on three days required four locomotives and six crews. From 2 October, the 3.25pm ex-Duffws and 5.00pm ex-Portmadoc would be discontinued; the 4.25pm ex-Duffws would run on six days instead of five; and the 9.00pm ex-Portmadoc and 9.10pm ex-Duffws would run on Saturdays only, instead of on Wednesdays, Thursdays and Saturdays, reducing mileage by 200 per week, and staff and fuel costs by £500 annually. He thought that the Duffws shunting engine was fully occupied for eight to nine hours daily, and about six hours on Saturdays in shunting and making trips between Duffws, Brookes' Siding, Ffestiniog Granite sidings and the LNWR and GWR yards. The Minffordd shunting engine was occupied for eight hours forty-five minutes on weekdays and five hours on Saturdays, and, could only be reduced this at the expense of altering the layout.

At the end of 1922, the company announced that Duffws Station would be closed to passenger and parcels from 1 January 1923, passenger trains starting from the Great Western station at the same time. Intending passengers were instructed to obtain tickets at the GWR station.

Set against this retrenchment, Portmadoc residents desirous of visiting relatives and friends along the railway on Christmas Day 1922 had a train provided for the purpose, leaving Portmadoc at 12.45pm and returning from Blaenau Festiniog, station unspecified, at 5.00pm.

There had been a *de facto* change in control of the company on 22 May 1922, when Davies and Jack transferred most of their ordinary stock, totalling £24,875, to the North Wales Power & Traction Company on Stewart's behalf, in payment for the NWPTC's interest in the Portmadoc, Beddgelert & South Snowdon Railway. To meet the agreed price for the PBSSR, £25,000, the remaining £125 came from five employees to whom Jack had transferred £25 each.

January 1923 was taken up by finalising the accounts covering the period of the Government's control. Inspectors had visited Portmadoc on

28 December, followed by investigators on 9 January. There were meetings with the company's solicitors, too, that might have taken place in London. The company received £1,356 6s 4d of its claim for £2,600 for new boilers obtained in 1919, 1920 and 1921. The Government had argued that the cost was disproportionate to the pre-war cost, even allowing for inflation, and that the Government had not received much benefit from the expenditure. The company also had to refund £399 overpaid for arrears of maintenance in 1918.

In anticipation of the light railway order about to be made, on 12 January 1923 Tyrwhitt was instructed to make arrangements to discuss with the Ministry of Transport a scheme for eliminating the railway's signalling, or reducing its expense, as soon as possible. The engineers, Sir Douglas Fox & Partners, were instructed to produce the necessary plans and specifications for the construction of the junction railways, and the erection of a new station adjoining the Great Western Railway. With a budget of £5,000, they included the renewal of track in the long tunnel and the provision of two observation cars. Fox was to obtain a tender for the works from Sir Robert McAlpine & Sons, requiring the work to be completed by 31 March. Working on projects for the Aluminium Corporation, Fox and McAlpine were keen to secure additional work whilst they had resources based in Wales.

Palmerston on the public wharf, Portmadoc, in 1922. Despite the accessibility of the location very few photographs were taken of railway activity on the harbourside.

(FR Archives)

On 2 February 1923, the directors discussed their proposal to combine the Ffestiniog and Welsh Highland Railways under one management and resolved to centralise accounting control at the Aluminium Corporation's Dolgarrog offices. The accountant, Robert Evans, was asked to work at Dolgarrog and to make arrangements for conducting the non-transferable work at Portmadoc. Tyrwhitt was asked to produce a list of employees and their wages or salaries with the objective of reducing expenditure and transferring superfluous staff to the WHR when it was completed.

Distribution of the annual report to shareholders on 17 February 1923 was accompanied by a circular letter from Jack. He said that when the present directors took office in June 1921 the undertaking was being run at a serious loss. Economies made since then had reduced the loss in 1922. The light railway order that had been made on 30 January relieved the company of the requirement to pay passenger duty on fares and opened the way for other savings to be made.

The railway's fortunes would only be improved, he continued, if the holiday traffic was expanded. The Welsh Highland Railway was about to be opened, and a working arrangement would be made to enable the operation of trains between Blaenau Festiniog and Dinas. The LRO authorised the creation of £20,000 of new capital; £10,000 of that would be issued to secure a bank loan of £10,000. That would be used to pay for the new works required at Portmadoc, estimated to cost £6,000. Jack did not mention that although the loan would enable the boiler expenditure to be capitalised, it would also permit the overdraft to be cleared.

The Board of Trade did not require traffic information to be reported from 1914. 1919 was the last year a return was made for the operation of mixed trains: 12,097 miles.

£10,000 of 5 per cent debenture stock was issued to Branch Nominees Ltd, a subsidiary of the National Provincial Bank, to secure a new overdraft for that amount on 16 March 1923. McAlpine signed the tender to contract to widen the bridge, and construct the junction railways and the new station, for a fixed sum of £3,500 on 20 April. The contractor undertook to complete the work ready for a ministry inspection not later than 12 May, in order that the railway could be opened by 19 May.

After Williamson's appointment terminated on 31 March 1923, Davies arranged for Colonel Holman Fred Stephens, an engineer with several light railways under his management, to consider taking the position on both the Festiniog and Welsh Highland Railways, and to visit them on 16 April. No doubt Stephens' efforts to have light railways excluded from the Railways Bill had brought him to Davies' attention. One source says that Stephens

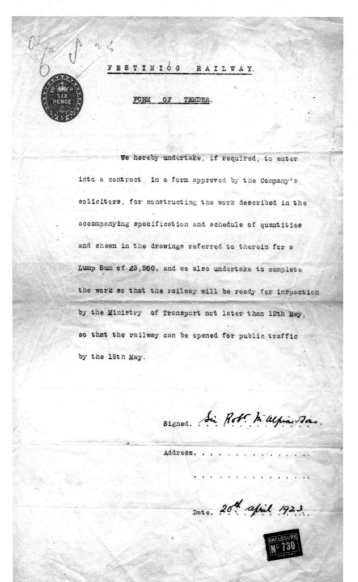

The tender submitted by the McAlpine partnership agreeing to contract to build the junction railways in Portmadoc in 1923.

James Spooner at the new Portmadoc Station in 1923. The FR owned the land on either side of the embankment.

visited the FR in 1918, but there is no record of such a visit in the company's archives. His appointment as engineer and locomotive superintendent of both railways with a salary of £100 plus expenses was approved on 27 August and backdated to 1 May, his remit excluding the Welsh Highland Railway between Portmadoc and Rhyd Ddu whilst it was maintained by the contractors.

By reputation, Stephens was a brusque man with a military bearing. He ran his empire from his Tonbridge office, communicating by letter and telegram, making occasional visits or sending his assistants in his stead. In 1926, he wrote to his assistant, W.H. Austen, 'The people on the FR are quite different to our people, as you have found out by now. I found it out a long time ago. They can't help it, it's their nature. We have got to put up with it whilst we have the job.' What does come across, though, is that he would recognise the efforts of those who worked in the company's best interest.

A trial run was made over the junction railways on 12 May and on 19 May a train comprising a bogie engine and three carriages ran from Portmadoc to Dinas, passengers including E.R. Davies and H.J. Jack. 'Certain difficulties' with the track on the Britannia bridge delayed the inspection until 24 May.

Colonel A.H.L. Mount, who also inspected the WHR, reported on the junction railways and the new station on 1 June. Located on an embankment on the existing Croesor Tramway, the new station's loop and platforms were 150ft long, and a corrugated iron building 40ft x 12ft would accommodate a waiting room, parcels and ticket offices and conveniences; the building was under construction at the time of his visit. A footpath to the GWR station had been made and a water tank was to be erected. The question of lighting would have to be considered if trains ran after dark.

Railway No.1 was in substitution for the original Ffestiniog line across the bridge – Mount said

Wreathed in steam, *James Spooner* crossing from junction railway No. 2 to junction railway No. 1 in 1923.

Croesor in error – and was 3½ chains (77 yards) in length. Railway No.2, 4½ chains (99 yards) long, formed a junction with Railway No.1 at the western end of the Old Sluice Bridge and crossed the main road to terminate by a junction with the existing Croesor Tramway via a 3½ chain radius curve. The existing track between the original Ffestiniog Railway station and Railway No. 1 had been relaid, and the existing Croesor line that crossed the main road had been relaid on a new alignment, although the old line remained in situ. Mount did not think that the longitudinal timbers laid between the rails would make a satisfactory surface for heavy traffic. Angle iron was used to form a check rail on Railway No. 1 and ordinary check rail on Railway No. 2.

The points in Madoc Street, at the termination of Railway No. 2, were unsuitable for that location and required changing; he suggested that it might be better to route all traffic from the Welsh Highland for the harbour via the old station and take up the direct line.

No attempt had been made to make the new track level with the road surface, or to bring the road up to

rail level, with the result that the highway engineer, who attended the inspection, complained about the lack of drainage. Mount agreed that the works had not been carried out to meet the council's reasonable requirements. The new station, he concluded, could be approved for passenger traffic, but whilst the junction railways were fit for passenger traffic, he was not prepared to approve their use until the company had reached a settlement with the council.

He had referred to the junction railways in the summary of the Welsh Highland inspection, which he had concluded by recommending that approval be given to the operation by passenger traffic for a temporary period of six months, when the whole would be reinspected, 'with a view to ascertaining, under the special circumstances in which this line has been constructed, whether the works are complete, and what, if any, additional requirements may be necessary,' which rather leaves one thinking

The FR guards' logs show that the Welsh Highland Railway's 0-6-4T *Moel Tryfan* regularly worked to Blaenau Ffestiniog, but this is the closest that anyone came to photographing it on the FR.

that he would have been more restrictive had he not understood that there was some sort of political pressure for the railway to be opened without further delay or expense. The Ministry's request to be informed of the settlement reached with the highways engineer and, when Mount's requirements had been carried out, was overlooked.

Sufficient agreement was reached with the highway engineer, however, to enable services to start on 1 June, a Friday, the same day that Mount compiled his report on the junction railways. The first train, at 8.10am, was hauled by *Princess*. At Waunfawr it crossed the first train from Dinas, which was hauled by *Prince*, so the Ffestiniog Railway had a high profile on the Welsh Highland Railway's first day.

It is not clear from the newspaper reports if trains carried passengers over the junction railways on 1 June. On 27 August, however, the directors minuted that it had formally been opened on 2 June, when a through train had been run from Blaenau Festiniog to Dinas.

In pursuit of the directors' desire to make more of tourism, they had already agreed to give the Snowdon Mountain Tramroad exclusive rights to establish and operate refreshment rooms, and book

stalls at stations. The annual rent was £50 on a twenty-one-year lease, renewable for seven, fourteen or twenty-one years, that started on 1 August 1923. Attempts to obtain more land for a refreshment room and other purposes at Tan y Bwlch came to nothing. Davies had agreed with the LMSR and the GWR to offer through tickets to stations on both railways, and to promote circular tours. He was, in April 1923, confident that the LMS excursion from Llandudno to Betws-y-Coed would be extended to Blaenau Festiniog.

The land used for the path linking the new station with the Great Western station belonged to Portmadoc Urban District Council. The company had agreed to make it up to a road within three years, but the council wanted the work to be done within six months. It eventually conceded this point, substituting a new demand for the company to erect a substantial stone wall to demarcate the road from the council's remaining property. In August 1923, the directors resolved to adhere to the draft conveyance; neither road nor wall was built.

Stephens dealt with the Ministry of Transport, concerning the signalling instead, of Tyrwhitt. On 27 August, the directors were informed that the application to dispense with signalling had been

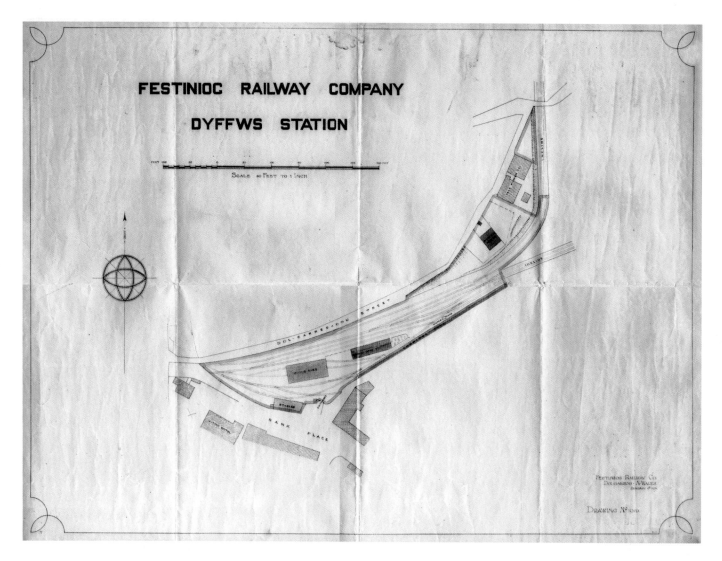

FESTINIOC RAILWAY COMPANY

DYFFWS STATION

A plan of Duffws showing the company's land boundaries, produced in January 1924, whilst company work was being undertaken at Dolgarrog.

approved with regards to the section between Portmadoc and Tanygrisiau, which they expected to result in a reduction in staff and a substantial saving.

Robert Evans had been visiting Dolgarrog to deal with the accounts on two or three days a week, but the division of his labour between Portmadoc and Dolgarrog proved inconvenient to him. A.G. Crick's offer to work full time there if a house could be found was accepted, the directors agreeing that he would be in charge of the accounts of the Ffestiniog and associated companies, and that his hotel bill would be paid until a house became available.

When Tyrwhitt gave notice to terminate his employment with effect from 30 September 1923, the directors decided to defer a decision on the appointment of a successor. Instead, Captain John May took the position of superintendent on a temporary basis for £5 per month. Born in

Llanybyther, Carmarthenshire, in 1867, May had joined the Manchester & Milford Railway as a clerk at the age of fourteen and worked for Irish narrow-gauge railways from 1893, leaving the Londonderry & Loughswilly Railway, where he had been traffic manager, in 1916, to take a commission in the Royal Engineers. He had left the Army earlier in 1923.

At the end of 1923, £3,656 16s had been spent on the junction railways, including land purchase and the new station. The light railway order had cost £400. Other capital expenditure made during the year was £376 13s 6d on a petrol tractor for shunting and £1,016 0s 9d on six coaching vehicles. The 40hp

The FR's first move towards using internal combustion came in 1923, with the acquisition of this protected 40hp First World War Simplex, used for shunting at Minffordd and in Portmadoc. Photographed at Boston Lodge on 4 August 1958.

(J. J. Davis)

petrol-engined 'Simplex' locomotive had been made by Motor Rail in Bedford for use during the war. The *Railway Gazette*, 9 November 1923, reported that the locomotive had been subjected to trials, including a trip from Portmadoc to Dinas and back, and the Bryngwyn branch, with a train of two carriages and acquitted itself well, apart from an interval when it required attention because the driver did not have the competence that would accompany experience. No comment was made about the amount of petrol that must have been consumed on such a journey.

The carriages were Hudson bogie semi-open toastracks intended for the tourist traffic; it was intended that three of them should be sold on to the Welsh Highland Railway, but that part of the transaction was not completed. Davies described them as observation cars.

With a view to making more savings, the directors had inspected the railway on 28 December 1923, agreeing a number of changes on 19 February 1924. The offices at Portmadoc should be arranged to allow the first floor of the building to be converted to living accommodation; the layout at Minffordd should be changed to increase capacity and efficiency, using the tractor for shunting in preference to steam locomotives; and that ways should be found and implemented to reduce the cost of operating the signal cabins at Glan y Pwll and Blaenau Festiniog. They also resolved to provide more wagons to meet the requirements of the quarry proprietors.

Davies had been in contact with the Great Western Railway, obtaining the services of engineering staff to inspect both railways, and make recommendations regarding savings and operations. A report had been submitted on 7 December 1923 that does not appear to have survived. Davies was authorised to continue negotiations with the GWR's superintendent regarding closer co-operation.

This, no doubt, was responsible for the appointment of Eric Harry Raymond Nicholls as managing director, agreed on 14 May 1924, and effective from 17 May. His £500 salary included his directors' fees and his services as general manager of the Welsh Highland Railway. Born in 1895, he had worked for the GWR before joining the Royal Welch Fusiliers in 1916 and relinquishing his commission on 30 September 1921. Whether he returned to the

Six open toastrack carriages were bought from Robert Hudson, Leeds, in 1923 with the expectation that the Welsh Highland Railway would pay for three of them. As carriages they did not last long, being converted to flat wagons by 1928 or out of use by 1929. No.38, seen here, became a flat wagon in 1926. Behind, to the left, is the Cleminson six-wheeled wagon, known as the 'iron bogie'.

Sir John Henderson Stewart Bt was buried in Kinnaird Churchyard, near Perth. (Author)

GWR before moving to Wales is not known, but it appears that his uncle was R. H. Nicholls, the GWR's superintendent.

Sir John H. Stewart's resignation as a director had been submitted on 29 December 1923 and accepted on 1 January 1924. He died by his own hand on 6 February, having transferred all of his stock and shares to Jack on 31 January. At a creditors' meeting held on 5 July, questions were asked about Stewart's involvement with 'Welsh railway shares'. The creditor who asked 'Is it not a fact that these were not disclosed because it was a political matter?' went unanswered. Stewart was replaced as a director by George Westall, a surveyor and estate agent, on 18 March.

The state of the footpath across the embankment was of concern to Portmadoc Urban District Council in 1923-4, which twice, about a year apart, approached the company about it. On each occasion, the council was informed that the section of the footpath within the company's boundary, about 300 yards, was in good order and that it, the council, should ask the owner, the Tremadoc estate, if it wished the remainder to be dealt with.

Another source of traffic had come under attack from 7 February 1924, when the Crosville Motor Company started operating a bus service between Portmadoc and Blaenau Festiniog at lower fares. Davies had visited the company's Chester offices, and secured agreement on the issue of return tickets valid by bus one way and train the other. Jack was to investigate the options for issuing return railway tickets at cheaper fares.

A busy scene at Minffordd. (Gwilym Phillips collection)

Nicholls soon got to work, making a series of recommendations to the directors on 18 June 1924. They agreed that he could sack John May at his discretion, but not later than 30 September; make arrangements with the GWR to oversee the railways' operation; dispense with the signalling at Blaenau Ffestiniog; approach the railway unions about reducing the number of employees and wages; develop the use of tractors; dispense with the annual issue of staff uniforms; reorganise the allocation of wagons; and develop a trade in sand at Blaenau Ffestiniog using the sand from the pit at Boston Lodge.

Colonel Stephens had resigned: the reason is not known, but there might have been territorial issues between him and Nicholls. Territorial issues were almost certainly the reason behind May's dismissal. In October 1924, he was appointed secretary and manager of the Ashover Light Railway in Derbyshire, a railway which had Stephens as its engineer.

Nicholls also had thoughts about the agreement made with the erstwhile Cambrian Railways in 1871

concerning the use of Minffordd Yard and exchange traffic, the directors agreeing to obtain advice on it.

On 14 May 1924, the North Wales Power & Traction Company sold £24,875 of its FR ordinary stock to the Aluminium Corporation for a nominal £500. As the NWPTC was about to be given responsibility for supplying power throughout North Wales, the Electricity Commissioners had advised that its operations should be confined to those of a public utility.

A proposal made by the Welsh Highland Railway that it should be managed by the Ffestiniog Company for £10 a week, backdated from 12 May 1924, was accepted. Purchase of the land from the council required for the joint station was completed on 26 May, a transaction that probably accounted for the overdraft being increased by £1,500 to £11,500 in January, the increase being secured by a £2,000 debenture. Despite this, the company did not have sufficient funds to pay £533 owed to Sir Douglas Fox & Partners for the work done on the junction railways and the new station, issuing a debenture for that amount. A debenture was also issued to William Hebburn McAlpine for £966 12s in respect of construction work that was unpaid, but this was not minuted. During the year, £2,539 8s 8d was spent on capital works, the final land purchase and construction costs for the junction railways.

The prospect of the Great Western Railway having an oversight of the railways' operation and engineering came to an end at a meeting held at Paddington on 5 August 1924. The GWR said that whilst its engineering staff could act as consulting engineers, they could not take any responsibility. As a result, H.J. Jack returned to Colonel Stephens and secured his consent to act until satisfactory permanent arrangements could be made.

Several proposals made by Nicholls were adopted by the directors on 5 September 1924. Not only had May gone, but F.G. Crick, the accountant, too, on 1 September. Crick got Portmadoc Urban District Council to intercede with the Ministry of Transport on his behalf, but to no avail.

Nicholls' scheme to reduce the winter service to four daily return trains, plus the quarrymens', and operate it with only two locomotives was particularly satisfactory, although allowances would have to be made to the 'old servants' whose services were dispensed with 'in order to secure an alert and efficient staff to run the company's service'. In this regard, Robert Williams at Boston Lodge was told that Nicholls was responsible for all appointments and dismissals.

As the question of wages had not been settled with the railway unions, Nicholls was told that he could terminate the existing agreements with them to enable him to reduce wages to a level that the company could afford. Priority should be given to allocating the company's houses to employees, but they should be charged an economic rent.

Wishing to strengthen the company's direction, Jack again approached Colonel Stephens and obtained his acceptance of an offer to take a seat on the board. The agreement was put into effect on 29 October 1924. On 20 November, acting on medical advice, Jack stood down as chairman. Nicholls' resignation, to take effect from 22 April 1925, was accepted on the same date.

News of a gravity train derailment caused by a broken axle that had occurred on 30 June was reported in the *Lincolnshire Echo*. Several of the forty-six wagons had overturned and a considerable amount of track had been damaged, whilst the two brakesmen escaped without injury.

The end of 1924 was balanced by good news and bad news on the financial front. A refund of £431 8s 9d had been received in respect of passenger duty paid on certain third-class fares, whilst £227 16s 6d income tax was due on the Railways Act compensation. An appeal was to be made because no allowance had been made of depreciation of track and rolling stock. The trades unions had been prepared to make some concessions on wages, but not enough to prevent the company operating at a loss, calculated at £60 a week since the winter train service had started on 22 September. Despite their efforts to make savings, the company's financial position had seriously deteriorated since 1919, as shown in Appendix 2.

CHAPTER 2

1925-1931: MANAGEMENT FROM TONBRIDGE

The terms of Colonel Stephens' appointment as chairman and managing director were agreed on 16 December 1924, a salary of £200 payable in addition to the remuneration paid to him as engineer and locomotive superintendent, and including service in respect of the Welsh Highland Railway. He would take over as managing director when Nicholls left.

Fares were reduced in February 1925. Notices published in *Gloch*, a Welsh newspaper, included what was essentially a 'use it or lose it' message, reminding readers that the railway was essential to the slate trade and that they had more reason to use it now the fares had been reduced, making them cheaper than some other means of transport.

Failing to obtain agreement over reducing the wages, and employees voting against concessions the unions supported, the directors decided to appeal directly to the workforce, arranging a

meeting at Boston Lodge on 6 April 1925. They thought that if there was a strike or an appeal for public sympathy, the company's position would be strengthened by doing so. By 21 July, a 25 per cent reduction had been agreed, with overtime payable at ordinary rates until ten hours had been worked in any one day. The men had accepted these proposals, the directors minuted, and were working normally. The unions reserved the right to re-open the discussion if the company prospered.

The basis on which the directors decided to appeal against its rating assessment were not recorded. In 1924, the assessment had risen to £1,189 13s 11d from £932 16s 3d the year before. The Ffestiniog Union's offer to reduce the 1925 levy by 50 per cent, provided the 1924 rate was paid in full resulted in an appeal to the Merionethshire & Caernarfonshire quarter sessions, the Southern Railway's rating surveyor appearing for the

Princess running light engine past the Glaslyn Foundry, close to the point where FR junction railway No. 2 connected with the Welsh Highland Railway.

A view across the embankment looking towards Boston Lodge. The signal post was relocated from Glan y Pwll. The railway's communications installation is on the right, whilst that on the left belonged to the General Post Office. On the left is the iron fence erected and painted white in 1887, for R. H. Bleasdale to use as a photographic backdrop.

company as an expert witness. The result was a credit of £177 6s 7d on the 1925 assessment. In 1926, the company paid just £180 10s 5d.

Payment of income tax was also causing problems for the company. The Inland Revenue wanted some payment on account, but the company replied, in the spring of 1925, that it was unable to do that unless passenger receipts showed an appreciable uplift during the summer months. A warrant for £326 2s 1d was followed by a further demand for £537 18s 7d. The company's position was explained on 9 November 1925, when it was agreed to suspend proceedings.

New working instructions devised to cover both railways were brought into effect on 1 October 1925. Issued under Stephens' name, they took account of the abolition of the FR's signalling.

Jack resigned as a director on 9 November, once more citing medical advice as the reason. The date was a week after the Aluminium Corporation's Eigiau Dam collapse, the resulting flood killing sixteen residents in Dolgarrog. It has been held that

Jack's resignation as chairman was a consequence of him taking responsibility for the Welsh Highland Railway's poor performance and then as a director because he took responsibility for the dam collapse, but this seems not to be the case. No accusations were made at the inquest and he did not leave the Corporation until 1928. If he did not find it necessary to leave the Corporation when sixteen people had been killed, then it seems unlikely that he would have felt obliged to resign over the WHR. He continued as chairman of the Snowdon Mountain Railway Company until his death in 1946.

Concerned about the overdraft, the bank required the £1,000 New South Wales Government

Kerr, Stuart No. 4415, the makers' prototype diesel locomotive, photographed during a break in activity at Minffordd. (FR Archives)

Palmerston by the coaling stage at Portmadoc.

3 per cent loan stock to be sold. The realisation of £812 8s paid to the loan account was reported on 12 November 1925.

More rolling stock was acquired during 1925: a 45hp Baldwin petrol locomotive (£248 13s 4d); four 5-ton bogie goods wagons (£140); and three inspection trollies (£13 10s), war surplus stock

no doubt sourced by Stephens. The locomotive had been built in 1917 for the French Government artillery railways. In 1926, the company bought spares for the locomotive (£2 15s 8d); carriage lighting equipment (£38 4s); two wagon bodies (£35); and three more inspection trollies (£22 13s 7d).

The FR's second venture into internal-combustion locomotion was this 45hp Baldwin tractor purchased in 1925. Like the Simplex, it was also made for use during the First World War, although it was delivered after the war ended. In the 1930s, it was photographed on the junction railway alongside the goods shed at Portmadoc, probably taking cooling water from the tank erected to serve steam locomotives passing between the FR and the Welsh Highland Railway. (FR Archives)

The general strike initiated by coal miners aggrieved by the post-war reduction in wages ran from 3-13 May 1926, with transport workers and those in heavy industry supporting the miners. Writing to Robert Evans, the accountant, on 10 May, Stephens said that every effort should be made to run a service if the buses were running, although it does not appear that in this instance any of the company's employees withdrew their labour. On 12 June, he told W.H. Austen, his assistant, that he had, 'told Williams to put all the shirkers in Boston Lodge on four days a week short time starting Monday = thirty-two hours a week each. The wages bill must be reduced.' In November, Stephens reported that coal supplied by the Great Western Railway had been of poor quality, delaying services to a considerable extent in some cases.

Disruption to coal supplies during the strike and afterwards also had a negative effect on the output at Boston Lodge, deferring some repairs to 1927 and increasing that year's expenses. Summarising 1927's results for shareholders, Stephens also said that goods traffic had been affected by weak demand for slate and granite, and passenger traffic had been considerably affected by strong omnibus opposition, themes that were not going to change, regardless of the directors' efforts.

Passenger train revenue during October and November 1927 had fallen to £53 per week, of which £38 was derived from the quarrymen, the remainder from school children and ordinary passengers. On 25 November, the directors decided to make further savings by discharging Robert Williams, the works foreman, paying him an honorarium of £1 1s per week and giving him free use of his house until he obtained another job; to dispense with the services of the permanent way inspector, paying one of the workmen 5s a week extra to act as ganger; and to cut two return trains from the winter timetable, making the men affected redundant, putting them on half-time or splitting their shifts to reduce their working days to eight hours, saving overtime payments.

The embankment was breached by a storm that occurred on 28 October 1927. A quarrymen's carriage was also blown across the embankment from Portmadoc and turned on its side. Although the breach took nearly four months to repair, with services terminating at Boston Lodge, the directors

Palmerston with a short train on a quiet day.

Seen in 1934, the station buildings erected by C. E. Spooner have served the railway well.

were only concerned about the company's liability for repairing the wall that separated the railway on the embankment from the road below. The 1869 Act had simply obliged the company to construct it and was silent on the subject of its maintenance.

Stephens consulted with the Tremadoc estate about it and a flurry of letters descended on Evans from Tonbridge. 'During daylight, traffic can be worked between Portmadoc old station and Boston Lodge old signal box under protection of a flagman.' [7 November] 'Whilst ballast was dumped on the footpath, notices were erected warning that its use was at own risk, to be removed.' [10 November]

'What gaps had been made in the iron fence [200 yards] and the masonry parapet wall [420 yards]?' [16 November] '[Permanent way inspector Lewis] Griffiths had been instructed to ballast the track, tell me if he changes his mind and does something else, the men were working slowly on Monday when I saw them.' [16 November] 'When do you expect the gap to be closed, we do not want complaints from farmers being flooded before the gap is closed?' [31 December] Not all of Evans' responses have survived.

With damage to the Great Western Railway's coast line sustained during the same storm putting Minffordd Yard out of action, the quarry proprietors

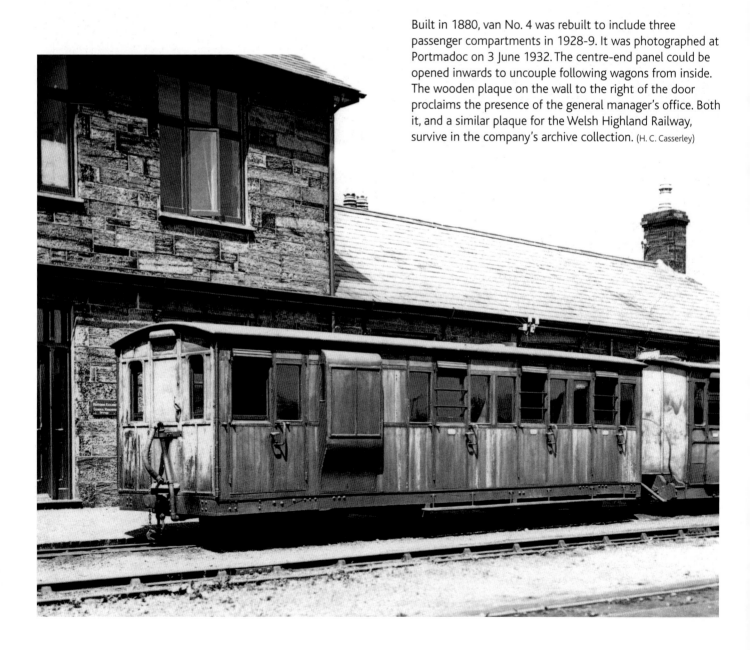

Built in 1880, van No. 4 was rebuilt to include three passenger compartments in 1928-9. It was photographed at Portmadoc on 3 June 1932. The centre-end panel could be opened inwards to uncouple following wagons from inside. The wooden plaque on the wall to the right of the door proclaims the presence of the general manager's office. Both it, and a similar plaque for the Welsh Highland Railway, survive in the company's archive collection. (H. C. Casserley)

Rebuilt with passenger accommodation in 1921, van No. 2 is seen with van No. 3 at Portmadoc in 1924. No. 2 has been turned to work on the Welsh Highland Railway.
(J. P. Richards/FR Archives)

found it convenient to make more use of the London, Midland & Scottish Railway's facilities at Blaenau Ffestiniog to the detriment of the FR. Greaves even used FR wagons for the purpose; Evans did not know if it would be politic to charge Greaves for using them and asked for advice.

Griffith Williams, a long-standing employee, died on 3 January 1928. Born in 1848, he had lived all his life at the family home, Bryn Tirion, Minffordd, and had a reputation as a litterateur and antiquary. When he had retired in 1925, the *Lancashire Evening Post* reported that he had worked on the railway for fifty-four years, managing the Minffordd weigh office. Evans arranged for a wreath to be sent to his funeral on Stephens' behalf; it cost 18s 6d. Williams' estate, valued at £2,196 3s 7d, probably included inherited property, but suggests that he might have had a more comfortable living than many of his colleagues.

In March 1929, the railway was used to try out the latest in internal combustion. The Stoke on Trent-based locomotive builders Kerr, Stuart had built a 60hp diesel locomotive, the first such, in 1928. After trials on the Welsh Highland Railway, mainly on the Bryngwyn branch, it was transferred to the FR,

where its cab had to be altered to suit the more restricted loading gauge. Used to shunt at Portmadoc and Minffordd, it was returned to its makers after a few months. After running on the 3ft gauge Castlederg & Victoria Bridge Tramway in Ireland, it was re-gauged again and sold to a sugar plantation in Mauritius in 1934. Not used regularly from 1962, it was displayed on a plinth in 1972 and returned to Wales in 1997. Restoration to working order was started at Boston Lodge in 2015.

In 1929-30, the 1880 brake vans were rebuilt with passenger accommodation, following the 1873 van rebuilt similarly, losing its 'curly roof', in 1921. The latter and one of the others are known to have been turned to place the brake end facing Blaenau Ffestiniog, for working on the Welsh Highland Railway.

W.R. Huson's resignation as secretary had been accepted on 25 April 1929. He was 75-years-old. He

was replaced by Cynan Evan Davies, E.R. Davies' eldest son, another solicitor. George Westall, the director who succeeded Stewart in 1924, died on 28 January 1930, aged eighty. He was succeeded by his youngest son, Hubert Lander Westall, a company secretary with the Snowdon Mountain Railway in his portfolio.

Sixty-five years of continuous passenger service were ended in April 1930, when the directors decided that the most effective way of saving money on it was to suspend it, except the quarrymen's trains, completely. On 30 April, E.R. Davies reported that a considerable saving had been made. A seasonal tourist service of two return trips was started in July. The directors did not think to tell the shareholders of this change in operations, merely saying that circular tours had gone well. Noting the discontinuance at the end of the season, on September 20 the

Palmerston is prepared for service outside the loco shed as *Prince* passes by on 31 August 1926. (H. C. Casserley)

Seen outside the Boston Lodge loco shed towards the end of its career, *James Spooner*, the railway's second bogie engine, was condemned in 1933 after several years out of use.

Merddin Emrys at Minffordd in August 1928. The loop line was only used by mineral trains until the 1920s. Colonel Rich, the railway inspector, had objected to the location of the shelter on the left when he had inspected the station in 1872. (E. A. Gurney-Smith)

Manchester Guardian said that passengers had declined with the growing popularity of bus services. The *Locomotive* of 15 October reported that 'this once prosperous line closed down on 20 September', adding that goods and slate traffic, and the daily quarrymen's train, would continue. It also claimed, in error, that all of the Fairlie locomotives had been scrapped.

Thanks to a correspondent who had visited Boston Lodge in August, on 15 December, the *Locomotive* was able to explain that *Merddin Emrys* was approaching the end of an extensive overhaul, that *Livingston Thompson's* boiler had been returned from the Avonside Engine Company, where repairs undertaken had included fitting a new firebox, and that *James Spooner* and *Palmerston* were in need of

heavy repairs. In the 'scrap yard' were the remains of *Taliesin* and *Little Giant*. The traffic was, therefore, being handled by *Princess*, *Prince* and *Welsh Pony*. When *Livingston Thompson* was returned to traffic in 1932, it did so bearing *Taliesin's* name.

The roof and chimney of the Boston Lodge engine shed had been damaged by fire after the cleaner, G.H. Jones, dropped his flare lamp in the pit on 9 July 1930. The lamp had ignited petrol that had

An assortment of wagons is stabled in the goods shed siding at Penrhyn as *Prince* passes with a passenger train.

leaked from the Baldwin tractor that was in for repair. The roof was patched at the insurance company's expense.

Colonel Stephens' resignation as chairman owing to 'continued ill health' was accepted on 30 April 1931 and E.R. Davies was elected chairman in his stead. He died at the Lord Warden Hotel in Dover, where he had been in residence for several years, on 23 October; his predecessor, Andrew Durham, had also died there on 8 October 1876. Although Stephens had attended the general meeting and board meeting held on 20 April 1930, his signature in the minute books had been weakening for two years. During that period the only matters dealt with by the directors had been those that had not required his participation, mainly the registration of share transfers.

At this distance it is hard to understand why no action had been taken to relieve Stephens of his responsibilities. He had had a stroke in January 1930 and the evidence of the signatures suggests that he had had one in 1928, too. By the time he made his

will in January 1931, he was unable to speak and barely had the strength to initial the document.

Data in Appendix 2 shows the decline over the period of Stephens' control, with big reductions in passenger numbers and freight, the figures from 1930 reflecting the cancellation of all-year-round passenger services. No petrol locomotive operation was reported in 1926-7; the figure of 980 miles operated in 1926 was back-reported in 1927, when the layout of the table reverted to that used in 1925, the low figure and absence of shunting data being indicative of lack of availability for reasons unknown. From 1928-30 the negative balance carried forward was maintained at the same level by transferring funds from reserves, a sleight of hand that would not have fooled any financially-literate shareholders. Cynan Evan Davies, E.R. Davies' eldest son, replaced him as a director.

CHAPTER 3

1932-1945: LEASING THE WELSH HIGHLAND, THE END OF PASSENGER SERVICES

One of the issues that E.R. Davies had to deal with was releasing the unused land at Duffws back to the Newborough estate. In September 1931, agreement was reached for the company to surrender the leases, except for a plot still required, and for the rent arrears to be cancelled. It was minuted that the arrears were substantial, but the amount was not stated. In a list of rents payable in 1921, the only item payable to Newborough was £8 1s due annually for land at Blaenau Festiniog.

Another issue for him was the road bridge at Duffws, built by the railway in substitution for the original level crossing. The Ffestiniog Urban District

and the Merioneth County Councils had been pressing for it to be maintained. He had convinced them that the company did not have the resources to undertake the work and they had agreed to release the company from the liability in exchange for the land affected, about 445 square yards. The conveyance discharging the company's liability in favour of the county council was dated 10 October 1931.

During his decline, Colonel Stephens had devolved his duties to members of his staff, who had worked under Davies' direction. The cost of this operation, including Stephens' salary, was £578 6s 8d a year. Dealing with Stephens' successor, W.H. Austen,

A view over the wall at Duffws as *Prince* pauses during shunting operations in 1934. The objects on the ground could be beams from the old road bridge, replaced in 1933.

(William Mackie Low)

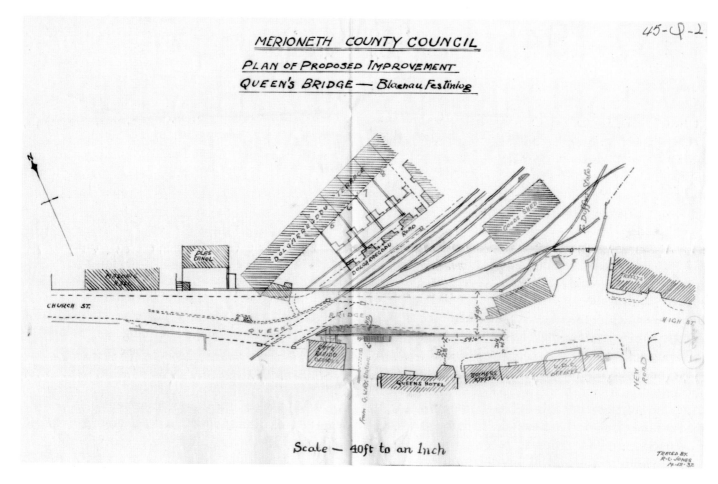

45-φ-2

MERIONETH COUNTY COUNCIL

PLAN OF PROPOSED IMPROVEMENT

QUEEN'S BRIDGE — Blaenau Festiniog

Scale — 40ft to an Inch

TRACED BY
R. C. JONES
19.12.32

A plan showing the extra land required by the county council when the road was widened and bridge rebuilt at Duffws in 1933.

who had acted as his resident engineer and office manager, Davies had arranged for Austen to take over as engineer and locomotive superintendent at a salary of £55; J.A. Iggulden, accountant and audit accountant, received £100; locomotive and permanent way assistant J.A. Levitt's salary was £40; and Davies, as managing director, was paid £320, the entire arrangement resulting in an annual reduction of administrative expenses of £263 6s 8d. A minor administrative change introduced at the same time saw salaries paid monthly by cheque, instead of from the petty cash.

Iggulden's appointment as accountant lasted until 30 April 1932, when the auditors' recommendation to appoint J.W. Coggins on a reduced salary of £30 instead was accepted. Iggulden's salary was reduced to £70.

Some tidying up of the accounts was approved the following month. £189 8s 1d owed by the Great Western Railway prior to 1925 was written off because it was not recognised by the GWR and an unspecified amount owed by the Welsh Highland

Railway was cancelled to bring the two companies into alignment with the WHR's receivers accounts. £1,331 9s 3d owed to the life tenant of the Tremadoc Estate was written down to £540 payable in three instalments by agreement. On 26 May, £900 kept in a special reserve account since 1896 was transferred to the general reserve account.

A rearrangement of the permanent way staff agreed with Austen was approved on 6 January 1933. Roberts, the telegraphs manager, was made permanent way foreman on a three-month trial for an extra 6s per week. The former foreman, William Williams, became 'an ordinary workman' and two men aged over sixty-five years were put on half-time. A younger man was also to be employed. Presumably Williams was also no longer in the first-flush of youth; the younger man would be expected to perform most of the physical work whilst the others told him what to do.

E.R. Davies had made enquiries about reducing costs by obtaining a diesel locomotive, but the lowest estimate had been £3,500, which the company could not afford. Austen had agreed that two engines could be reconditioned to provide sufficient power to run an increased passenger service in 1933. Sufficient carriage stock to provide 1,000 seats was to be made available.

Always keen to encourage more tourists from North Wales, Davies had persuaded the LMS to run a new train from Caernarvon to Afon Wen and the GWR thence to Minffordd, the FR adjusting its timetable to make the most of the connections. Robert Evans estimated the additional cost at £12, per week presumably.

Davies also considered providing accommodation for tourists, in the form of a hostel developed in a house at Boston Lodge that had been vacant for several years. The neighbour would look after the property and take a profit from provision of meals, incurring no expense to the company. A promotional leaflet was printed.

More arrears were dealt with in November 1933; the amounts concerned, especially with regards to repayments, do give an indication of how the company was struggling financially. Sir Joseph Bankes, who received tolls for slates crossing his land at the long tunnel, had agreed to accept £180 in three instalments in lieu of £236 4s 11d. More seriously, the Inland Revenue was owed £1,135 19s 1d, accumulated over ten years. Davies had written many letters and made numerous visits before being informed, on 14 November, that his offer of £568 payable in twelve instalments had been accepted.

For their efforts, Davies' firm, Evan Davies & Company, was paid 50 guineas. Davies himself had disbursed £54 18s 3d in expenses since April 1931, so he was reimbursed that amount and paid £26 5s annually for his expenses in future.

Iggulden's position with the accounts was reduced further when the directors decided to reward Evans' efforts by putting him in charge of them for £50 increase in salary, leaving Iggulden as audit accountant for £20, and paying Coggins £50 more to oversee them. Iggulden must have complained because, on 4 May 1934, his salary was increased to £26, the equivalent of 10s a week. Evans's £50 increase was changed to a bonus.

The 1933 tourist season had been successful, prompting Davies to solicit quotations to put *Merddin Emrys* back into service before the 1934 season, enabling the operation of an extra train to attract more traffic.

Another item being dealt with by Davies concerned the land leased from the Tremadoc estate for the station at Portmadoc. In this case, the

Its bulk meant that the Welsh Highland Railway's Baldwin 4-6-0T No.590 could go no further on the FR than Boston Lodge, where it was photographed on 9 August 1935.

Taliesin at Minffordd. Next to the locomotive, van No. 2 was one of several vehicles repainted with its mouldings highlighted in a contrasting colour.

payment had only gone into arrears on 6 September 1932. He not only negotiated a new lease at half the £125 annual charge previously incurred, but reduced the tonnage payable from 1½d to 1d as well.

Faced with continuing losses on the Welsh Highland Railway, the investing authorities had decided that it should be closed from 1 January 1934. Davies, however, thought that traffic in 1933 had been good and that in 1934 it would be better. Therefore, he commenced negotiations with the object of the Ffestiniog Railway leasing the WHR.

It took a while to agree that the FR did have the power, to lease another railway and the WHR the power to be leased, before terms were agreed for a twenty-one-year lease, renewable for twenty-one years, effective from 1 July 1934. A sticking point, which concerned the maintenance of the overbridges, had been resolved when the Ministry of Transport pointed out that if the county council adopted the roads concerned, they would qualify for a ministry grant.

The rent was £1 for the first six months, with a break clause allowing the FR to withdraw. Thereafter it was 10 per cent of gross income for thirteen years, followed by 10 per cent plus 5 per cent of any gross income over £2,000; a review would then be carried out. The big weakness, and surely an oversight on Davies' part, was that rent was payable on the gross and not the net income.

Services under the new arrangement started on 9 June 1934, the entire stock on both railways being repainted in varied colours, 'as a novelty', reported the *Locomotive* on 15 August.

Other items that came to the magazine's attention, were the operation of six trains to Blaenau Festiniog on weekdays, but only five back to Portmadoc, a 3d supplementary charge for riding in an observation car, which would have been one of the Brown, Marshalls or Hudson semi-opens, and the 'lady stationmaster in picturesque Welsh national dress' at Tan y Bwlch. According to the magazine, a locomotive named *Little Clara* was amongst those that had been scrapped, an error for *Little Giant* surely.

In preparation for taking over the Welsh Highland Railway, on 8 June 1934 Davies had said that he needed some technical assistance locally, proposing the appointment of the Snowdon Mountain Railway's manager, David Henry Roberts, as a director. The proposal was accepted. Davies' desire for technical assistance might be related to a comment that he had made in the report to shareholders on 26 April, that the company had to face the stern necessity of past neglect to maintain and improve the permanent way and rolling stock, which might imply that, notwithstanding local decisions made concerning cuts, there had not been as much supervision from Tonbridge as there should have been.

In the same report, he had said that the slate traffic was showing a gradual improvement, whilst tourist revenue showed a gratifying increase. Improvements to the general financial position had been made by discharging accounts that had been in arrears, whilst negotiations were now in hand concerning the arrears on the debentures. He had first mentioned this on 16 November 1933, when he thought that it might be possible to cancel the arrears and pay a flat 4 per cent interest to all holders.

This was not possible, and neither was a scheme to pay 50 per cent of the arrears in scrip, monetised certificates. Finally, the debenture holders settled for

40 per cent of the arrears in cash and 4 per cent interest in future. New certificates with a face value of £27,799 12s were issued to the thirty-seven holders on 19 July 1934. As well as reaching a resolution with the existing debenture holders, it was anticipated that the new arrangements would make the debentures marketable and increase their value.

Evan Robert Davies died suddenly on 2 December 1934, aged 63, family mythology saying that his doctor had declared him fit a few days before. He was replaced by his brother Walter Cradoc Davies, another solicitor, as a director and chairman on 15 December.

E.R. Davies was responsible for the FR taking a lease on the Welsh Highland Railway in 1933, but he died in 1934. His grave is in Pwllheli's public cemetery.
(Author)

Nearly 60-years-old when photographed at Boston Lodge on 3 June 1932, this Brown, Marshalls carriage was looking well past its best.
(H.C. Casserley)

The emptiness of the wharves indicate that the slate industry was in decline when this photograph was taken. The three-masted ship has probably made its last commercial journey, but there is still work for two locomotives. (Photochrom)

Close to the *Oakeley Arms*, two smart gents pose for a picture with the sign directing them to Tan y Bwlch Station.

The operation of the Welsh Highland Railway had not gone as well as he had expected. In January 1935, *Railway Magazine* reported that a special fare had been offered to holders of LMS 10s holiday tickets as an inducement to travel from Dinas to Blaenau Ffestiniog via Portmadoc, but that this had had a poor response, the more spectacular route from Llanberis to Portmadoc via Pen y Pass, Pen-y-Gwryd and Beddgelert offered by competing road vehicles having greater appeal to the public.

The prospect of the railway's centenary in 1936 generating publicity, and more passengers, had to be tempered with the minimal service that had operated during a strike by Ffestiniog quarrymen

Prince, captured during a break in shunting in Blaenau Ffestiniog, with the market hall and the North Western Hotel as a backdrop. (Martin Fuller collection)

that started on 14 March and lasted nine weeks. The company's immediate reaction had been to reduce its workforce, effectively to hibernate. However, the quarry proprietors said that they would use their foremen and administrative staff to perform tranship work at Minffordd if the railway remained open, having previously made veiled threats to close their outlets at Portmadoc and Minffordd if they were at all inconvenienced. More than 1,500 tons of slate was carried by working two or three days a week, but the £276 revenue thus earned had cost £348, despite some men being laid off or put on short hours. The company was probably too intimidated to ask for the cost of the service to be underwritten. Because of the strike, debenture interest and arrears due on 15 July were not paid.

Centenary publicity extended to a red flash on the timetable posters, 'The Ffestiniog Railway attains its centenary this year. It has a very interesting history, and is one of the most wonderful and popular toy railways in the country.' Holders of LMS and GWR

holiday contract tickets were encouraged to 'take a trip by the toy train thro' faeryland'. On production of their contract tickets they could obtain reduced rate tickets to do so.

Updating his co-directors about the Welsh Highland Railway on 25 May 1936, W.C. Davies had said that the situation was far from satisfactory. He had met the investing authorities in the spring of 1935 because Rhos Tryfan had stopped using the railway, undermining the company's business case for operating it. The summer passenger service had incurred a loss of £496 plus £100 rent. During the winter, merchandise had been carried by operating on one or two days a week, employing a driver and a fireman as required. On 23 April, he had sent copies of the accounts to the county council and

asked for the rent to be waived, adding that unless there was a considerable improvement in 1936, the company 'would have to consider seriously whether it was justified in running the railway'.

The hostel, one of E. R. Davies' ideas, had not been a success and was closed after the 1935 season. The house was let to a Mr L. de Thierry on a ten-year lease for £26 in June 1936. He stayed there until his death in 1985, aged ninety-seven. His grandson became a locomotive volunteer on the revived FR.

In September 1936, the directors considered J.W. Greaves' request for a further reduction on the slate rates. The full charge from Blaenau Festiniog to Minffordd was 4s 2d per ton. The company already gave a rebate of 6¾d and the GWR allowed 2s 3¾d so, although Greaves only paid 1s 4d, they wanted another 6d. The directors decided that the company

OPPOSITE: One of a set of photographs taken to commemorate the railway's centenary in 1936 and published as postcards. The photographer had managed it all, even getting the LMS driver to sound his whistle at the right moment. And on the FR, the loco crew and guard all make sure they can be seen by the camera. (Valentine)

Taliesin, the erstwhile *Livingston Thompson*, arrives at Portmadoc with the rebuilt van No. 2.

Anyone who did alight at Boston Lodge for Port Meirion, as the sign suggests, would have found they were in for a good walk before reaching their destination. The house beyond the turntable once used to turn locomotives, on which a slate wagon is stabled, was used briefly as a walkers' hostel. (H.C. Casserley)

The Welsh Highland Railway's Baldwin 4-6-0T No. 590 taking water in the FR station. It says much about how little the loco was regarded that it was never named, but it appears in many photographs and must have been well used.

(Martin Fuller collection)

could not afford a further reduction and resolved to ask for a meeting with the GWR, as that company would lose more if Greaves diverted its traffic via the LMS. On 2 December, the GWR said that it was prepared to offer another 3d per ton, if the quarry proprietors agreed to send an agreed proportion of their output via this route. Meeting on 8 December, the directors decided that if the proprietors were not prepared to guarantee a minimum traffic then the company would close during the winter months and merely run a summer passenger service for tourists.

The directors' decision to put some staff on short time, and to lay off the boilersmith without consulting him, caused W.H. Austen, the engineer, to take offence and to resign with effect from 31 October 1936. At first he accepted the request of the secretary, C.E. Davies, to reconsider, but then changed his mind. On 8 December, the directors appointed S. Alexander, the Snowdon Mountain Railway's resident engineer, as engineer and locomotive superintendent, at a salary of £30.

A notebook containing a daily record of work carried out by Boston Lodge personnel for twelve months from August 1936, provides a snapshot of activities. As well as work on the home fleet and wagons, work on Welsh Highland Railway locomotives was also done. On 19 October, Monday,

the works and railway were closed for the thanksgiving festival; in days gone by this would have been an opportunity to run extra trains for celebrating residents. From February 1937, there were regular entries for work undertaken for the Snowdon Mountain Railway.

The centenary year was concluded with a radio broadcast from Bangor on 8 October and repeated on 12 December, both dates rather too late in the year to encourage any visitors. Robert Evans and enthusiast/historian Charles E. Lee participated in the programme.

Promoting it, the *Nottingham Evening Post* commented on the railway's unusual features, 'a woman station master who wears the traditional Welsh costume, a gauge of only two feet, and a pair of Siamese twin engines', adding that, 'since the slump in the slate trade, the railway has been used considerably less, but is still patronised by hundreds of visitors during the summer.'

Continuing poor results from the Welsh Highland Railway prompted a special directors' meeting on 16 February 1937, when W.C. Davies gave them a copy of the minutes of a meeting that he had attended with the local authorities on 31 December 1936. Briefly, he had told the committee that operating the WHR had lost £506 in 1934, £498 plus £100 rent in

1935 and was likely to have lost the same in 1936. The FR had publicised the WHR and encouraged the LMS and GWR to provide connecting trains, but it had lost the slate traffic, and the Crosville Bus Company, in which the LMS was invested, was competing for both Blaenau Festiniog-Portmadoc and Portmadoc-Caernarvon traffic. The situation was aggravated by the effect of the strike on the FR's revenues and the estimated £1,000 expenditure to make the WHR fit to run another season.

It was most unlikely that the councillors would agree to Davies' request for the company to be relieved of its obligations under the lease and they did not. They asked him to write explaining why the company should not pay the rent so that an opinion could be obtained from the treasury and the Ministry of Transport. On 16 February, the directors thought they were justified in deciding to cease running the WHR. If the investing authorities would not agree terms for surrendering the lease, then the company would have to face whatever action they took.

Counsel's opinion, already obtained on the likely outcomes if the company defaulted on the lease, was that the investing authorities would be entitled to judgment for the arrears of rent and damages. The directors thought that the authorities would have little to gain by taking such action as, if they obtained judgment, any attempt to enforce it could be forestalled by the company's debenture holders appointing a receiver.

A formal decision not to run the Welsh Highland Railway from 1 June was made on 14 May 1937. Robert Evans was instructed to have all the wagons assembled at Dinas and check them against the lease inventory, and to have the locomotives stabled in the shed at Dinas.

Negotiations with Greaves and the other quarries over the rates had been continuing with input from the Great Western Railway. By January 1937, they

wanted a reduction of 8d a ton, from the net 1s 4d. They settled on 4d a ton; if the volume exceeded 15,000 tons a year, then the company would rebate another 1d per ton. The GWR was asked for 6d per ton, but would only agree to 4d.

The new rates were introduced on 22 March 1937, 1s per ton to LMS or GWR stations in Blaenau Festiniog and 3s 10d Blaenau Festiniog to Minffordd and direct to Portmadoc. No charge was made for slate shipped from Portmadoc to Minffordd for despatch via the GWR although 7d per ton was charged to carry slate from Minffordd to Portmadoc.

A unilateral 5 per cent increase in freight rates applied by the Railway Clearing House was put into effect on 1 December 1937, when the local rate was increased to 1s 1d and the Minffordd/Portmadoc rate to 4s. The Minffordd-Portmadoc rate was left unchanged. At the same time, the quarry proprietors had been reminded that the shortage of wagons was due to them being kept under load at Portmadoc and elsewhere, and not because there was a shortage.

Alexander's appointment as engineer was short-lived and had been terminated on 30 August 1937, when he had also left the Snowdon Mountain Railway. W. C. Davies had reported that he was

There are many photographs taken of 'station mistress' Bessie Jones at Tan y Bwlch. This is one of two taken in colour in May 1937. Living in the station house with her husband Will, Bessie met the trains wearing her Welsh costume, posed for photographs, sold picture postcards and served refreshments from her front room. Will, who worked on the track, is also pictured, carrying the haversack. The photograph shows that the locomotives were no longer kept in pristine condition. (Rev Stuart Marsh)

A busy scene at Tan y Bwlch, with carriages loaded with tourists. The brightly-coloured carriage is No. 23, the Ashbury obtained from the Welsh Highland Railway in exchange for wagons. Bessie Jones talks to passengers and sells them picture postcards of the station and herself.

Tan y Bwlch seen from the back of the train one afternoon in 1933. (T.P. Griffith/Meg Davies collection)

dissatisfied with his performance on 14 May. In substitution, Davies had recruited James Williamson, the engineer from May 1921 until March 1923, on a salary of £50 plus expenses from 1 October. He was expected to carry out an inspection and report on the track immediately, and then to spend one day per month on the railway.

It was not until January 1938 that the directors realised that Williamson had no experience or qualification to sign the locomotive superintendent's certificate in the annual report, resolving to appoint Boston Lodge chargehand Morris W. Jones as acting locomotive superintendent with effect from 1 January. He had a Board of Trade chief engineer's certificate.

On 15 February 1938, the secretary, C. E. Davies, writing to Caernarvonshire County Council about the Welsh Highland Railway, asked if the company might be allowed to keep the WHR locomotive *Moel Tryfan*, then at Boston Lodge. It had, he said, failed its boiler test in 1934 and the company was not, therefore, obliged to restore it to pre-lease condition. Once it became clear that the Welsh Highland Railway lease was not going to be resolved quickly, the directors decided, on 9 May, that until it was clarified, no further debenture interest, or arrears, should be paid. On 1 September, the investing authorities decided that the company could keep *Moel Tryfan* provided that it paid £600 in settlement of claims arising from the lease.

Two level crossings were widened to better accommodate road traffic in 1938. At Penrhyn, after negotiations that had taken two years, Merionethshire County Council paid £130 for 546 square yards of land and £75 to compensate the company for the additional cost of maintaining and operating the enlarged crossing. Only 180 square yards of land was required at Glan y Pwll and the council paid £25 for it.

Some remarkable initiative was shown when the track through the Moelwyn Tunnel was relaid during the first half of 1938. The company was allowed to take lightly-used rail from a wharf owned by the Tremadoc estate at Portmadoc and replace it with the old rail when the relaying was complete.

Williamson reported that the track would benefit from the employment of two additional labourers installing 200 new sleepers per month for six months. New chairs were also required; as the foundry was

Taliesin and train near the Garnedd Tunnel in 1935. (R. W. Kidner)

unable to produce the number required, tenders should be obtained.

In October 1938, a review of the year's traffic revealed that there had been 3,000 fewer passengers and 1,000 tons less slate and goods. Passenger revenue had been slightly increased because of a fare increase and more bookings at Portmadoc; circular tour and through-journey bookings earned less because of the commission given. Thanks to the 5 per cent increase, goods revenue was only £30 down. Later, Evans reported that the loss up to 9 July, when the passenger service started, had been £1,002. When it ended on 26 September, the loss had been reduced to £110, but increased to £758 by the end of the year, so

The Boston Lodge locomotive watering arrangement spanned the track alongside the engine shed, as seen with *Taliesin* on 3 June 1932.

(H.C. Casserley)

the passenger service had made a profit of £892 whilst the goods and minerals had lost £1,650.

The directors also knew that it would make sense to cancel the quarrymen's train during the winter, but knew that if they did that, the quarrymen would use road transport and not return to the railway in the summer, losing £250 revenue annually. The table, taken from the year's annual report, shows the figures. Without the quarrymen, the average fare would have been 1s 1.22d and the company would have been saved the cost of operating six trains a week. The quarrymen would have stayed with the railway because it was cheaper, and they knew that they could not bully the bus company into reducing its fares for them.

Locomotive working could probably be made more efficient, the directors thought. The locomotive

that worked the quarrymen's train spent the day assembling the slate train, and the locomotive that returned the empties from Portmadoc and Minffordd had to return without a load. A tractor also worked between Portmadoc and Minffordd, shunting as required. It ought to have been possible for the first engine to make a return trip to Portmadoc during the day, taking the loaded slate wagons and returning with the empties.

Operating the railway and Boston Lodge were considered in more detail in December 1938, D.H. Roberts reporting on the former and the Snowdon Mountain Railway's locomotive superintendent, T.G. Jack, on the latter. The directors approved £200 expenditure on *Prince*, the work to be carried out by the Dinorwic Dry Dock Company, and ordered a scrap drive to dispose of the remains of *James Spooner*, *Taliesin* and *Little Giant*, as well as disused wagons and other unwanted material.

In January 1939, the directors resolved on salary reductions for the chairman (from £120 to £100); secretary (£225/£200); accountant (£78/£50); and manager (£334/£300). The audit accountant would

Class of passenger	Number	Receipts	Average fare
1st	675	£55	1s 7.56d
3rd	36,497	£2,016	1s 1.26d
Workmen	21,916	£299	3.27d
	59,088	£2,370	9.63d

retain the same fee, but the auditors would be asked to revert to that charged before the Welsh Highland Railway was taken over.

Six men were also sacked: O. Owens, Portmadoc porter, £3 6s 9d; H. G. Griffith, Tanygrisiau clerk, £2 10s 6d; Wilson, blacksmith striker, £2 9s 6d; J. Roberts, carpenter, £2 9s 1d; W. H. Jones, blacksmith, £2 12s 10d; B. Jones, extra cleaner, £2 0s 1d. As Owens occupied the Portmadoc station house for a nominal 1s per week, he was allowed to stay if he cleaned the offices and station.

Rents for some properties on the company's estate were also revised from 1 January 1939; W. Lloyd, Glan y Pwll crossing, to 5s from 2s 1d a week, and William Jones, Tan y Bwlch station house, 2s 6d / 1s. Mary Davies, the tenant at 2 Boston Lodge, not an employee, had her rent increased from £6 5s a year to £10 8s, 4s per week.

The directors had realised that there was still a deficiency in the railway's professional supervision, in that the foreman fitter, Morris Jones, did not have appropriate locomotive qualifications. On 1 February 1939, they appointed T.G. Jack, from the Snowdon Mountain Railway, as locomotive superintendent on a salary of £2 14s 6d per month plus £1 per month travelling expenses. He was expected to spend two half-days a week at Boston Lodge. He was not related to H.J. Jack.

Two incidents of trespass were recorded in 1939, the first for many years, although there must have

By rooting around Glan y Mor Yard the inquisitive enthusiast could find *Little Giant's* saddle tank and *James Spooner's* cab amongst the detritus dumped there.
(H.W. Comber/FR Archives)

been many unrecorded occurrences. A bicycle run over by the down light-engine on 25 January belonged to the grocery delivery boy delivering to Tyn y Pistyll, the cottage near the waterfall at Tanygrisiau, who told the police that he did not know of any other way to reach the property. In November, Williamson told Evans about children who had been seen playing on the track at Blaenau Festiniog; Evans replied to the effect that prosecutions in the past had not acted as much of a deterrent. He asked the police superintendent to visit local schools.

A fine view of the Boston Lodge engine shed with Cnicht and part of the Cambrian Railways' Glaslyn Bridge in the background. 3 June 1932. (H.C. Casserley)

Merddin Emrys makes a spirited departure from Tan y Bwlch in the 1930s. Next to the loco is 1873-built van No. 2, rebuilt with two passenger compartments in 1921. Without its footbridge and fences the station looks very bare. (F. U. Sergeant)

On 19 January 1939, there had been another fire at Boston Lodge, this time involving machinery and line shafting, although Evans' report gave no details of its cause or circumstances. The *Liverpool Evening Express* said that it had started near the oil engine and that employees' efforts to quell the flames had been hampered by the limited water supply. The fire brigade had only succeeded after two hours, by using 'giant chemical extinguishers'. The insurance claim was settled for £705 and the roof was replaced by corrugated iron.

The directors visited the works during their June meeting, deciding that an architect should be appointed to produce plans to alter the layout to improve working efficiency. They also visited Penrhyn Station and Capel Nazareth Underbridge. Whilst Williamson recommended demolishing the station building except for the booking office they thought that the booking office, and the waiting room, which had recently been leased to the Llanfrothen Co-operative Society, should be retained, but the remainder, including the urinal, should be pulled down due to their dilapidated condition. The Co-op had rented land at the station for a store shed since 1918.

They visited the bridge because a complaint had been made to the Ministry of Transport, claiming that it was too narrow for the motor vehicles using it and calling on the company to widen it. They found evidence of vehicles scraping its sides and of a gate across the road on the uphill side. It was, they felt, quite evident that when the bridge was built it was for nothing more than an accommodation road, sufficient for the requirements of the traffic until recently. They did not consider that the company was liable to widen it.

In advance of the tourist season starting, the directors approved a tender of £20 for the external woodwork and railings of Portmadoc Station and goods warehouse to be painted.

The declaration of war on 3 September 1939 brought an immediate end to the passenger service and a reduction in the already low slate traffic. The directors met on 15 September, following the government's 29 August notification that it had no intention of taking over light railways. C. E. Davies'

Taliesin being coupled on to its train at the Great Western platform in Blaenau Ffestiniog. *Isallt*, the house behind, accommodated the railway's shop and booking office when services were restored in 1982.

optimism, in a letter to Robert Evans, that the situation would change when, after an emergency, road transport became short, proved to be misplaced.

Evans reported that for the year to 8 July, passengers had increased by 245, increasing receipts by £28 whilst slate revenue was reduced by £100. Economies had saved £268, reducing the loss to £807, whilst passenger traffic from 9 July until 2 September had reduced it to £28 so the £739 profit on the passenger service had been wiped out by the loss on the goods service of at least £1,075.

Forecasting a loss on the traffic that had been carried since 2 September, Evans said that the average weekly load from 1 January until 2 September, 636 tons, had fallen to 542 tons since. The lower volume would generate about £70 a week whilst a normal week's expenses was £115. As some quarries were closing one or more weeks per month and Oakeley was not working on Saturdays,

he recommended withdrawing the quarrymens' train, with receipts of less than £4 a week, to enable the operation of a shorter working day. He pointed out that the volume was likely to fall further because the Government had placed restrictions on new housing schemes and there might not be any passenger traffic to make good the loss on the mineral traffic in 1940.

After meeting the quarry proprietors, the directors decided that drastic measures were called for and that from 18 September, the railway would be opened on three days a week, Mondays, Wednesdays and Fridays, from 25 September 1939.

The LNWR station and yard in the 1930s, showing empty slate wagons awaiting return to the quarries. The roof of the FR station is visible on the left.

Whilst the country faced up to the realities of being in a state of war, the railway was not entirely forgotten. The MP for Caernarfonshire, Goronwy Owen, asked the Minister of Transport to explain why the company was not being taken over as it had been during the 1914-1918 conflict and whether any financial support was available if the company found itself unable to continue because of the war conditions. In a written reply on 17 October, the minister said that only the railways deemed to be necessary for essential transport had been taken over. As a narrow-gauge line, the Ffestiniog Railway did not form an integral part of the main line system or provide an alternative route for heavy traffic; he had no funds with which to provide financial assistance.

In September 1938, the FR had been included in a list of ten 'lesser' undertakings to be taken under Government control in the event of a national emergency, but on 27 March 1939, the Ministry of Transport had asked the railway executive committee to review the list as, 'at first sight it is difficult to see what justification exists for taking such a line as the Festiniog into control' A recommendation to exclude the FR, with the observation, 'This is a narrow-gauge line, and no operating or commercial reasons are seen for Government control' had been made on 11 April and accepted by the ministry on 26 April.

Left to their own resources, the directors did what they could to maintain a minimal service for the quarries whilst reducing expenses. The locomotives were in poor condition. In January 1939 *Palmerston* had been out of use, *Prince* dismantled, and *Merddin Emrys, Taliesin, Princess* and *Welsh Pony* were all marked as 'overdue for thorough examination'.

Princess had a firebox patch that leaked, and *Welsh Pony* had several leaking tubes and stays.

Repairs to the embankment carried out by the Tremadoc estate's contractor, J. Llewelyn Davies of Barmouth, brought in some extra revenue in 1939-40. Before work was started, the company and the estate waltzed around each other to determine where the rights and responsibilities lay. The estate was responsible for maintenance and entitled to have access for that purpose, but it was not entitled to interrupt the railway's traffic; the company was entitled to charge for any carriage provided. Correspondence had started in April 1939.

Evans persuaded the estate that it would be better to deliver stone to site from Blaenau Ffestiniog by rail rather than by road from quarries on estate property and the rate of 2s 5d per ton, payable by the contractor, was agreed. He also persuaded the contractor to pay a wayleave of £5 per annum for the right to have concrete and other materials conveyed to site by using his men to push a wagon under the railway's supervision, and £1 to site a shed on company property near the station. On 23 August, the contractors were allowed use of a company-owned crane; whether this was the rail-mounted crane obtained to unload materials for the shell factory is not clear; £1 a week was charged for its use. In December, 18s was charged for repairs to telephone wires damaged by the crane and settled by the insurance company.

The repairs included constructing the concrete wave wall along the sea-side of the embankment. The passage of time has shown that the work was done well as there have been no further incidents of the embankment being breached since it was constructed. The work started in July 1939 and took twelve months.

The memory of Boston Lodge being used by the Government in 1915 was obviously not forgotten, as an advertisement published in the *Manchester Guardian* on 17 December 1940 reveals: *RAILWAY ENGINEERING WORKS AVAILABLE FOR WAR WORK immediate possession. Full particulars from Manager, Ffestiniog Railway Company, Portmadoc.* There was no response.

Some five years after it had last been operated, the company was closer to being relieved from the responsibility of running the Welsh Highland Railway. The Ministry of Supply had requisitioned the track on 13 March 1941, after the investing authorities had indicated that they would not contest an order. George Cohen, Sons & Company Ltd, bought the requisitioned assets and started removing them in August 1941. The summons releasing the company from the lease was heard in September, when £600 settlement became due, £200 immediately, the remainder in four annual instalments starting one year after end of the war or any armistice. On payment of the settlement the company would be entitled to retain *Moel Tryfan*.

Repairs to bomb-damaged buildings brought a brief and welcome revival in the slate traffic in 1941, but it was not sustained. On 5 March 1941, C.E. Davies was prompted to ask the Ministry of Transport if the minister could change his mind and make the railway one of the controlled lines, but on 13 March, the railway executive committee informed the minister that there had been no change in the circumstances which made it desirable to control the FR. As the war progressed, the quarries were unable to meet the demand for slate because they had lost their skilled labour to the forces.

On 29 May 1941 it was reported that C.E. Davies, the secretary, had been commissioned into the Royal Air Force so his duties were again transferred to his brother, Ninian Rhys Davies. A few days later, the Davies brothers transferred £100 of their jointly-held ordinary stock to Robert Evans and William Hugh Davies, their Pwllheli clerk. Whilst no explanation for the transfer was recorded, it did at least ensure that the directors could be joined by ordinary shareholders at general meetings.

C. E. Davies resumed his duties on 20 December. T. G. Jack had joined up so Morris Jones was again appointed acting locomotive superintendent, back-dated to 1 January 1940.

Director H.L. Westall died on 28 February 1942, aged sixty-three. On 3 April, he was replaced by N.R. Davies after £500 of the joint stock holding had been transferred to him in his own right. Westall's ordinary stock, £2,243 16s 6d, was bequeathed to Henry Jack Macinnes, who had been known as Henry Joseph Jack until 6 June 1933.

Although the company's advertisement offering the use of facilities at Boston Lodge for industrial purposes in 1940 had been fruitless, the company was able to provide some accommodation for Government departments. A list of rentals minuted in 1943 includes: War Department, Boston Lodge, £6 10s, from 2 September 1941; War Department, Portmadoc Station, £83 4s, 10 April-30 June 1942; Portmadoc Station, £120, from 10 July 1942.

Another tenant moved into Boston Lodge in November 1942, Portmadoc's Glaslyn Foundry. With reference to the Location of Industry (Restriction) Order which had been made in October 1942, the foundry was licensed by the Board of Trade to use Boston Lodge to produce components for the Ministry of Supply, providing sufficient facilities were allowed to the company for its own purposes and to the Britannia Foundry if required. An agreement was dated 16 November 1942. It will have been as a consequence of this arrangement that *Palmerston*, which had been awaiting repairs since 1935, was moved to a location alongside the foundry to provide steam for the belt-driven equipment.

In June 1941, Maenofferen had complained of the inconvenience incurred by working on two wharves at Minffordd and Robert Evans had been instructed to consult with the other tenants to see what improvements could be made. It took until February-May 1943 to complete new leases, the revised arrangements earning £176 7s a year instead of £75 10s.

As well as increasing some of its rentals, the company was also able to dispose of some surplus stock. The 6-ton mobile hand crane, obtained to unload wagons whilst Boston Lodge was under Government control during the First World War and retained afterwards, was sold to the Broughton Moor Green Slate Quarries Ltd for £142 10s, after commission, in 1943. The vehicle had proved to be something of a white elephant.

In 1942, two batches of ten slate wagons had been requisitioned by the War Department to be used for target practice on the Welsh Highland Railway near Hafod Ruffydd, a compensation of £33 each being paid. The archives reveal that the company did quite well out of this as the wagons were on the books at £20 each and the War Department also paid £5 5s to cover the cost of negotiating the compensation. There was some internal debate as to whether the wagons had been replacements, chargeable to

revenue, or additional, chargeable to capital, whilst the company actually had no renewal funds. The Ministry of Supply paid £420 for fourteen wagons which it requisitioned, £30 each. N.R. Davies reported that even without these wagons, the company still had sufficient to meet its obligations to the quarry proprietors.

Two years after the court hearing where approval was given to releasing the company from the Welsh Highland Railway lease, the matter was still not resolved. In 1943, the WHR receiver agreed that £50 incurred in legal fees on his behalf could be offset against the £600 compensation owing for surrendering the lease. The surrender agreement was dated 12 August 1945 and the first instalment of £100 paid on 30 August.

The directors did not involve themselves too much with the company's affairs during the war. In 1942-3, four meetings, two only dealing with stock transfers, were written up, but not dated and obviously never happened. The general meetings of 1943 and 1944 were conducted by N.R. Davies on his own, acting with the support of proxies, the second, adjourned from 26 July until 21 October, being the last held under the Davies regime. Some forty years later, Davies told the author that these meetings had been the most unusual feature of his period in office.

Apart from dealing with the sale of a plot of land in 1945, from 1943 the directors only dealt with share transfers. The land was a part of that bought from Portmadoc Urban District Council to be used as the road between the new station and the Great Western Railway station in 1923.

Despite the reduced expenses and rental increases, the reduced service operated during the war still ran at a loss. In the report for 1944, produced in November 1945, W.C. Davies explained that 1944 had been worse than 1943 because the quarry output had been affected by shortage of labour, and the cost of essential maintenance on rolling stock and track had tended to increase. He did not say so, but the directors had run out of ideas for keeping the railway going.

CHAPTER 4

1946-1954: CLOSURE AND ABANDONMENT

The local authorities were concerned about the effect the railway's possible closure would have on the locality. Meeting on 15 July 1946, they had no solution although one councillor did suggest, presciently, that the emphasis should be on promoting the railway as a tourist amenity.

The first outsider known to take an interest in the railway's future was William J. Brown of Stoke-on-Trent. He had written to Portmadoc UDC on 11 July to ask about the railway re-opening. He received a detailed reply after the meeting, and was asked if he had any ideas for reviving it or if he could exert any influence. Brown was a benefactor of the revived railway, enabling the restoration of *Taliesin* to be completed sooner than might otherwise have been possible. Upset when the loco was re-named in 1961, he transferred his allegiance to the revival of the Welsh Highland Railway.

The Ministry of Transport had informed Robert Evans that it would not make a grant to repair the track unless the railway was essential to the quarrying industry. There was no formal decision to close it but on 2 August 1946, Evans informed the quarries that the company was not in a position to accept any further traffic and that they should gather together the company's wagons ready to be collected.

On 24 July 1946, the photographer captures what appears to be a timeless scene at Minffordd. *Princess* simmers as the driver oils round and the fireman readies the fire ready for another trip to Blaenau Ffestiniog. Neither of them knew that a few days later, on 2 August, the staff would receive twenty-four-hours' notice that their jobs no longer existed and the railway would be closed. The crude alteration to the worksplate recording work carried out in 1937 is quite clear. (B.B. Edmonds)

The last of the Welsh Highland Railway promoters who took control of the FR to further their aims, Henry Joseph Jack, who had adopted the name Macinnes in 1933, died in 1946 and was buried at Ann's Hill Cemetery in Gosport, Hampshire. (Author)

He also told the remaining employees, apart from Morris Jones, that they no longer had jobs, giving them twenty-four-hours' notice. Jones was kept on for a few months, and was presumably responsible for collecting the wagons and stock. Whilst he obviously had no idea if the closure was permanent or temporary, it is to be regretted that no consideration was given to preparing the locomotives for a period out of use; it would have taken very little effort to drain them down and to remove damp slack from their bunkers, actions that would have prolonged their use when the revival started.

The railway's closure came shortly after the death on 2 January 1946 of the last member of the triumvirate that took over the company to secure the development of the Welsh Highland Railway in 1921; Henry Jack Macinnes had died in Tunbridge Wells, aged seventy-six.

In response to the closure notice, J.W. Greaves, operators of Llechwedd, tried to find another source of free wagons, approaching the London, Midland & Scottish Railway, which provided wagons to Oakeley, and the Ministry of Works' director of roofing, with no result.

The quarries subsequently combined to make an agreement whereby they leased 650 yards of the railway between Duffws and the LMS, originally LNWR, yard that they could operate themselves on payment of 1s per ton, minimum £5 per week, the arrangement starting on 7 October 1946. The quarries also rented wagons, Greaves paying £5 a week for fifty-five. It thought this amount was excessive and argued, fruitlessly, that £3 was more reasonable.

From 1946, the company received a steady stream of letters from enthusiasts asking for information, old tickets or permission to visit. On 25 February, J.I.C. Boyd, who was to make a name for himself as a writer on narrow-gauge railways, asked if he and his wife could travel on a goods train; he enclosed an indemnity signed over a 6d postage stamp. On 10 September, P.B. Whitehouse, who became one of the railway's patrons, and whose son became company chairman, asked about visiting.

J. K. A. Firth was the first to suggest that the railway might be re-opened if it changed hands. Writing from Radley College, Oxfordshire, in October 1946 he said that he had seen the railway's remains whilst on holiday and asked if its rights could be acquired. There was nothing from his letter to indicate that Firth was a 16-year-old schoolboy and nothing more was heard from him after he had written once more. He was to lose his life in the Korean war.

Captain J.P. Howey, the owner of the 15in gauge Romney, Hythe & Dymchurch Railway in Kent, visited and met Evans, but was not inspired. If he had been, he had the resources to take the railway on and to make a considerable investment in it.

In 1947, W.B. Broadbent, a young engineer working for the LMSR at Crewe, started a correspondence with Evans and visited the railway.

Merddin Emrys forms the centrepiece of this view of the Boston Lodge engine shed on 24 August 1946. Just visible on the left is the Simplex tractor whilst the partially dismantled Welsh Highland Fairlie *Moel Tryfan* is on the right. (B B. Edmonds)

With his friend Michael Low, he devised a business plan, but nothing came of it; they were too busy developing their careers and starting families. Bill Broadbent held influential positions in the railway's direction and management from 1955 until 1998.

To start with, Evans accommodated requests for visits and there are several photographs of him taken at Boston Lodge, but then he found that the motives of some were suspect and from 1948 he started to refuse them, although there were those who realised that his refusal could be circumvented by writing to the secretary in London.

Later, one of the tenants at Boston Lodge, Reverend Timothy Phillips, the son of a Boston Lodge fitter who retired there in 1949, acted as guardian to the works, accosting those he found roaming the site, and securing doors and windows.

The directors found themselves in a difficult legal situation. The company's Acts of Parliament gave them powers to build and operate the railway, but not to close it. There was uncertainty about whether control could be held through the ordinary stock or the debentures, although they themselves only held ordinary stock. There was also no advantage from

In the erecting shop in the same day, the photographer found *Taliesin* and *Prince's* wheeled frames awaiting the installation of it's new boiler, visible on the left. (B.B. Edmonds)

disposing of surplus assets because any realisations had to be applied to the capital account, for the benefit of the ordinary stock holders, and not to the current account, for the benefit of the creditors.

At some point, George Cohen, the scrap merchant who had dismantled the Welsh Highland Railway, had offered £4,000 to do the same for the FR. In 1948, another scrap merchant, probably W.O. Williams of Harlech, offered £7,000 for it, offers that seem to have influenced the directors' response when enquiries were made about taking over the railway.

A meeting held in Portmadoc to discuss the future of the slate quarry industry on 7 August 1948,

revealed that it, too, was in poor condition. Of the 8,550 quarrymen in North Wales, only 700 were working full time, 1,300 were unemployed and the remainder were working short time. Wages had been reduced from £3 15s per week in 1921 to £2 9s. No benefit was being gained from the construction of new council houses, because the Housing (Financial Provisions) Act of 1924 insisted on the

Outside at Boston Lodge, *Palmerston* had been plumbed in to supply steam to the works' stationary engine. (B B. Edmonds)

use of the cheapest materials so the Welsh industry was being undercut by imports. The report published in *The Times* on 13 August, said that the company had been represented by Evan R. Davies, an impossibility, as he had died in 1934. On the proposal of the company's representative, a committee was appointed to draft a memorandum extolling the virtues of Welsh slate for circulation to county councils.

Narrow Gauge Railways to Portmadoc, J.I.C. Boyd's book about the railway and the other narrow-gauge railways that had served Portmadoc, was published in the spring of 1949, generating a lot of interest amongst enthusiasts wanting to know more. Several were keen enough to want to find some way to preserve it and looked to him as their leader.

Boyd spent the remainder of the year promoting the cause of Edward 'Teddy' Eustace Smith of

Corbridge, Northumberland, as a candidate to take over the railway. Smith, who was allegedly wealthy, failed to make an offer that exceeded the scrap merchants' and Boyd gave up, convinced that the directors were not interested, not knowing that W.O. Williams had increased his offer by £1,000 during the year. When Smith died in 1979, his estate was valued at £82,110 so he probably was not as well off as Boyd had thought.

The failure to make any progress with this scheme persuaded the directors that the only option available to them was to obtain an abandonment order, sell off the assets and liquidate the company. A shareholders' meeting in October 1950 was followed by an application for an order, which was rejected on 4 December, the Ministry of Transport saying that it was not empowered to make an order, confirming its position on 9 February 1951.

By 1949 the abandoned rolling stock in Portmadoc Station became something of an attraction and a few photographs were taken in colour. Brake van No. 3 was beyond repair, its re-creation becoming an ambition from the early days of restoration. (David Elliott)

Dereliction at Minffordd in 1949. Maybe the paint scheme on the ground-floor window frames will be reinstated one day. (David Elliott)

This behind-the-scenes activity spilled over into the local press, attracting letters of complaint and calling upon the town council to take action. In response, James Boyd wrote to say, in *Y Rhedegydd* published on 7 December 1950, that once it was known who was going to dismantle the railway, he and some friends were prepared to buy a double engine; he had already asked the council for help in leasing or buying the Portmadoc goods shed in which to display it and other items. If it proved to be impossible to keep the intended collection in Portmadoc, then a home would be sought elsewhere; he considered the railway museum at York and had made contact with the national museum of Wales, but they were already full.

On 18 December, the Portmadoc Chamber of Commerce decided to look further into a member's suggestion that a miniature train running along the embankment would be a fine attraction for the town.

The enthusiast fraternity appeared quite determined that something could, and should be done, for there was a buzz surrounding the Talyllyn Railway in southern Merionethshire, which was on the cusp of becoming the first preserved railway. Following the death of its owner, the former MP for Merionethshire, Sir Henry Haydn Jones, on 2 July 1950, a supporting society had been formed and, on 8 February 1951, an agreement was reached with Jones'

widow, leading to it becoming the first railway to be operated with an input from volunteers on 14 May.

Boyd was soon involved with the TR, in March 1951 writing to newspapers about the FR from its North Western Publicity Department. On 20 April, he addressed a meeting of councillors and others in Portmadoc, saying that they should offer 'something' for the company's shares and get the money back by selling surplus stock and machinery for scrap, then they could try and make the railway pay by relying on tourist traffic. If it did not work, they would not have lost anything. They must not rely on enthusiasts for 'heavy financial support' and must find the resources themselves, he told them. At his suggestion, a committee of thirteen was formed to take things forward. Boyd himself and J.C. Wilkins, owner of the 15in gauge Fairbourne Railway, were appointed technical advisers.

It appears that this committee only met once, on 28 June 1951, when the members made it clear that the railway could expect no financial support from local sources, the WHR debt was still being paid off and residents had no enthusiasm for further railway ventures. It was suggested that the company should be asked if the railway over the embankment and some stock could be hired for a trial to be operated in 1952, further developments depending on its success.

At around this time, Boyd discovered that he was not the only person who had been in contact with the company to establish whether it would be possible to take it over and revive the railway. Leonard Heath Humphrys was only a 17-year-old school boy in 1950, but deciding that something should be done to prevent the railway's abandonment, he wrote to Robert Evans in February and then in June commenced a correspondence with C.E. Davies.

Late in 1950, he started writing to magazines looking for support, the first letter being published in the *British Locomotive Journal* in January 1951. He made contact with Boyd, who virtually told him that he was wasting his time, at the same time that

The wagons abandoned by the harbour were not photographed so often, or as well as those in the station.

In October 1954 the British Electricity Authority commissioned a photographer to visit the railway, presumably with the intention of demonstrating that it was beyond restoration. Not being knowledgeable about railways, however, he managed to show it in a better light than perhaps his employers intended. At Pen Cob the remains of the signal box stand on the left, whilst a war-time pill box had been built on the embankment with little regard for the possibility that train services might one day be resumed.

(British Electricity Authority)

Davies offered every co-operation. He attended the 20 April meeting in Portmadoc as an observer.

Around seventy enthusiasts expressed their interest and support, so Humphrys arranged a meeting at the Bristol Railway Circle's club rooms on 8 September, sending out hand-written invitations. Twelve attended with sixteen apologising for absence. He arrived late, delaying the revelation that he was still at school. After a discussion, an ad hoc committee was formed. At a second meeting, held at the *Old Bull Inn* in Barnet, North London, on 8 October, it was decided to form the Ffestiniog Railway Society with the objective of reviving the railway and to appoint a legal committee to deal with any complications that might lay ahead.

Participants in these first meetings included Allan Garraway, who became a founding director of the society and then the railway's general manager; Fred Gilbert, who conducted the negotiations with the company; and Vic Mitchell and R. W. Winter who both became society directors. Others played a role in other railway preservation enterprises. As he was about to be called up for National Service, Humphrys stood down as secretary. In his absence,

and without consulting him, W.G. Rear of Crewe was appointed secretary. It is thanks to Gilbert's tenacity that the nascent society did not fold at this point, for letters to Rear went unanswered.

Some correspondence between C.E. Davies and the Ministry of Transport and the Ministry of Supply in January 1952 gives an insight into the legal situation, the latter being keen to facilitate the disposal of the scrap in the national interest. The Ministry of Transport had been advised by the treasury solicitor that, although the company could not be wound up without further legislation, there was nothing to compel it to operate the railway and therefore no legal objection to the disposal of the rails and rolling stock. Davies replied that he had legal advice that no one had power to sell the stock and that any receiver would be unable to sell it either.

Thereafter, Davies communicated with L. Taylor Harris, Gilbert's solicitor, on 5 February 1952 informing him that on 31 December 1950 the company owed £9,068 on the debentures, which accrued at £632 a year, owed £11,407 19s 9d to the bank and had unsecured long-term trading debts of £460. At 30 November 1951, £454 of rents payable

Looking towards Boston Lodge, Morris Jones had left a few carriages outside, only partially sheltered by the wall.
(W. G. Rear)

Constructed in 1879-80, Penrhyn Station has been thought to contain elements of the first station at Portmadoc, but expenditure totalling £441 19s 9d suggests that that might not be the case. (W. G. Rear)

were in arrears as were £209 of rents receivable. The company had not paid any of its £1,111 war damage contribution and had a liability of £478 in connection with the Welsh Highland Railway lease surrender.

Gilbert got his accountant, R.L. Houghton, to work out what the stock might be worth. He thought that as the company was 'hopelessly insolvent' and trading at a loss, the ordinary stock and preference shares were worthless, and that the debentures were only worth whatever could be realised from the sale of scrap. He was also surprised that the bank had not served a winding up order. He suggested offering 1 per cent for the ordinary stock and preference shares, and 2½ per cent for the debentures, giving a cost to acquire control of £1,390, if acceptances were received for half of it.

At a public meeting held in London on 20 April 1952, the '(proposed) Ffestiniog Railway Preservation Society' was formed, although without the company's approval to use the railway's name, with a new committee. L. Taylor Harris was elected chairman in recognition of the work he was undertaking. John Bate, an engineer who had attended the Bristol meeting and who became chief engineer of the Talyllyn Railway, submitted his report on the railway's track and structures with an estimate that they would cost £13,100 to make safe.

On 6 May, C.E. Davies informed Gilbert that the National Provincial Bank had said that it would

Near Tan y Bwlch the BEA photographer failed to find much to obstruct the view of the super-elevated track and C.E. Spooner's parabolic curves installed to speed the gravity trains. Had he gone a little further he would have found the way impassable. (British Electricity Authority)

accept £2,000 to discharge its £12,000 debentures if settled within two months, but would require a separate settlement in respect of the current overdraft. The Aluminium Corporation had said that it was prepared to donate its ordinary stock to the society providing the other holders did likewise.

When Gilbert reported to a committee meeting held on 25 May, it was felt that there would be a reluctance to donate to an appeal to 'buy' the railway if it was known that the money, or some of it, was going to 'enrich' shareholders. He returned to Davies with a counter-offer; 2 per cent for the 5 per cent (£467 4s) and 1 per cent for the 4½ per cent (£270 4s) providing the other 4½ per cent holder would agree to sell at 1 per cent and the bank was willing to negotiate over the debenture settlement. He would also seek to acquire a majority of the other debentures for not more than 2 per cent.

Davies thought this was unreasonable. He had already secured more than half of the ordinary stock for no cost at all and could give the society more than half of the 5 per cent preference shares and nearly half of the 4½ per cent preference shares for what was really a nominal sum. The committee should take this into account. Its position would be much more difficult without his cooperation. He was, however, prepared to accept £1,000 for the preference shares held by him and his brother, but it was wrong to make any purchase of additional 4½ per cent preference shares conditional on the price being the same as that paid to the Davies brothers. Any explanation that control of the company had been acquired for little more than £1,000 could not,

Davies was prepared to match that offer in respect of the £19,527 that he controlled, providing the society acquired his preference shares by purchase. This gave a valuation as shown in the table:

National Provincial Bank – debentures	£2,000
National Provincial Bank – overdraft	£600
Davies - £23,360 5 per cent preference shares	£1,168
Davies - £3,660 4½ per cent preference shares	£183
1,341 4½ per cent preference share from other holders to give class control	£67 1s
Total	**£4,018 1s**

Looking towards Portmadoc, over the bridge that replaced the earlier level crossing at Tan y Bwlch, it's clear that the right of way was being used as a footpath.
(British Electricity Authority)

Apart from the rotting doors, Tan y Bwlch goods shed looked quite sound.
(British Electricity Authority)

The loading dock at Tan y Bwlch was rarely photographed before it was demolished. (W. G. Rear)

Beyond the short tunnel there was little overgrowth and the track looked quite sound although it would not have stood up to too much traffic.

in his view, be criticised or regarded as other than a token payment.

Nevertheless, the bank was not prepared to budge on the £2,000. The committee thought that the prospect of raising up to £4,000 to acquire control and the further funds for restoration would be too difficult. It would have to find other means to achieve its objectives.

Despite this apparent contretemps, Davies and Gilbert established a rapport and continued communicating. Letters about the railway were published in the *Daily Telegraph* during the summer. Shareholders, asked to contribute their holdings as gifts, responded to the extent of £3,000. On 1 October, Davies suggested approaching the Cowper family, representing £4,860, via him as they had not replied to direct requests from the society; he thought that having this holding would help the society considerably. The Cowper family, which had inherited its holding from Florinda Thompson, Livingston Thompson's widow, in 1897, did not reply to Davies either. It is still on the share register at the time of writing.

On 24 December 1952, Davies told Gilbert that he had told the Ministry of Supply that there were 'prospects of the railway being acquired for the purposes of re-opening' and that it would not be

available for the acquisition of scrap. He was clearly of the view that the society would succeed with its bid and Gilbert soon had news in that regard.

At this point the story gets complicated, in that it involves a network of people who knew people. Gilbert wrote to Davies on 11 February 1953 to explain. Fellow committee member, and neighbour of Gilbert's, Thomas A. King was deputy surveyor at Finchley Borough Council where L.J.W. (Les) Smith was the town planning officer. Smith was a railway enthusiast; with his friends H.T.S. (Trevor) Bailey

and Alan Francis Pegler, who had been at Radley School together, he ran enthusiast excursions on the Eastern Region of British Railways. Working for the family firm, Pegler was wealthy by the standards of the day so Smith and Bailey suggested that he might like to involve himself in taking control of the Ffestiniog Railway.

The idea appealed and the trio went off to Portmadoc on a wet Saturday in January 1953. There they met Robert Evans, visited Boston Lodge and Blaenau Festiniog, and rode down through the long

tunnel from Tanygrisiau on an unbraked wagon. Returning full of enthusiasm for the railway, despite the rain and the air of dereliction that surrounded it, Pegler decided that he would try and take control. He met the committee on 5 February.

Initially, he was prepared to lend the society £3,500. In April, Trevor Bailey's brother-in-law, Ernest John Routly, had become involved as a solicitor. Various options were investigated over the following months, including the possibility of taking the Welsh Highland Railway (Light Railway) Company out of receivership and using that company to take over the FR. In January 1954, the society learned that Pegler would provide the money only if he appointed the company's directors and that he would not provide funds for the railway's restoration, that would be the society's responsibility. This was hard for the society to accept, and some members never did, but there were no other alternatives.

Attention turned to thoughts of operating, Bill Broadbent seeking a meeting with the chief inspecting officer of railways at the Ministry of Transport, Lieutenant Colonel G.R.S. Wilson, on 24 March. The meeting took place on 13 April, when it was agreed that Colonel Dennis McMullen, who had inspected the Talyllyn Railway in 1952, would visit the railway

Approaching the long tunnel.

The abandoned 1836 formation near Tanygrisiau. The railway is now located even closer to the waterfall.

(Bob Jones)

Tanygrisiau Station. Of these buildings, only the goods shed, at the far end of the range, survives.
(W. G. Rear)

The Cwmorthin quarry incline at Tanygrisiau.

to advise on essential works to be carried out before passenger services could be resumed.

When Alan Pegler mentioned to his father that he planned to take over the railway and intended to obtain a bank loan to pay for it, his father offered to provide the required funds. Pegler, Trevor Bailey and Bill Broadbent met Pegler's parents for tea at their Hyde Park Hotel suite in May. There, the enthusiasts watched a cheque being written out. Unfortunately, none of them looked closely at the amount; subsequently Pegler said it was for £3,000 whilst Broadbent said that he had paid close attention and that it was for £2,000. At the first Lands Tribunal hearing in 1960, John Routly said that 'about £1,500' had been paid for the preference shares, and that 'about £1,500' had redeemed the National Provincial Bank's debentures and cancelled the overdraft, so the larger amount seems more likely. In later life Pegler said that he thought that his parents decided to lend their support in this way because they knew and trusted Bailey.

The new regime took over on 22 June 1954, at a board meeting attended by the Davies brothers and John Routly. After the Aluminium Corporation's £25,000 ordinary stock was transferred to Routly, he, Pegler, Bailey and Les Smith were elected directors, and the Davies family members resigned.

Routly acted as Pegler's trustee. When the new board met for the first time on 28 June, more stock was transferred to him. The bank's £12,000 debentures were transferred to Pegler. Qualifying holdings of £500 ordinary stock were transferred to Pegler, Smith and Bailey on 29 June.

Considering that E.R. Davies had been the only member of his family to enter into railway proprietorship by choice, and that neither he nor his brother and sons previously knew anything about running railways, it was perhaps remarkable that the FR lasted as long as it did. During the 1930s it had become apparent that the railway could make money from carrying tourists but the directors lacked the courage or wisdom to stand up to the quarry proprietors when it became clear that their business was being carried at a loss. The underlying problem was the decline in slate traffic that had started with the arrival of the standard-gauge railways in Blaenau

During the closure period, the area around the Glan y Pwll engine shed became a timber yard. (C.H.A. Townley)

Glan y Pwll level crossing and crossing house viewed from the footbridge to Glan y Pwll school. The roof of the engine shed can be seen to the right of the crossing house.

A view from the GWR footbridge, looking towards Glan y Pwll. A stop block on the standard-gauge line protects users of the FR crossing to and from the GWR yard. The recess in the wall on the right indicates the former location of a private siding.

Ffestiniog in the 1880s, which led to the inability to make enough money to service the debt. The borrowing to fund the junction railways and the new station in 1923 merely aggravated the problem. It is unlikely that the outcome could have been any different without it.

To advise the new regime, Colonel Dennis McMullen visited the railway on 18 August 1954, accompanied by Pegler, Bailey, Broadbent, Humphreys and Gilbert. Just as it was during Pegler's first visit, the weather was appalling. Reporting on 27 August, McMullen reviewed the entire length of the line even though it was obvious, because of the overgrowth, that services could not be immediately operated throughout its length. Although the rails and chairs were in good condition and had plenty of life, large numbers of sleepers and keys were rotten. Provided speeds did not exceed

15mph and all curves were fully sleepered, straight sections could be operated with two out of three sleepers spiked, approximately 1,200 per mile instead of 2,000 as originally provided. This seems to be a very pragmatic view, especially as he was putting it in writing, appearing to recognise that resources to take care of the track properly would not be available unless the railway could earn money from operating trains.

He was unhappy at the prospect of amateur drivers working trains through the long tunnel

The end of the line at Duffws. The Maenofferen incline is straight ahead whilst the Rhiwbach line curves off to the left.

because of the limited clearances but if, as he had been told, a former driver was employed, that would be acceptable providing carriage doors were locked. He thought that none of them had any real idea of the enormity of the task they had taken on. The decision to proceed would be theirs and they would be responsible for safety.

He was, of course, right that they did not understand what needed to be done to restore the railway to operating condition, but that was surely the point. If they had done, they would have walked away.

Led by Mike Elvy, from London, the first working party took place shortly after McMullen's visit, clearing the track in front of Boston Lodge, entered for the first time on 20 September 1954. The former chargehand and superintendent Morris Jones had been recruited to assist a team that comprised Allan Garraway and his friend D.W. Harvey. They got the Simplex tractor running and, on 21 September, ran across to Portmadoc for the first time, to get petrol. On 23 September, they took two carriages across for a local reporter. Despite a landslip above Boston Lodge that had required the track to be supported with

sleepers, a way was also forced through to Minffordd. These trips must have been undertaken with great caution and trepidation, as McMullen had said that nearly every sleeper on this section was rotten.

When the directors met on 1 October, they agreed to employ Jones as a fitter and, subject to the availability of funds, to relay the track over the embankment. Trevor Bailey was authorised to negotiate the sale of scrap to raise funds. The sale of 3 acres of land in Portmadoc, bought for the new station in 1923, was to be investigated. Another money raiser was the stock of 150,000 tickets, which took nearly thirty years to clear.

Regarding the society, it was decided that it should have the power to appoint a director and a trustee if a trust was established; in return the company would expect the right to appoint two society directors. Afterwards, the directors decided that the Society could use the railway's name, but it should be registered as a limited company as they could not, or would not, deal with an unincorporated body. A draft agreement produced to be used as a basis for negotiation covered the use of society subscriptions and donations to resuscitate and maintain the railway;

the transfer of company shares to a trust devised with the objective of repaying the settlers, ie Alan Pegler; the cost of acquiring the shares and devoting any income to the same objects as the society's; and the disposal of the shares or compensation if the railway could not be resuscitated satisfactorily.

The disposal of wagons for scrap was started and the sidings by the harbour, at Portmadoc Station, Boston Lodge and Glan y Mor were cleared. On 2 October 1954, the power unit and boiler of the Welsh Highland Railway's single Fairlie *Moel Tryfan* was towed across to Portmadoc ready to be scrapped.

Robert Evans' sixty years with the company was marked on 6 November, clearance of overhanging branches permitting the operation of a train of two carriages to Minffordd. Afterwards the party moved to the Queen's Hotel in Portmadoc, where he was presented with a clock.

In November John Routly was deputed to handle negotiations with the society and Bill Broadbent was appointed to represent the society as a director and trustee. Other appointments made included Allan Garraway as mechanical and permanent way engineer. Working with Trevor Bailey, he was to

proceed as he thought best with regards to the available funds. Henceforth, the directors decided, locomotives should be painted dark green and the carriages dark green with ivory – colour samples were pasted into the minute book.

Penrhyndeudraeth Urban District Council had removed the tarmac from the level crossing by the time of the December working party and the Simplex managed to push its way through to a point above Bryn Mawr, 6 miles from Portmadoc. A member paid for the reinstallation of mains electricity at Boston Lodge and work started on re-assembling *Prince*; the means by which the company had managed to acquire a new boiler for this locomotive in 1945 remain unknown, but its availability was a valuable asset.

The Festiniog Railway Society was registered as a company limited by guarantee on 24 December 1954, the word preservation being deliberately omitted as it was felt that the railway could not be preserved in a museum sense.

After one or two working parties, there is already a big improvement to be seen at Portmadoc Station.
(British Electricity Authority)

CHAPTER 5

1955-1958: REVIVAL – BACK TO TAN Y BWLCH

The year 1955 opened with attention focused on establishing a service over the embankment and clearing the formation. At Boston Lodge, priority was given to *Prince*. Behind the scenes, the directors were planning to object to the Parliamentary activities of the Central Electricity Authority.

In 1944, the North Wales Power Company had devised an extensive system of hydro-electric power stations and associated reservoirs with the intention

of reducing dependency on coal for power generation. No progress had been made when the industry was nationalised in 1948, but in December 1951, the British Electricity Authority gave notice of its intention to deposit the North Wales Hydro-Electric Power Bill, for powers to build four new reservoirs and other works that would supply water to new hydro-electric power stations. Of relevance to the railway was work No. 22, a reservoir to be formed across the Afon Ystradau, which would have flooded the railway between the long tunnel and Tanygrisiau. C.E. Davies told Fred Gilbert that he had received a notice about this in February 1952.

When the Bill received its second reading in the House of Commons on 1 April 1952, it came in for some criticism from the MP for Kidderminster, Gerald Nabarro, who later was chairman of the Severn Valley Railway. On this occasion, it was not the railway that concerned him. He thought that the scheme was extravagant and that the BEA was misleading Parliament by introducing innocuous schemes that were really part of a much larger plan. If the generating station at Connah's Quay was operated at its design load of 80 per cent, North Wales could be supplied with electricity without any difficulty, he claimed. Goronwy Roberts, the MP for Caernarvon, also objected, saying that the authority was asking for everything and conceding nothing, the scheme would damage the area's natural beauty, and the livelihood of a large proportion of the inhabitants, and deprive industrial workers in the English north-west and Midlands of one of their favourite holiday retreats. Provisions of the National Parks Act

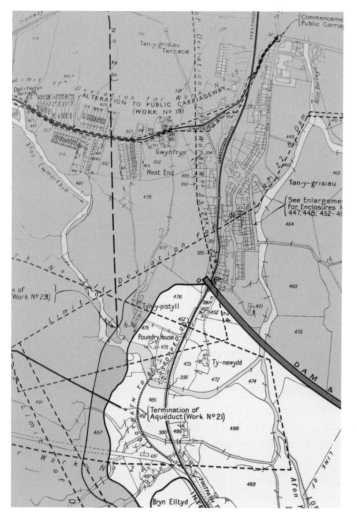

An extract from the deposited plans of the North Wales Hydro Bill of 1951 showing the area around the railway at Tanygrisiau that would have been flooded. (Parliamentary Archives)

The area around
the tunnel mouth
that would have
been flooded by the
1951 scheme.
(Parliamentary Archives)

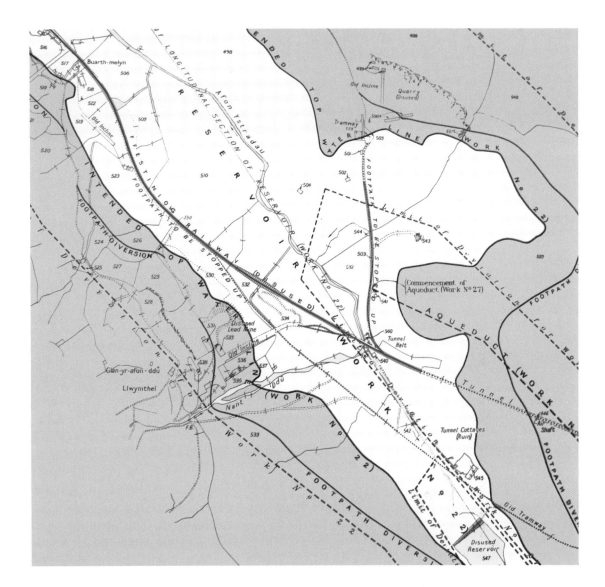

and the River Boards Act would be set aside in favour of the authority.

The MPs were told that whilst the scheme's capital cost of £3,325,000 compared with £2,328,000 for a coal-fired power station, its running costs would be only £21,000 compared with £265,000. It would also save 65,000 tons of coal a year. The Bill got its second reading, but in May, the authority announced that it was discontinuing the promotion of the Ffestiniog scheme in response to new information provided about the geological conditions affecting the proposed reservoir at Cwmorthin. Further action would be deferred to allow for a review and possible modification of the works.

Most likely those involved with the railway overlooked this caveat, but in December 1954, the authority returned with another Bill, seeking powers

for schemes at Tanygrisiau, called Ffestinog, and Cwm Rheidol, near Aberystwyth. In the intervening thirty months, the Ffestiniog scheme had been reinvented as a pumped-storage development that comprised two reservoirs, 1,000ft apart. The higher reservoir was to be provided by enlarging the existing Llyn Stwlan by constructing a dam 90ft high and 1,100ft long (Work No. 1) whilst the lower reservoir was to be created by damming Afon Ystradau near its junction with the Afon Cwmorthin, (Work No. 3). Work No. 2 was an aqueduct, intended to be mostly underground, that linked the reservoirs via a hydro-electric power station constructed alongside the railway formation, on the west side of the lower reservoir. The railway was also affected by the power station access road, which was to cut across the formation near the LNWR exchange

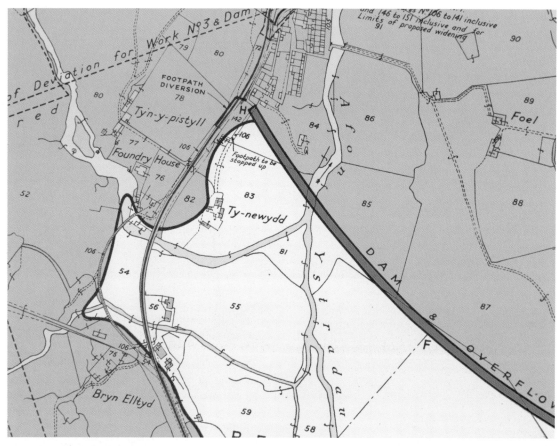

The 1954 North Wales Hydro Bill reduced the area to be flooded at Tanygrisiau.
(Parliamentary Archives)

FR property affected by the 1954 scheme to make way for the Central Electricity Generating Board power station access road near Blaenau Festiniog station.
(Parliamentary Archives)

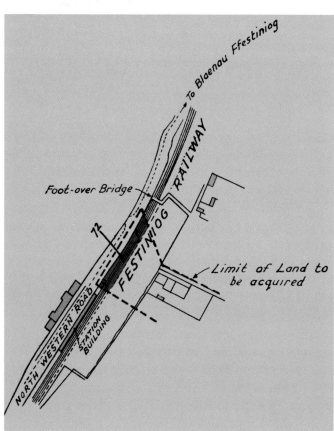

station. It would cost £14.79 million, a remarkable increase on the original scheme, considering that the authority had said that one of the reasons for abandoning it was that it was too expensive.

News of this proposal had become public in September 1954, when the local authorities' opinions on it had appeared in local newspapers. The company had not been consulted and had found out by chance when Fred Gilbert met one of the authority's surveyors in a pub in August.

Trevor Bailey complained in the strongest terms about the way the company had been treated on 14 September 1954, and asked for a meeting. He would have been unaware that it is considered most improper for a statutory authority, like the BEA, to take unilateral action against another statutory authority, like the Festiniog Railway Company.

The BEA's chairman, Lord Citrine, replied on 20 September, explaining that the authority would only consult with those affected by its proposals after it had consulted with the local authorities. When Bailey and Alan Pegler met seven BEA officials in London on 3 November 1954, an apology

From the train, a fence prevented passengers seeing very much at Boston Lodge. Allan Garraway had it removed for their benefit. Double-decker buses running between Portmadoc and Blaenau Ffestiniog were a regular feature until the 1960s.

was offered, but they were told that the company would be dealt with as a landowner rather than as a railway company. Bailey explained that the railway was not as bad as some people imagined, the structure was sound and the track could be renewed in stages. Pegler probably did their credibility no favours, though, when he suggested that the railway could be used to carry construction materials.

The meeting's chairman summed up by saying that the authority would do what it could as good neighbours, but he did not think that the company could make a success of its undertaking. There was no change in the authority's opinion when it became the Central Electrical Authority on 1 January 1955 and, despite the company's best efforts, this attitude prevailed. The authority also persuaded itself that the scheme to restore the railway was merely a device to extract compensation from it, no doubt one

reason why John Routly persuaded Alan Pegler to place his shares in trust later in 1955.

At a meeting with members of Merionethshire County Council and the Snowdonia national park joint advisory committee held in January 1955, a CEA spokesman overstated, by around 2 miles, the extent that the railway would be flooded and understated the revival effort, by saying that its reopening was merely being 'considered'. It was implied, if not stated explicitly, that there could either be a power station, with its promise of jobs, or the revived railway, not both. Two weeks later, the county council decided to rescind its resolution opposing the hydro-electric Bill.

A meeting with CEA representatives on 5 February 1955 left the directors feeling that progress had been made, with an agreement on a diversionary route, but within a few weeks they were told that there was

The Simplex tractor and carriage No. 10, formerly Van No. 2, at Pen Cob. This combination was often used on lineside clearance excursions. The carriage was not restored for regular use until 1991.

no such agreement. What happened is unclear. It seems that the authority's engineer had proposed a viable route apart from its gradient and had left the meeting saying that he would improve it. His masters obviously did not agree with that course of action.

Deciding that they would not object on principle, the directors petitioned for changes to the reservoir to protect the railway. When the Bill was heard by a House of Lords committee starting on 29 March, the authority's barrister opened by saying that the railway no longer justified itself and would not do so again; public funds could not be spent on it.

Pegler gave evidence on 30 March, admitting that diverting the railway would be more practical than altering the reservoir. He gave details of a deviation route that included a tunnel 2,200ft long and costed at £123,000, but his request for a new clause to be inserted into the Bill, providing for a deviation to be constructed at the authority's expense if railway services were resumed to Tan y Bwlch by 1 January 1958, as certified by the Ministry of Transport, was refused. No matter how good the argument, the authority would do nothing to favour the railway. The company had incurred legal expenses of £800 to make its case heard.

The compensation claim was brought to an end on 5 December 1955, when Lord Citrine wrote to say that the authority, working on the basis that the railway was worthless, could not accept the company's claim for equivalent reinstatement.

Meanwhile, a reporter and photographer from the *Liverpool Daily Post* had visited Boston Lodge on 9 January 1955, to find a gang working to restore *Prince* to working order. With the volunteers were Morris Jones, the former superintendent, and Arwyn Morgan, described as an assistant fitter, but actually the apprentice. The day before, volunteers from as far away as Scarborough and the Isle of Wight had spent twelve hours clearing two miles of undergrowth near Tan y Bwlch. The reporter was particularly impressed to hear about Mrs Valentine of Dolwyddelen, who, with her 10-year-old daughter, 'worked as hard as any of the men.'

At the same time, a comment had been made in the *Manchester Guardian* about the difficulties likely to be encountered in restoring the railway, noting that the railway's Portmadoc terminus seemed 'to have decayed more quickly than even the most unkempt of British Railways stations'. The whole atmosphere of desuetude is heightened by a nearby fence consisting of no fewer than 43 iron bedsteads.'

The society had started to function as a corporate body on 10 February 1955, when the directors met for the first time. Regarding his task as completed,

At Easter in 1956, *Merddin Emrys* was taken over to Portmadoc for photography. In this photograph the sewer that ran along the platform, and which regularly blocked with increased usage, was being excavated and cleared.

L. Taylor Harris stood down as chairman. Bill Broadbent was elected chairman of the meeting and Fred Gilbert as secretary. Broadbent handed over the society's first financial contribution, £234 7s 7d, to the company on 29 March; the society regarded the money, raised by the unincorporated society, as grant in aid but the company issued a receipt recording it as a gift.

A report on the condition of the rolling stock had been obtained from the British Railways shedmaster at Bangor, J.M. Dunn, who visited Boston Lodge with his boilersmith on 22 February. *Princess, Welsh Pony, Taliesin* and *Merddin Emrys* had been damaged by damp slack left in bunkers, and water left in boilers and tanks. The carriages that had been operational in 1939 had been left outside, whereas those stored under cover had various defects.

Outside, the Simplex had reached Glan y Pwll on 31 January and, hauling carriage No. 17 and No. 1 van, reached Blaenau Ffestiniog on 5 March. Apart from being a boost for the volunteers involved, these trips were used to recover wagons and lineside equipment until concerns about the hazards of running through the long tunnel brought them to an end.

On 20 May 1955, the directors decided to appoint A.G.W. 'Allan' Garraway as manager with effect from 6 June and dispense with the services of Robert Evans from 18 June. Working for British Railways, Garraway was not inspired by the forthcoming modernisation and withdrawal of steam locomotives and had intimated that he would like to work for the FR. The decision to appoint him and dispense with Evans seems to be linked to a report Garraway had submitted in April, and £900 owed by the scrap merchant, apparently unpaid. One of his priorities was to negotiate a new contract for the disposal of scrap. Given a pension of £1 10s a week, Evans died in Prestatyn on 29 February 1960.

Services between Portmadoc and Boston Lodge started on 23 July 1955, with the Simplex tractor hauling two carriages. The front cover has been removed from the tractor to improve ventilation around the engine and radiator.

Progress was sufficiently advanced for 22 July 1955 to be set as the target to start operating trains. Colonel McMullen returned on 21 July and thought that the section between Portmadoc and Boston Lodge could be opened without undue risk. In his report of 27 July, he described the railway concerned, just over a mile long, almost level until it swung sharply to the left when it rose on a gradient of approximately 1 in 70. The rail heads were considerably worn, most sleepers were poor and did not hold their spikes and, at the rail joints, the sleepers had been replaced by second-hand standard-gauge sleepers cut in half. Before *Prince* was put into service, each 24ft rail length should have at least four good sleepers, including the joint sleepers. The excessive super-elevation on the curve at Boston Lodge should be reduced, also before *Prince* entered service. The pillbox erected on the embankment during the war restricted clearances and should be removed; clearance could be improved by slewing the track until it was done.

Train working would be one engine in steam and a staff should be provided, along with clear, simple and brief instructions issued to everyone on the railway. Train speed should not exceed 8mph, trains approaching Portmadoc should stop short of the facing points and proceed at walking pace. When

Prince was ready, it was to be run light over the section twenty times to assess its effect on the track.

Being given verbal approval to start operating, Allan Garraway immediately telegrammed active volunteers to say that the inspection was satisfactory and that the railway would be opened on Saturday, 23 July. The Simplex hauled two carriages; No. 12, a passenger brake built as a brake van in 1880 and rebuilt in 1929-30, and No. 23, a 56-seat Ashbury carriage built for the North Wales Narrow Gauge Railways in 1894. Because there was no loop at Boston Lodge, the train was propelled back to Pen Cob and a chain-shunt performed to put the locomotive on the front of the train for the return journey. McMullen had made no comment about the use of this technique, which had been banned on main-line railways many years before. The fare was 1s return.

Janet Jones, the year's Welsh tourist queen, performed the official opening on 29 July. She was accompanied by local dignitaries and Bessie Jones, the pre-war 'station mistress' from Tan y Bwlch.

After a great deal of hard work, *Prince* entered service on 3 August. For the first time a Ffestiniog Railway locomotive was equipped with the same chopper couplings used on the bogie carriages. They had previously used hook-and-eye couplings that could only connect to wagons and four-wheeled stock.

11,371 passengers had been carried when the season ended on 24 September, generating £439 15s 9d revenue. Other income had been £108 12s from souvenirs, £152 12s 7d from the sale of old tickets and £473 16s 5d for tonnage/use of the railway at Blaenau Ffestiniog, but there was less than £10 in the bank and debts of £1,021, including £630 for the petition against the power station Bill. At the directors' meeting on 5 October, Garraway was instructed to prepare a budget based on extending services to Minffordd in 1956. To control expenditure, they wished any matter not connected with routine operating to be referred to them, approving expenditure of £100 on a bathroom in the first-floor offices at Portmadoc that Garraway had converted into accommodation, £15 on a water tank and, with reluctance, £47 14s 9d on oxy-acetylene equipment. Garraway was to reimburse the cost of the bathroom at £1 a week.

When the society held its first annual general meeting in Portmadoc on 8 October 1955, it had 650

Simply decorated with flags, *Prince* made its first appearance hauling trains on 3 August 1955.

On 20 August, *Prince* was ready to set off with another full load. Allan Garraway's bike leans against the wall. (A. E. Rimmer)

With no loop at Boston Lodge it was necessary to shunt the carriages past *Prince* using a chain. Here the loco is about to couple on ready to return to Portmadoc. (W. G. Rear)

On a fine day during the summer of 1955 *Prince* stands at Boston Lodge Halt, waiting to set back to run-round its carriages at Pen Cob.

members, including 50 who had joined at Portmadoc since July. Members were still being enrolled to the unincorporated society because deficiencies in the incorporated society's articles did not allow for membership to be renewed or suspended in the event of non-payment. Five new directors had been co-opted to the board the previous week: Norman A. Pearce; J.B. White; R.H.R. Garraway (Allan's father); Vic Mitchell and Lt Col R.H. Rudgard. Allan Garraway reported that the first priority had to be in restoring the track.

Some of the members were unhappy about the relationship between the company and the society, particularly with regard to the shares. William Kenneth Nelson, the treasurer, who had been involved since the London meetings, thought that they should be held by the society. A member pointed out that there were other shares in circulation that could be acquired.

Alan Pegler put his ordinary shares into a private trust on 7 December 1955, appointing John Routly and Trevor Bailey as trustees, reserving to himself the right to appoint and remove trustees, and adding the society's Rudgard and R.H.R. Garraway by 1957. Income was to be devoted to the repayment to him of the cost of acquiring the company and in pursuit of the same objectives as the society. He stood down as a company director on 19 December, continuing as chairman.

The unincorporated society was formally taken over by the incorporated society on 31 December 1955, although it remained in existence for junior members, who could not be members of a limited company.

Extension of services to Minffordd from 19 May 1956 was approved at the directors' meeting on 1 February. They were allocated functional responsibilities with limited approval to authorise

On 19 August 1955 there had not been sufficient passengers to justify the use of two carriages.
(J. F. C. Plowman)

expenditure. A statement of organisation was devised to improve communications; at the next meeting, on 7 March, Allan Garraway was instructed to adhere to it. He was then asked to increase scrap sales to £100 per month. Against an estimate of £650, the Vulcan Foundry was given an order to repair *Taliesin*.

The question of the shares was raised again at the society's second general meeting on 24 March. Bill Broadbent replied that money could be better spent on the track than on buying shares, but the debate appears to have become heated and was not fully recorded.

Colonel McMullen returned to inspect the line to Minffordd on 14 May 1956. A train of three carriages hauled by *Prince* was run for him. He found the track to be in good order except for one length which, from his description, had been overlooked. Minffordd level crossing had only one gate and should be provided with two. Sighting of the road crossing to the yard also required improvement. He was satisfied that trains could be run without risk, providing speed was limited to 10mph generally and 5mph on the facing points at Minffordd.

He also looked at the track on the embankment, finding it in need of attention; there were instances where three adjacent sleepers were providing no support for the rails. At Portmadoc, a point had been moved to shorten the loop; although it had not been

completed, the work was in good order and he recommended its approval. It was not too long before the loop required extending again.

A small event, featuring Bessie Jones in her Welsh national costume, launched the extension of services to Minffordd. J.B. White, the company's press officer, who had flown to Portmadoc from London in an Auster aircraft, invited journalists to fly with him over the route of the railway; the location of the local landing strip was not reported. A detailed report in *Railway World* magazine explained that track work was being led by Will Jones, Bessie's husband, who had worked on the track in the 1930s. Another gang working on the lineside was repairing the telegraph pole route preparatory to installing an omnibus telephone system. At Boston Lodge, volunteers from Merseyside were building a new inspection pit on the site of the pedestrian entrance that had been filled in, the Baldwin tractor had been equipped with a Gardner 3LW 35hp diesel engine by volunteers from Derby locomotive works, and the double engine *Taliesin* had been retubed.

For passengers, the fare for the extended journey was doubled to 2s. They also had the opportunity of using the train to travel to the beach at Pen Cob, where a halt was opened. The third carriage was No. 11, another 1880-built van that had been rebuilt with passenger accommodation in 1928-9. It was

Services were extended to Minffordd on 19 May 1956.
(Martin Fuller collection)

Vans 4 and 5, now Nos. 11 and 12, running together at Minffordd.

marshalled, so that there was a brake van at each end of the train. Somewhat surprisingly, it was found that passengers would pay extra to travel in the compartment that had upholstered seat backs so when 1876-built Brown, Marshalls bogie carriage No. 17 re-entered service on 24 July, it had its first-class compartment restored.

An evening excursion was run as far as the long tunnel for members of the Stephenson Locomotive Society on 27 June 1956. The society's organiser, the photographer H.C. Casserley, had approached Allan Garraway the previous October, to ask if it would be possible to organise a trip to Blaenau Ffestiniog before the track was lifted. Initially he was rebuffed, insurance and ministerial difficulties being cited, but on 14 December 1955, Garraway wrote 'Strictly *entre nous*, I do have to run up to the tunnel about once a week to help keep the line clear. Normally quite a

In an attempt to attract more traffic, Pen Cob was made a request stop in 1956, although it was closed at the end of 1957.
(Martin Fuller collection)

A stop for photographs by the Stephenson Locomotive Society excursion which ran as far as the tunnel on 27 June 1956.

Several trips were made to Blaenau Ffestiniog to recover materials before the tunnel was judged to be unsafe. After the first time, when the party was met with suspicious silence, crowds of small children gathered round to ride on the train. In the background, British Railways is replacing the LNWR station building with a brick structure.

number of locals and any volunteers here join me entirely at their own risk, but making a contribution to the funds' and suggesting that such a trip might be possible if arranged nearer the time of the intended visit.

On 28 May, Garraway informed Casserley that, 'the trip up the line must be referred to as a works train, when SLS members joined in with clearing the track for future years' extensions.' The train comprised the Simplex and carriage No. 10, the 1880 van rebodied to include passenger accommodation in 1921, which was often used as a personnel carrier at the time. The party toured the works and visited the loco shed the next day.

The Central Electricity Authority had broken the line near the LNWR station, Garraway had told Casserley on 14 March, and intended to make a further break at Tanygrisiau after a final trip on 15 March. This second break seems to have been deferred, as the society magazine reported that the Baldwin tractor made two trips to Blaenau Ffestiniog to collect telegraph poles over the summer bank holiday weekend in August.

Fitted with a new engine, the tractor had been moved under its own power during July. On 3 October, the directors decided that it should be named *Moelwyn*, not only the name of the mountain

through which the railway runs, but a pun on its maker's name, *moel* meaning bald in Welsh.

Taliesin's repairs had cost more than £1,000 when it was first steamed on 2 September 1956. After making some trips as a light engine, it was attached to the four-carriage train and ran to Penrhyn, the

Seen here at Clogwyn Daniel, track lifting on the section of railway to be flooded by the Central Electricity Generating Board took place in 1957. (J. W. Lloyd)

In use, the Baldwin tractor was found to be rough riding; before the closure it had not been used on long runs or, probably, where time was critical. Therefore, during 1957, it was semi-permanently coupled to an old four-wheeled brake van, numbered No. 1 since 1955. The loco was named *Moelwyn* in 1956 but nameplates were not fitted straight away.

Towards the end of 1956 *Taliesin*, seen at Pen Cob, made several appearances in grey primer. Workers from the Vulcan Foundry at Newton-le-Willows, Lancashire, finished restoring it in 1957.

After a loop had been constructed, services resumed to Penrhyn on 20 April 1957. By this time the two former vans had been turned to bring their guards' compartments together and No. 12, the former No. 5, adapted to enable refreshments to be served.

first steam there since 1946. The same combination was used on 12 November, when the general manager of British Railways' Western Region, K.W.C. Grand, visited with two of his officers. After travelling to Penrhyn on the train they were driven to Tan y Bwlch to meet Bessie Jones wearing Welsh national dress and taken up to the long tunnel on a train hauled by *Moelwyn*.

A loop was needed at Penrhyn before passenger services could be resumed. At Christmas 1956, work started to relocate the turnouts from the crossover near the weigh house at Minffordd. In January 1957, the track affected by the power station scheme was lifted; the authority had taken possession on 3 February 1956.

Terms of the society agreement were accepted by the directors on 21 January 1957; it was signed on 8 March. The society was allowed to make use of the railway's name, required to transfer funds, subscriptions and donations to the company to be used for the purposes of the railway, and recruit volunteers. The company would give privilege travel to society members. Each organisation would have representation on the board of the other and Alan Pegler would give the society first refusal if he decided to sell his preference shares or debentures. A draft version of the agreement, which differs

significantly, was mistakenly published in the society magazine in 1970.

Despite Lord Citrine's attitude regarding compensation, negotiations did continue. Commenting on the House of Lords' minutes of evidence, in 1956 the British Electricity Authority's valuer said that the authority's counsel had said that reinstatement was not proper, but that the company would be entitled to compensation for severance. However, although he could not accept Alan Pegler's claim that the railway would be commercially successful, he wanted to recommend that the authority paid more than the low value of the land taken. If the value of the complete railway was valued before and after the severance, the outcome was still a low figure because its original value was assumed to be the £3,000 that Alan Pegler had paid for it. He wanted more information.

Under pressure from the authority to reach a settlement, on 11 April 1957 the directors decided that the company should take every opportunity to emphasise that no part of the railway had been abandoned, that it was determined to restore services to Blaenau Ffestiniog and that timetables should list all the stations with the words 'services temporarily suspended' against those to which services had not been resumed.

A 1956 view of Portmadoc Station with the wharves disused and overgrown, and small leisure craft starting to take over the harbour.
(Dennis)

Prince passing the ex-Glan y Pwll trident signal in 1957. It collapsed during a gale in February 1967.

Prince was repainted, with the fleet number as shown, during 1957. The timetable is displayed on the blackboard, 'there and back in 30 minutes.' The iron plates on the ground are the covers of the carriage inspection pit constructed in the platform road in the nineteenth century.

Services to Penrhyn were started at Easter 1957, 20-22 April, the earliest they had been run, and fully justified by the 1,135 passengers carried. Clearance had been given despite McMullen not making his inspection until 21 May. He reported on 3 June.

Between Minffordd and Penrhyn, some track had been completely relaid with new sleepers; in other places, sleepers had been replaced at the rail joints, but others had not been touched. Once again, McMullen asked for at least four new sleepers per rail length, and five where the track was on a curve. He noticed that one of the underbridges that used thick slate slabs as girders was starting to fail; it should be watched.

He thought that speed should be limited to 10mph, but when any portion, not less than a quarter of a mile in length, had been completely resleepered it could be increased to 20mph. Re-visiting the section between Portmadoc and Minffordd, he

found it in much better condition and applied the same restrictions regarding speed.

The main operating season was from 5 June until 28 September. Two more halts were opened, at Boston Lodge and Pen-y-Bryn, near Penrhyn. The sale of lemonade to passengers on an ad hoc basis since July 1955 had demonstrated the demand for on-train catering, so in 1957, carriage No. 12 was modified with the construction of a buffet counter. Turning carriage No. 11 and making a corridor connection between them increased the size of the

The former brake van No. 5 became buffet car No. 12 and was repainted in this form in 1962. Over the winter of 1962/3 it was mounted on a steel underframe and extended by 5ft, the interior layout being altered too.

Carriage No. 20, built by the Gloster Wagon Company in 1879, was returned to service in 1957, but required more attention by 1961, cheap paint and exposure to the sea air not doing it any favours.

market in an instant, creating an essential part of the railway's operations ever since.

During July, Allan Garraway responded to a local bus strike by fitting lighting in three carriages and running evening trains, a move which attracted local publicity and goodwill, and objections from the Transport & General Workers' Union.

Carriage No. 20 re-entered service on 5 August, the bank holiday. When it had been tried on 1 August, to see how *Prince* could cope with five carriages, a spring

hanger pin had fallen out of one of its bogies and three compartments had been damaged externally.

Having received a quote of £1,500 to return *Merddin Emrys* to service, the directors decided to spend £500 on buying a Peckett 0-6-0ST built in 1944 for the Harrogate Gas Works. With transportation, it had cost £585 10s by the time it reached Portmadoc in August 1957. Although the directors decided that it should be named *Volunteer,* and some sketches were made showing how it could be adapted, it was

Taliesin catches the afternoon sun as it arrives at Minffordd during 1957. The driver is Tom Davies, who worked for the company before the war.
(Martin Fuller collection)

Seen from the signal post, *Taliesin* and *Prince* cross the embankment together on 2 September 1957.

Acquired in 1957, very little work was done on the Harrogate Gas Company's Peckett 0-6-0ST. It was dismantled for assessment in 1987 and sold for £12,000 in 1989. Taking inflation into account, the sale price was about double what had been paid for the loco in 1957 before it was sold in 1989. (Martin Fuller collection)

actually too big for the railway and was eventually sold in 1989.

During the summer of 1957, Allan Garraway and the volunteers spent their evenings clearing the line up to Tan y Bwlch using *Prince* and carriage No. 10. The task of removing the stumps of trees that had taken root during the closure would have been easier had the trunks cut off in 1955-6 been there to pull on. Tan y Bwlch was reached on 6 September, carrying a working party from Chace School, Enfield, other volunteers and guests who were met by Bessie Jones in her Welsh dress. The track still required a great deal of work to make it suitable for regular trains, especially as it was now policy to remove the turf.

At the end of 1957, receipts had been £2,946 compared with £1,671 in 1956 but there was still a negative balance of £1,527 8s 11d. One train had been cancelled, due to weather conditions on the embankment. An experimental winter Saturday service, run on the directors' instruction for shoppers, was cancelled on 18 December; on one day in November it had only carried two passengers and earned 1s 9d.

The riding of the Baldwin tractor, *Moelwyn*, was much improved by the addition of a leading bogie made using a wagon wheelset and made the loco capable of working passenger trains when required. Another modification made in December 1957 was the conversion of carriage No. 11 into an observation car with the insertion of windows in the end and using seats obtained from withdrawn Mersey Railway carriages. The railway had advertised observation cars before the closure but, apart from the compartment in the old van No. 5 after its 1929-30 rebuild, they did not have windows.

With services extended to Tan y Bwlch at Easter, 4-7 April 1958, on 7 May the directors considered the future, deciding that the company should consolidate its position before considering extending further. Colonel McMullen made his inspection on 16 May, reporting in two parts, on 20 May recommending that approval be given to its use by passenger trains subject to speeds not exceeding 20mph on straight sections that had been completely relaid and 10mph elsewhere. He wrote in more detail on 10 June. The rail was mostly 48½lb double-head in 24ft lengths although there was also some 50lb bull-head. The lighter rail had been worn down to about 40lb. The loop at Penrhyn was not in use whilst that at Tan y Bwlch was 'of great length' and was to be shortened.

For about a mile above Penrhyn level crossing, the track had been completely relaid and was in good

Whereas excursionists had to make do with internal-combustion motive power, steam did venture beyond the limit of public working for the benefit of track clearing volunteers, who often went out in the evening, after a day's train operating. (Martin Fuller collection)

In 1958 a better way was found to improve *Moelwyn's* ride, by extending its frame at the front and fitting a spare wheelset as a truck, in which condition it was photographed at Boston Lodge on 18 August 1967. (J. J. Davis)

1958 was about the resumption of services to Tan y Bwlch, which occurred on 5 April, 7½ miles of abandoned railway being restored in three years. Of course, there was still a lot to do.

Even with services resumed, parts of Tan y Bwlch station still had an air of abandonment.

Soon after the services had been extended, on 26 April *Taliesin* was seen arriving at Tan y Bwlch. Towards the end of its operational career it was often seen shrouded in steam, especially, but not only, on cooler days.

condition. Elsewhere, the track was in reasonable condition with some sleepers renewed and some re-spiked, but he did find places in urgent need of attention. The one-engine-in-steam staff had been replaced by train staff and ticket; he had been told that electric token instruments were to be installed with a block post at Minffordd and an intermediate instrument at Boston Lodge. Asked to comment on the policy of locking carriage doors, he said that he thought the policy was correct.

Reporting to the directors about the inspection, Allan Garraway said that McMullen had not been able to pull out any spikes by hand and had not been so complimentary before.

The peak service comprised three return trains with an evening train on four days a week. The fare was 5s. Things did not always run smoothly, one week in July experiencing two loco failures and a derailment. The last, in which *Taliesin* had derailed whilst running round the morning train at Tan y Bwlch, gave the passengers an unusual experience, for they were put into carriages Nos. 11 and 12 and returned to Penrhyn by gravity, *Moelwyn* meeting them there and taking them back to

Portmadoc where they arrived only two minutes late. Quite what McMullen might have thought of this may be imagined.

Demand for the popular 2.30pm departure, aggravated by the big lunchtime gap in the timetable, was such that it was decided to return three of the four-wheeled Brown, Marshalls carriages to service, to run with a four-wheeled van as a relief train. Work started on 31 July and the train went into service on August 5, the day after the August bank holiday. The intention to run the relief to Penrhyn was thwarted by demand after the first run, so it always ran to Tan y Bwlch thereafter. Some embarrassment was caused on 7 August, when one of the carriages carrying McMullen and his children derailed near Hafod y Llyn. Alan Pegler was also on the train.

Two 'new' carriages were acquired within a few weeks of each other in 1958. On 26 October, the body of North Wales Narrow Gauge Railways 1894-built Ashbury, No. 26 in the WHR/FR fleet, was obtained from a farm in Groeslon. It had been sold when the Welsh Highland Railway was dismantled in 1941; using bogies from the similar, but withdrawn, FR vehicle, No. 21, it was soon restored to service. In

Increased demand for passenger accommodation saw the four-wheeled stock quickly returned to service in 1959. It makes a fine sight with *Merddin Emrys* at Whistling Curve in 1961.

Merddin Emrys arrives at Tan y Bwlch in 1961.

Ashbury built carriage No. 26 for the North Wales Narrow Gauge Railways at the same time that it built Nos. 21 and 22 for the FR. When the Welsh Highland Railway stock was sold in 1943, the body of No. 26 was bought by a farmer in Groeslon and used as a chicken hut, where it was photographed in November 1958, when it was acquired for re-use. Equipped with bogies from No. 21 and fitted with a new floor and seating, it was returned to service in less than six months.

November, Allan Garraway and others visited Devon to assess what use could be made of an abandoned Lynton & Barnstaple Railway carriage. He bought it for £2 10s, saying that its bogies, brake gear and doors would be suitable as spares, and it was recovered over two weekends in April and May 1959.

To develop a new route to bypass the power station, the company asked Charles Goode, a society member, to survey the area and suggest a route, which he produced in 1958. No technical details, if there were any, are known to have survived. A plan of the area showing the alternatives produced by Les Smith's office in 1971 shows an alignment leaving the original line to the north of Dduallt Station, climbing through a tunnel a little shorter than the old tunnel and following the old route as closely as possible at a higher level, immediately behind the

power station and rejoining the original route on the approach to Tanygrisiau Station.

During 1958, the company appointed Livesey & Henderson as consultants to examine Goode's suggestion and suggest alternatives. John Routly had known one of the partners at Cambridge University. On 30 October, they reported that Goode's route was feasible, although the steep side slopes of the rock would have required fairly heavy rock cutting works. However, the apparently empty space behind the power station shown on the CEGB's Parliamentary plans, all that was available to the company, would be occupied by switchgear and ancillary buildings. Pushing the railway alignment further west would require a second tunnel and was likely to be the subject of considerable opposition from the CEGB. Further difficulties arose

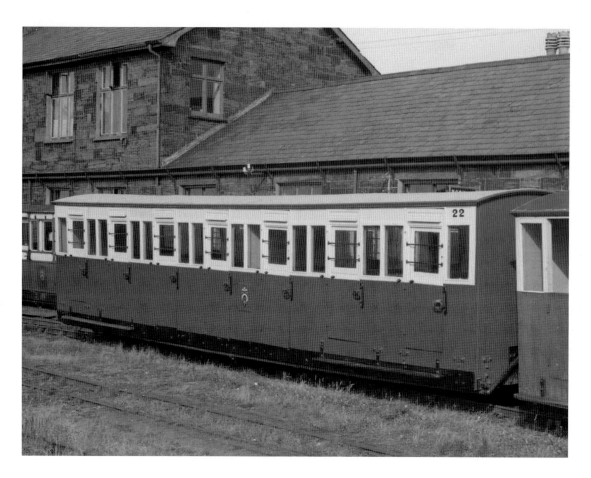

Photographed on 1 August 1958, carriage No. 22 was bought for quarrymen and tourists sixty years earlier. It was no more comfortable then than when it was new and had a distinctive droop in its roof as well. It was put on a steel underframe in 1967 and was re-bodied with a higher roof in 1984. (J. J. Davis)

with the levels approaching Tanygrisiau Station, where there was insufficient clearance for a bridge over the power station access road.

Livesey & Henderson investigated a route to the east of the reservoir, passing to the west of Moel Ystradau, that required a tunnel 1,860ft long, 340ft shorter than the existing one, but there was a problem achieving a connection with the old alignment near Tanygrisiau Station. A bridge downstream of the dam would be longer than the dam and expensive to build. Crossing immediately below the dam, on the made-up ground provided as landscaping, would be feasible, with bridges across the spillway and some sort of structure where there was no made-up ground. The most economical solution, and the most satisfactory solution from an engineering perspective, would be to locate the railway on the dam, with a light structure to carry it over the spillway, as the service road on the top of the dam had already been graded to suit railway purposes. Crossing the power station access road on the level, the new alignment could then join the old a little way beyond Tanygrisiau Station.

Pointing out that a diversion would be required to allow for the changes in levels made by the access road where it crossed company property near the LNWR station, and excluding land purchase, the new Tanygrisiau Station, the bridge over the Dolrhedyn road removed by the local authority and preliminary expenses, Livesey & Henderson thought that the work required could be carried out for £168,000. Considering this in July 1959, the directors were concerned that the route's ruling gradient was 1 in 67.5 compared with the railway's norm of 1 in 79.82.

The CEGB submitted an application for a determination in respect of the FR's property with the Lands Tribunal on 5 December 1958, starting what became the longest legal case in British jurisprudence.

By the end of 1958, the company had £3,287 in the bank with creditors owed £650, plus £636 owed to Vulcan Foundry for the restoration of *Taliesin* and two £100 instalments due on the Peckett. The directors decided to spend £1,000 on restoring *Merddin Emrys*. They also promoted Allan Garraway to be general manager.

CHAPTER 6

1958-1962: TRAFFIC BOOMS

Development of another incursion into the railway's property for a power station had started in 1958, arising from the need to provide the nuclear power station at Trawsfynydd with a rail link. At a meeting to discuss this with British Railways' officers at Crewe on 1 December 1958, Allan Garraway had said that when the FR's services were restored to Blaenau Ffestiniog, he expected to exchange traffic with BR's services at North station and/or with Crosville buses. It would be necessary, he said, for the FR to cross the proposed standard-gauge link to cater for slate traffic to Portmadoc. In February 1959, a drawing was produced showing how this might have been

achieved, showing the FR crossing the standard gauge opposite the market hall at an acute angle. The gradient was 1 in 60, stiffening to 1 in 45 to reach Duffws, which would have been quite a challenge for loco crews.

However, although Liverpool Corporation had obtained powers in the Liverpool Corporation Act 1957 for Work No. 10, to build a diversion of the Bala & Ffestiniog Railway where it was affected by the construction of the Tryweryn Reservoir, which could

Services to Tan y Bwlch had resumed on 6 April 1958. *Prince* makes a spirited departure soon afterwards. (W. G. Rear)

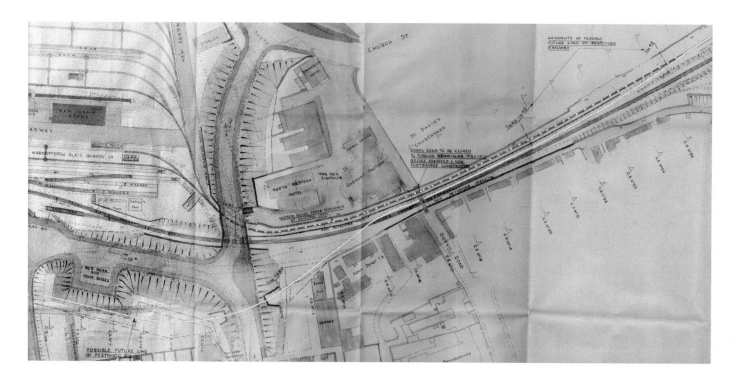

have maintained rail access to Trawsfynydd, British Railways wished to close that railway and the former GWR line to Ruabon it connected with at Bala. The matter was resolved on 27 August 1959, when it was announced that the corporation had agreed to pay not more than £180,000 to the British Transport Commission to fund the connection between the ex-LNWR line and the Bala & Ffestiniog Railway at Blaenau Ffestiniog, and up to £540,000 to

What Allan Garraway asked for. An extract from a plan made by British Railways showing the proposed connection between the LNWR and GWR termini in Blaenau Ffestiniog following a meeting at which he had asked for the FR to maintain access to Duffws. The FR route has been highlighted in yellow, the track used by the quarries in red and yellow. (National Archives)

Seen c1956, the original Rhiw Plas bridge. Minffordd cemetery lies just beyond it. (Mike Elvy/FR Archives)

Merioneth County Council for road improvements. Why the link line should not have been the responsibility of the power station contract is not understood, although it was no doubt considerably cheaper for the corporation than building a 3½-mile diversion.

Included in the British Transport Commission Act of 29 July 1959, therefore, were powers for Work No. 32, 'a railway (362 yards in length) commencing by a junction with the railway between Llandudno Junction and Blaenau Ffestiniog, and terminating by a junction with the railway between Bala and Blaenau Ffestiniog at a point 110 yards east of the bridge carrying Dorvil Road over the Ffestiniog Railway.' Operational from 20 April 1964, no provision was made for the FR to cross, as requested by Allan Garraway in 1959. Ironically, the quarries had ceased to use 'their' railway in 1962. The directors once referred to a compensation claim in

Rhiw Plas Bridge was rebuilt to accommodate transformers being transported from Portmadoc harbour to Trawsfynydd Nuclear Power Station, traffic being diverted over a temporary level crossing on the Portmadoc side. The Simplex is seen passing the site shortly after the bridge was completed in 1960.
(John Neville)

respect of the land taken, but the minutes are silent on the outcome.

During 1959, work started on the restoration of *Merddin Emrys*. John Summers & Sons Ltd, the Shotton steelmakers, agreed to new tanks, smokeboxes, chimneys and other components at no charge. The company also sent a welder to Boston Lodge to repair *Prince's* foundation ring. The Vulcan Foundry repaired the boiler, installing new tubes and stays.

Strengthening the road between Portmadoc and Trawsfynydd for the transport of heavy loads for the nuclear power station under construction at the latter place affected the bridge over the railway at Rhiw

Plas. It required rebuilding and was made longer to accommodate the wider road. Work started later in 1959, a temporary level crossing taking traffic across the railway being commissioned on 7 January 1960.

Allan Garraway persuaded British Railways to market circular tours on six Tuesdays during the 1959 peak season, running an extra train during the lunchtime break for participants. The extra train attracted so many ordinary passengers that it was soon run daily, taking the pressure off the popular 2.30pm.

From 1 January 1958, responsibility for electricity generation, including the Ffestiniog power station,

This cattle truck was built by the Great Western Railway for use on the Vale of Rheidol Light Railway in 1923. It was subsequently transferred to the Welshpool & Llanfair Light Railway and was bought from British Railways in 1958. Between 1964 and 1968 it was restored as a parcels van by members of the society's East Anglian group. After several years out of use it was sold to the Vale of Rheidol Railway in 2015.
(Ken Rangeley)

had been passed from the Central Electricity Authority to the Central Electricity Generating Board. Despite their concerns about the gradients on the Livesey & Henderson route, the directors decided to adopt it when the company's claim for reinstatement was heard at a Lands Tribunal hearing on 11-13 May 1960. The hearing had been postponed from several dates in 1959, due to the length of time it had taken to produce an agreed statement of facts. A further request by both parties to postpone the hearing until 30 May had been refused because of the length of time the case had been in abeyance and the postponements previously granted.

Eight witnesses were presented by the company, none by the CEGB. The claim hinged on the interpretation of section 2, rule 5, of the Acquisition of Lands Act, 1919, whether its use of the word 'may', with regards to reinstatement, was mandatory on an arbitrator or whether he had discretion.

Under examination, Alan Pegler said that he had been aware of the 1951 scheme, but had assumed that it would not be reinstated. The CEGB made much play of the existence of a map with the railway

marked as abandoned, which had not been the case when the North Wales Power Company had first started developing its plans. It also claimed that the company would only proceed with the deviation if it won its claim. Francis Wayne cited the case of the Lochaber scheme, where the Aluminium Company had paid for the diversion of the West Highland Railway when it had raised the level of Loch Treig in the 1930s.

Expenditure of the order contemplated, argued the CEGB, could not possibly be justified by the additional traffic that might be generated. A reasonable return on £180,000 invested in a deviation, allowing for depreciation, might be £30,000, which equated to 1,000 extra passengers a day. It was impossible.

Summing up, chairman Sir William FitzGerald MC QC, said that he accepted the argument put by the CEGB, that if the cost of reinstatement in relation to the value of the undertaking was out of all proportion, then it would be unreasonable to order reinstatement. With Alan Pegler having paid only £3,000 to take control and the company

An undated plan produced by the Central Electricity Authority showing a proposed deviation route alongside the eastern side of the reservoir.

(National Archives)

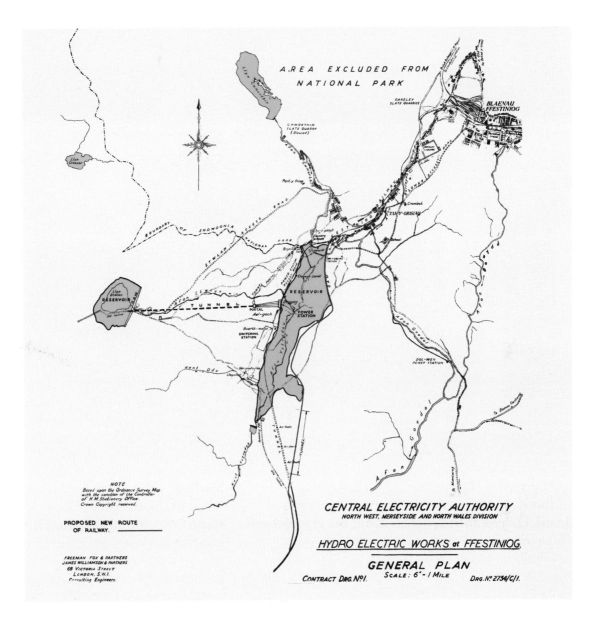

claiming £180,000, it was impossible for the company to bridge the difference. He rejected the claim and ordered the company to pay the CEGB's costs, £1,541 3s 2d. Unhappy with the outcome, the company lodged notice to appeal on 22 August 1960.

Meanwhile, at Portmadoc, passengers found the station altered on the side of the building facing the town, by the insertion of doors, one into the booking hall and one to the offices. The layout of the booking hall had been altered and a souvenir counter provided. A large sign promoting the railway's location was also erected on the town side of the building.

A £100 guineas facilities fee was earned when the BBC made a thirty-minute live broadcast from the railway on 13 July 1960. Garraway hoped that it would boost passenger numbers, 1,000 down because Easter had been late. The results for the week of the broadcast and the five weeks following are shown in the table. For the first time, more than 100,000 passenger journeys were made during the year. The staff were rewarded by a party at the Queen's Hotel and Garraway's salary was increased by £100.

Week ending	17 July	24 July	31 July	7 August	14 August	21 August
Bookings	1,918	3,032	4,628	5,046	5,591	5,700
Revenue	£526 3s 2d	£676 1s 10d	£963 10s 6d	£1,017 17s 1d	£1,116 6s 4d	£1,114 10s 3d
Sales	£101 2s 1d	£126 15s 2d	£235 2s	£257 16s 4d	£309 12s 5d	£268 1s 3d

Earl of Merioneth's fireman couples up to the train on 6 September 1962. Carriage destination boards were out of service by the end of the decade. Stabled outside the goods shed is wagon No. 63, one of three ex-War Department bogie wagons built by Hudson and purchased from Smiths' potato estates, Lincolnshire, in 1960. No. 63 had been adapted from an ambulance van and was later piped for vacuum brakes to be able to run in passenger trains.

The wall at the end of the platform at Portmadoc provided a fine vantage point for observing activities in the Station.

Living at Tan y Bwlch stationhouse, Will and Bessie Jones soon got to know the railway's personnel. Will joined the staff and trained a few of them on the art of track maintenance with limited resources. Bessie resumed greeting the trains in Welsh costume and serving refreshments from her front room. They retired in 1968. The Simplex tractor, which became known as *Mary Ann*, and the Wickham trolley are seen outside the cottage. The trolley was bought from British Railways in 1962 and regauged; it had fallen out of use by the 1970s.

With the railway's operations becoming more complex since the extension of services to Tan y Bwlch, the railway inspectorate had become very interested in the railway's operation. A report, obviously prepared by Garraway, but signed by Alan Pegler, was given to Colonel McMullen on 1 December 1960, containing what might best be described as some 'unusual features'. Briefly, a light engine running between Portmadoc and Pen Cob could do so without being in possession of either the staff or a ticket; when two trains were in operation, block working was observed between Penrhyn and Tan y Bwlch, 'and elsewhere when possible, otherwise 15 minutes headway is allowed.' Sometimes, an intermediate block post was set up between Penrhyn and Tan y Bwlch to control it. It was admitted that some methods appeared to be unorthodox.

Colonel Ernest Woodhouse went through it, producing a closely-typed two-page critique of its weaknesses, and Bill Broadbent was summoned to a meeting, held at the United Services Club on 23 February 1961, for three inspectors to explain their

concerns. Their report was passed to Garraway, who wrote to Woodhouse on 9 March to explain himself. The intermediate block had only been put into effect when *Taliesin* had been running short of steam and some 'telephone boys' had been working in the section at the time; time-interval working was avoided 'where possible'.

Time-interval working had been banned on British railways with the enactment of the 1889 Regulation of Railways Act. A long-standing society member and volunteer told the author that the intermediate block post, at Bryn Mawr, was only operated once. The correspondence was continued for several months before the inspectorate was satisfied that it was getting the answers it wanted. On 16 April 1961 Woodhouse filed one of Garraway's letters with the comment, 'It shows what an argumentative chap Garraway is.'

In London, the company's appeal against the Lands Tribunal decision was heard on 11 and 12 December 1961, when its claims that the rules had been applied incorrectly; that no account had been

A young passenger scrutinises *Prince* whilst the driver and guard chat. They are not ready to go – the vacuum pipes are not connected and the destination board on the van needs turning over.

Prince was repainted again in 1959, but was needed in traffic before the job was finished.

Carriages would also be put into service with the paintwork incomplete, sometimes still wet. This is No. 15 in 1960.

For a time, *Princess* was put on display at Portmadoc, with a description saying that it was 'the next engine to be restored'.

Volunteers undertook, and still do, many tasks throughout the railway, including restoring and maintaining the telephone network. (John Neville)

taken of the improvements carried out since 1955; that its value of the business, not the open market value, should have received more weight; and that undue weight had been placed on the CEGB's claim that 1,000 extra passengers a day would have to be carried to justify the expenditure, were rejected.

The railway inspectorate's Colonel Woodhouse attended both hearings. Reporting briefly, 'I think this is the end of it', he reckoned without the determination of railway enthusiasts. Maybe the society would not have been so keen to present him with a 'centenary of

steam' medal in 1966 had it known how sceptical he had been of the railway's chances.

The company's attempt to make provision for its eventual return to Blaenau Ffestiniog, with regards to the construction of the standard-gauge link line, was effectively rejected in February 1961. In advance of a meeting with British Railways' estates department, the directors decided that their determination to complete the restoration should be emphasised and that provision should be made for slate traffic as well as passengers, and for the railway to pass through the Benar Road Bridge. Merioneth County Council was also to be informed that if it adopted the power station access road, which breached the company's property near the former LNWR exchange station, it would do so subject to a claim for reinstatement of the railway. The directors were, of course, unaware that the general managers of the Western and London Midland regions had already decided that they should take no account of the company's requirements when constructing the link line.

Changes made to the company's financial structure in 1961 were probably the result of the comments made about its value at the Lands Tribunal hearings in 1960. As the debentures were effectively a variety of preference stock and there was no intention of paying the interest, then the amount previously reserved for it was cancelled, increasing the company's value. To overcome the misleading aspects of nineteenth-century railway accounting, which assumed that assets were maintained as-new and never deteriorated, the assets were also revalued and shown by a £1 million fixed asset replacement account, balanced by a capital reserve of the same amount.

Attempts were made to improve the relationship with the society during the first months of 1961. Alan Pegler decided to withdraw the reimbursement clause from the trust deed and to appoint society chairman Bill Broadbent as an additional trustee, and the Company decided to allocate £1,000 5 per cent preference shares to the society in acknowledgment of an equivalent donation. The gesture was criticised at the society AGM on 22 April, when treasurer W.K. Nelson, who had always been unhappy that the society did not control the company, pointed out that they were worthless. He thought that restoration of

PLAN

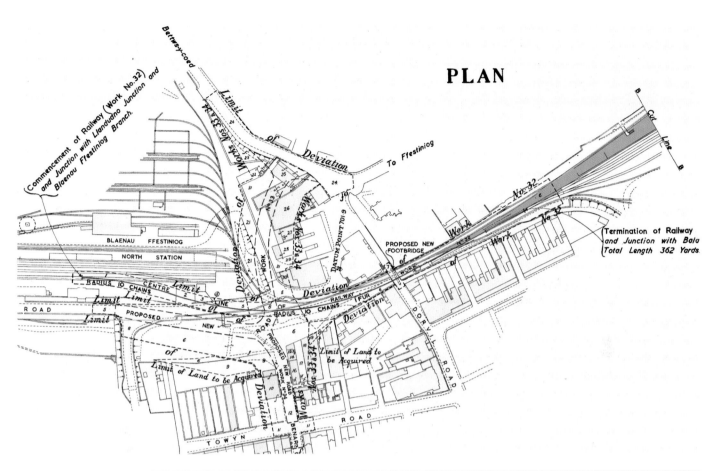

An extract from the deposited plans that accompanied the British Transport Commission Bill later in 1959. Work No. 32, the standard-gauge connection, has been highlighted in red, the FR route, for which no provision was made when the link was built, in blue.
(Parliamentary Archives)

Taliesin appeared with its paintwork modified in 1959, its domes, cab fronts and boiler barrels painted green instead of black.

In a move that was not universally liked, *Taliesin* was renamed *Earl of Merioneth* on 22 April 1961.

the railway had outrun the society membership and that trains would be running further than Tan y Bwlch if the society was in control.

Earlier in the day, and without notice, the directors had arranged for *Taliesin* to be renamed *Earl of Merioneth*. The name is one of the Duke of Edinburgh's titles and permission had been obtained from Buckingham Palace to use it. No explanation was given for the change, although it was felt in some quarters that the directors aspired for the railway to benefit from a royal visit. *Taliesin* had been chosen to be renamed because it had been built as *Livingston Thompson* in 1886 and renamed in 1932 so, they reasoned, it had only carried its name for a short time, failing to understand the affection with which it was regarded as the first Fairlie to be restored under the new regime.

The renaming ceremony was carried out by Oswald Thomas, former chairman of Portmadoc Urban District Council. It was the subject of some debate at the AGM and afterwards there were several oblique references to the fact that the change of name had not been universally welcomed.

One landmark of the weekend was the appearance of *Merddin Emrys*, double-heading with the *Earl of Merioneth* on the society's special trains, the first time that two bogie engines had been

steamed since before the war. A film made by the BBC was broadcast three times. Without a cab and with incomplete paintwork, *Merddin Emrys* entered service on 3 July 1961.

Oswald Thomas showed Allan Garraway a letter that he had received seeking support for the restoration of the Welsh Highland Railway, Bob Honychurch from Shrewsbury writing that there was vast financial and practical support available for it. Reporting this to the directors, Garraway was obviously unhappy about the prospect of competition, suggesting that if there was money available it should be used to extend the FR, or even the Talyllyn or Welshpool & Llanfair Light Railways.

Keen to promote the growing number of narrow-gauge railways in Wales collectively, Garraway organised a meeting in Shrewsbury for representatives from the railways to meet officers from the Wales Tourist Board. Honychurch attended, but when the board agreed to produce a leaflet promoting the existing railways, and the Welshpool & Llanfair because it would soon be reopened, the meeting decided that the WHR should not be included 'because it was not very practical'.

In an attempt to manage overcrowding during the peak, on 17 July 1961 the directors decided to increase the Tan y Bwlch return fare by 6d from 1

August. There was no comment on whether the increase had the desired effect, and only FR and Talyllyn Railway members, who had free travel, commented about the fare increase. Garraway also noted that a four-wheeled carriage on one of the relief trains had gone out with twenty-five passengers.

Bill Broadbent had been investigating sources of 'new' rail. 75lb was affordable, but too heavy, 60lb cost more, £27 per ton, because there was demand for it from industrial users. The Penrhyn quarry railway was due to be closed, however, and he hoped to be able to get its 50lb bullhead rail for £13 per ton. He warned that to get all of it would cost around £3,000. The company offered to match the price offered by scrap merchants and decided that the worn rail being replaced could be sold.

For 1962, Allan Garraway decided to recast the timetable to give a more even spread of departures, but requiring operation of two distinct trains instead of a main train and a relief. Looking ahead to the completion of the Lynton & Barnstaple carriage, he

In 1961 *Merddin Emrys* was returned to service although without a cab and a temporary paint scheme. At Tan y Bwlch, the sidings are still covered in grass and thoughts were turning to ways of making sure that motor vehicles did not encroach on the track. 22 August 1961.

discussed the options for building new carriages at Boston Lodge. Timber bodies built on steel underframes should be designed to harmonise with the existing fleet. A centre corridor would allow tickets to be inspected on the move and give standing room for busy times; fewer doors would reduce loading times. New stock should adopt the Lynton & Barnstaple profile.

There was around this time clearly some conflict between the manager and his staff, a subject that he and the directors returned to several times. Hindsight suggests that problems arose because there was no proper structure and that maybe some individuals were determined to cause trouble. Some

One fine day in the early 1960s, *Earl of Merioneth* arrives back at Portmadoc. There appears to be another train, or at least a locomotive, on the embankment behind it.

A view from the back of the train at Cei Mawr. Apart from the height of the embankment, tree growth has made this location almost unrecognisable.

To address the shortage of locomotives capable of handling the traffic, in July 1962 arrangements had been made to hire *Linda*, one of the Penrhyn quarry railway's large Hunslet 0-4-0STs. Shortly after arriving at Boston Lodge it was photographed with the weed-killing wagon coupled acting as a tender.
(Ken Rangeley)

employees became concerned that volunteers would take their jobs and tried to make them unwelcome. An organisation chart was published, and conditions of service, including arrangements for rest days, produced.

On 16 April 1962, Garraway told the directors that no locos were available for traffic yet the service was due to start on 18 April; he blamed mismanagement in the works. He was not going to work all hours to sort it out and would not expect anyone else to. *Merddin Emrys* was made ready in time to start the service. The works manager, Richard Hilton, left in June. He had joined the company in 1959 and had become locomotive superintendent in 1960. It seems that he was unwilling to take instruction from the manager.

Through the summer, problems with the locomotives developed or came to light, a broken axle box on *Earl of Merioneth* in June, leaking stays and distorted crown sheet, evidence that the firebox had been overheated, on *Merddin Emrys* in July. *Prince* was still in bits, its winter service incomplete. With only the *Earl of Merioneth* available in July, Garraway had no option, but to delay the start of the two-train service.

To overcome these difficulties, he arranged to hire Hunslet 0-4-0ST *Linda* from the Penrhyn Quarry Company for £50 a week. The purchase price for the

three suitable locomotives was £1,500 for *Linda*, £2,500 for *Blanche* and £500 for *Charles*, which needed a new boiler. He felt the price had been inflated by inquiries from enthusiasts, which made the quarry think the market for them was bigger than it was. The alternative was overhauling *Princess* or *Welsh Pony* at a cost of at least £3,000; they required new tanks and boilers, and would have to be sent away.

Prince was tested on 12 July, but its wheels had been put in the wrong way round and its valves were operating in reverse; it entered service on 15 July and the two-train service was started. *Linda* had arrived at Minffordd by rail from Port Penrhyn the day before, and was unloaded and steamed on 15 July. With six carriages, it reached Cae Mawr before running out of coal and water. Garraway thought that it was too lively to run at FR speeds, but could be made useful if it had a tender. During another test on 21 July, it went off-beat at Gwyndy. The quarry's engineer had no solution and agreed to forego the rent until it was fixed.

Problems with *Prince* in August, a broken piston and a leaking fusible plug on different days, saw *Linda* put into service, still with its wheels set to 1ft 10¾in gauge and without continuous brakes. This came to a sudden end on 5 September, when *Linda* was piloting *Prince* on the 2.15pm departure

and derailed in Cutting Budr, above Cae Mawr. The remains of an occupation crossing slewed the locomotive round and only the coupling with *Prince* prevented it from falling down the hill. A passenger in the quarrymen's carriage reported being bruised and shocked, but otherwise there were no injuries. The service was suspended for the rest of the day and re-railing was completed after dark.

Track being loose to gauge was thought to be the cause, made worse by *Linda's* narrower wheelsets pushing against the rails. The incident, known in FR mythology as '*Linda*'s leap', was not reported to the railway inspectorate as it should have been, although it cannot have been entirely coincidental that an enquiry was made about the railway's procedures for dealing with 'foreign' locomotives a few weeks later. *Linda*, which sustained damage including a broken eccentric, was put away until its future was decided.

A letter to the ministry from Broadbent in December 1962, that included details about the availability and use of locomotives, gave the new chief inspector, Brigadier C.A. Langley, an opportunity to ask Alan Pegler, as chairman, specifically about the use of *Linda* and vacuum

brakes, drawing attention to the relevant legislation and asking for a report describing the circumstances under which it became necessary, as opposed to convenient, to use *Linda* as train engine following *Prince's* failure, and in contravention to the 1890 Regulation of Railways order, and an assurance that it would be complied with in future.

Broadbent replied on 16 January 1963, saying that whilst the company wished to comply with every safety requirement, including the use of vacuum brakes, the ministry had misunderstood the rules as applied to the Ffestiniog Railway. He closed by saying that he was not suggesting that the Company should be exempt from the regulations, that it wished to comply with both the spirit and the letter of the law, and that the obvious answer was not to allow non-vacuum fitted locomotives to be booked on passenger workings 'in future'. In a separate letter, he asked for a copy of the 1890 order as it had not been possible to find a copy in the archives.

Langley naturally replied, to Pegler, that Broadbent was wrong and repeated his request for a report and assurance. Francis Wayne now became involved, telling Broadbent that the company's interpretation of the legislation was correct and helpfully enclosing a second copy of his letter to be passed on to the ministry. When the treasury solicitor confirmed that he stood by his interpretation, Pegler was once again asked for a report and assurance.

The request, and a reminder in April, were both ignored, but an incident involving *Linda*, regauged and equipped with vacuum brakes, at Penrhyn Crossing on 8 June, triggered another reminder that was followed by a rebuke for not reporting the incident in compliance with the rules. Both were ignored.

When the quarries had stopped using the isolated section of the railway between Duffws and the LNWR yard during 1962, Maenofferen bought the 103 wagons previously rented for £375, Allan Garraway telling the directors that there were still enough wagons available to resume carrying slate to Minffordd if necessary. In January 1963, he discovered that no provision was being made for the FR in the construction of the standard-gauge link-line.

Earl of Merioneth was dismantled, enabling its boiler to be examined in February 1963, and revealing wastage under the regulator glands and manifolds and, when rust was cleared away, a hole in the barrel. It might be possible to repair by welding, Garraway informed the directors, but a new boiler would be required within five years, recommending an order be placed for one that had increased steam spaces, superheating and steel instead of copper fireboxes.

Whilst no agreement had been reached on the purchase of *Linda*, the Penrhyn Quarry Company had offered to hire it for £150 a year and to deduct such a charge from the sale price. Modifications to the wheel treads and the installation of vacuum brakes were authorised to be undertaken with immediate effect. The wheelsets were sent to Hunslet, the locomotive's builder, to be altered, and the broken eccentrics replaced by those that had belonged to the original *Taliesin*, dismantled in 1932.

A big celebration to mark the railway's steam centenary, with a budget of £1,000, was organised in 1963. Garraway had been most unhappy about the idea when the directors told him about it, saying

A few minutes later he went to investigate why silence had suddenly descended after the train had passed from sight, to find this sorry sight.

that the passenger centenary two years later was more significant and doubting that it would attract the 9,000 extra passengers necessary to recoup the expenditure.

Nevertheless, a programme was devised. On 20 April, the society's AGM day, a special train from London was hauled part-way by ex-LNER 4-6-2 No. 4472 *Flying Scotsman*, purchased by Alan Pegler just four days before; on 22 May, the railway hosted a visit by twenty-seven journalists and on 4 August, the bank holiday, an extra carriage was added to the 2.30pm for society members. The railway benefited from reports published in twenty-four newspapers and periodicals immediately following the press visit.

Located in the grounds of Plas Tan y Bwlch, Plas Halt was opened on 1 June 1963, having been built the night before. The property had recently been acquired by shipping magnate John Bibby, who was building chalets in the grounds. It was subsequently sold to Caernarvonshire County Council and became the Snowdonia National Park's study centre.

On 22 May 1963, the railway celebrated its centenary of steam with staff and volunteers dressed in costume, joined by members of the Women's Institute and their children in costume, too.

Linda was back on its wheels in June, but its ejector had not been connected to the steam supply and it could not make a vacuum, so it could only go out double-headed. It derailed at Three Gates, near Tan y Bwlch, on 8 June. The leading axleboxes were too tight and too low in the horns, reported Garraway, one of the penalties of having inexperienced staff at Boston Lodge, he said. Equipped with a tender adapted from one of the England tenders and carrying sixty gallons of water in barrels, *Linda* was approved for use in case of failure after it had made a run to Tan y Bwlch with five carriages on 13 July 1963.

In contrast, buffet car No. 14, the Lynton & Barnstaple carriage, which entered service in June, was an immediate success. As well as accommodation for twenty-three passengers, it had a small kitchen with a calor gas oven for cooking and water heating. A dynamo provided power for an ice-cream fridge and lighting. Advantage was taken of licensing laws that permitted the sale of alcohol whilst on the move without a licence, which proved to be extremely popular in an area of Wales that remained dry on Sundays for many years. During its first week in traffic, on-train sales had doubled those of the same week the year before.

Celebrations for the steam centenary on 25 August 1963 entailed decorating *Prince* and staff, volunteers and members of Portmadoc Women's Institute wearing Victorian dress. Journalists from national newspapers produced fulsome reports about the day, no doubt encouraged by the draught beer on offer in the buffet car. The society arranged for the production of commemorative silver medals that were sold with the promise of travel on the first passenger train to run to Blaenau Ffestiniog.

A decision on the purchase of *Linda* and *Blanche* was urged on the directors by Garraway in September. Having two similar locomotives would enable one to be kept going using parts of the other.

He did not expect *Merddin Emrys'* boiler to last until its next five-year examination; its fireboxes were not as good as those on *Earl of Merioneth*, there were problems with its foundation rings, and its bottom-end bogie required new cylinders and steamchest. It should be kept in reserve for two or three years and then be reboiled. The directors resolved to buy *Linda* (£1,000) and *Blanche* (£2,000 as its boiler was only five years old) on 27 September 1963. *Blanche* was delivered on 17 December. At Felin Hen, where the loco had been kept, a Penrhyn employee scratched '*Blanche* 1963 *ffarwel yr rhen hogan* [farewell old friend]!' on the slate shed wall.

On the same date, the directors responded to Garraway's earlier request for two or three new carriages to be built with corridor connections and first-class compartments by deciding that ten new carriages should be built, one of them an observation car. Garraway had already explained that the corridors would increase revenue from the buffet car and that building new would be more cost effective than adapting existing stock. They would be 35ft long and be similar to No. 14 in outline. The first

When *Blanche* was obtained from Penrhyn in December 1963, it was regauged straight away and ran regularly in 1964, running with the tender that had been temporarily attached to *Linda*. Running round at Tan y Bwlch, 3 August 1964, the driver has found a convenient hook for his tea caddy.

Just as it was before the war, in the 1960s Glan y Mor Yard became a place where enthusiasts could find abandoned locomotives. This was *Palmerston*.

carriage, put in hand straight away, would be treated as a prototype.

Later in 1963, Bill Broadbent produced an undated report on the condition of the locomotives and their future availability. *Merddin Emrys* would require a new boiler within four years; *Earl of Merioneth's* boiler was in fair condition, the loco would not require attention for some years; *Prince* had a new boiler in 1955 and had new cylinders, in good order for many years to come; *Linda's* boiler was in fair condition, mechanical condition greatly improved after modifications carried out at Boston Lodge; *Blanche*, not yet at Portmadoc, mechanical condition believed to be sound, to be modified as *Linda*; *Volunteer* required firebox repairs, mechanically excellent, intended to reduce driving-axle loadings with the addition of a pony truck and tender.

He forecast that in 1968, six steam locomotives and three stand-by diesels would be available for traffic. *Prince* was out of traffic within ten years,

Volunteer never ran in service on the FR before it was sold. Due to influences not yet developed, *Earl of Merioneth's* story took a very different turn.

Instances of theft from Boston Lodge reached their nadir over Christmas 1963. During December, *Linda* had been fitted with a five-chime whistle from the ex-LNER 'A4' 4-6-2 No. 60015 *Dominion of New Zealand,* which had been donated by that country when the loco had been built. When the works reopened after the holiday, it had been stolen. Garraway thought that it had been targeted by 'souvenir hunters' as other collectible items, including *Linda's* own whistle, had been left. Other items, including the Peckett's worksplates, one of *Princess's* number plates, and several wagon plates, had been stolen as well. In April the directors decided that members of the public should not be allowed to visit Boston Lodge and that society members should ask permission before looking round.

CHAPTER 7

1963-1970: CONSOLIDATION, DEVIATION, DDUALLT

A solution to the question of finding an affordable means of deviating the railway around the reservoir was developed in 1963, coinciding with the power station's opening.

On 9 July 1963, company secretary Francis Wayne wrote to the Ministry of Transport to ask if the ministry would be prepared to make a Light Railway Order to empower the construction of a deviation route. He explained that two previous surveys had been made, one along the west side of the reservoir, made impossible by a changes to the CEGB's plans, the other surveyed by Livesey & Henderson, and which involved a long gradient of 1 in 67½ and a tunnel 700 yards long. A new survey had been made to find a route with a gradient that did not exceed 1 in 80, compensated on curves, to reduce the amount of tunnelling or deep cuttings, which enabled work to be undertaken by volunteers if the compensation proved to be insufficient, and to reduce the £180,000 estimated cost of the Livesey & Henderson route.

Although the route was longer, no curve was sharper than 200ft radius, the cutting was 22ft deep at its greatest, and preliminary estimates indicated that it could be built for £125-150,000, less, depending on the amount of voluntary labour used. Negotiations had been started to purchase the non-CEGB land required and the board's engineers had been asked to supply details of its requirements for crossing the dam of the lower reservoir.

The new survey had been made by Cambridge University student Gerald Fox and a group of friends earlier in the year. The requirements for gradient and curvature had been met by inserting a spiral into the route at Dduallt. With the tunnel a mere 90 yards long, the route passed to the east of the reservoir, and crossed the dam and the power station

With construction of the deviation starting on 1 January 1965, even with no powers in place, there was great excitement about what was happening. This plan, a tracing of the original, showing the old route and the options considered for a deviation was submitted to the Lands Tribunal hearing for compensation.

(National Archives)

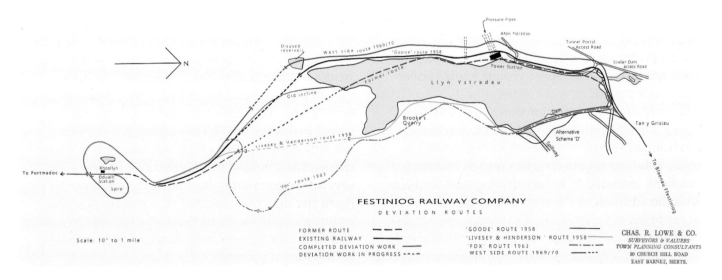

FESTINIOG RAILWAY COMPANY
DEVIATION ROUTES

Scale: 10" to 1 mile

FORMER ROUTE
EXISTING RAILWAY
COMPLETED DEVIATION WORK
DEVIATION WORK IN PROGRESS

'GOODE' ROUTE 1958
'LIVESEY & HENDERSON' ROUTE 1958
'FOX' ROUTE 1963
WEST SIDE ROUTE 1969/70

CHAS. R. LOWE & CO.
SURVEYORS & VALUERS
TOWN PLANNING CONSULTANTS
10 CHURCH HILL ROAD
EAST BARNET, HERTS.

access road to join up with the original route at Tanygrisiau Station.

Fox had also made contact with the CEGB and on 27 September 1963 was told unequivocally, by the secretary of the north-west region, that the CEGB was unable to consent to the siting of the railway on the west side of the power station. With regard to making use of the dam, there were several requirements to be met: access to vehicular traffic was required at all times, except when a train was passing; pedestrian access was required at all times, even when a train was crossing; the train service must be suspended at any time and without notice; maintenance works attributable to the railway on the dam were to be carried out by the CEGB and at railway company expense; modifications to the levels, to accommodate the railway, must leave the drawpits easily accessible; there was no objection to running on the CEGB's land, but the railway company would be responsible for the diversion of any public rights of way; details would be required of any works below lake level; there was no objection to a bridge over the spillway; a level crossing over the access road was preferable to a bridge to avoid difficulties with the transportation of large loads to the power station; and proposals for landscaping the railway's work must be approved by the CEGB.

The access requirements were still not very practical for either party and, notwithstanding the region being reasonably co-operative, it did not signify that the relationship with the headquarters legal department was improving. On 8 November 1963, the CEGB asked John Routly to verify Fox's *bona fides*, and seeking his, Routly's, assurance that the company did intend to reinstate the railway and was not, 'investigating these schemes merely on the assumption (which, as you know, would be quite unwarranted) that the Board should pay for reinstatement.'

The chief inspector of railways, Colonel J.R.H. Robertson, who was sceptical that the company might be able to construct a deviation, asked for information about how the lengthened railway was to be run and how the deviation was to be financed. He asked the treasury solicitor if there were any grounds for refusing to make an order, 'we are not too happy about the plan to extend their railway in this way. They have a very narrow financial margin

as it is and are sometimes tempted to work unsafely to keep the traffic moving and the passengers' cash coming in,' he wrote, asking for advice on whether a new LRO could be made to apply to the deviation only, or include safeguards not contained in the 1923 order, and what the position would be if the CEGB compensation was conditional on the deviation being built, but was insufficient, in his view, to cover the cost of construction and the extra stock needed to work it safely.

There was no reason why a new order should not include new safeguards applicable to the remainder of the railway, Robertson was informed, the only problem was likely to be opposition from the applicants. The solicitor doubted that anything could be done about the company's financial arrangements. Robertson should specify his safety requirements and leave it to the applicants to find the money.

In a letter to Bill Broadbent on 8 November 1963, Robertson referred to the last point by citing article 6 of the 1842 Regulation of Railways Act, which covered the reasons the Board of Trade could apply to postpone the opening on a new railway, including the 'insufficiency of the establishment for working such railway'.

Francis Wayne and Martin Barradell, the accountant, compiled a report entitled 'potential gain from the upper section' on 18 November 1963, the day after the directors had met at Alan Pegler's house in Nottinghamshire to discuss options for the deviation. Concerning potential traffic, Wayne and Barradell noted that most passengers made the full return journey available; there might be a diminishing return per mile at some point, but doubling the mileage and increasing the fare at slightly less than *pro rata* could generate more than twice the income from the same number of passengers.

Operating a longer mileage would require some increase in locomotive and carriage stock, not as much as double, and justify commitments already made. One new carriage a year would meet peak demand with a reasonable reserve and provide a larger proportion of centre-gangway stock.

Referring to a Government report on Welsh tourism published in 1963, they noted that North Wales attracted 58 per cent of the four million visitors to Wales in 1961, Caernarvonshire attracted

A feature of peak operations from 1963 was the operation of the 3.00pm departure from Portmadoc as *Y Cymro* (*The Welshman*), non-stop to Tan y Bwlch. One such is seen approaching Rhiw Plas.

over 25 per cent and Merioneth about 300,000. As 74 per cent of visitors to North Wales visited beauty spots, it could be that 750,000 of the visitors to Caernarvonshire were potential visitors to the Vale of Ffestiniog and therefore potential passengers. Commenting that drawing conclusions from statistics was notoriously difficult, they observed that there were more holidaymakers on the North Wales coast than around Portmadoc and thought that re-opening Blaenau Ffestiniog Station should, with adequate car parking, attract at least as much tourist traffic as between the wars.

The directors considered the report on 25 November 1963. As the railway below Tan y Bwlch was in 'admirable shape' and required little spending on it, unless receipts were depressed in some way, more funds would become available to be spent above Tan y Bwlch. The board, however, had two options, to complete the restoration to Blaenau Ffestiniog or to maintain the status quo. Whilst either was theoretically possible, the only realistic one, the directors concluded, was to complete the restoration, for several reasons.

It had been the objective since the current board had been appointed, they minuted, and was shared with the FR Society; voluntary labour and gifts were partially contributed on the basis that the restoration would be completed. Increasing numbers of passengers were prepared to pay the current fares and, by implication, would not resist fares increasing as the length of journey increased. Revenue in excess of expenditure would need to be applied to the railway; it would be wrong and unprincipled to apply any of it to payment of a dividend, since it was the fruit of voluntary labour and, in any event, any dividend paid on the majority holding would be returned to the railway by virtue of the trust deed under which it was held.

The return anticipated from completing the restoration justified it if the funds were available. Some compensation was bound to be received from the CEGB. No matter how small, it would have to be applied to the purposes of the railway. In view of the excellent condition of the railway now being operated, it must therefore be spent on a part not yet operating.

To reopen to Blaenau Ffestiniog would cost £140,900 for the deviation, plus other expenditure on reinstating the bridge over the Cwmorthin road at Tanygrisiau and building a new terminus. Some work could be done by volunteers and local paid labour, reducing the cost to £95,000. The directors still thought that the CEGB should pay for the cost of the deviation and should do so on the basis of the contract price, as insisting on its reduction by using volunteers would extend the construction time, postpone giving the benefit of the deviation to the company, and hence increase its cost.

If the compensation was less than the contract price, then the shortfall could be funded at the rate of £3,000 a year from operating surpluses, albeit with completion delayed. A bank loan could not be obtained without guarantees and there was no one available to guarantee the funds required. If there were no compensation, then there would have to be a public appeal, when the circumstances of the compulsory acquisition would be made known. The best course was to proceed with the compensation claim and to rely on public sympathy if the outcome did not meet the company's requirements.

The £140,900 construction price had come from Livesey & Henderson when they had validated Gerald Fox's plans. Their own estimate had been £165,000, but they had reduced it to allow for the use of Penrhyn quarry rail.

Wayne submitted what he called a formal application for an LRO on 4 December 1963, but this was not in accordance with the prescribed rules for applications. An application in the correct form was not submitted until July 1966.

The question of archaic railway company accounting, where expenditure on maintenance or renewals was treated as a charge against the year in which the money was spent, only showing a true picture if the assets were maintained at a consistent level, was addressed in 1964, when the fixed assets were revalued in terms of their estimated cost of replacement, less the estimated cost of bringing them up to standard, arrears of maintenance, reflecting the process of restoration and the gifts, cash and labour that had made it possible. Dealing with gifts had been a particular problem of the old system, because donations were treated as capital receipts, but the expenditure they funded was made from revenue.

Concerning the revaluation, the railway had cost £6,000 a mile, about £81,000, to build, or £810,000 in 1963 allowing for inflation. The estimate for building the deviation was £142,000, or nearly £50,000 per

mile, producing £675,000 for 13½ miles. However, the Fox route contained no earthworks exceeding 25ft high or deep, whilst the sections from Cae Mawr to Coed y Bleiddiau and above Tanygrisiau contained heavy earthworks. Land below Penrhyn and above Tanygrisiau would also cost more on a replacement basis, indicating that if the railway had not been built, it would cost at least £800,000 to build in the 1960s. As both calculations produced a similar figure it was reasonable, the report noted, to value replacement of the land and permanent way at £800,000. Other valuations are given in the table.

	Standard replacement value 31 December 1962	Estimated restoration cost
Buildings	£76,425	£8,825
Locomotives	£79,750	£8,900
Carriages	£66,000	£11,000
Other rolling stock	£12,380	£2,050
	£234,555	£30,775

With the revaluation, the balance sheet was re-drawn in compliance with then-current standards and the revised arrangement applied to the accounts for 1963. These were accompanied by the first post-revival chairman's report, although very few people would have seen it, and it was not repeated until after the 1987 share issue.

Terms for buying the locomotives and rail from the Penrhyn Quarry Company were settled in January 1964, £3,000 for the locomotives, less £75 rental for *Linda*, and £8,000 for the rail, a total of £10,925. A cheque for 30 per cent, £3,187 10s, was authorised to be sent straight away.

A suggestion that the Penrhyn quarry railway should be preserved, that was published in the *Railway Magazine* in January 1964, attracted a response from Allan Garraway, who said that before restoring, more railway enthusiasts should consider the needs of the four narrow-gauge lines already operating in Wales, or about to start operating in the case of the Welshpool & Llanfair Light Railway. There was also, he observed, an organisation seeking to revive part of the Welsh Highland Railway, declaring, 'The prospect of another 2ft gauge line on its own doorstep is not regarded with favour by the Ffestiniog authorities, especially when it has its own line to extend.' Regarding the Penrhyn proposal, he thought that the land would be impossibly

Merddin Emrys, seen at Portmadoc coaling stage, ran in 1963 without its cab roof. Its weakening fireboxes meant that it did not seen much use until it was reboilered in 1970.

expensive and two of the main-line locomotives were already at the FR whilst the third was at the Penrhyn Castle Museum. Of the smaller locomotives, those in reasonable condition were still being used in the quarries and the remainder required expensive repairs. There was no suitable passenger accommodation.

A letter from R.J. Hunter, a former society director, complaining that it did not represent the company's view, caused the directors to prepare a statement to be read at the society's AGM, saying that Hunter had misunderstood the facts, that Garraway was entitled to express his views, that they did not oppose any scheme and did not know of one likely to diminish appreciably the FR's traffic receipts.

Hunter had also complained that some of those connected with the FR had a belligerent attitude that meant that 'many of us are no longer ready to help it'. 'In the old days', he said, 'when they had few

paid staff and no "paid" volunteers we were prepared to do a lot, but the Ffestiniog Railway cannot be said to be a friendly line and the letter unfortunately illustrates this.' He appreciated, however, that an efficient railway could not have the fairground atmosphere 'many' would like. In response the directors expressed their appreciation of the 'ever-growing army of volunteers, and the ever-growing membership of the society, and all our other friends whose steadily increasing support has given us such encouragement. To any who misunderstand us, we still offer our sincere friendship and no "belligerent attitude".'

With the cab roof modified to improve clearances in the Garnedd Tunnel, a repaint and *Welsh Pony's* tender modified to suit, *Linda* entered service, usually with Allan Garraway at the regulator. Not long before her retirement in 1968, Bessie Jones chats with the fireman.
(John Neville)

For *Blanche*, a tender cab was made at Boston Lodge in 1965, the loco entering service in July in this temporary black livery. It was painted green in October.
(Martin Fuller collection)

On learning that the company had been awarded a certificate of merit for its contribution to Welsh tourism by the Welsh Tourism & Holidays Board, the directors were determined to make an impression. Alan Pegler arranged for them to arrive at Cardiff, where the certificate was presented on 18 March 1964, travelling in an observation car hauled by his ex-LNER 'A3' 4-6-2 No. 4472 *Flying Scotsman*. A headboard featuring the FR's crest was carried.

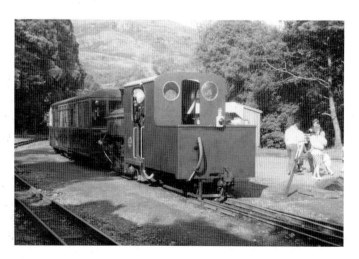

Arising from the event, the Mayor of Cardiff visited the railway on 15 April.

The directors also commissioned a ciné film, to be in colour with sound, and noted that the artist Terence Cuneo had been commissioned by Alan Pegler to paint a picture featuring the railway; he visited to make sketches on 14 May 1964. Pegler gave the company the reproduction rights to the painting, and it produced a poster that was used for publicity and for sale in the shop. In 1971, John Routly bought the painting for the company; it appeared in the accounts as a fixed asset valued at £578 for several years. The artist was given one of three 'centenary of steam' medals that the company bought, the others being given to Allan Garraway and P.B. Whitehouse, the author of a book about the railway's revival that had been published in 1963.

Some of the society's area groups found quite imaginative ways to help the railway off-site; in 1964 the Midland group delivered a four-wheeled passenger brake van, built at Bickenhill, Solihull, comprising a timber body mounted on a steel frame and using the running gear from a quarrymen's

Tan y Bwlch one fine morning c1966. None of the three carriages nearest the camera had been on the railway ten years earlier. Observation car No. 100 (left) was so numbered to commemorate the centenary of passenger services in 1965, when it entered service. No. 14 (centre) is the buffet car built making use of the Lynton & Barnstaple Railway carriage No. 15 retrieved from Devon in 1959; it entered service in 1964. No. 24 was the first of the new stock built using the Lynton & Barnstaple profile and also entered service in 1965; it was renumbered No. 104 in 1967.

carriage. The guard shared his accommodation with up to eight passengers, whose accommodation was quite primitive. The project leader was Tony Hills, whose eventual establishment of the Brecon Mountain Railway in South Wales came about because he was not allowed to restore *Welsh Pony* as a homework project. The carriage was transferred to the S&T department in 1987.

Although the company had no powers to build the deviation, in December 1964 the directors had agreed that Gerald Fox should establish a civil engineering section that would be responsible to the general manager and to allocate £1,000, plus donations, to the 'Blaenau fund', towards constructing the route, including £250 for land purchase. Two landowners had donated 4 acres of land at Dduallt for the deviation, but others proved to be somewhat intransigent.

Fox took a small group up to Dduallt on 2 January 1965 and, after a ballot, invited one of them, academic Dr Michael Lewis, to cut the 'first sod'. This was particularly appropriate because Dr Lewis's researches into the origins and construction of the railway were about to be published. None of

the directors, company or society, or Allan Garraway, attended and for several years, construction of the deviation was undertaken as if it was something that had nothing to do with the railway, with tension between the operators and the builders.

The builders became known as deviationists, which seemed rather *outré* at the time. They came from a wide range of backgrounds and most of them were not enthusiasts, but people who enjoyed being involved in something that was completely different from their normal routine. Gender was no barrier to participation and it was soon noticed

Some deviation volunteers stayed in the old permanent way hut near Dduallt, using a trolley to carry their possessions.

(M. Costello/Irish Railway Record Society)

Digging out the cutting to make the embankment towards the site of the new bridge at Dduallt.

(John Neville)

As well as making use of a barn at Dduallt Manor, a mess was established for volunteers working on the deviation on the widened formation near the old tunnel mouth. The locomotive was a 20hp Motor Rail built in 1940. It was built for the St Albans Sand & Gravel Company in Hertfordshire. (M. Costello/Irish Railway Record Society)

that the male output increased when there were women in the party.

Deviationists established themselves in the barn at Dduallt Manor, rented by the company, and later in a mess constructed of portable timber buildings located on the widened formation by the old tunnel mouth. The railway thence remained in place and in use for the conveyance of volunteers, their baggage and supplies; a platform and siding were also constructed at Dduallt Manor, named Campbell's Platform after the property's owner, Colonel Andrew Campbell, for their and his convenience. As a licensed shot-blaster, he provided a useful service during the deviation's construction for several years.

Looking further ahead, Ffestiniog Urban District Council had asked the company to clarify its intentions with regards to its terminus in Blaenau Ffestiniog. The company had intended to restore the route to the GWR station and Duffws, as both were close to the centre of the town and had land available for car parking, but the route had been severed by both the CEGB's access road and the standard-gauge link line. Restoration to Duffws, the directors noted

in November 1964, would provide a link with the slate quarries, but slate production had been declining so potential slate traffic was uncertain. Therefore, they decided that to assist the council they would agree to restrict passenger services to the LNWR exchange station site, providing adequate facilities for a terminus and car parking were available there, and providing there was an adequate connection with any slate quarries still operating.

After ten years with carriages painted green and ivory, a change was made when No. 24, the first of the new carriages, entered service on 24 August 1964, for it was turned out in a simple varnished livery, a development intended to save on paintshop time. It was followed in March 1965 by No. 26, the former

When work on the link line at Blaenau Ffestiniog was started there was still a good stock of slate, and a good number of FR wagons, in the LNWR yard.

Work in progress to make the standard-gauge link line in Blaenau Ffestiniog on 5 July 1963, seen from the end of the LNWR platform.

(J. J. Davis)

The quarries stopped using the FR line between Duffws and the LNWR yard in 1962, and the track became overgrown and covered by rubbish. Seen a few weeks before the link line was opened on 20 April 1964, the ballast train's loco was the last steam here until 1982.

(Geoff Charles/National Library of Wales)

Welsh Highland Railway carriage rescued from Groeslon. It had been given a steel underframe in 1964 and its original half doors had now been replaced with full doors. When the directors met on 12 April 1964, there had been few comments about the livery and few of them adverse, reported Garraway. Therefore, they resolved, any carriages that required painting in future would be scraped down and varnished. Inconsistent weathering proved to be its downfall.

The second of the new carriages, observation car No. 100, was launched to mark the centenary of passenger services on 24 May 1965. A donation of £1,500 had allowed its construction to be brought forward. The armchairs in the saloon had been obtained from the former Pullman works at Brighton. From 1966, a supplement of 2s 6d was charged to travel in the vehicle. No 24 was renumbered No. 104 in 1967.

The logistics of recovering the Penrhyn rail were not as straightforward as at first appeared. Leeds Metal Traders' offer to do the work for £4,000, payable at the rate of £1,000 per month after the track had been lifted to the satisfaction of the quarry company, which seems remarkably generous, was accepted in April 1965. Closer to home, Allan Garraway had

negotiated the purchase of 3,000 tons of ballast from the former GWR line near Trawsfynydd, for £1,500 including haulage. It was intended to use 3 miles of the rail on the deviation and the remainder to replace worn rail elsewhere.

Some 60 yards of deviation formation had been constructed by May 1965, although the Company still had no powers or planning permission, and the latter was required before a light railway order application could be submitted.

Planning approval for the route over the dam was granted on 29 June 1965 but, finding the CEGB's requirements for its use too onerous, an application was also made for a downstream route, which was refused because the CEGB objected to it on the grounds of visual amenity. The directors thought that this was unfair because the CEGB's requirements had

prevented the route over the dam from being progressed. An appeal lodged in October was withdrawn in December 1966, the company reserving its right to make a fresh application.

An element of frustration is detected in the minutes of a directors' meeting held on 13 October 1965. The land had been taken in 1956, but nine years later there was no sign of a resolution of the compensation claim or an agreement for a deviation route around the reservoir.

The possibility of acquiring another locomotive, Beyer, Peacock's first Garratt, was discussed in November 1965. The Manchester locomotive builder was closing down and sought a new home for the locomotive which it had repatriated from Tasmania in 1947. Allan Garraway thought that it would be useful for hauling peak-load heavy trains and that its height could be reduced to suit the FR loading gauge. The directors, however, decided to defer purchase until there were fewer demands on the

The first Garratt, *K1*, had been repatriated from Tasmania by its makers in 1947. There was, allegedly, a risk that it might be sold overseas had the FR not bought it. It was displayed at Portmadoc for a few months before being stored at Boston Lodge. For several years there was talk of it being cut down to fit the FR loading gauge, a move that would have required some serious butchery. (John Neville)

cash available. Garraway seemed to have been unaware that reducing the height of the loco to suit the FR would have made it difficult for the crew to stand up and that there would also have been problems with the width. Society members raising £1,250 to buy and transport it, it arrived at Portmadoc on 23 March 1966. It was displayed in the station for the remainder of the 1966 season before being moved to Boston Lodge for storage until 1976, when it was loaned to the National Railway Museum. It was

A consortium of Boston Lodge-based staff and volunteers bought Hunslet 0-4-0ST *Britomart* from the Pen-yr-Orsedd Quarry in 1965 and steamed it for the first time in 1966. This photograph was probably taken on the occasion of one if its first steamings; it usefully also shows the track that was once connected to the line across the Britannia Bridge.

returned to the railway in 1995, when restoration to working order was started; it entered service on the Welsh Highland Railway in 2006.

When Alan Pegler bought the preference shares in 1954, he took over responsibility for the £11,480 bank loan, which had been cancelled by the bank, holding £12,000 debentures as security, later transferring them to the trust. No interest had been paid, although provision had been made for it in the accounts. On 24 November 1965, the directors agreed that, in agreement with the trust, the loan be treated as satisfied by the debentures already held by the trust and the loan account closed. This transaction was a precursor to the trust becoming a charity, its registration being effective from 3 March 1966. The trust, which held nearly three quarters of each class of stock, was governed by a deed made on 10 November 1964 and amended on 24 May 1965. The trustees were then John Routly, Trevor Bailey and Ron Garraway. Power to appoint new trustees was vested in Alan Pegler, as founder, during his lifetime and by the company, in consultation with the chairman of the society, thereafter.

Notice of intention to apply for a Light Railway Order was published in the *London Gazette* on 12 July 1966. Powers were sought to make railway No. 3, a line 1 mile 7 furlongs and 9 chains in length,

commencing by a junction with the existing railway north of Dduallt Station and terminating near Brookes' Quarry on the eastern side of Llyn Ystradau, the power station's lower reservoir. The proposed order did not seek powers for a complete route because, although the CEGB had modified the dam to accommodate the railway, it had been impossible to obtain an agreement over its use, or for an alternative in the vicinity. It was also intended to amend the 1923 order and to authorise the abandonment of part of the existing railway,

Brookes' Quarry, the destination approved by the 1968 Light Railway Order. (M. Costello/Irish Railway Record Society)

between Dduallt and the tunnel. Railways Nos. 1 and 2 were the junction railways authorised by the 1923 order.

A review of the company's insurance cover in 1966 included obtaining £10,000 death by accident cover on Allan Garraway. Membership of the BUPA health insurance scheme for monthly-paid employees was also investigated.

I	LAND TAKEN	£	£
(a)	Strip of land, some 2 acres in extent from centre of Moelwyn tunnel to Tanygrisiau station	10	
(b)	Fixtures and fittings comprising permanent way materials destroyed or damaged beyond repair by Central Electricity Generating Board	2,113	2,123
II	DISTURBANCE		
(a)	Cost of construction of new line of railway, excluding cost of acquisition of land and making allowance for additional permanent way required having regard to I(b) above and also the additional length of the diversion route over the original route	140,900	
(b)	Cost of signalling equipment at the dam and provision of safety measures that may be required (See Note A below)		
(c)	Loss of profits based on the expectation that the line would have been opened throughout from Portmadoc to Blaenau Ffestiniog by 1960 and that the earliest date now possible for resuming such services is 1970.	32,307	173,207
III	SEVERANCE		
(a)	Strip of land, some 1 acre in extent from centre of Moelwyn tunnel to Dduallt	5	
(b)	Maintenance of above	200	
(c)	Making safe tunnel shafts	75	
(d)	Maintenance between Tanygrisiau and Blaenau Ffestiniog for ten years (1960-1970)	90	370
			£175,700

We should also add:
(A) The cost of the following items will have to be added when the requirements of the Ministry of Transport and/or the Central Electricity Generating Board are known.
   (i) Signalling requirements across the dam
   (ii) Safety measures on the diversion route which may be required
(B) DISTURBANCE – any claim arising in respect of the access road at Blaenau Ffestiniog North Western station has been omitted.
(X) No figure has been included to represent surveyors' and consultants' fees for the preparation of proposals and designs, for contract documents and site supervision etc, which can only be agreed once the items in Parts I, II, and III are settled.

Provision of accommodation for volunteers was discussed several times during 1966, with the society anxious to restore and adapt Penrhyn Station for the purpose. With an estimated cost of £3,200, the company directors' initial reaction was to think that the money could be spent with more benefit to the company's and society's objectives, such as (possibly) the locomotive and carriage programme. Hostel accommodation could be provided more cheaply, they thought, by using sectional buildings or a scrap standard-gauge sleeping car and dining car located in Minffordd Yard. After a meeting with the society directors, the Penrhyn proposal was accepted; planning permission for a trial seven-year period was obtained in 1968 and the premises opened for use in 1971. Mary Roberts, one of the nearby residents who had been vociferous in her objection to the concept, discovered that the volunteers were quite normal people and became the warden for several years. The company gave her a travel pass when she retired in 1988.

The CEGB had continued to be uncooperative over the matter of the company's compensation claim. In March 1962, the directors had decided that there was no point in taking the Lands Tribunal appeal decision to the House of Lords and in February 1963 had agreed to proceed with a fresh application for compensation including an element for loss of profits. The company's solicitors submitted a formal claim, shown in the table, on 24 December 1963. Apparently, sporadic discussions took place between the parties, on 25 April 1966 the CEGB informing the Lands Tribunal that negotiations had taken place 'with a view to narrowing the field of dispute. Agreement has been reached on several points, but on 21 September 1967, nearly a year after the company had sent a reminder, the CEGB declared that it disputed all of Part II of the claim.

Some brief respite had been had from the CEGB's negativity in 1966, when it had accepted the claims for the land taken and severance, paying, after some badgering, £3,406 19s 7d, which included interest at 6 per cent, £1,555 14s 2d, less £641 14s 7d income tax, on 13 October.

Nevertheless, the company was not deterred from its ultimate goal, and work to bring the railway between Tan y Bwlch and Dduallt into service had

Services were extended to Dduallt, two miles from Tan y Bwlch, on 6 April 1968; the official opening, by Sir Leonard Cooke, London Midland Region board member of British Rail, was on 19 June. Sadly, no passengers saw it like this, for the formation was widened to the right of the conifers to make space for a run-round loop. 25 April 1964. The conifers have since succumbed to disease and the weather. (M. Costello/Irish Railway Record Society)

Learning from previous experience, the track between Tan y Bwlch and Dduallt was completely relayed, some of the work being carried out by troops on exercise. This steam working must have been in preparation for the opening. The bridge carrying the deviation crosses the line at the spot where the old footbridge crossed. (John Neville)

Another glimpse of the track before it was renewed, at Garnedd Tunnel on 25 April 1964. Rope tails once hung from the gantry to remind gravity train brakesmen to keep their heads down going through the tunnel. The telegraph follows the original formation to the left of the tunnel.
(M. Costello/Irish Railway Record Society)

started over the Easter weekend in March 1967, with a gang of more than eighty volunteers deturfing and ditching. The formation for a loop at Dduallt was created by excavating the hillside to preserve the trees planted to beautify the place in the 1920s, the stone removed being used to start the embankment beyond the station. Employees and volunteers completed the track laying, excepting Garnedd tunnel and Dduallt Station, by 24 October 1967 and spent the following 10 weeks ballasting it with 600 tons of new stone bought from Minffordd Quarry. Notice was given to the Ministry of Transport that the company intended to extend the passenger train service to Dduallt from 6 April 1968.

The ultimate location of the railway's terminus was discussed again on 13 September 1967, when the directors decided to inform the Ffestiniog UDC that terminating the railway at the GWR station site would be acceptable, providing the council and other bodies concerned would bear the additional cost of going beyond the LNWR site. The council was in the process of acquiring the GWR site.

The Light Railway Order public inquiry was held in Blaenau Ffestiniog on 26 and 27 January 1967. Objections had been received from the CEGB, and the Country Landowners' Association, representing

Rhys and Aneurin Davies, who also objected individually and jointly. The CEGB's objection was to ensure the inclusion of a protective clause that restrained the railway from being constructed lower than the highest permissible water level of the reservoir, forbad the construction of a station on its property, controlled the use of explosives, retained access to pylons and for agricultural purposes, provided for the dispersal of spoil, and the location of power lines above and below the railway. The terms were accepted by the company and the objection withdrawn.

The Davies brothers, who farmed adjoining properties, were concerned about the effect on agriculture, severance, fire risk, access to Rhoslyn, the lake, for cattle and severance of the water supply to Rhoslyn cottage. They did not give evidence. An after-lunch discussion between solicitors on the second day produced what was described as a tentative agreement on a clause protecting the Davies' interests and the inquiry was adjourned in order that it could be refined and submitted for inclusion in the order.

In addition to payment of £750 plus £85 costs for his land, Aneurin Davies was to have the land occupied by the section of railway to be abandoned

Earl of Merioneth approaching Dduallt. The full load, fresh ballast and the strategic positioning of the photographer suggests that the photograph was taken on 6 April 1968, the first day services were extended beyond Tan y Bwlch.

(John Neville)

With the extension of services to Dduallt, work was started to improve facilities at Tan y Bwlch. When *Earl of Merioneth* arrived with an AGM special on 27 April 1968, work had already started on restoring the goods shed and converting it to a café. The token has been collected by John Harrison, who had moved into the station house with his wife, Nell, after Will and Bessie Jones retired.

(M. Costello/Irish Railway Record Society)

conveyed to him free of charge, but he dragged his feet when it came to committing himself to an agreement to this effect. In contrast, Rhys Davies, who was paid £400 plus £45 for his land, was more co-operative, leading to him being paid a further 15 guineas in expenses and being given the right to remove timber from the land concerned.

The Ffestiniog Railway (Light Railway) (Amendment) Order 1968 was made on 9 February and effective from 21 February. This was a momentous achievement, a declaration that the Minister of Transport thought that the deviation was in the public interest. It was also significant in that its termination at Brookes' Quarry clearly would not be a permanent terminus, yet the company had no idea of how it would progress from that point. In modern times, such an order would not have been made.

In addition to powers to construct and operate railway No. 3, the order also incorporated, amended and excluded parts of the 1923 order, particularly to ensure that the Regulation of Railways Act 1889 was applicable to all parts of the railway. Article 8 was for the protection of the CEGB and article 9 for the protection of 'certain landowners', i.e. the Davies brothers. Fifteen years were allowed for construction and no part was to be used for the public conveyance of passengers without the permission in writing of the Minister of Transport.

A foot and mouth disease outbreak caused work on Dduallt loop, and the deviation, to be suspended for two and a half months. The chief inspector of railways, Colonel J. R. H. Robertson, inspected the extension on 31 March and it was opened as planned on 6 April 1968, albeit with the loop incomplete and a second locomotive, usually *Prince*, being used to shunt the carriages in order that the train engine

The tracks at Tan y Bwlch realigned to make space for an island platform, an excavator being hired for two days to speed the work, completed in time to be used for the first time on 25 May 1968.

(John Neville)

could change ends. The loop was brought into use on 20 April.

During 1968, the layout and facilities at Tan y Bwlch Station were examined by a sub-committee of directors. Work was started on the adaptation of the goods shed to create a catering facility, shop and booking office on the proviso that it would not be paid for until June.

Whilst the company was in control of developments at Dduallt it was not in control of those at Portmadoc, where a developer had taken control of the former Hafod y Llan wharf, built an access road to it across the car park in front of the station, and pre-empted the company's car-parking rights on the wharf. It transpired that Tremadoc Estate had sold the land without referring to the company's interest in it and that the planning application for the development had not disclosed the Company's interest in it either, although, unfortunately for the company, that did not invalidate the application. The developer, who

owned a campsite in Portmadoc, was not always easy to deal with and it is not clear, from the written record, whether he intended to do everything that he said he wanted to do, including the construction of a dance hall over the station tracks, or whether he was just trying to upset Allan Garraway.

Running to Dduallt resulted in a significant boost in passenger numbers, nearly 20,000 more than in 1967, generating a profit of £25,382, enough to cancel the current deficit and for the balance carried forward to be a positive sum for the first time since 1924. It had quickly become apparent that on the busiest days the railway would not be able to cope with the traffic offering. On Mondays to Thursdays

The company leased land on the Hafod y Llan Wharf for car parking, making a crossing across the tracks near the water tower to give access; the sign was photographed on 19 August 1958. The arrangement was to cause problems ten years later, when a developer obtained the rights to the wharf and wished to continue using the company's access for all traffic.

Paintwork complete, *Blanche* arrives in the down platform at Minffordd with a train of modern stock. Most of the trees on the left have succumbed to disease and strong winds since the photograph was taken. (John Neville)

in August, therefore, a revised timetable was put into effect, with trains crossing at Penrhyn to permit operation at forty-five-minute intervals during the afternoon. On one day, when the 10.00 and 10.40 trains had left without any empty seats, a more intense service was run.

Capacity was slightly increased by the entry into service in July of a new carriage, 'super buffet'

Work on adapting Penrhyn Station as a society hostel started in 1969. Here, the foundations have been dug for an ablutions block that connected the building to the former Co-Op.

No. 103, with seventeen seats, a serving counter and kitchen. An opening window in the kitchen permitted off-train sales whilst stationary at Dduallt. By this time, the company's ice cream supplier had found what were claimed to be the only three 12v DC fridges in the country and on-train ice cream sales joined the draught beer as features unique to the FR amongst narrow-gauge railways in the UK for many years.

No. 103 was the last vehicle turned out in the varnished livery. On 6 August 1968, the directors inspected No. 16, painted in unlined cherry red livery, and approved of it. The new colour was thought to be harder wearing, easy to apply and a good match when coupled to vehicles in teak livery. The society's internal newsletter for regular volunteers reported that the livery was for 'old' stock, and five nineteenth-century bogie carriages and six four-wheelers were repainted in 1969. The four 'new' bogie carriages were then repainted in 1970, however, and other vehicles followed when they received works' attention.

In September 1968, the accountant had reported that the cash balance was £23,500, sufficient to take the company through to May 1969 without an overdraft. In reward for their efforts, Allan Garraway was given a bonus of £200 and the other employees shared a pool of £1,000. The commercial

After being serviced at Boston Lodge and fitted with an enclosed cab, the 'new' *Mountaineer* was launched on AGM day, 26 April 1969. There were still doubts about its capabilities so *Blanche* was coupled inside. To improve draughting it had been fitted with *Linda's* chimney. The original *Mountaineer's* bell was mounted on top of the smokebox. The installation of brass window frames awaits funding.
(M. Costello/Irish Railway Record Society)

manager, Maurice Bolton, was paid 2 per cent commission instead of the 1 per cent agreed when he was employed in 1966; he left the company in May 1970.

Suggesting that a passing loop should be built between Penrhyn and Tan y Bwlch, Garraway thought Budr would be a suitable location, telling the directors that it would enable trains to run at thirty-minute intervals and equate to having five extra carriages in service. He was instructed to produce estimates.

A new locomotive, First World War Alco 2-6-2PT No. 3-23, entered regular service in the spring of 1969. Built in 1916, it had seen service in Belgium with the 13th (Canadian) Light Railway Operating company as War Department No. 1265. Society director John Ransom had bought it from the Tramway de Pithiviers à Toury in 1966, because he thought it might be useful for a tourist railway, he told the author, and a year later offered it to the company in exchange for £500 5 per cent preference shares. The shares being allocated on 13 September 1967, it arrived at Portmadoc on 16 October and was

steamed two days later, but repairs and modifications to adapt it to the FR kept it out of service for most of 1968. Bill Broadbent's suggestion that it be named *Mountaineer*, in recognition of the England 0-4-0TT withdrawn ninety years before, had been accepted by the directors on 3 November 1968. The naming took place on AGM day, 26 April 1969.

The budget for a five-year £29,500 locomotive overhaul programme had been discussed in February 1968, a significant item being a new boiler for *Merddin Emrys*. On 20 June, Allan Garraway submitted tenders from Andrew Barclay in Kilmarnock and Hunslet in Leeds for two Fairlie boilers. Barclay's price was £4,235 each, to be paid in full on delivery, whilst Hunslet wanted £5,200, payable 10 per cent on completion and 10 per cent every four months for three years, which suggests that Hunslet had a better idea of the company's financial position. The directors decided to order from Barclay if payment in three four-monthly instalments could be negotiated. With a price of £4,250 each, payable in two instalments, the order went to Leeds. Having parallel barrels and small

A train of carriages freshly painted in cherry-red livery at Portmadoc on 25 April 1969. (M. Costello/Irish Railway Record Society)

superheaters, the boilers were delivered to Minffordd on 8 October 1969.

The increase in traffic and the administration that accompanied the company's expansion had increased the load on Allan Garraway. He must have been relieved when the directors accepted his recommendation to appoint Alan Heywood as traffic manager, from 24 May 1969. An experienced guard, Heywood became general manager himself in 1996.

An undercurrent of unhappiness with the railway's management is detectable in the minutes. When Garraway produced a proposed organisation chart in February 1969, the directors decided that they should confine themselves to policy and that he should function as the chief executive. Two months later, they decided that relations with the deviation leadership, known as the *junta*, should be brought under his control. Later in the year, Paul Dukes was appointed Boston Lodge works manager.

On the deviation, Michael Schumann's report proposing a route from Gelliwiog to Tanygrisiau via the west side of the lake, behind the power station,

was considered by the directors on 10 June 1969. 1,000 yards shorter than the east-side route, it would be cheaper to build and operate, and removed all difficulties associated with the dam. The directors observed that whilst it was an improvement on the present intention to cross the valley on or near the dam, they recalled that an earlier west-side scheme had been unilaterally rejected, without an explanation being offered, by the CEGB in 1958. Whilst they regretted that Schumann's proposal could not be taken further, they still hoped to receive an explanation from the CEGB.

In this regard, they applied pressure on the CEGB. Les Smith made contact by telephone, John Routly by letter, resulting in both being told that a west-side route was not possible. Alan Pegler, as chairman, then wrote to the CEGB's chairman to ask for better co-operation regarding the route and received a reply that encouraged the directors to write again to clarify the position. This approach paid off, for by 11 November 1969 the CEGB had agreed to discuss the west-side route.

A meeting with the power station superintendent, H.W. Golding, and his deputy was held there on 5 December 1969. After a discussion they intimated that, subject to certain safeguards and approval of detailed drawings, the route could be permitted.

The safeguards were that the railway was to be 'generally some 20ft to the west of the position shown on the map'; the installation of continental-style barriers on the Stwlan Dam road level crossing; between Buarth Melyn and the summit north of the power station, the railway was to be at least 60ft horizontally from any pylon conductors; a bridge with provision for access was required over the high pressure pipes with guard rails on this section to minimise the risk of derailments; 'this work', in the vicinity of the power station, was to be carried out by contractors, 'not by voluntary labour'. There were to be no stations on CEGB property, but there was no objection to a passing loop south of Tanygrisiau Station or to the proposed route from Buarth Melyn southwards and, subject to approval by the CEGB's landscape consultant and the planning authority,

there appeared to be no objection so far as landscaping was concerned.

Michael Schumann recalls that the first proposal for a west-side route had been put to the CEGB's chairman by Alan Pegler and Les Smith. Whilst he agreed to give consideration to the west-side route, he immediately rejected the idea of passing the rear of the power station in the switchyard roadway, tramway style, which explains the requirement to move the alignment 20ft further west, higher up the hill. Level crossing requirements were, of course, the purview of the Ministry of Transport.

On the ground, land owner Aneurin Davies had refused to complete the verbal agreement made concerning his land at the Light Railway Order Public Enquiry in 1967, forcing the company to use its compulsory purchase powers. He might have regretted his reluctance as in 1969 the Lands Tribunal had valued the 1½ acres concerned at £675, a reduction on the £750 plus expenses offered by the company.

A brief hiatus occurred in the new relationship when the company submitted its planning application for the new route on 14 February 1970. On 5 March, the CEGB's executive officer at Llandudno Junction asked Merioneth County

Looking ahead to changes in Minffordd Yard, in 1970 the roof of the slate shed was raised to enable it to be used to store carriages. The standard gauge sidings remained in place until 1973.

Council to defer consideration of the application because it had not been supplied with the detailed plans promised at the 5 December meeting. This was because the required surveys had not been completed; the plans were submitted on 3 February 1971.

Planning for another Light Railway order application had been started when the directors met in March 1970 and the siting of Tanygrisiau Station was being discussed with the CEGB, on whose land it was located, and the council. The MP for Merioneth had already expressed his support and it was agreed to make an announcement in the society magazine.

One of the unexpected difficulties that accompanied the company's growth arose because it outgrew the facilities available at the manager's discretion at the Portmadoc branch of the National Provincial Bank, the company's banker since at least 1869. John Routly investigated and reported that it would be worthwhile transferring the account to a branch in the City of London, the £15,000 overdraft immediately available, if required, being nearly double that available locally.

With track laying, albeit of a temporary nature, having commenced on the deviation, the project's first paid employee started work on 16 May 1970. David 'Bunny' Lewis, a former member of the Special Boat Service, was already well known to the deviationists, having been one of them for several years. On 27 June, his duties were defined in a statement of intent agreed with the company and the deviation *junta*. In addition to co-ordinating volunteers and organising their work, he was also to keep the general manager informed, and to encourage the development and happiness of the volunteer effort on the operational railway.

A claim for £70,537 plus interest loss-of-profits compensation from the CEGB had been lodged with the Lands Tribunal on 19 November 1969. On 8 September 1970, the directors noted that the CEGB had twice asked for a two-month extension to the time allowed to proceed to the next stage. 'This request had been granted despite the fact that the land was taken 14 years 4 months ago.' Lands Tribunal records reveal that four extensions had been requested and granted.

The hint of frustration over the time taken by the CEGB to deal with the company's claim probably represents the view of secretary Francis Wayne as much as it did that of the directors. On 26 October 1970, he circulated them with his thoughts on the company's financial situation and its budgeting. The year's traffic revenue and passenger journeys had both increased by 10 per cent over budget, great achievements he thought. He also commended the two-speed approach of 'possible' and 'desirable' expenditure shown in the budget for 1971, Allan Garraway's initiative, he thought.

However, he noted that although income was £4,100 better than budget, expenditure had exceeded it by £4,685, so the gain had already been spent. In the past, the company budgeted for the same income as the previous year, leaving improved earnings and society donations as a safety margin. However, the 1971 budget included [forecast] improved earnings and society donations; if the actual receipts were the same as in 1970, there would be a shortfall of £1,200 on the 'possible' expenditure. In other words, he explained, so long as revenue increased by 10 per cent every year things would be alright, but if receipts ever fell the company would be in difficulties.

An increasing proportion of the budget is fixed, he continued, adding that in 1971 the wages bill would be almost half of income. He had pointed out before that fixed expenditure should be limited to two-thirds of the total, because in the event of some unforeseeable set-back, the company did not have the resources to stand a loss and would have to make cuts.

Each year revenue and expenditure had been budgeted to increase by about one-seventh. An increase in expenditure from £70,000 to £80,000, however, meant that £40,000 was needed to see the company through the winter, but in recent years the autumn bank balance had not increased in proportion to meet this commitment. The balance would be influenced by end-of-season stock levels and the company should keep watch on them. He questioned whether a £15,000 overdraft would be sufficient.

His impatience was explained, Wayne said, because there was one obvious solution, without saying what it was, but continuing, 'It is quite wrong that we should incur considerable expenses over many years and then be expected to have yet further delays,' and concluding by observing that the 1971 budget was based on receipts of £80,000 compared

With Evan Davies at the regulator, *Earl of Merioneth* passes Pen Cob with wagon No. 63 carrying station benches, summer 1970. (John Hunt)

with actual receipts of £50,000 in 1968 and £61,000 in 1969; a considerable increase in motive power and passenger capacity would be necessary before services were extended to Blaenau Ffestiniog.

When the directors met on 10 November 1970, they discussed, in Wayne's presence, the future appointment of the company secretary and accountant. Immediately afterwards they illustrated his concerns by agreeing to increase budgeted expenditure to £91,400 out of £96,600 estimated revenue. With net deposits of £7,500, an overdraft was likely from January. Wayne's resignation was accepted on 13 January 1971, the distance he had to travel from his home in the north of Scotland to meetings being given as the reason. Martin Barradell, the accountant, had submitted his resignation, without explanation, on 7 November, but his letter had not arrived before the November

meeting. R.D.I. Scott, society secretary since 1966 and an accountant, was appointed secretary.

An 'inconsistency in signalling' at Pen Cob had allowed a passenger train to be diverted into the 'long shed' at Boston Lodge on 2 July 1970, the train engine, *Mountaineer*, colliding with *Earl of Merioneth* stabled in the shed. Allan Garraway reported the incident, saying that the driver had misread the signal, but it was not interlocked with the ground frame and a driver could be misled as to the way the points were set. He was also a little economical with the truth, merely saying that the train had gone into the yard, not that it had gone into the shed.

The timing of the incident was rather unfortunate as Garraway was engaged in correspondence with the Ministry of Transport's inspector, Major P.M. Olver, on the subject of signalling at stations. To control the passage of trains on the single line, the electric train staff (ETS) system of train control had been introduced in 1961 (Portmadoc-Minffordd, intermediate instrument at Boston Lodge) and extended to Tan y Bwlch (1965) and Dduallt (1968), with signalling at stations by means of flags. Remote operators designed and built in-house had been installed to permit the release of tokens when the remote station was unmanned, which was likely to be the case for most of the year. By 1970, the increasing traffic being handled made the installation of signals at stations a priority.

As an intermediate measure, colour-light signals were installed at Tan y Bwlch, becoming operational on 16 May 1970. There had been some concern, apparently, that the installation would seem out of place, but on 22 May, Garraway told Olver that they had not generated any complaints. Olver was not happy to be told, however, that the signals were being used in a 'slightly unorthodox' manner, as route indicators, green to indicate that the points were set for the main route, the yellow aspect to indicate that they were set for the loop, not the interpretation found on the national network.

He informed Garraway that whilst this was acceptable for the temporary installation, the permanent installation would have to be in line with British signalling practice. A revised scheme submitted in July was acceptable when the station was manned, but not when it was unmanned. He proposed an alternative that required trains to be stopped at the inner home signal and for a member of the train crew to walk to the signal box, open it up and signal the train in, which would cause several minutes' delay.

On 30 November, Olver gave provisional approval to a scheme that involved interlocking the advanced starting signal with the token and using directional treadles to put the outer home to danger when the station was unmanned. It was, he said, a tremendous advance on anything previously proposed and should be adopted at the other main crossing stations.

Realising that other railways would have the same problems in understanding and complying with the inspectors' requirements, Garraway approached the Association of Railway Preservation Societies, of which the society was a member, with a view to forming a sub-committee of operating railways. Whilst the idea gained support, he also discovered that the Association of Minor Railways, one of the organisations established to lobby against the 1920 Railways Act, was extant if moribund. At a meeting of interested railways, the association was revived and Garraway was elected chairman; the AMR later amalgamated with the ARPS, the combined organisation becoming the Heritage Railway Association.

Earlier in 1970, Garraway, encouraged by the Wales Tourist Board, had called the meeting that led to the formation of the joint marketing panel known by its slogan, 'the great little trains of Wales', to give the railways concerned a better marketing presence.

Despite the extensions of time granted to the CEGB to respond to the company's claim for compensation, on 10 November 1970 it formally replied that 'there were no profits from the intact undertaking for many years prior to the date of entry, therefore the valuation in respect of a claim for disturbance is NIL'; therefore, it would ask for costs, too.

The year 1970 ended with an innovation that has become well established in the railway's calendar, the operation of Santa trains in December. One of the chapels in Penrhyn asked the company to run a Christmas train on 19 December, the Saturday before Christmas. A fare was agreed and the chapel started selling tickets to its members, leading to a request being made for another train for the church. The venture was so successful that three trains were run, one on 19 December and two on 20 December. Headboards were carried by the engines, one of which was *Linda*, burning oil for the first time on public trains. 300 children received presents from Father Christmas at Tan y Bwlch, and entertainment and refreshments were provided there. The highlight of the weekend for Alan Heywood, one of the guards, occurred on the Sunday, when the two trains crossed at Tan y Bwlch and the passengers spontaneously started singing carols. It was a magical atmosphere, he recalls, but unrepeatable. The Oakeley Silver Band was employed to lead the singing in 1971 but it was not the same, he said. Carol singing at Tan y Bwlch remains a feature of the Company's Santa train operation.

CHAPTER 8

1971-1977: PURSUING THE DREAM

Francis Wayne's pessimism about the adequacy of the overdraft proved to be well-founded. It had been increased to £20,000 by the time the directors met on 13 January 1971. On that occasion, Allan Garraway obtained approval to issue cheques up to £50; he and the secretary continued to sign cheques for more than that amount. He also received approval to pay wages by cheque providing a pro-forma authorisation system that could be audited was put in place.

Garraway distributed a report, *'Expansion Through The Seventies'*, to the directors, apparently on his own initiative. They agreed that it was an excellent move on his part, but did not have much to say about it. Based on an expectation of 10 per cent growth per annum, then three or four more locomotives and twenty-three new carriages were required, along with the loop at Budr and an expansion of Boston Lodge, by 1980. In April, they decided to discuss the company's requirements with the Wales Tourist Board to see if any funding would be available.

Since the railway had been re-opened, land along its boundaries between Rhiw Goch and Garnedd had changed hands, the new owners planting conifers. Despite being warned that the railway operated coal-burning steam locomotives they persisted in planting up to the boundaries, and then complained when there were fires. The issue had first been raised with the directors in February 1969, when Garraway had reported discussions that he had had with the manufacturers of oil-firing equipment, Laidlaw Drew, and been given approval to spend £350 on a trial. He had said that its cost would be recovered by reducing the cost of fire watching and claims.

Now, he told the directors that conversion of locomotives to oil firing was a viable proposition and should be carried out as soon as possible; the advantages to be gained from the avoidance of forest fires were immense. In 1970, fires had cost £1,000. The cost of equipping six locomotives would be £4,000; in addition to the saving of £1,000 he forecast considerable savings in fuel handling; the conversion was not irreversible and the locomotives could be converted back to burn coal 'in one day' if required.

The Economic Forestry Group, owner of some of the affected property, had offered to lend £1,000 to convert two locomotives. Bill Broadbent's observation that the expected economies might not arise owing to the increased cost of oil was disregarded and work on the conversion of *Linda*, Garraway's regular steed, had been carried out in time for the loco to be tested in December 1970. The results were sufficiently encouraging that in April 1971 the directors decided that the conversion of the locomotives in regular use should be completed in 1972.

In May 1971, Garraway explained to the directors that he wished to investigate the use of aluminium-bodied carriages built by contractors. After agreeing that new carriages could not be built at Boston Lodge because its resources were devoted to maintenance, the directors authorised him to make further inquiries provided no commitment was made until the 1972 budget had been reviewed in September. The quotation of £4,329 already obtained excluded bogies.

One of the most visible features of the deviation is the bridge crossing the existing railway at Dduallt. Designed to be erected on a remote site by volunteers using minimal equipment, it comprises four pairs of two 18in-diameter reinforced concrete pillars joined by a capping beam capable of carrying three 5m-long pre-cast concrete beams. The pillars and capping beams had been built in January 1969, and a temporary deck added to facilitate the

The first stage of constructing the Rhoslyn Bridge was completed in January 1969, a signal to passengers that the railway was serious in its intent to return to Blaenau Ffestiniog.

(M. Costello/Irish Railway Record Society)

transport of spoil. The beams were delivered to site in November 1970 and lifted into place in January 1971. Using ready-mixed concrete delivered by rail from Tan y Bwlch, the deck was poured on 20 March 1971, an operation timed to be completed before the 14.30 train arrived from Portmadoc at 15.20.

Further along, the spiral was close to completion, with activity reaching close to the point where the east-side and west-side routes diverged. Garraway asked for the deviationists to be given a 'firm instruction' not to move on to CEGB property prematurely, so clearly communication between Portmadoc and the far side of Dduallt was not as good as it could have been.

Les Smith and Michael Schumann attended a meeting to discuss the west-side plans at the CEGB headquarters in London on 17 June 1971. The proposed route had been pegged out on the ground and the power station superintendent, H.W. Golding, said that in his opinion it was satisfactory. Studying the plans, several more requirements were called for. As the meeting ended it was noted that the route would not adversely affect the CEGB's interest and improved the position when compared with the east-side route, that the CEGB would grant an easement for at a nominal rent and its officers would recommend the scheme's approval, allowing the planning application to be resolved. Schumann still remembers

Golding saying, 'I realise now that you will do exactly what you want to do and there is nothing that I can do to stop you.' At long last the company's ambitions were being taken seriously.

Temporary track had been laid as far as Barn Cutting and on 1 July a test train hauled by *Linda* ran onto it, the loco reaching the bridge. In the train was carriage No. 37, a semi-open vehicle newly constructed at Boston Lodge on a Hudson bogie-wagon underframe; on this occasion its doors had still not been fitted. This was a cheap solution to the capacity problem and created a slightly modernised version of the Hudson carriages obtained in 1923; No. 38 followed immediately afterwards and No. 39, although ordered, was not built. In 1992, however, a local engineering company built a replica of the 1923 vehicles on a Hudson wagon underframe. Given the number 39 it was funded by donations, some of them in memory of Trevor Bailey, and was launched at the company AGM on 16 September 1992.

In 1969, *Linda's* boiler had been sent to Hunslet to be fitted with a new firebox and a superheater. Whilst the boiler was away, a pony truck was fabricated, using a wheelset from the bogie of *Moel Tryfan* that had been retained when the remainder of the locomotive had been scrapped, and fitted. In May 1971, Garraway reported that with these modifications it was giving excellent performance

and recommended that *Blanche* should also be fitted with a superheater during the winter of 1971-2, when the loco would be dismantled. The directors authorised him to order one at a price estimated to be less than £2,000.

Higher smokebox temperatures generated following the conversion of *Linda* and *Mountaineer* to oil firing damaged the paint, resulting in their smokeboxes being painted silver until a suitable heat-resistant black paint could be obtained, a somewhat controversial development in the eyes of some enthusiasts. It was in this form that *Mountaineer* was running on 11 August 1971, when fireman Douglas Dick was injured by hitting his head on a gate pillar at Boston Lodge whilst checking the injector overflow. Whilst he had obviously chosen the wrong place to apply the injector, the locomotive's greater bulk compared with the other locomotives, with clearance of only 6in, was also a contributory factor.

When he reported the incident to the ministry, Allan Garraway was asked about the clearance. The

Increased fire risk along the railway, following new woodland planting close to its boundaries, resulted in the adoption of oil-firing for the locomotives instead of coal. Equipment was first fitted to *Linda* during 1970. The appearance of *Linda* and *Mountaineer* with silver smokeboxes caused controversy amongst purists until a high-temperature-resisting black paint could be sourced. At the same time as the oil-firing conversion, the loco was altered from 0-4-0STT configuration to 2-4-0STT to improve its stability at FR speeds.

In the background, the appearance of a window in the end of the station building is evidence of offices being created in the roof space.

officer dealing with it reported to Colonel Robertson, asking for, this thoughts, saying that moving the pillar and gateway would be 'a big operation for these people'; some kind of notice might suffice. Robertson replied 'The FR always claims to be a "proper railway", it should obtain and fit British Rail-type limited-clearance plates to the post'.

Garraway replied to say that after another incident involving a driver on 31 October 1971, a survey had

As shown, *Mountaineer's* spark arrester was removed as soon as the oil-burning installation was deemed to be satisfactory. It is clear that the high temperatures were close to the limit tolerated by the silver paint.

Mountaineer's oil tank replaced the coal bunker at the back of the cab. It is seen leaving Tan y Bwlch under the footbridge erected in 1971.

Linda at Dduallt, with the top of its oil tank visible in the tender. The chimney colour has reverted to black although it looks in need of renewal.

With silver paint still in situ, *Linda* arrives at Tan y Bwlch with Allan Garraway at the regulator, a crowd of expectant passengers hoping to find seats. Covering the platform with slate dust, whilst cheap, was not an ideal solution as it was carried into the carriages, damaging the carpets in the first-class compartments.

been conducted, identifying three gateposts at Boston Lodge which had now all been removed. With *Mountaineer*'s cab being so big, a hole with a grating had been put in the cab floor so that firemen could watch the injector overflow without leaning out. Concerning the injured fireman, he said he was, 'an experienced person just being thoughtless, which no amount of notices will combat.'

The temporary colour-light signalling installation at Minffordd had been commissioned on 27-28 February

1971. It remained in use for much longer than most people would consider to be temporary.

Another venture onto the deviation with a train had been made on 20 July 1971, for the president of the Lands Tribunal. The hearing had been scheduled for 5 July, but the CEGB had again sought a postponement saying that it needed more time to consider the FR's 'unexpectedly high claim'. The hearing started on 4 October and lasted for six days. Maybe the directors realised that the railway's luck was

Merddin Emrys as converted to oil burning in 1973.

At Minffordd, the standard-gauge tracks were removed from the yard in 1973. A boundary fence was erected later.

Two mates chatting, a timeless scene at Minffordd in 1973. Ron Lester (left), then responsible for the permanent way beyond Dduallt, and Paul Dukes, then the works manager. They lived at opposite ends of the station building.

about to change, for on 20 September 1971, the CEGB had formally accepted Michael Schumann's west-side route subject to conditions relating to detail - and negotiations over the terms for access had already been started.

During the hearing, counsel for the CEGB claimed that the reason for objecting to the original west-side route was that it was too close to the switch compound, that it was only using the spiral to place the railway higher up the hill that made it acceptable, whereas local officials had told railway personnel that any crossing of the pipelines was an unacceptable engineering complication. It is likely that the CEGB was eventually influenced by the realisation that the west-side route was the lesser of two evils and, once construction was finished, it would be much less inconvenient than having trains running over the top of the dam at regular intervals.

At the start of the hearing the CEGB's position was that no compensation should be awarded, although towards the end a willingness to pay £25,000 was mentioned. The decision was announced on 19 November 1971, fifteen years since the land was taken, thirteen years since the claim was launched, nine years since the last hearing. Assuming that without the CEGB's intervention, services would have been restored to Blaenau Ffestiniog in 1962, and that they would in fact be restored in 1977, £59,693 was awarded for loss of profits after tax and £5,228 for preliminary expenses in establishing the alternative route, rounded to £65,000 plus interest, £41,710, and costs, £3,209.

The subject of costs was the topic of a legal debate after the award had been announced, the CEGB's QC attempting to have the issue deferred to await the outcome of an appeal on the costs of a rating case, and then suggesting that only a proportion should be allowed to compensate the CEGB for abortive work carried out on earlier stages of the company's claim. The chairman accepted the FR's

response, that the only basis for not awarding costs in full was if the company could have got the £65,000 by some means that avoided the expense of the tribunal, but it had no choice. It would be, the FR's barrister said, 'a most novel, and outrageous proposition if we were to have our costs cut down' The company was awarded its costs 'on the High Court scale', £15,688.96 against a claim for £17,793.47.

Reporting the award on 20 November, the *Guardian* quoted John Routly as saying that the company expected to spend £245,000 on reinstating the railway, and that the deficiency would have to be met by voluntary effort and funds from sources other than those from which, morally if not legally, they should be derived. The paper also cited the trial of Warren Hastings (nine years) and the Tichborne case (thirteen years) as other long-running legal cases.

On 25 November, the Lands Tribunal sent the CEGB a copy of the decision with a request for payment of the £250 hearing fee. It took the CEGB some six months to remit the award, asking the company to prove its title to the land before it would pay. Whilst the organisation's doubts about the motives for taking over the company and the likelihood of the railway's revival being successful can be understood, its treatment of the company as the years passed was quite appalling. The time it took to bring the claim to a conclusion may be a record in the British judiciary, but not one of which

Construction of the pumped storage power station at Tanygrisiau was approaching completion when this photograph was taken in June 1962. The high-pressure pipelines, visible here, were subsequently covered up and then partially re-exposed when the railway formation was built across them.

(R. G. Roscoe)

the CEGB should have been proud. Its legal expenses over the years must have been quite substantial.

Writing about the 'misleading nonsense' of railway company accounts in *The Accountant* published on 3 February 1972, Francis Wayne said, 'It is an unfortunate fact that the great public bodies are incapable of treating claimants as reasonably as their individual officers would wish. This in turn greatly adds to the difficulty of their obtaining public support for their new schemes. The sixteen year delay [from taking possession] in obtaining compensation in the Ffestiniog case will hardly improve their reputation in this respect.'

For its part, the company in the 1950s was quite naïve, despite the qualifications of the various directors. In verbatim reports of the various hearings, which may not give a true impression, Alan Pegler, in particular, comes across with an air of flippancy. When it came to the appeal against the Rule 5 decision, John Routly, Francis Wayne and the company's advisers must have known that they were wasting their time, and the company's money, in claiming that 'may' should be interpreted as 'must'; this element of the case, incidentally, was cited as an example in the Law Commission's 2003 review of the compensation component of

compulsory purchase. Years later, Routly was to claim that the delay had been in the company's interest and implied that it had been partially engineered, but that is not an opinion supported by the records available to the author.

Wayne was obviously very frustrated by the constant delays in settling the claim by the time he retired. He is believed to have been involved in the publication of the Society of Individual Freedom's advertisement that complained about the treatment accorded to the company by the CEGB published in the *Daily Telegraph* in 1972. Wishing to work in harmony with the CEGB, the directors were quick to disassociate themselves from it.

In his article in *The Accountant*, Wayne said of the award, 'The result can satisfy nobody, since the acquiring authority must now pay roughly double the cost of incorporating alternative track in their scheme; while the railway company, having spent nearly 16 years in obtaining agreement to a reasonable new route, receives about half the cost of building its own new deviation.'

Nevertheless, it had not taken long for the deviationists to take advantage of the rapprochement. On 16 October 1971, the power station superintendent, H.W. Golding, participated in a first sod ceremony on CEGB property, breaking out the first stone from the old dam. When it had formally agreed to the route, the CEGB proposed making a contract to cover the works, including submission of drawings, specifications and programme of works to the CEGB, access to the company's works for construction traffic, indemnification of the CEGB against losses, damage and consequential losses, use of explosives, headwalls of culverts and fencing.

When the railway was completed, its operation would at all times be subservient 'in all respects' to the CEGB's operations. The company must indemnify the CEGB against losses of up to £7,000 a day if it caused any damage that closed the power station and undertake to review that figure annually. As the company had said that the maximum frequency of trains would be two trains per hour, a maximum of 26 journeys per day would be included in the contract.

Although the suggestion that a halt might be provided near the visitors' reception centre had been rejected for fear of overloading the power station with train loads of passengers, there was no reason why the idea might not be further considered if satisfactory financial arrangements could be made.

The reduction in passenger numbers that started in the 1980s means that the company has never been at risk of breaching the limit on the number of trains operated. Security issues eventually brought an end to power station tours, and the visitor reception centre's closure and partial demolition, leaving a privately-operated café for visitors to the area.

Buoyed with confidence by the award, the directors investigated sources of grant funding. The Wales Tourist Board offered 49 per cent of expenditure up to £19,400 on projects for tourist coaches, toilet facilities at Tan y Bwlch, Dduallt Station and Gysgfa [ex-Budr] loop. Construction of the tourist coaches seem to have been missed by the directors. As the coaches and the toilet facilities had been completed, the grant was applied to Dduallt Station and the loop. The Carnegie Trust and the Department of the Environment were also investigated; the latter had been making 85 per cent awards to British Rail for new rolling stock. Blaenau Ffestiniog Urban District Council had made a grant for improvements to Tan y Bwlch station house.

Some society members and volunteers had become concerned that in meeting the demand for increasing passenger numbers the FR was at risk of losing its heritage, the very thing that made it interesting and worth preserving. The autumn 1971 issue of the society magazine published a letter from a group of forty volunteers under the name 'Active

After tests at the end of 1970, *Merddin Emrys* appeared in traffic with its new boiler in 1971, albeit with a dome cover only at the uphill end. It was 1973 before the fireman's side was fully enclosed, and for the same shade of green paint to be used throughout. The 'Active Forty' wished to avoid changing the appearance of the *Earl of Merioneth* to the same extent.

Forty', expressing concern about the impending rebuild of the *Earl of Merioneth* to accommodate its new Hunslet boiler. It was, they wrote, the only FR engine in service to retain its original form and Victorian appearance. With the new boiler and oil tanks, radical changes to its appearance could not be avoided. They suggested that a new locomotive could be built using the original bogies and the new boiler, and the old superstructure could be stored until the old bogies became available for it to be displayed as a museum piece. A fund should be established to reimburse the company for the parts that it could not re-use.

Within a few weeks, more than £1,000 had been raised and the company had embarked on the construction of a new locomotive to be named *Earl of Merioneth*. The old *Earl of Merioneth*, ex-*Taliesin*, was henceforth to be known by its original name, *Livingston Thompson*. Its last day in traffic was 31 October 1971, when it ran as far as Barn site on the deviation. Plans by the 'Active Forty' to restore the superstructure for museum display failed to materialise under their direction.

In March 1972, Garraway asked about the programme for completing the restoration to Blaenau Ffestiniog. Word had got back to him that one of the directors had told one of the society's area groups that services would be resumed in 1978, probably based on the assumption contained in the loss-of-profits calculation that services would be resumed in 1977. How was it to be done and how was it to be equipped, he asked? He was asked to prepare a paper for circulation.

Having taken his locomotive, 4-6-2 No. 4472 *Flying Scotsman*, on a prolonged excursion to the USA, Alan Pegler resigned as company chairman. Accepting his resignation on 9 May 1972, the directors appointed him president of the company and elected John Routly company chairman as well as chairman of the board. Changes to the board over the previous ten years had seen C. W. Bellamy, who had retired in 1961, replaced by David, Viscount Garnock, on 8 November 1962 and Trevor Bailey, who resigned on 26 April 1966, replaced by Garard (Gerry) Fiennes, a career railwayman, on 17 January 1968.

Expenditure on several items that would support the company's expansion was agreed, £5,000 on an extension to the erecting shop in 1972 and £7,000 on a

new carriage shop in 1973. On the deviation, clearing the ground for making the new tunnel was started by letting a £2,600 contract to create the north cutting.

With this expenditure authorised, the directors were concerned to be told that the company owed £36,000, including £20,000, to the bank. Garraway was reminded of the instruction he had been given in December 1971, to ensure that the heads of departments made every effort to control expenditure during 1972. Perhaps news of the award made some think that constraint was no longer necessary.

A two-storey extension to the station building at Portmadoc was approved, without reference to cost, in July 1972. It would include an enlarged shop and a café with seating for forty on the ground floor and offices on the first-floor. Linking the existing building with the goods shed, the end wall of the latter was to be opened up to enable it to be adapted as a museum, and intended to be temporary until permanent facilities could be provided. The directors decreed that the need for exterior painting should be eliminated or reduced to avoid a recurring maintenance expense, which must account for the white uPVC cladding that adorns it. Once started it must be completed, Garraway was instructed, to avoid disruption. It was built by the company's building department, men who had been employed by a local contractor who had apparently been added to the company's workforce without formal prior directorial approval.

The notice of intention to apply for the second Light Railway Order was published in the *London Gazette* on 20 June 1972. Railway No. 4 would be 1 mile 5 furlongs 6 chains, or thereabouts, in length and start at a junction with Railway No. 3, 5,180ft from Dduallt, passing to the west of the abandoned Moelwyn Tunnel through a new Moelwyn Tunnel, to

the west of the reservoir, behind the power station, across the penstock and Stwlan Dam access roads, across the Cwmorthin, past Ty'n y Pistyll and terminate by a junction with the existing railway at the site of Tanygrisiau Station.

What appears to be another dispute with Aneurin Davies was settled in September 1972. The details were not recorded except to say that the sum of £1,200 covered all claims arising from the 1968 order.

Meeting on 17 November 1972 and discussing the 1973 budget, the directors continued to express their concern about the trend for the margin between wages and revenue to reduce over the past three years. What was wanted was fewer but better-paid staff and more volunteers. Throughout the 1970s

Constructed by the company's building department, the extension was designed by Eddie Jones, a volunteer who was an architect for one of the national banking chains. The public areas were finished in 1976, when the café was named the *Little Wonder*. The offices were finished the following year.

The station work was not the only construction carried out in Portmadoc in the 1970s. Across the road, the Britannia Foundry buildings had been demolished and an office block erected for the Inland Revenue. *Merddin Emrys* departs with a society special on 28 May 1977.

The Cwmorthin bridge at Tanygrisiau was constructed in 1976 using pre-cast beams made in Gloucester. Beyond the bridge, the formation for the new station is under construction. (Author)

there was agitation from some employees for their wages to be improved, to achieve parity with British Rail. This must have been partially triggered by a feeling that the company had more money available since the CEGB award had been made, but also by inflation, which reached 24.89 per cent in 1975. Such high levels also had an effect on the value of the company's cash reserves, of course. The directors were not prepared to consider a 25 per cent increase, to achieve parity with BR's basic rates, which would bring them into conflict with the Government's pay restraint policy. They did, however, decide to set up a company pension scheme.

John Routly's pursuit of grant aid from the Department of Trade & Industry bore fruit in January 1973. He reported that regional development schemes would contribute 20 per cent capital expenditure on buildings and equipment, and had established that the projected work at Boston Lodge would qualify. The schemes under consideration were:

	Cost	Grant
New buildings at Boston Lodge	£22,200	£4,500
Equipping workshop Glan y Mor	£7,000	£1,400
Smalley excavator	£6,000	£1,200
	£35,200	**£7,100**

Furthermore, if employment was increased by 50 per cent, six posts at Boston Lodge and four on permanent way, then 'selective assistance' grants would be available. If required, the Department was also prepared to make loans of up to 50 per cent repayable over five or eight years, interest-free for the first three years, 7 per cent thereafter.

Taking expenditure on a road crane (£2,000) and carriages (£100,000) into account meant that capital expenditure of £137,200 could be made for a cash outlay of £68,600 and a loan of £61,500. Allan Garraway was instructed to process the paperwork. The excavator was wanted for the deviation; after the engineer, Michael Schumann, launched an appeal to pay for it with Green Shield savings stamps, a plant-hire contractor provided a machine on free loan in August 1973; the stamps collected were used to buy other deviation equipment.

With local government reorganisation scheduled to take effect from 1 April 1974, the authorities of Merionethshire and Caernarfonshire merging with Anglesey to form Gwynedd County Council, the directors decided that the councillors elected to the new authority should be invited to travel on a special train on 7 July 1973. With a budget of £1,000, they wanted to obtain support for the railway and the company's plans to reinstate services to Blaenau Ffestiniog. The train ran on to the deviation and terminated at Barn site, where a temporary platform had been made of sleepers, and a buffet lunch was served. The venture was considered to be a great success.

Construction of the passing loop between Penrhyn and Tan y Bwlch was started at Rhiw Goch in 1973. Originally to be at Budr or Gysgfa, the site was changed because the company owned the land and it did not require any engineering work apart

from site clearance and track laying. The site had been used to pass trains until the introduction of steam locomotives in 1863. The Wales Tourist Board made a grant for the work.

The tourist board also agreed to make a grant contribution of £150,000, paid over three years, toward the company's £550,000 'getting through to Blaenau Ffestiniog' project. This would be funded, the directors were informed in June 1973, by £100,000 CEGB compensation, £200,000 volunteer effort, £100,000 operating profits and the WTB grant. The anticipated Department of Trade & Industry grants would act as capital reserve. No indication was recorded of how the £550,000 figure had been calculated and at the next meeting, in September, Gerald Fiennes cast some doubt on the volunteer and profits elements as they could not be budgeted.

As construction of the deviation progressed, in both physical and legal senses, the directors started to consider the work required to bring the section of the original route beyond Tanygrisiau back into operational condition. It would not be as straightforward as dealing with the railway below Tan y Bwlch. The bridge built by J. S. Hughes at Tanygrisiau in 1900-1 had been removed by the CEGB in 1957 and Merionethshire County Council had subsequently removed one of the abutments. The Barlwyd River Bridge, near Glan y Pwll, required replacing and residents had been using the railway formation as a footpath.

Les Smith thought that the council's actions at Tanygrisiau had been illegal and was authorised to obtain legal advice on the issue. After the council's obligations had been taken over by Gwynedd County Council in 1974, he found a letter undertaking to replace the bridge, which was held to be binding on the new authority and accepted by it in 1975.

In September 1973, the directors had learned that the council had approached the CEGB to see if part of the Stwlan Dam access road could be incorporated into a diversionary route to Dolrhedyn, a development that removed the pressure to maintain headroom for large vehicles on the original road; the concept had first been mentioned at a meeting held at the power station on 21 September 1964, when Alan Pegler, Les Smith, Allan Garraway, and the company's newly-appointed landscape consultant,

Clough Williams Ellis, had joined power station officers and officials from Merioneth County Council and Ffestiniog Urban District Council to discuss the company's planning application for the east-side route.

Some months after it had been submitted, Gerald Fiennes' resignation was accepted on 8 November 1973. Acting as liaison between the directors and those building the deviation, he had been well regarded. He was replaced by Air Marshall Sir Ben Ball.

Earlier in 1973, Hugh Eaves, a footplate volunteer, offered his services to the directors as an accountant. He was recruited as financial secretary and in January 1974 produced a cash flow forecast for the year. Items in the capital budget included 5,000 jarrah sleepers at £2.25 each (2 miles of track, £11,250); 100 tons of 60lb rail, £7,500; Portmadoc Station improvements, £18,300; Atcost buildings at Boston Lodge, £5,000; underpinning retaining walls at Tanygrisiau, £2,000; bridge over high-pressure pipe and rehabilitation work at Blaenau Ffestiniog, £37,000; and house at Minffordd, £7,000. The last arose from a scheme of Les Smith's, to buy houses that might be suitable for company purposes; this one was next to the crossing house at Minffordd, but it was not bought and the scheme seems to have been quietly forgotten.

Obtained from British Steel at Workington, the minute indicated that the rail had been paid for at £7,500, but Allan Garraway subsequently reported that it had cost £9,277. Another 100 tons was ordered. In February 1973, the directors had decided that new rail should be used on the deviation as it would be more convenient to handle, a lesson learned from dealing with the Penrhyn rail.

Back-dated to 1 December 1973, the employees' pension scheme cost the company 7¼ per cent of payroll expenditure with waged employees contributing 1½ per cent of income and salaried staff 2½ per cent. The company also paid ½ per cent to fund contributions from 1969.

A curious, but useful, postscript to the Lands Tribunal hearing is to be found at the National Archives. When the company's costs were assessed in December 1973, the registrar noted, 'This case should be marked for preservation as of historic interest before return to central store, but when taxation is completed papers should be reduced to essentials and remainder shredded for waste.' Whether the files were 'reduced to essentials' is not clear, they are certainly not as well ordered as they might be, but do contain much of interest that has been of use in compiling this account.

Although the trust had been registered as a charity in 1966, the trustees did not meet until 18 May 1973, shortly after an announcement in the society's magazine that it intended to play a more active part in the railway's heritage. The first secretary was the society's financial secretary, Bryan Chicken, who had suggested that the trust should be more active.

At Boston Lodge, the condition of *Mountaineer's* boiler was giving cause for concern, so in April 1974 the directors decided to order a replacement. Hunslet had already quoted £9,000, but the company would also have to pay £3,000 for the flanging block required.

An offer to buy the remains of *Palmerston* for £350 was made by a group of enthusiasts led by a former employee in 1974. On 14 May, the directors agreed if the locomotive was to be run in public in the future its first appearance should be on the FR, but on 6 June they agreed to sell it for £450 on receipt of an undertaking that it would not be run in North Wales. There was, apparently, some concern that it might be used in competition with the FR on a revived Welsh Highland Railway.

Notwithstanding the wishes of the local authorities that the railway should terminate in the centre of Blaenau Ffestiniog, in 1974 Gwynedd County Council advertised its intention to obtain the company's first preferred site, opposite to the LNWR exchange platform, in order to dispose of the spoil from the Glan-y-Don tip, being reclaimed under a £600,000 Welsh Office derelict land reclamation programme. By June 1975 the council was expected to sell the land to the company, in compliance with an informal agreement made with the now-defunct Merionethshire County Council, if the proposed central redevelopment scheme did not go ahead.

The application for the second Light Railway Order had required fresh negotiations with the landowner, Aneurin Davies. On 12 September 1974, Les Smith had reported that he would be paid

The spiral in 2006. The route to Porthmadog is at the top of the picture. When the deviation was being built volunteers swam in the lake, but it doesn't look so appetising now. (Author)

£3,500 for all of the land taken for both orders; whether this amount was inclusive of the £1,500 already paid was not specified. It did include compensation for the dumping of peat, which he claimed had poisoned the ground, an allegation the deviationists had shown was unfounded by growing potatoes in it.

Deviation engineer Michael Schumann reported on the options available for building the new tunnel on 17 December 1974 and the directors accepted Ben Ball's recommendation, to build it by direct labour, on 2 January 1975. The work had been estimated to cost £40,000, but Sir Ben thought that £50,000 was a more reasonable figure. Before the work could proceed, however, the directors required the Wales Tourist Board to confirm that grant aid would be available. Terms with a team of three miners with experience in South Africa and Cornwall were settled at £1 per hour for a sixty-hour week, each, plus £3.33 each per metre progress and £750 each terminal bonus, producing estimated costs of £9,318 if the work took thirty-four weeks or £11,535 if it took forty-two weeks, figures that did not appear to include consumables. Tunnelling started in September 1975.

The Wales Tourist Board's award of a grant of 49 per cent of the estimated £100,000 expenditure for the 'Dduallt to tunnel north' project was noted in April 1975 and probably included a contribution for the new rail. To keep construction going whilst the grant was being negotiated, John Routly arranged bank borrowing of £50,000 for the tunnel and £35,000 to cover the seasonal revenue shortfall. Discussions on the availability of grants continued throughout the year.

The retirement of Robin Scott as secretary prompted John Routly to suggest that the positions of clerk and treasurer called for by the 1832 Act of Parliament should be reinstated. Hugh Eaves had therefore been appointed treasurer on 2 January 1975 and Mark Wright, Routly's son-in-law, as clerk on 12 June.

Operation of an independent shuttle service over the deviation as far as Gelliwiog, a derelict cottage alongside the railway nearly a mile from Dduallt, had been started on 26 May 1975. Stone from the tunnel had been used to make up the ground to enable a separate platform to be constructed at Dduallt and the service was provided by *Moel Hebog*, a Hunslet mines engine that had been rebuilt for push-pull working, and the first of the steel-bodied carriages, No. 110, which was incomplete for the first few weeks the service operated. The push-pull element of the operation was restricted to allowing

The Gelliwiog shuttle soon after it had started operating in May 1975. Work continued on both the carriage, which had no windows at this stage, and the locomotive during the summer. 15,000 passengers were carried during the year, but it only ran on a few days in 1976, before the track was given over to works trains. (Author)

the guard, located in a driving compartment at the downhill-end of the carriage, to sound an alarm or apply the brakes in an emergency and to communicate with the driver by means of a bell system, control of the locomotive remaining with the driver.

The service, which ran as required, was intended to allow passengers to view the works in progress, and to generate revenue from the deviation, although it was not as popular as expected, probably because passengers could not get off the train at Gelliwiog although there was nothing to stop them

walking to the construction site to get a closer view of the works. Whilst the train was stopped at Gelliwiog, the guard gave a brief discourse to the passengers explaining the purpose of the deviation and how it was being constructed. In 1976, the shuttle was only run during the Spring bank holiday week, the transport of crushed stone from the tunnel to be used as ballast taking precedence, although the directors expressed concern about the loss of £500 per week in ticket revenue.

Major Olver had inspected the extension on 12 June 1975 and submitted his report on 12 June. He noted that installation of the facing-point lock protecting the main line at Dduallt, and its controlling ground frame, had not been completed. Accompanied by Allan Garraway, he inspected the line on foot, observing that clearances were greatly improved compared with the railway between Porthmadog and Dduallt.

The track comprised serviceable 75lb rail with staggered joints 'to assist in maintaining the correct

Demand for travel from Tan y Bwlch to Dduallt at peak time was so great that a diesel-powered shuttle service was operated in between the main trains. Carriage No. 37 was one of two semi-opens built on Hudson wagon underframes at Boston Lodge in 1971.

Once the track was laid there were several excursions onto the spiral for staff, members and dignitaries. This photograph was taken on 18 July 1971, when *Blanche's* conversion to oil firing was being tested.

alignment on the many curves'. Several joints had been secured with only two bolts instead of four and there was a short closure rail, 4-5ft, at Spooner's Hollow. There was also a temporary tipping siding at Spooner's Hollow that needed a point lock and ground frame capable of being worked by the train staff.

At Dingle Curve, the track had been slewed to increase its radius to 200ft and eliminate the need for check rails, but leaving it with an irregular cant until it was properly ballasted. Garraway assured him that all his requirements would be dealt with before services commenced.

Although it had been agreed that the service would be operated at 10mph, Olver tested the push-pull train at 15mph; he was pleased to see that there was no sign of the carriage wheels lifting off the rails or of wheel flanges climbing the sides of the railheads when the carriage was being propelled through Dingle Curve.

He required a sealed undertaking that the extension would be worked by the 'one train on line' staff method, and required a revised sealed undertaking to cover the new method of working between Penrhyn and Tan y Bwlch, with the introduction of the passing loop at Rhiw Goch, which he inspected on the same occasion.

At Rhiw Goch, the facing-points had been well-constructed from 1 in 6 75lb flat-bottom turnouts and were in all cases correct to gauge; the facing-point locks had been correctly adjusted. Electric depression bars positioned in advance of the facing points ensured that a signalman could not replace a signal to danger prematurely and move the points in the path of a train. An additional depression bar was located on the up main line opposite the fouling point with the down loop at the Penrhyn end to ensure that the last carriage of an up train standing at the up starting signal was not foul of the down loop starting signal. All the depression bars operated correctly.

Operating flexibility was improved from 14 May 1975, when the loop was commissioned at Rhiw Goch, replacing that at Penrhyn which was too short for the longer trains being operated at busy times. Both lines were signalled bi-directionally and controlled from the signal box using colour-light signals. The photograph is of the first crossing to take place there. (Author)

As fireman Phil Girdlestone prepares to surrender the Dduallt-Tan y Bwlch token to the signalman, the much larger token he is about to receive, apart from the appropriate engraving, tells him that short-section working is in operation and that he will be crossing another train at Rhiw Goch.

In 1969 *Princess* had been displayed outside the Queen's Hotel in Blaenau Ffestiniog as a contribution, the *'Croeso 69'* celebrations of the Prince of Wales' investiture, remaining there afterwards to remind the town of the company's intention to restore rail services from Portmadoc. To leave a notice that only used English in such a location would now be considered insensitive and an invitation to vandalism. September 1970. (John Hunt)

Checking the sighting of the colour-light signals, Olver found that the red aspects were adequate in all cases, but the yellow and green aspects were dim, particularly when first cleared, and required them to be adjusted as a matter of urgency. Olver did not comment on the loop lines being signalled in each direction. The loop was used to cross trains for the first time on 14 May, one of the trains being a special operated to launch John Winton's book about the railway, *The Little Wonder*. Regular use was started on 17 May.

The second Light Railway Order was made on 17 June 1975 and came into operation on 27 June. Principally, it authorised the construction of railway No. 4, 2,735 metres in length, including a tunnel, and the abandonment of part of railway No. 3. It also applied parts of the Regulation of Railways Act 1889, and gave the company power to take and use the land shown in the deposited plans, and to borrow up to £500,000 by mortgage and/or the creation and issue of debenture stock. The clause protecting the rights of the CEGB took up three of the order's eight pages. It required, *inter alia*, the company to employ

an approved civil engineering contractor to construct the railway behind the power station, the installation of check rails or barriers on that section, and restricted the number of trains using the level crossings to no more than four per hour and forty per day.

Before the order had been made, the CEGB had agreed to grant the company a ninety-nine-year easement for the land behind the power station for £10 per annum, commuted to £71. A similar easement granted for the land required for Tanygrisiau station was commuted to £70.

A highlight of 1975 was the visit by HRH Princess Margaret and her children on 25 July. The royal party joined a train at Minffordd and travelled to Dduallt to view the deviation works, and then travelled back to Tan y Bwlch. The railway did not benefit from its royal visit as much as it might have done, however, as the report in the *Court Circular* referred only to visits made to the Snowdonia National Park Study Centre at Plas Tan y Bwlch and Llechwedd Slate Caverns later the same day.

Amongst enthusiasts, the railway must have benefitted from the display of *Princess* at the Stockton

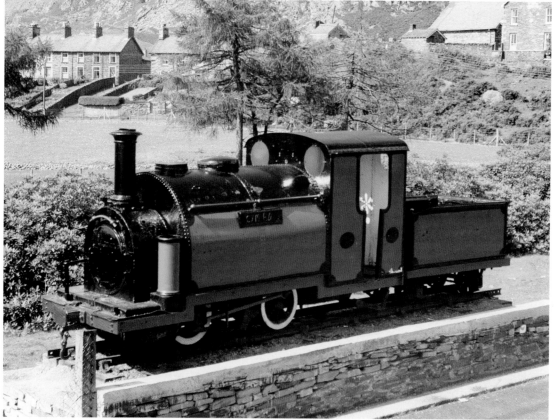

In 1975 *Princess* was displayed at the Stockton & Darlington Railway 150th anniversary celebrations at Shildon, County Durham.

Returning to Wales, a new home was created for *Princess* on a plinth constructed on the former station site opposite the British Rail station. It stayed here until 1980.

& Darlington Railway 150th anniversary exhibition in Shildon, County Durham, in August. From 1969, the loco had been displayed outside the Queen's Hotel in Blaenau Ffestiniog. On returning to Wales it was mounted on a plinth constructed on the former station site opposite the BR station.

There was much activity around the station at Portmadoc on several fronts during 1975. Perhaps most significantly, after twenty years, Allan Garraway had moved out of the station flat in April. He was awarded a £500 salary increase, apparently in recognition that he would be paying his own utility bills in future. The directors also agreed that the company should pay for his telephone.

Looking ahead, and realising that the station site lease was due to expire in 1996, when the £75 annual rental could be expected to be increased to account for inflation and improvements made, the directors decided to offer £3,000 to purchase the freehold, including the car park. In the car park, an offer to sell the company part of the stone building there for £1,500 had been countered with an offer of £1,000 which was refused; in the longer term the company would have found that extra £500 a worthwhile investment.

The shell of the station extension having been completed, the priority should be, the directors decided, to relocate the ladies' facilities along the platform in order that the shop could be completed and brought into use. Paul Dukes, the works manager, had submitted a long report in favour of completing the first-floor offices first.

At the same time, the volunteers converting the goods shed into a temporary museum sought assurances that their labours would not be wasted if it was decided the space could be better used by extending the new café into it. Having inspected the site, the directors agreed that their fears could be well-founded and proposed a meeting with the society to discuss the issue, in November 1976 dismissing the idea of enlarging the museum to make space for 'eventual bar facilities'. It was twenty-three years before the museum was usurped from its home by the catering department.

The year 1975 ended with news that the company had succeeded with an application for support from the Manpower Services Commission, a grant of £27,350 paying for the employment of twelve men to

work on the deviation for twelve months. Established by the Employment and Training Act in 1973, the commission had a remit of co-ordinating employment and training services that included providing temporary employment for the unemployed. Another grant was obtained to complete the new *Earl of Merioneth* and to build new carriages, identified as Nos. 30-2 in the minutes, although they never carried these numbers in service.

Carriage No. 30, later No. 110, which had entered service on the Gelliwiog shuttle, seated forty-two passengers in an open saloon and had a driving compartment to enable it to work in push-pull mode with *Moel Hebog*. Entering service in 1977, No. 31 (No 117 when it entered service) was the first of five steel-bodied carriages built on underframes acquired from Isle of Man Railways; the others were Nos 118-121.

The new shop at Porthmadog was brought into use before the end of 1975 and the café, named *The Little Wonder* following a competition for society members, followed in 1976. The first-floor offices were not completed until 1978. It appears that no estimate was produced before work started and that no quotation was obtained from a contractor to establish if using the company's own workforce would be good value for money. The cost of the construction was not separated out from other expenses in the accounts. It would be expected that a contractor would have taken less time to complete the work, enabling the new assets to earn their keep sooner. On 21 January 1976, the directors complimented Hugh Eaves for reducing audit costs by keeping better accounts. The plan to move the booking office closer to the harbour, to enlarge the booking hall, was never put into effect.

The tunnel bore was completed on 1 May 1976 although by July, 70m of it still needed to be opened out to the loading gauge. Sir Alfred McAlpine (Northern) Ltd, successors to the Scottish railway builder, took a management contract to build the underground bridges over the power station pipelines that started in October 1976. The railway company provided the labour, forty-two posts paid for by a £98,461 Manpower Services Commission scheme. One of the largest grants made by the commission, the contract included the Cwmorthin River Bridge and the two level crossings on CEGB property. Meanwhile, planning was started for the

Started on 1 September 1975, the tunnel bore was completed on 1 May 1976 although it still required opening out to the loading gauge. (Author)

To shunt wagons in the tunnel, a battery-electric locomotive was acquired, stabled and charged in temporary accommodation located at Dduallt station, where an electricity supply was installed, at some expense, for the purpose.

construction and opening of a temporary station at Buarth Melyn in 1977.

Gwynedd County Council's withdrawal of the subsidy for little-used Saturday evening bus services in 1976 gave the company an opportunity to show that it could provide a useful service to the community. At the council's request, it covered the last bus to Penrhyn, which had been well-used as it ran just after pub-closing time. Running at 22.35 from Porthmadog, use of the Gelliwiog shuttle train, *Moel Hebog* and carriage No. 110 avoided the need to run-round at Penrhyn. Loadings varied from five to thirty, averaging at twelve. When the council decided

Temporary track in place on the Tanygrisiau-side tunnel cutting, with the route cut through the old dam. (John Hunt)

to reinstate the subsidy, the train ran for the last time on 4 September. To mark the occasion, a buffet car was added to the train, which ran full.

Keeping the railway running whilst balancing income and expenditure on the deviation was no mean juggling act. The overdraft forecast for 1976 was £96,000 despite the bank having only approved £90,000, secured by a mortgage of the railway's assets. In May 1976, the overdraft was only below the forecast because £25,000 of cheques had not been issued and grant payments had been received early. The situation was alleviated a little by the easement granted for use of the company's land whilst the Glan-y-Don tip was being cleared, which earned £12,500 plus interest.

With inflation at its maximum there was pressure on wages too. When Allan Garraway remarked that the situation was stressful, he was told that work for 'ordinary organisations' could also be stressful. His relationship with the company's employees had also become stressed and many joined one of the rail trade unions, the National Union of Railwaymen becoming particularly aggressive in promoting its

This dramatic view from above the tunnel mouth shows the state of affairs when track had been laid from Dduallt and dismantling the tunnel construction site compound had been started. Surprisingly, there is a motor car on the old incline formation.

In 1976 the company was paid for the use of its property at Glan y Pwll whilst the Glan-y-Don slate tip was removed, evidence of the large vehicles used visible in this photograph. The nineteenth-century signal post remained in place until the railway was reinstated.

Viewed from above Glan y Pwll Junction, the Glan-y-Don tip, once served by the Welsh Slate Company's viaduct, is in the centre of this photograph, which also shows the 1836 alignment to Dinas and Rhiwbryfdir, and the line to the Nidd y Gigfran quarry incline on the left. (John Hunt)

The authorities or the contractors, it is not clear which, were encouraged to modify the landscaping to accommodate the reinstatement of Glan y Pwll Junction and the Dinas branch if required. The Barlwyd river bridge is at the bottom of the picture. In the centre, a DMU is passing the site of the carriage storage shed built as part of the strategic development scheme in 1996. (Author)

claim for recognition. Although the directors thought that it wanted to secure wages parity with British Rail and eliminate the use of volunteers, a satisfactory agreement with the union was made on 10 January 1977.

A job assessment and grading exercise was also carried out, comparison with wages paid by other minor railways showing that the company paid poorly, the directors becoming amenable to the idea that the regrading exercise should be accompanied by increases in pay. Grievance and disciplinary procedures were also put in place. Whilst these developments, including the NUR's desire for recognition, were consequential on the Employment Protection Act of 1975, it is quite clear that there were problems in the relationship between management and employees.

It was around this time that a meeting between John Routly and the employees was held in the new café. It came to an end when Routly, conscious that many staff had previously been volunteers, said, 'You are the only group of employees I know whose jobs are underwritten by volunteers. But for them

you would not have jobs at all – and also you are doing work you really want to do – and in any case it's jolly good fun.' The last three words really made an impact and, before too long, reminders of them, in the form of the initials 'JGF', had spread throughout the railway, on wagons and locomotives, and on the podium when the railway to Tanygrisiau Station was opened. At Boston Lodge it was noticed that the three words had twelve letters so the erecting shop clock had its numerals replaced by the letters 'jolly good fun', where they remain. Routly became aware of the new life taken by his phrase and would often repeat it, accompanied by a grin, in later years. In 2001 he explained its origins in the society's magazine, too.

On the railway, buffet car No. 103 was returned to service after an overhaul and kitchen refit in the spring of 1977. The directors had decided that the buffet cars should be named after well-known historical personalities associated with the railway and its antecedents. No. 103 was the first to be so treated, with the name *Charles Spooner* painted on simple wooden plaques fitted to its body sides. The other names were *Samuel Holland* (No. 12) and *William Madocks* (No. 14). Whilst it might be possible to understand the logic behind the directors' thinking, there was a feeling that naming carriages was 'not very Ffestiniog', the names were not liked and were soon removed. Maybe the lack of elegance in the nameplates' design also contributed to the disdain with which they were regarded.

The largest group, 996 passengers, accommodated by the railway was carried on 12 June 1977, a record that still stands. Organised by the *Leicester Chronicle*, the party had travelled by two trains from Leicestershire, one train travelling to Blaenau Ffestiniog, the other to Minffordd. After making a single journey on the FR, participants returned home by the opposing route, making a circular tour. At one point during the afternoon,

The clock in the erecting shop, modified after chairman John Routly told staff that working for the company was 'jolly good fun'. (Author)

At Boston Lodge, this view shows some of the capital works carried out during the 1970s, the offices constructed after the chimney was demolished, the new erecting shop and the carriage shed. The temporary corrugated walls of the erecting shop remained in place for more than twenty years. The flat-roofed building is the mess, paid for by donations contributed by members in memory of Ron Garraway, a society membership secretary and father of Allan. The items acquired 'because they might be useful' have now all gone, as has the caravan. (Author)

Seen at a quiet moment, whilst it was a terminus, Dduallt must at times have been the busiest station ever located 'in the middle of nowhere'. The second carriage in the *Earl of Merioneth*'s train is No. 103, a buffet car with a large kitchen designed to serve customers at Dduallt, built in 1968. Re-bodied in 1990 and re-equipped in 1993, in 2009 it was replaced by a 35-seat saloon allocated the same number.

every available carriage except one, and three steam locomotives, were at Dduallt.

On the deviation, track laying through the tunnel had been completed on 2 February 1977, but the extension of services to the temporary platform, named Llyn Ystradau, was unexpectedly delayed. The consultants validating that the new infrastructure had been built to a standard acceptable for public use recommended that the tunnel should be lined with sprayed concrete, which caught the directors unawares as the old tunnel had been unlined.

A trial with *Mountaineer* hauling the wagon-mounted loading gauge to check clearances run on 28 May found that more work was required before the proposed concrete-spraying method, called 'shotcrete', could be started. Meeting the requirements of Major Olver, who made his first inspection on 29 May, and completing outstanding

work, delayed public opening until the afternoon of 8 July. There had been two special workings previously, a filming train for the BBC's *Go with Noakes* TV programme on 15 June and the 'opening' train for 200 invited guests on 25 June. On the second occasion, the MP for Merioneth, Dafydd Ellis Thomas, cut a ribbon across the track before the train entered the tunnel. Olver made a second visit on 6 July and completing the shotcrete was deferred until the winter.

Mountaineer and Major Olver's inspection train near Llyn Ystradau on 29 May 1977. (Author)

From 19 May 1977, Bill Broadbent had been appointed chief executive to strengthen the company's management on a six-month contract via a private company in which he had an interest. In addition to a fee and expenses, he was to be paid a bonus of 10 per cent of any cash generated above the forecast. The minute recording the decision noted, 'The chairman and the deputy chairman had consulted throughout with the general manager and it was expected that the chief executive would have full support from the general manager in fulfilling his assignment.' The appointment was not warmly received in all quarters and was widely seen as a move towards dispensing with Allan Garraway's services. When Broadbent stood for re-election at the society's 1978 AGM, he received the lowest number of votes of the successful candidates.

In July 1977, Hugh Eaves reported that as a proportion of receipts, wages were high and rising, and the percentage of new works expenditure on labour had also risen; in November he reported overspending of £40,000 on the tunnel and £8,000 on the power station contract.

Broadbent's July proposal to grade non-management staff into four bands was accepted to be put into effect by 1 August, despite increasing the wages bill by 7 per cent. He had also arranged for the Manchester Business School to advise the company on management training for a fee of £500; as this was not referred to again it might not have been put into effect.

When the budget was discussed a few weeks later, there was concern about shop profitability and stock levels; a railway book publishing boom had resulted in large stock-holdings. The figures are shown in the table opposite; before 1972 stock for resale had been included with stores. In 1978, Allan Garraway was instructed to reduce the figure to £25,000. David Garnock suggested that the number of lines stocked should be reduced and the mark-ups increased. Borrowing in 1978 was forecast to peak at £250,000 compared with £190,000 in 1977. Hugh

Planet diesel locomotive *Upnor Castle*, bought from the Welshpool & Llanfair Light Railway in 1968, was regularly seen on passenger trains during the 1970s. The first carriage is No 26, repainted silver to celebrate the Queen's Silver Jubilee in 1977, one of Bill Broadbent's schemes whilst he was chief executive.

On the left, the McKenzie & Holland somersault home signal had been installed in 1971.

Eaves called for increased fiscal discipline, saying that there had been a tendency for over-optimism on revenue budgeting in recent years.

	1972	1973	1974	1975	1976	1977
Stock for resale	£7,833	£13,581	£26,621	£40,450	£33,736	£32,787

Gwynedd County Council was anxious that the railway would bring to Blaenau Ffestiniog the economic benefits it had already delivered to Porthmadog. The town's population had fallen to 4,500 from its peak of 13,500 100 years before. On the edge of the town, the Llechwedd and Gloddfa Ganol (ex-Oakeley) quarries were attracting some 300,000 visitors each annually, and the power station and Stwlan Dam were also popular attractions, but they provided little economic benefit to the town or its inhabitants. If the railway terminated at its chosen site, 400 yards from the nearest shops, few of its 250,000 passengers would venture into the town. Both the council and Cyngor Dosbarth Merioneth, the district council, claimed the credit for promoting the concept of encouraging the FR to adopt a new terminus in the centre of the town.

The council's planning, highways and transportation committee gave its support to a combined BR/FR station in the town on 25 October 1977. This had not been straightforward, as the Gwynedd Health Authority had bought the GWR station site to develop a health centre. However, the authority's acceptance of an alternative site in May 1976 enabled a scheme for redeveloping the site to provide facilities for both railways, and reclaiming derelict land at Duffws to increase the amount of car parking available, to be promoted. Funding was to be sought from various government agencies and the European Economic Community's regional development fund. A target date of Easter 1980 was set for the new station to be operational.

A change to the board took place on 4 November 1977, when R.H.N. 'Dick' Hardy, executive member of British Rail's central engineering training group, replaced Sir Ben Ball, who had died on 24 January 1977. His remit was to advise on training.

The question of the company's senior management was resolved, so far as the directors were concerned, on 4 November 1977. They decided that a 'chief general manager' should be appointed, to be accountable to the board for all aspects of running the business with direct responsibility for personnel, publicity, administration, new works and planning. Allan Garraway, as 'general manager (operating and engineering)', and the commercial manager (responsible for sales, catering, travel and the booking office) would report to him.

CHAPTER 9

1978-1985: BACK TO BLAENAU, BUT NO POT OF GOLD

Although 1978 opened with the prospect of services resuming to Tanygrisiau, signifying the completion of the deviation, the largest such project ever undertaken on a heritage railway, which many had believed, and stated, could never be done, it was still a difficult time for the company.

At the directors' meeting on 10 February, John Routly opened by thanking Allan Garraway for running the railway in difficult times. Concern was expressed, however, at the apparent repetition of teething troubles with the shotcreting. The society's magazine reported failure of hydraulic and concrete pumps, theft of a battery and freezing weather as contributory factors to the delays.

Garraway's future was further considered by the directors on 7 April. After a meeting with John Routly and Les Smith, he had had second thoughts about his situation and had consulted the Association of Railway Preservation Societies' chairman, solicitor

David Morgan. The directors decided that he should be offered three choices: underpinning with a deputy or a joint general manager and taking retirement at age fifty-five; remaining in post with altered duties and reporting to a chief general manager; or taking redundancy.

Major Olver returned to inspect the new line on 7 June, submitting his report on 19 July; he referred to a report dated 27 September 1977, a copy of which has not been found. He had gauged the cuttings between Tanygrisiau and the tunnel, and found all clearances to be satisfactory. In the tunnel, he found that a lot of rubbish had accumulated on the side of the track, obstructing drainage, and some areas of the shotcrete lining obstructed the structure gauge. He had previously asked for barbed-wire entanglements to be erected above the tunnel portals to prevent vandals from climbing onto them to drop items on the track in front of approaching trains or

Joining the deviation to the existing line at Tanygrisiau required further rock shifting to bring the levels and alignment into line. (John Hunt)

Whilst Tanygrisiau was a terminus, provision was made for locomotives to take water and refuel. Immediately beyond the station was the first of four footbridges crossing the railway that needed to be rebuilt to a higher level to maintain clearances for rolling stock introduced since 1955.

with the intention of wounding a locomotive driver or fireman. This had not been done, it was not satisfactory and an effective barrier should be provided forthwith; it never was done.

At Tanygrisiau, he asked for a notice to be erected at the end of the platform, prohibiting passengers from walking towards Blaenau Ffestiniog along the trackbed, and another to warn drivers of locomotives running round their trains to look out for passengers using the foot crossing to reach the platform. The level crossing access to Ty'n y Pistill, at the Porthmadog end of the station, required signs warning users to 'stop, look and listen before crossing the line' and to 'shut the gates'. The two-lever ground frame controlling the points at this end of the station locked them satisfactorily, but required locking by a padlock with the key kept on the train staff. The fencing was incomplete; it did not need to be completed before the official opening on 24 June, but should be completed before the railway was opened to the public.

Whilst a strategy had been agreed for dealing with the level crossings over the CEGB's private access roads to the Stwlan Dam and the penstocks, it could not be put in place before the line was opened. Therefore, in the short term, manned barriers, which could be locked in the down position, needed to be

erected on the Stwlan crossing and the gates already erected on the penstock road had to be capable of being locked across the road. Olver was prepared to accept, however, that this would not be done before the official opening, but insisted that the crossings should be manned and pennants put across the road to indicate to car drivers that they should not cross. Otherwise, when public services started they must be fully operational, complete with interlocked white lights to indicate to locomotive drivers that it was safe to proceed.

Olver agreed with Garraway's suggestion that both crossings could be manned by a single crossing keeper, but required a telephone to be installed in order that the approach of trains could be notified. The author remembers working these crossings before they were automated but has no recollection of any phone being installed. He also remembers getting very wet.

On the subject of signalling, Olver noted that the installation at Dduallt was incomplete at the time of his visit, adding that Garraway had agreed that it would be complete by the time passenger services started to Tanygrisiau. He also raised the issue of the signalling at Tan y Bwlch, started 5-10 years before and still incomplete, and Minffordd, started before Tan y Bwlch and also still unfinished. The

Hauled by *Merddin Emrys*, the second train to arrive carried company and society officers and guests. The headboard had been made by the BBC, which had made a children's TV programme about building the tunnel. The goods shed (left) and store are all that remain of the original station, and show how much higher the new one is. (Author)

On 24 June 1978, a day of heavy rain and low cloud, the deviation to Tanygrisiau was opened. The construction of 2½ miles of new railway in difficult terrain with limited resources was a remarkable achievement. Hauled by *Blanche*, the first train to arrive at the new station carried a few of the volunteers who had helped to build the new railway. John Gibbons stands by the groundframe ready to reset the points after the train has passed.

situation was most unsatisfactory and both schemes should be completed as matters of urgency, the Tan y Bwlch scheme before services were extended beyond Tanygrisiau.

The railway's signalling projects had suffered from a lack of focus, changes in specification and personnel changes. The colour-light signals commissioned at Tan y Bwlch on 16 May 1970 had been considered a temporary solution pending the installation of a complete semaphore system controlled from the signal box that has never been used for its intended purpose.

The official opening to Tanygrisiau took place on 24 June 1978. Having started with the Prince of

Even for a temporary terminus, facilities at Tanygrisiau were quite basic, with tired Terrapin portable buildings providing space for booking office, shop and tea bar. Toilets were located closer to the water and sewage connections. By 1980 work was still in progress to improve the station's appearance. On 11 May 1980 woodland fires below Tan y Bwlch had resulted in a train being stabled at Tanygrisiau overnight. A few minutes after taking the photograph, the author discovered that he was expected to be fireman on the empty stock working to Boston Lodge. (Author)

Wales, and approaching the chairman of the Wales Tourist Board and the secretary of state for Wales, the directors settled for the Manpower Services Commission's director, Dewi Jones, to perform the opening ceremony, driving home a golden (copper-plated) spike. To the railway's crest which decorated the podium from which the speeches, kept short by heavy rain, were made, the letters 'JGF' had been introduced.

Public services started with the 15.00 departure from Porthmadog, but passengers found facilities very limited beyond the island platform. A shop / booking office and conveniences were located in second or third-hand portable buildings sited in the small car park.

Constructing the deviation was, by any measure, a remarkable achievement. That much of the work was carried out by volunteers made it even more remarkable. From this point no-one could ever say that any heritage railway scheme was impossible.

The CEGB's claim that the enterprise was not worthy of compensation had been rejected by the Lands Tribunal and ignored by other Government departments, the Wales Tourist Board (£178,000), Manpower Services Commission (£142,000) and the Development Board for Rural Wales (£42,500) contributing £362,500 to the eventual £610,000 expenditure, much inflated over earlier estimates. The CEGB compensation covered only a fraction of the cost of reinstatement, and rampant inflation after the award had been made reduced its value further. To complete the task, the company had been dependent on profits and borrowing. By the end of 1978 it had £239,741 in outstanding loans and was faced with

Beyond Tanygrisiau a great deal of work was done to restore the overbridges and boundary walls in a manner sympathetic to their surroundings, with volunteers learning stone-walling techniques.

the task of completing the restoration to Blaenau Ffestiniog with a serious lack of funds.

In two respects the CEGB might be said to have done the company a favour. The route eventually adopted between the tunnel and Tanygrisiau gives passengers much better views than that which it replaced, a subjective opinion, based on a few old photographs. Being forced to find a new route did have the benefit of avoiding the need to address the problems of the old tunnel and its sub-standard loading gauge. Only the old stock would have been capable of running through it and late twentieth-century passengers would have been much more vociferous about their dislike of it than their predecessors. Although it was possible to employ Blaenau Ffestiniog rockmen to improve the clearances on the shorter Garnedd Tunnel on a part-time basis, the length of the long tunnel would have made it much more difficult, and expensive, to alter.

On 14 July 1978, the directors agreed that there should be a period of consolidation. They thought the company would be unable to move on from Tanygrisiau before the end of 1979 in any event.

Meanwhile, progress had been made on the development of clearly-defined staff negotiating machinery; on the same date, terms negotiated with the National Union of Railwaymen by Dick Hardy

were approved. Three tiers of committees were defined, with three departmental committees at the lowest level. Whilst the departmental committee members had to belong to the NUR, they were elected by all employees with more than six months' service. The disciplinary procedure had also been adjusted to bring it into line with British Rail practice.

Conditions for Allan Garraway's departure were sealed on 20 September. A letter that he had circulated to his friends had been considered libellous by the directors, but as he had distributed a 'letter of amends' they decided to take no further action. Legal expenses amounting to £688 had been incurred to deal with the matter.

By November 1978, the overdraft limit had been set at £270,000; Hugh Eaves reported that whilst most creditors had been paid, he anticipated that there would be substantial outstanding bills by May 1979 to keep within the limit. In January 1979, it was reported that a revised cash forecast had reduced peak borrowing to £300,000, but failed to provide for its reduction. Reviewing the options available to them, the directors decided to increase the income forecast and reduce the wages budget by reducing the number of staff employed, imposing upon Garraway responsibility for controlling expenditure and engagement of staff.

At Glan y Pwll the remains of the old loco shed were incorporated into a larger building for use as a workshop. The steelwork is being moved into place using the company's road crane. (Author)

They were still concerned about stock levels, which had reached £51,000.

Two possible sources of income that might ease the situation were being pursued. The Wales Tourist Board had been asked about making a supplementary grant in respect of the tunnel and power station overspends, and John Routly had started negotiations with the Development Board for Rural Wales, to see if it would agree to work to stabilise a rockfall at Penlan, Tanygrisiau, that had occurred in 1975, being transferred to the Wales Development Agency as a land reclamation scheme, with a 100 per cent grant available, releasing DBRW grants for other projects. Eventually, no supplementary grant was forthcoming; the WTB's chairman was supportive, but his board was not.

Beyond the Penlan repair works and Dolrhedyn Bridge reinstatement, the directors had no strategy for completing the remainder of the railway's restoration. It was not going to be as straightforward as it had been in the 1950s. Residents, and sheep,

had been using the trackbed as a footpath, and the boundaries were in poor condition. As well as clearing the formation for tracklaying and making the boundaries secure, four pedestrian overbridges required rebuilding to accommodate higher locomotives and carriages, the Barlwyd River Bridge near Glan y Pwll needed to be replaced and a means of controlling Glan y Pwll level crossing that avoided the need for a crossing keeper had to be developed and approved.

The 'senior general manager', Percy Royston 'Dick' Wollan, was appointed with the title of chief executive and took up his appointment on 19 April 1979. Recruited by a head-hunting firm, he was a Welshman who took early retirement from a senior

The permanent way department put a re-gauged standard-gauge Matisa tamper into service in 1978. It had been built for British Railways in 1958 and acquired by the railway ten years later. Its adaptation to the railway's requirements was carried out at Boston Lodge by Steve Coulson, a volunteer who had moved to Porthmadog to support the railway. It was photographed in action on the mineral line at Minffordd. (Author)

position with ICI's Mond Division to join the FR. In an interview with ICI's house magazine, he explained that the appointment came about because the directors were having to involve themselves in running the business and Allan Garraway could not be expected to handle the load imposed by dealing with labour legislation, health and safety regulations, cash flow projections and budgetary controls as well as operating the railway.

Later, Garraway said that they worked well together, there was no conflict and they became good friends. One of the first things Wollan did was to tell the directors that a co-ordinated programme was needed to complete the railway's restoration to Blaenau Ffestiniog. He also introduced the practice of holding an annual planning and budget meeting for the directors and the departmental managers.

The year 1979 was a time for celebration. In January, the Association of Railway Preservation Societies presented its award for an outstanding contribution to voluntary railway preservation to the society 'for the significant part that it played in the work leading to the completion of the Festiniog Railway deviation, project in 1978'. Strictly speaking, the society had not played that great a part in the deviation but the company was not a member of the

ARPS. Lord Downe presented the trophy to Michael Schumann and the society chairman Gordon Caddy at the ARPS AGM, held at York on 27 January.

Earl of Merioneth, the new Fairlie, made its first appearance in steam on 12 June 1979. Despite the retention of some old parts, the directors had decided that it was to be regarded as a new locomotive. It was formally named by Allan Garraway at Porthmadog on 23 June, one of several events commemorating the twenty-fifth anniversary of the company's revival. A dinner was held for the company's employees and honorary officials at Gloddfa Ganol, the tourist centre then located on the site of the Oakeley Quarry.

The new locomotive entered service on 19 July. It had nothing of the elegance that George Percival Spooner imbued on its precursors, and was rather functional in appearance. Built with the resources and skills available, it epitomised what some regarded as the company's brutal approach to its history. Large angular tanks gave it the capacity to operate to Blaenau Ffestiniog without taking water at Tan y Bwlch, but no advantage could be taken of this capability whilst the remainder of the fleet still needed to stop there. Its predecessor, the old *Earl of Merioneth*, the erstwhile *Taliesin*, was put into store.

New locomotive, new railway. *Earl of Merioneth* approaching Tanygrisiau, crossing the CEGB's Stwlan Dam road, which had been made public as far as Dolrhedyn. The level crossing is still being worked manually. Although the train is still heading up to Blaenau Ffestiniog, the gradient here is falling to Tanygrisiau. The second carriage from the end is No. 119, recognisable by its toilet compartment window, built on an Isle of Man Railways underframe and completed in 1980. The fifth and sixth carriages are Nos. 117 and 118, both built in 1977 on Isle of Man underframes. (Author)

In contrast, *Moelwyn* is climbing up to the power station summit on its way down to Minffordd. (Author)

Mountaineer has just breasted the summit. Carriage No. 23 had been painted in 1950s livery in recognition of the society's silver jubilee in 1979. The third carriage from the front is No. 116, built by Edmund Crow in Cumbria and which entered service in 1972. It is clad in aluminium.

Built around the second boiler supplied by Hunslet in the 1960s, the 'new' *Earl of Merioneth* was named by Allan Garraway at Porthmadog on 23 June 1979, with centenarian *Merddin Emrys* standing alongside. It entered service on 25 August 1979. Although it contained many old components, some from *James Spooner*, much was made of it being the first new Fairlie locomotive for sixty years and the first new locomotive built at Boston Lodge since 1886. (Author)

The bridge over the old road from Tanygrisiau to Dolrhedyn, originally an occupation crossing that had been replaced by a bridge in 1901, had been removed in the 1950s and the road level raised to improve the gradient for motor vehicles. Agreement with the CEGB for part of its Stwlan Dam access road to be adopted to give access to Dolrhedyn facilitated the reinstatement of the rail bridge. (John Hunt)

Allan Garraway was again the focus of attention with the publication of the Queen's birthday honours list on 25 June, announcing that he had been awarded an MBE. This was the first time that anyone associated with what was then called a 'preserved railway' had received such an award. It rather looked as though the nomination and the invitation to name the locomotive were attempts to address the offence caused by the appointment of the 'chief general manager'.

For the society, its twenty-fifth anniversary was marked by a celebratory open weekend on 15-16 September 1979, with 1,780 visitors conveyed to Boston Lodge by the shuttle train, the first time public access had been permitted on any scale. A dinner was held there on 15 September.

During 1979, the company introduced a scheme to appoint patrons, distinguished railway enthusiasts both from the UK and the US and Canada, whose names might lend stature to the railway. They included Leonard Heath Humphrys, who had started the railway's revival; Sir Peter Parker, then the chairman of British Rail; and the Hon Sir William McAlpine Bt, the enthusiast

member of the construction family known for its use of mass concrete when building railways in Scotland. There were eventually nine in total. At the time of publication only Sir William is still alive, becoming a trustee in 1999. The others were not replaced on their deaths and the scheme faded away.

A rock-bolting scheme for repairing the Penlan rockfall was devised during 1979 and McAlpine's £78,000 bid, plus £175 per additional hole, was accepted in 1980; a grant obtained from the Development Board for Rural Wales helped to pay for the work. Gwynedd County Council adopted part of the CEGB's private access road to Llyn Stwlan to make a new route to the hamlet at

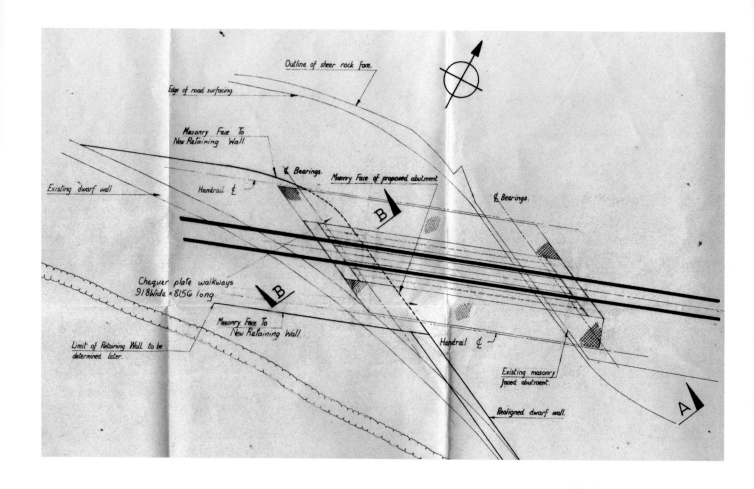

Outline of sheer rock face.

Edge of road surfacing

Masonry Face To
New Retaining Wall.

Existing dwarf wall

Handrail ℄

℄ Bearings.

Masonry Face of proposed abutment

B

℄ Bearings.

Chequer plate walkways
918 Wide × 8156 long

B

Masonry Face To
New Retaining Wall.

Handrail ℄

Limit of Retaining Wall to be
determined later.

Existing masonry
faced abutment.

Realigned dwarf wall.

A

An extract from a plan of the replacement bridge at Tanygrisiau produced by Gwynedd County Council in 1975.

The new bridge was completed in 1980. On 2 May 1981, it was seen being crossed by a works train carrying sleepers to the head of steel. Once served by the railway, the Groby Granite Quarry is in the centre distance. (Author)

Dolrhedyn and the replacement railway deck was poured in December 1979. Contemporary references in the society's magazine are undecided as to whether the bridge's construction 12in higher than previously was by prior agreement or the result of a devious scheme by the council to maintain headroom for cars contrary to expectations.

Work on the new joint station at Blaenau Ffestiniog was started in February 1980, with Lilley Construction Ltd undertaking most of the work. Although the estimated £860,000 was beyond the sponsoring authorities, the interdisciplinary nature of the project encouraged support from eight public bodies, including the Welsh Office, as trunk road authority; the Welsh Development Agency, for land reclamation and environmental improvements; the Development Board for Rural Wales; the European Economic Development Fund; and three local authorities. The European funding was the first obtained in connection with a heritage railway scheme.

Writing in the *Railway Magazine* in April 1980, John Routly justified the expenditure of public funds on the company's new station at a time of cutbacks by pointing out that Porthmadog had been dead when the railway's revival had started in 1955. Now, 79 per cent of passengers surveyed said they visited the town to travel on the railway, and the town and railway had grown together. Blaenau Ffestiniog was still a dead town, but before the railway closed it had attracted 60 per cent of the passenger traffic; the railway would bring prosperity here, too, he wrote.

As the company required a station wherever it terminated, the funding contained no contribution for the FR, but it did include £11,000 for the extra track required to extend it beyond the 7-acre site.

In an article published in *Railway World* in July 1982, the county council's planning department explained, inter alia, that space was created for a second FR track from Glan y Pwll to the new station

Seen from the Gloddfa Ganol Tourist Centre, the bridges for the new FR formation through to the central station had been completed by 1981. (Author)

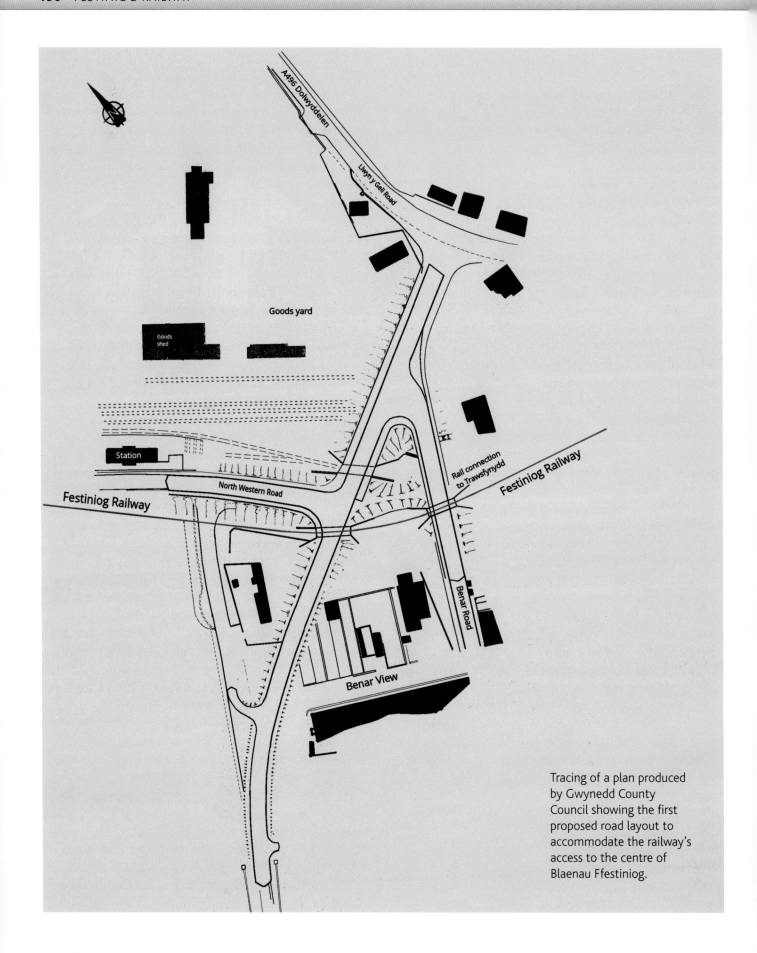

Tracing of a plan produced by Gwynedd County Council showing the first proposed road layout to accommodate the railway's access to the centre of Blaenau Ffestiniog.

Track was washed out at Bron Madoc, near Rhiw Plas, on 11 March 1981. Until a permanent repair could be carried out at the end of the season, this temporary arrangement was put in place with a 5mph speed restriction.

(Author)

in order that a shuttle to Dinas, the first terminus, and the slate quarry tourist attractions could be operated at a later date. Facilities provided for British Rail included a parcels office and loading dock, although the parcels service was withdrawn shortly after the station was brought into use. Associated works included: demolishing the road bridge over the rail access to Duffws; constructing a wall along the boundary between the station and the school that had been built on the GWR goods yard site, providing parking for 250 cars; and accommodation for the FR, the national park visitor centre and the North Wales Visitor Council in Isallt, a house adjacent to the footbridge that crossed both railways. There was no contingency allowance and when the cemetery wall required greater reinforcing than anticipated, the North Western Road layout was not simplified as planned.

After being out of use since 1969, *Prince* was returned to service in March 1980. With the company's priorities focused on larger locomotives, it had not been until 1974 that the society took the initiative to start its overhaul, establishing a volunteer team of retired engineers for the purpose. Work carried out included replacing the firebox; replacing the tubeplates to permit the installation of superheating; converting it to oil firing; and raising

the cab in order to accommodate twentieth-century man, and woman. Cleaning old plate to bare metal revealed evidence of paint and lining on the cabside that dated from the 1890s, some of which was preserved, and wrought iron plate on the tender that had probably originally been made for a side tank of one of the England engines in 1863-4.

Also during March, militant Welsh politics brought the railway into the media spotlight when an incendiary device was found on the window ledge of the new café at Porthmadog. The police were called and it was made safe without causing any damage. The incident might have been linked to a campaign of arson against English-owned second-homes in remote areas of Wales over the winter of 1979-80 and the placing of thirteen incendiary devices outside Conservative Party offices and public buildings subsequently. The incendiary offences and most of the arson attacks remain unsolved.

A notice for the Light Railway Order application for the new station, with Gwynedd County Council, British Rail and the company as joint applicants, was published in the *London Gazette* on 24 June 1980 and a company extraordinary general meeting was held to approve its part in the application on 26 July. John Routly told the bank that there was no likelihood of the borrowing being reduced during the next two

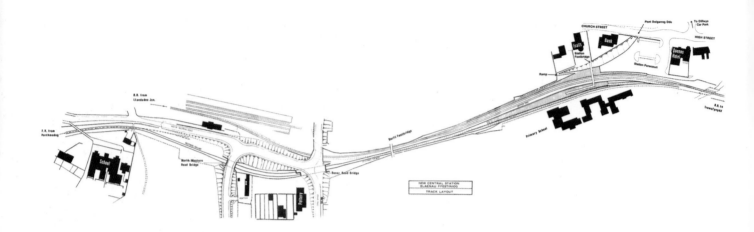

years as it was essential for the company to respond to this Government scheme.

Elsewhere, the company struggled to find the resources to complete the restoration between Tanygrisiau and the new station. Appeals to deviationists that the work was incomplete and that the railway still needed their help largely fell on deaf ears; after thirteen years of railway building they went to develop careers, relationships and families, although some returned twenty years later to assist with the Welsh Highland Railway. Dick Wollan's concept of a co-ordinated programme to complete the restoration was taken forward by encouraging functional and area groups to take on micro-projects in which participants could have a sense of ownership. Launched under the title 'project Blaenau' in July 1980, over seventy projects, including four footbridges, three underpasses, ten culverts, and over 1,500 yards of boundary walls and fencing, were offered with completion by May 1982 as the target. Seven men employed on a twelve-month Manpower Services Commission scheme from May 1981 were mostly utilised on walling.

The Blaenau Ffestiniog (Central Station) Light Railway Order 1981 was made on 20 January 1981 and effective ten days later. The British Railways Board was authorised to construct and use a railway 482m long commencing by a junction with the Trawsfynydd branch railway a point where it was crossed by the Benar Road Bridge and terminating by a junction where it crossed the Afon Bowydd. The FR was empowered to build and use a railway 636m long that started with a junction with the existing railway 56m west of the embankment carrying the A496 road at its south-western approach to the

Benar Road Bridge and ending at a point 28m west of the Afon Bowydd.

Additional powers were given to the company to borrow up to £750,000 by means of mortgage, creation of debentures or by bank loan or overdraft. Article 8 of the 1975 LRO, power to borrow up to £500,000, was revoked. The directors' intention to include power to borrow by overdraft in the 1975 order had been overlooked; its inclusion in the 1981 order formalised an irregular situation that had been in place since 1914.

Tracklaying was sufficiently complete to enable the Barlwyd Bridge beams to be transported from Minffordd in July 1981 and for a steam-powered ballast train to be run to Glan y Pwll on 11 December. The first works train reached the new station in January 1982.

At the end of 1981 some work was left undone, and vacancies left unfilled, to improve the cash-flow position. Dick Wollan and Allan Garraway had not taken the salary increases awarded. Tyddyn y Bwlch, the Penrhyn crossing keeper's house, was put on the market for £15,000 to employees, £1,000 more to others; the sale was not completed until 1983. 1982 fares were increased by 10 per cent and wages by 6½ per cent, but the latter was not accepted by the staff.

Installation of major exhibits in the goods shed museum, which had started in 1979, was completed with the setting up of *Princess* therein during 1981.

By twenty-first-century standards the work at Blaenau
Ffestiniog seemed to take a long time, although maybe
that did not matter, because the FR was unable to move
any faster than it did. Here, the pre-cast footbridge
sections are on site, but the new formation for the
standard-gauge tracks has not been made. (Author)

At Porthmadog, the
goods shed was
developed as a
museum in 1979, the
hearse van making a
rare appearance in
the open air as it was
moved into place by
members of the
building department.
(Author)

British Railways started using its section of the new station on 22 March 1982. The footbridge has been erected, the FR tracks are laid and the water tower base constructed, but the platform is incomplete. (Author)

The loco's period of display on the plinth at Blaenau Ffestiniog, where it had been exposed to the weather and at risk of vandalism, had been ended in 1977-8.

Notice was given for another light railway order on 23 February 1982. Its main purpose was to deal with the requirement of the 1832 Act to provide a lodge at the Glan y Pwll level crossing, but it also legislated for the level crossing on the Stwlan Dam access road and authorised the company to enter into agreements with other railway companies, including the British Railways Board, and shipping companies. This last came about because in 1966 the company had started to sell rail tickets as an agency for British Rail following the withdrawal of personnel from Minffordd Cambrian Station. This had developed into a worthwhile business that had grown further when the company started operating its own tours in the 1970s. The order was made on 13 October 1982.

With the completion of the works in prospect, the directors decided that the restoration of services to Blaenau Ffestiniog, 'NOT to be called an "opening"', should take place on 25 May 1982, to commemorate the 150th anniversary of the 1832 Act of Parliament. They soon realised that any official visit to mark the event would have to be deferred to another date. An attempt to arrange a visit from the Prince and Princess of Wales proved fruitless, and various

Government ministers were considered before an invitation was extended to the speaker of the House of Commons, George Thomas MP.

From January, the directors were submitting suggestions for guests to be invited to travel on the first train to Dick Wollan. Managing 'first-day travel' would prove to be quite a logistical exercise as it had been calculated that some 850 supporters were entitled to it.

British Rail started using its part of the new Blaenau Ffestiniog Station on 22 March. Ten days before, the directors had noted that an, 'FR steam-hauled service may be bringing materials to site on that day.' Sure enough, as the first BR train arrived from Llandudno Junction, *Blanche* appeared pulling a four-wheeled Hudson wagon and a van, the loco crew accompanied by a pair of grinning directors, John Routly and Les Smith. To his credit, the BR driver, although he must have realised that his moment in the sun was about to be stolen, slowed down and paced the FR's train into the Station, where a small crowd had gathered to observe the event.

The new Barlwyd Bridge was load-tested with *Earl of Merioneth* on 13 May, ready for Major Olver's inspection train, hauled by *Prince*, on 17 May. Olver submitted his report on 30 July; the report of a previous visit to this section has not come to light. The line between Tanygrisiau and Blaenau Ffestiniog had been worked as a siding. From the commencement of services to Blaenau Ffestiniog a new long-section staff would be made by welding together the existing Dduallt-Tanygrisiau and Tanygrisiau-Blaenau Ffestiniog staffs. Increased flexibility would be provided by the installation of electric token instruments at Dduallt and Blaenau Ffestiniog during the winter of 1982-3. An intermediate instrument would also be installed at the Glan y Pwll permanent way depot.

The points at Tanygrisiau would be locked out of use when services were extended as locos would no longer runround there. A more permanent solution would be arranged as soon as reasonably possible.

Footbridge No. 1 had been completed with galvanised parapets and a reinforced concrete decking. The handrail on the roadside of the line was an old type and required replacing. Footbridge No. 3 was incomplete and if it became obvious that it could not be completed before 25 May, then temporary arrangements should be made to prevent residents from crossing the track on the level.

Until the requirements of the 1982 Light Railway Order had been met at Glan y Pwll level crossing, it would be protected by the use of pennants and a flagman. He thought the company's pennants were

insufficiently conspicuous and suggested borrowing or purchasing a set of 'official level crossing pennants' from British Rail. He asked for 'stop until called forward' boards to be installed 25 yards from the down side of the crossing and 30 yards from the up side, adding that there would be no need for trains to stop once the flagman had put the pennants across the road, was satisfied that traffic had stopped and had given a green flag signal.

The Wakefield footpath crossing, near Glan y Pwll, had been provided with gates that should be made self-closing. Springs on the gates at Groby Junction were better, but should be regularly inspected to ensure that the mechanism continued to work properly.

He gauged the road-over-rail bridges that had been constructed using pre-cast box-section culverts to carry the railway under the A496 and Benar Road. Due to the difficulties, he wrote, in getting the correct road and rail alignments, there had been compromises in vertical clearances, between 3½in and 6in beyond the kinematic envelope on the A496 bridge, and 11½in to 11in on the Benar Road Bridge. The lateral clearances were 20in beyond the kinematic envelope on the A496 bridge and between 23½in and 28in at Benar Road. Whilst substandard, he thought that for all practical purposes and taking train speed into account, they were acceptable. He

In operation from 14 October 1982, the Ffestiniog Railway Light Railway (Amendment) Order 1982 authorised the Glan y Pwll and Stwlan Dam crossings. Seen at the former, *Mountaineer* had been fitted with a Fairlie-style cab and electric headlights earlier in 1983. (Author)

The FR's Blaenau Ffestiniog Station was opened on 25 May 1982, the 150th anniversary of the company's act of incorporation. Seen from the BR platform in 1984, a train has just arrived and passengers climb the ramp to leave the station. Since the opening, the platform has been partially tarmacked and temporary second-hand portable buildings installed. Notice the peeling paint on the observation carriage.

did not need to mention that the formation had made provision for a second track to be installed between the Station and Glan y Pwll, in case the Dinas branch was ever reinstated to make a connection with the tourist enterprise based at Greaves' Llechwedd quarry.

In the Station, the buffer stop on the headshunt required strengthening he said. At the tightest point, which was near the buffer stop, there was approximately 20in clearance between the kinematic envelope and the boundary wall. The distance between the outer edge of the FR track and the outer edge of the nearest BR track was 89½in, about the minimum clearance required.

Olver was concerned that passengers arriving on one railway would cross the track to get to the other. He persuaded Garraway to have signs erected, similar to those already erected on the BR platform, reading 'passengers must not cross the line and must use the railway footbridge'. The FR platform would be single-sided on the side away from the BR tracks, with a tubular-steel boundary fence 4ft 6in high in the course of erection. The platform was a minimum of 2m wide throughout its length, widening to 4 or 5m in the area of the footbridge ramp. Meeting Peter Marston, Gwynedd County Council's deputy planning officer, he discussed methods of preventing members of the

public climbing over the footbridge and asked for a deterrent, sharp random slate, to be concreted onto the school wall to prevent or discourage children or others from climbing over or sitting on it. A strategy for preventing trespass from Benar Road was also agreed.

The first 'normal' train from Porthmadog to the new Station, described as a training train, was run on the evening of 23 May, with Allan Garraway at the controls of *Linda*. It carried staff and volunteers, and anyone who happened to be hanging around. 'Training' being considered completed on the way up, the buffet car was opened during the journey back to Porthmadog.

On 25 May, the 09.55 departure from Porthmadog terminated at Tanygrisiau. Invited guests took the 10.10 departure hauled by the 'new' Fairlie *Earl of Merioneth*. More invited guests travelled on the 12.00 from Blaenau Ffestiniog, which established a record by making the journey to Porthmadog non-stop in fifty-two minutes.

At the new Station, passengers found the facilities quite primitive. The platform, intended to be tar-macked, was crushed slate. There was no shelter. The booking office and a small shop counter were in 'Isallt', a house owned by the county council located next to the pedestrian entrance. Les Smith's doubts about its long-term suitability, expressed to the directors in

1980, soon proved to be correct. The footbridge, combined with its long platform access ramp, was quickly shown to be a bottleneck at busy times and its gradient too steep for wheelchair users. The nearest toilets were in the old Duffws station building.

The uPVC cladding of the locomotive water tank, mounted on the top of what was then called the 'locomotive facilities building', was not erected until the autumn. Located on the widened formation where the Newbororough slate mill branch had once joined the railway, the base had been designed to match that of the parcels office on the BR platform.

So did the Festiniog Railway return to Blaenau Ffestiniog. Despite the CEGB's assertion that use of public funds on reinstatement could not be justified, the planning department estimated that some £1,640,000, of public money had been spent on the new station. The main headings were: site preparation (£385,000); roads and car parks (£360,000); bridges (£210,000); BR costs (£200,000); accommodation works (£150,000); fees and supervision (£140,000); statutory undertakings (£135,000); land purchase (£35,000); and FR costs (£25,000).

Despite the shortcomings, and strikes by BR personnel objecting to flexible rostering proposals, the trains were busy and by the end of the year traffic was increased by 2 per cent, with most of the increase accounted for by transfers from BR. Sometimes as many as 200 passengers transferred from BR's 11.07 arrival. In July, the directors recorded that the strikes had cost an estimated £2,000 per week in lost revenue. The increase was not quite what it seemed, however, as it was 20 per cent less than the number carried in 1974, the peak year. Rail tour operators found that the new Station increased the railway's attractiveness as a destination and several tours had been accommodated. Two of the society's area groups joined together to run four trains using Pullman stock, whilst another ran a circular tour using two trains from the East Midlands, running one to Blaenau Ffestiniog, the other to Minffordd/Porthmadog, their participants making a single journey on the FR before returning home in the opposite direction.

During 1982 there were some improvements of a minor nature to facilities. In July, the sales kiosk previously at Dduallt, and at Tan y Bwlch before that, was moved to the foot of the ramp and during the winter the toilets from Tanygrisiau were also relocated to the platform. The FR became part of the Red Star parcels service on 9 August, another benefit of the direct connection to the national network; the logo was painted on brake van doors.

The water tanks were soon concealed from view, as intended. The overhead pipeline was soon deemed unnecessary and removed..

Dduallt was a token station until 1988. For a time, trains crossed here, too.

George Thomas MP, speaker of the House of Commons, performed the official opening on 23 April 1983. Before leaving Porthmadog, he shakes hands with the company's archivist, Michael Seymour, who had painted the headboard. (Author)

Two outstanding matters concerning the deviation came to the directors' attention in 1982-3. They agreed to pay £3,500 to farmer Aneurin Davies to settle his claims for land taken and disturbance since 1973, but had not reached a settlement with Rhys Davies over additional land taken near the spiral.

A second award was made by the Association of Railway Preservation Societies to the society on 29 January 1983, recognising the support given to the company in restoring services to Blaenau Ffestiniog. The 'year of restoration' was effectively brought to an end by the official opening of Blaenau Ffestiniog Station by George Thomas MP, speaker of

the House of Commons, on 30 April 1983. He travelled on the train from Porthmadog, unveiled a slate plaque that is still to be erected in a permanent building, waved off trains on both railways and signed the locomotive headboard that bore his crest.

The court circular of that day, published in *The Times*, recorded that company chairman John Routly had, the previous evening, hosted a dinner at Bwlch y Fedwen, Penmorfa, for Mr Thomas, where the guests had been William George, Chairman of Gwynedd County Council and nephew of the famous Liberal politician; Alan Pegler; Viscount Garnock; Bill Broadbent; Les Smith; Dick Hardy; society chairman Gordon Caddy; society vice-chairman Norman Pearce; Dick Wollan; and Allan Garraway.

On a day of celebration, it went unremarked that it was also Allan Garraway's last day in service as general manager. When he had attended his last board meeting on 18 March, tribute was paid to his thirty-two years' involvement with the railway, first as a volunteer, as manager from 1955 and as general manager from 1958. His support for the cause of minor railways, the Great Little Trains of Wales marketing panel and work for the North Wales Tourism Council were also acknowledged. As his successor had yet to be appointed, he continued as acting general manager for the time being.

With services resumed throughout the length of the railway, the directors turned their attention to its future and its appearance. An 'image committee' was appointed to consider the issues and consult with the society. Its report was accepted in 1983, with the directors noting that there should be no pictograms 'except disabled'; the styles of hats worn by guards and station staff should be subject to further review; that train staff should be encouraged to be cheerful and welcoming rather than just civil and helpful; and that the Fairlie locomotives should be used to symbolise the railway and play a prominent role in publicity. The society saw the priorities as marketing, tidying up the 'tatty' railway and fundraising for special projects.

A second series of Pullman excursion trains promoted by the company in 1983 was brought to an early end when the train was withdrawn following the discovery of asbestos in the stock. On the up side, the increase in ordinary connecting traffic caused British Rail to convert the 12.10 departure from Llandudno Junction to locomotive haulage.

Concerned about the need to encourage volunteering in the wake of the resumption of services to Blaenau Ffestiniog, in 1983 Michael Schumann devised a sponsorship scheme with assets then valued at £120,000 put into a fund held by the trust. Over the next ten years, projects supported included the restoration of various buildings and structures along the railway, and three four-wheeled carriages.

David Pollock was one of two candidates for the position of general manager introduced to the directors on 7 July 1983. A first-class honours engineering graduate who had occupied senior positions with the Westinghouse Brake & Signal Company and Hawker Siddeley, he took up the appointment on 4 August. Dick Wollan retired as chief executive on 30 September, whilst Allan Garraway continued acting as a consultant on a part-time basis, working on proposals for the 15in

gauge railway at the International Garden Festival held in Liverpool in 1984.

The first challenge faced by Pollock was dealing with a serious reduction in receipts, the combined consequence of recession and poor weather according to an item in the society magazine. In the annual report, John Routly informed shareholders that the effort in restoring the line was justified by the knowledge that 30 per cent of the traffic now originated from Blaenau Ffestiniog, but that there had been a 3 per cent reduction compared with 1982 and a trading loss of £45,898. This was not what had been expected.

In response, seven people were made redundant from positions not involved in train operation in September, and one more in October. This came as quite a shock and there was talk of withdrawing labour amongst some volunteers. The secretary of the FR staff representative committee wrote to the magazine to thank volunteers for their support. Without their efforts, he wrote, the service could not have been maintained and the company would have been in more trouble. A local councillor also gave notice that he would call for a public inquiry into the company's use of public money unless he received a satisfactory explanation about the redundancies.

The underlying problem was not just related to recession and weather, of course, but to the borrowing needed, despite the various grants and gifts, to build the tunnel and complete the railway's restoration, as shown in the table. The increase in the amount due to the sundry creditors also suggests that the company was taking longer to pay its bills; up to 1973 the figure had been less than £10,000. The society loans, which included loans from the area groups and members from 1979, were interest free and repayable on demand, the intention being that they should mitigate overdraft interest. Costs were reduced by running some trains diesel-hauled whilst the offer of free travel to children in family groups had boosted traffic if not revenue.

	1975	1976	1977	1978	1979	1980	1981	1982	1983	1984
Sundry Creditors £	49,272	97,192	85,222	84,234	72,040	68,725	64,937	48,927	36,311	46,197
Overdraft: National Westminster Bank £	20,000	50,000	180,000	230,000	210,000	174,000	165,067	146,255	117,134	80,760
Interest bearing loans £		4,295	3,740	3,241	2,656	57,545	20,560	21,000	3,000	3,000
Loan: FR Society £	9,000	9,000	9,000	6,500	18,500	40,700	11,850	18.300	114,497	123,572
	78,272	160,487	277,962	323,975	303,196	340,970	262,414	234,482	270,942	253,529
Interest paid £	2,283	5,705	14,717	26,423	37,767	41,683	26,828	28,116	22,807	14,398

Mountaineer climbing across the CEGB's private penstocks road crossing. Although the road was privately owned, the power station manager insisted that the crossing be equipped to the same standards applicable to the Stwlan Dam road crossing. The road was subsequently closed, but the crossing apparatus had to be maintained until 2 April 2015, when a level crossing order downgraded its status. (Author)

In 1984, work to strengthen the embankment was carried out by the National Rivers Authority using this tracked crane to lift 3-ton boulders from rail wagons. The exercise was not repeated in this manner.

With the focus removed from restoring the railway and extending services, the attention of some turned to the railway's heritage. Although there had been a museum display at Portmadoc since 1956, moved into the goods shed in 1979, little attention had been paid to historic structures or rolling stock beyond the restoration of carriage No. 16 by Ron Jarvis, the engineer responsible for the

Seen leaving Tan y Bwlch from the 'wrong' line, *Linda* was converted to burn coal on the gas producer principle in 1985, a response to rising oil prices. A change in prices the following year meant the change was short-lived although the Lempor draughting was retained. Its Hunslet chimney was also reinstated. (Author)

Whilst resources were concentrated on rebuilding and restoring the route to Blaenau Ffestiniog in the 1980s, the up line at Tan y Bwlch required relaying. As an interim measure, up trains were swapped over to the down line and a temporary water crane installed, here being used to replenish *Blanche*. The track was relayed in the winter of 1985-6 and operations reverted to normal, the water crane being removed in 1992. Locomotive water capacity had been increased by replacing the original tank with one taken from a road vehicle. A new tank, with even greater capacity, was commissioned in 1990. The building, which was originally at Hafod y Llyn, was apparently under threat from demolition in 1967, a society newsletter published in 1968 reporting that it 'was saved by society members from certain destruction last year'. It has since been the subject of conservation and restoration work.

rebuilding of Bulleid Pacifics for British Railways. When he had completed No. 16 in 1969, he started on four-wheeled carriage No. 5, completing it in 1983. He then took No. 6 (now No. 2) to his home at Llanbedr, where it was nearly completed when he died in 1994. He was meticulous in his work, emphasising the importance of using original construction techniques, and inspirational to the company about the way the heritage stock should be treated. With regards to No. 16, things could have been so different, for a plan dated 1957 has recently come to light sketching out how it could be converted to be a buffet car.

In this enlightened environment the heritage group was formed, launched in the spring of 1984. It was soon involved in re-arranging the exhibits in the goods shed museum, restoring carriage No. 10 and surveying the buildings at Tan y Bwlch. Under David Pollock's leadership, the company, too, adopted its heritage as something that could be beneficial to its bottom line, and heritage-based activities, events and restorations are now an essential part of its undertaking.

Reflecting the changes to the route caused by the deviation, a new gradient diagram was published in the society magazine in 1979. (Andy Savage)

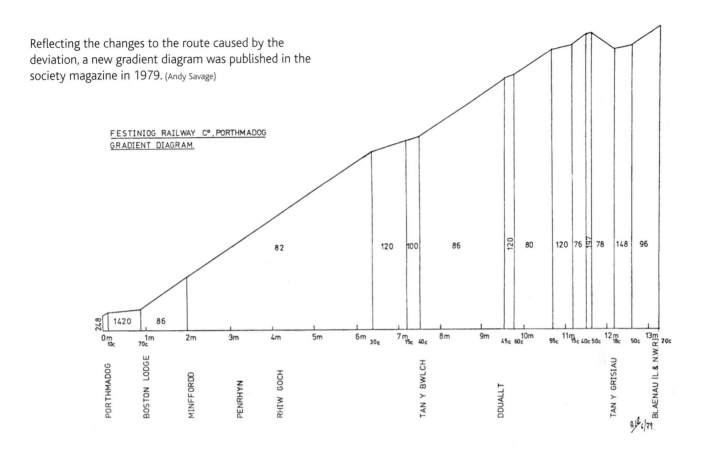

After a period on display outside the goods shed, in 1984 *Welsh Pony* was moved onto a plinth in the car park to promote the railway's presence. A second F was later added to the sign on the station building. (Author)

CHAPTER 10

1986-1991: 150 YEARS, AND THE WELSH HIGHLAND CONTROVERSY

Settling down under new management after so many years focused on the restoration of services to Blaenau Ffestiniog, attention turned to sorting out the financial position, tidying up the railway and putting on a big show to commemorate its 150th anniversary.

The latter was celebrated with a highly successful event over the weekend of 19-20 April. Exhibitions were laid on at Boston Lodge and Minffordd, a 7¼in gauge miniature railway at Tan y Bwlch and resident privately-owned Hunslet 0-4-0ST *Britomart* was joined by Leighton Buzzard Railway-based de Winton 0-4-0VBT *Chaloner* to shunt the wagons for gravity slate

The railway celebrated its 150th anniversary in several ways, but chiefly with a major event on 19-20 April 1986. Features included opening Boston Lodge to visitors, the operation of a miniature railway at Tan y Bwlch, demonstration gravity trains on Gwyndy Bank and a visiting steam locomotive, Alf Fisher's Leighton Buzzard Railway-based de Winton 0-4-0VBT *Chaloner*. The latter, which once worked at the Pen-yr-Orsedd Quarry, shared duties with resident privately-owned Hunslet 0-4-0ST *Britomart*, which was also a Pen-yr-Orsedd stalwart. *Britomart* and *Chaloner* are seen here with slate wagons, preparing for gravity to take over. The downside to the event was that the locomotive and operating volunteers supported it instead of their normal duties, costing the company an additional £3,000 in seasonal staff before the end of the summer. (Author)

train runs from Gwyndy to Minffordd, the first since the centenary of steam in 1963. The push-pull shuttle train ferried hundreds of visitors from Porthmadog to Boston Lodge, a facility not normally open to visitors.

Operating on vintage shuttles between Porthmadog and Minffordd, one of the major attractions was *Prince* repainted in the livery discovered when it was being overhauled during the 1970s. Approved by the directors on 10 January 1986, the work had been carried out under the aegis of the Heritage Group, a member encouraging a paint manufacturer to supply the materials required. The new livery had been launched on 24 April, when

In preparation for celebrating the railway's 150th anniversary in 1986, the Heritage Group arranged for *Prince* to be repainted in heritage livery, even organising the donation of paint.
(John Hunt)

The Tan y Bwlch road bridge was also brought into the celebrations, despite not being 150 years old, by being repainted, also with sponsored paint. Its deck had been replaced with reinforced concrete, whilst preserving the external appearance, the year before.
(Author)

When British Rail asked the company to participate in the launch of its Class 150 'Sprinters' on the Conwy Valley and the Cambrian Coast lines on 24 March, it was no surprise that *Prince* was chosen to represent the FR link, making its first public appearance in the new livery. Snow in March was not unusual in those days. (Author)

On 1 May 1986 John Routly named British Rail's Class 47 47 645 *Robert Fairlie Locomotive Engineer 1831-1885* at Blaenau Ffestiniog. Modern main-line diesel and electric locomotives are, of course, articulated. In addition to the nameplate, the loco was adorned with a cast version of the FR's 150th anniversary crest. (Author)

British Rail launched its Class 150 Sprinter trains on the Conwy Valley and Cambrian Coast lines.

Another heritage event saw the naming of a BR Class 47, No. 47 645 *Robert F. Fairlie Locomotive Engineer 1831-1885,* at Blaenau Ffestiniog on 1 May. John Routly performed the ceremony with

descendants of Fairlie in attendance. The climax of the year from a heritage perspective was a gravity train run on 3 November for visitors from other narrow-gauge railways. Comprised of seventeen slate wagons and three bogie Hudson wagons added to provide extra braking capacity, it ran from the

On 3 May 1993, Regional Railways' Class 37 No. 37 422 took over the name *Robert F Fairlie Locomotive Engineer 1831-1885*, previously carried by No. 47 645. General Manager Gordon Rushton unveiled the nameplates at Blaenau Ffestiniog.

On 3 November 1986 the company, hosting the narrow-gauge get-together' for employees of other narrow-gauge railways, operated a gravity train from the power station summit. At the end of the run, probably the longest since 1939, *Prince* fetched the wagons back across the embankment. The bogie wagons had been included in the formation in case additional braking power had been required. (Author)

summit near the power station and reached the home signal on the embankment.

The railway's contribution to the development of narrow-gauge railways had been recognised by the Institution of Mechanical Engineers on 9 April 1985, when a plaque was presented to John Routly in a ceremony at Porthmadog. In preparation for the event, members of the newly-formed parks and gardens group spent a weekend converting a strip of waste land at Minffordd Station into a garden. Fifteen tons of rubbish was removed, 2½ tons of manure applied and dozens of trees, shrubs and bulbs planted. This group eventually took on responsibility for tidying the lineside and the appearance of structures, which had

A last look at the FR's green locomotives/red carriages era which came to an end over the period covered by this chapter. Seen at Porthmadog, Hunslets *Linda* (left) and *Blanche* had become stalwarts since their acquisition in the 1960s, proving themselves very capable and versatile machines. (John Hunt)

Linda's driver whistles for Garnedd Tunnel, high above Llyn Mair. In a short time, the slope would be planted with conifers and the view obstructed. (John Hunt)

The barn next to the spiral became, and remains, a popular location for photographing the trains. *Merddin Emrys* was withdrawn for an overhaul, that would include cosmetic modifications, in September 1985. (John Hunt)

been much neglected during the 'back to Blaenau' years, under the name of 'detattyfication'.

Amongst some society activists there was a demand for change. Now that the railway's restoration had been completed, the society should have more say in how its money was spent instead of just handing it over to be spent as the company determined. At the AGM on 19 April 1986, therefore, Gordon Caddy, chairman since 1978, had retired and was replaced by Gordon Rushton. Bill Broadbent, one of the original society directors, had retired in 1984, but did not stand down as society nominee on the company board until 1986, preventing the society from nominating a successor until then; Andy Savage was his replacement. Broadbent remained a trustee and had been appointed a society vice-president in 1984.

The company board hosted a dinner to mark Allan Garraway's retirement on 20 March 1986, presenting him with an engraved decanter. Working a nominal two days per week since 1983, he had been excused from attending the office since the

Liverpool Garden Festival consultancy contract had been completed in 1984.

At Porthmadog, changes put in hand during the 1980s included installing a bar in the café; opening up the wall between the café and the museum; changing the shop layout to improve the flow of passengers through it; installing new gents' toilets; resurfacing the car park; paving part of the platform and erecting a canopy over it. The latter made a big improvement to the Station's capacity, as it meant that passengers would wait outside even when the weather was not so good.

In the booking office, a computerised ticket issuing system written in-house by a volunteer, Brian Bushell, had been introduced on 23 February 1985, pre-dating the national roll-out of British Rail's

In 1989 *Earl of Merioneth* was turned out in a revised green livery in an attempt to soften its angular appearance. Here, Ann Evans controls the fires as it leaves Minffordd. The carriages are in the *Mountain Prince* livery, which soon became the FR's standard colour scheme. (John Hunt)

APTIS system by more than a year. *The Times*, 7 May 1985, reported that a ticket could be issued in six seconds. Whilst some bemoaned the loss of the traditional Edmondson card tickets, booking clerks appreciated the ease with which the arithmetic and end-of-day calculations could be performed. The system attracted a lot of interest and was subsequently installed by the Romney, Hythe & Dymchurch, Brecon Mountain, Vale of Rheidol, Torbay Steam and Dart Valley Railways. The accountancy side was used by the Talyllyn Railway. From 1987, a railcard scheme allowed residents of Gwynedd and Clwyd to travel at reduced rates.

An automatic signalling installation was commissioned at Tan y Bwlch on 10 May 1987 and entered service the next day. Designed and built in-house, it allowed trains to cross without the use of a signalman. The sidings at the Porthmadog end of the Station were removed and replaced by others at the Blaenau Ffestiniog end. The signalling at Dduallt was decommissioned to eliminate the time taken to change tokens and make the published timetable achievable.

A new train service was launched on 25 May. Named the *Mountain Prince*, and hauled by *Prince* on the launch day, it was the 14.30 departure for Blaenau Ffestiniog and all seats, including third class, could be reserved. To distinguish it from the other services, a rake of carriages was painted in a new livery of red and ivory. Passengers, it turned out, did not want to reserve seats on the 14.30, but did want to reserve them on the off-peak 'early bird' train. The new livery, which had been approved by the directors on 14 November 1986, was liked so much that it was soon applied to most of the bogie stock.

This advertisement is not an invitation to subscribe for or purchase any shares or stock

THE FESTINIOG RAILWAY COMPANY

| Incorporated 23rd May 1832 | | Act 2 Will. IV cap. 48 |

OFFER FOR SUBSCRIPTION

of up to £400,000 4% Debenture Stock 2007/12 at par and up to £1600 Ordinary Stock at par

Sponsored by OCEANA ASSET MANAGEMENT LIMITED

(Members of the Stock Exchange)

★ A rare chance to invest in a unique railway company established by Act of Parliament in 1832.

★ The amount of Ordinary Stock available is limited by an 1869 Act of Parliament. In order to obtain this rare Ordinary Stock investors must also purchase a new issue of Debenture Stock in multiples of £250.

★ The Debenture and Ordinary Stock certificates have been designed to be similar to those issued by Victorian railway companies. The certificates will be limited in number and should be of interest to collectors.

★ The proceeds will be used to further the preservation of what is believed to be the world's oldest independent railway company.

★ Copies of the prospectus with an application form attached, on which basis only applications for Ordinary and Debenture Stock will be accepted may be obtained from the Booking Office at Porthmadog Station or Oceana Asset Management Limited, 16 Northgate Street, Ipswich, Suffolk IP1 3DB. Telephone: Ipswich (0473) 231342 (24 hour answering service).

The question of the borrowing was addressed by a combined share and debenture issue launched on 26 October 1987. The directors had first discussed the possibility of issuing some of the unissued capital in 1977, when they had decided that there was no need for it. Planning for the this scheme had started in 1985, with Oceana Asset Management Ltd sponsoring it for £7,500 and taking over management of the company's registry.

Subscribers for up to £400,000 2007/2012 4 per cent debenture stock were also allowed to subscribe for unissued ordinary stock in the ratio of £1 ordinary stock per £250 debenture. The purpose of the issue was to reduce short-term borrowing to release profits to be used to preserve and promote the railway's heritage; improve facilities at Porthmadog and Blaenau Ffestiniog; provide more covered accommodation at Boston Lodge; and a volunteers' hostel at Minffordd.

In addition to society members, who all received a copy of the high-quality thirty-two-page prospectus, the company hoped to generate interest from investors attracted by the idea of having a share in a nineteenth-century railway company. With interest at 9 per cent at the time of issue, the 4 per cent return on investment offered was not intended to be competitive although the rates did converge in 2001. The company's archivist, Michael Seymour,

To promote the debenture scheme to passengers, advertising cards were placed in carriages.

designed certificates reminiscent of the more ornate designs used on Victorian stock to appeal to collectors of such items.

With publicity in the national media, by the end of 1987 £158,200 had been subscribed, and the borrowing was reduced by £79,803. £269,500 was subscribed by 31 December 1989. One investor subscribed for twenty-five debentures (£6,250) to secure the £25 holding of ordinary shares that qualified him to vote at general meetings. No bank interest was paid in 1990, the first time the company had been in that enviable position since the First World War. Most of the investors did not claim their 4 per cent interest, either, the £10,780 annual liability averaging out at less than one third of that amount. In connection with the issue, attempts made to deposit the annual report with Companies House were rebuffed because the company was not registered.

The year ended with an air of satisfaction. There was progress on dealing with the debt, turnover exceeded £1 million for the first time, net profit was nearly doubled and the railway was named the

In the works for overhaul and restoration of Victorian features, required to operate post-Christmas trains in 1987, but with insufficient time to visit the paintshop, *Merddin Emrys* ran in black for a few days. With carriages in *Mountain Prince* livery, this was the scene at Rhiw Plas on 30 December. (Author)

With painting completed at Easter 1988, *Merddin Emrys* was also an attraction during Steam 125 gala in May. Features restored included curved edges to the tanks and circular smokeboxes replacing the 'D' shaped items supplied by Hunslet with the boiler. The rivets were fake. (Author)

independent railway of the year by publisher Ian Allan. A review in the society magazine noted that not only had traffic been 25 per cent below 1974 and 6 per cent below 1981, but that more people were travelling off-peak. In the 1970s, weekly passenger journeys would range from 1,500 in April and October to between 25,000 and 29,000 in August. In 1987 it had been rare for any week to drop below 4,000 or to exceed 20,000.

Michael Schumann's concerns about the smaller locomotives being altered to adapt them for work beyond their design capacity was not addressed, as

he had hoped, by the restoration of *Livingston Thompson* to working order. Instead, he contributed £100,000 for the restoration of original features to *Merddin Emrys,* which had been withdrawn for an overhaul in 1985. Its appearance had been rather brutally altered when it had been re-boilered and converted to oil firing in 1970. His offer was made on 1 January 1986 and accepted on 10 January. A contribution towards the cost of the overhaul was included in a Wales Tourist Board grant of £83,200, which also contributed to the cost of improving the toilets and installing the canopy at Porthmadog.

The loco was sufficiently complete to run the post-Christmas 1987 trains in a temporary black livery. Repainted in maroon Victorian livery, it was launched to an admiring public during the 'Steam 125' celebration of steam locomotives on the FR, held over the weekend of 30 April-2 May 1988.

It was overshadowed, though, by the appearance of Hunslet 2-6-2T *Russell*, the only surviving locomotive owned by the Welsh Highland Railway. Now owned by the WHR (1964) Company and restored to working order in 1987, it was equipped with vacuum brakes so that it could haul passenger trains as far as Rhiw Goch. On display at Boston Lodge was the partially-restored *Palmerston*, sold in 1974. Following a change in the locomotive's majority shareholding, it was now based at the FR for its restoration to be completed.

The directors were informed that some 4,000 visitors had attended the event. It had cost £19,000 including labour, which had been 'more or less' covered by revenue. There should be regular events from 1990, they decided, as they were beneficial

from the financial, local goodwill, publicity and staff and volunteer morale perspectives, but they should cost less to put on.

To boost volunteering input in train operation, David Pollock challenged the society to run a series of vintage trains, from preparation to disposal, on Saturdays during the summer of 1988. Hauled by *Prince*, the train included carriage No. 15 painted in a nineteenth-century livery, setting a precedent for the treatment of vintage stock in the future.

The overhaul of *Merddin Emrys* having released a set of bogies for *Livingston Thompson*, the society funded its restoration to display condition. A contractor undertook the work in Minffordd Yard and, on 16 October 1988, the loco was formally

On 9 April 1979 the Garratt was put on display at the National Railway Museum in York, company chairman John Routly formally handing it over to the keeper, John Coiley. The loco had benefitted from a cosmetic restoration carried out by museum staff. (Alan Bowler)

handed over to the National Railway Museum for display. The Garratt K1 had been loaned to the Museum in 1976, where it was restored for display in works grey livery.

Under the heading 'keep the wheels of history turning', from 1988 the trust raised its profile with a regular advertisement in the society magazine encouraging donations and bequests to be made in a tax-efficient manner. The advertisement's claim that the trust incurred no administrative costs was not quite true, as its expenses were paid by the company. Mike Hart, as company chairman, stopped this and the trust now pays its own way, its running costs of less than 2% comparing well with highly-regarded charities that spend 30 per cent or more on administration and fund raising.

Lack of maintenance over a long period and winter gales brought an end to the aptly-named 'long shed' at Boston Lodge in February 1989, twelve months after the directors had agreed to its demolition. Built in 1875 to store bogie carriages, since 1955 it had been used as the locomotive running shed. The inspection pit provided for that purpose remains in use, but with no protection from the elements for the locomotive crews.

A programme of capital improvements throughout the railway had a significant effect on its appearance from 1989. Named InCa (Increased Capacity), it followed a request from the Wales

After agreement had been obtained for the Garratt K1 to be restored by the Welsh Highland Railway Society for use on the WHR, it was withdrawn from the National Railway Museum and displayed in Minffordd Yard during the 'All Our Yesterdays' event in May 1995, then moving to Tyseley Locomotive Works for restoration to be started.

A view inside the goods shed, which in 1990 contained the museum and an extension to the *Little Wonder* café. The larger exhibits visible include the hearse van, complete with coffin, *Princess*, the horse dandy wagon and a wooden-framed slate wagon. (Author)

Tourist Board, which wished to promote Wales as an all-year-round tourist destination, to extend the operating Season. This attracted grants from the European Economic Community's national programme of community interest, for promoting tourism in Dyfed, Gwynedd and Powys, and the WTB itself. The awards totalled £430,000, then the largest made to the company.

At stations, Blaenau Ffestiniog was to get toilets, a sales kiosk and a canopy; Tan y Bwlch new toilets; and Porthmadog an improved connection between the café and museum. On trains, capacity would be increased by the provision of three new carriages capable of being used in the push-pull train; the *Earl of Merioneth* was to be rebuilt with a new boiler; and the permanent way department was to have a new locomotive. A two-road carriage shed was to be built in the Glan y Mor yard at Boston Lodge.

In development, the programme was modified in some respects. The new boiler, required as cracks had been found in *Merddin Emrys'* Hunslet boiler and it was not then known if they could be repaired

successfully, was used on a new locomotive. Carriages Nos. 117 and 121, built in 1977 and 1981 respectively, were refurbished to match the new stock and observation car/driving trailer No. 111, construction of which had been started in 1986, was brought in to the programme. In addition to the new toilets, the café at Tan y Bwlch was also extended.

The station works were all completed in 1990 and the Glan y Mor carriage shed the following year. The permanent way diesel locomotive was a modified Baguley-Drewry machine obtained in 1989 in part-exchange for the Peckett; it entered service in the spring of 1990 and was named *Harlech Castle/Castell Harlech* by the Secretary of State for Wales, David Hunt MP, and his daughter Daisy, in a

ceremony at Blaenau Ffestiniog on 24 April 1991. The locomotive transaction had been agreed by the directors on 4 November 1988.

Bodies of three new aluminium-clad carriages were built in Lancashire by Carnforth Railway Restoration & Engineering Services. Bogie construction and internal finishing, including

Funded by the InCa (Increased Capacity) scheme, the diesel locomotive *Harlech Castle/Castell Harlech* was built at Boston Lodge using some components made by Baguley-Drewry for a cancelled export order. It entered service with the permanent way department in May 1990. The photograph shows the loco with its train on the Tanygrisiau side of the tunnel, the 1836 incline running across the picture. Mess car No. 1111 is stood at the spot where the old dam was breached to make way for the deviation route.

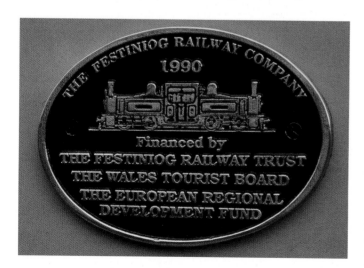

The naming of *Harlech Castle* took place during the operation of a 'thank you' train acknowledging the contributors to the InCa scheme. This plate was attached to the loco.

wiring, was carried out at Boston Lodge. Nos. 112 and 113, which each had a third-class saloon seating eighteen passengers and two four-seat first-class compartments, entered service in July and August 1991. No. 114 was a buffet car with a nineteen-seat saloon; it was delivered in 1991, but did not enter service until 1992. Fitted with gas heating and insulation for winter operations, these carriages, with Nos. 117, 121 and 111, were capable of being locomotive-hauled as well as operating in the push-pull train, distinguished from other stock by being painted in a green and off-white livery. As repairs to the 1960s-built timber-bodied stock became necessary,

During the 1960s it became clear that the original water supply and tank at Tan y Bwlch were inadequate to replenish locomotives working the intensive peak summer timetable. A larger tank recycled from a road vehicle was installed on a temporary basis in the 1970s, and construction of a much larger permanent tank plumbed to accommodate two locomotives was started in the 1980s. The latter was photographed a few months before it was completed in 1990. (Author)

In 1987 a retaining wall near Tanygrisiau collapsed. Seen in February 1990, its repair took several years. (Author)

they were rebuilt and modified to match the higher-quality internal finish of the Carnforth vehicles.

Along the line, the automatic signalling system at Minffordd had been commissioned on 18 March 1989, Rhiw Goch being closed as a staff station whilst remaining as an intermediate siding. When required all trains were crossed at Minffordd and/or Tan y Bwlch. A scheme for signalling Tanygrisiau to break up the long section between Tan y Bwlch and Blaenau Ffestiniog was mooted.

Boosted, perhaps, by the confidence attached to building a new locomotive in-house, the 'Taliesin 2000' scheme was launched to society members in April 1989. If a minimum of 200 would subscribe at

Earl of Merioneth passes the site of the former Blaenau Festiniog Station with eight carriages. Carriage No. 15, next to the loco, had been turned out in 'heritage' livery in 1989. The penultimate vehicle is No. 121, built with a steel body for the push-pull train. Its experimental push-pull train cream and green livery proved impractical, and the colours were reversed. (John Hunt)

The push-pull concept was developed to provide a heated train that could be operated all year round with minimal staff and time-saving from not having to run-round. Developed by Boston Lodge staff and volunteers, it was a part of the InCa (Increased Capacity) grant-aided project. Controlled from the driving compartment in No. 111, *Conway Castle* propels the push-pull train at Minffordd.

The bodies of three new carriages, Nos. 112-4, were made for the push-pull train by Carnforth Railway Restoration & Engineering Services in 1991. No. 114, the buffet car, awaits attention from the carriage workshop to complete it, on 16 May. (Author)

least £60 per year for ten years, then a new single Fairlie, a replica of the 0-4-4T *Taliesin* that had been withdrawn in 1932, could be built. The subscriber base was soon reached and construction was started in 1995. One of the promoters' objectives was to provide work, and an income stream, for Boston Lodge.

The Earl of Lindsay, who, as Viscount Garnock, had replaced Bill Bellamy on the company board in October 1962, died on 1 August 1989. A man with many useful contacts, he had started his career with the LNER before moving on to carpet manufacture and then other aspects of tourism. He was replaced by Mike Hart, an enthusiast running his own business in the railway industry, who had been a Boston Lodge volunteer at the age of sixteen and who had brought *Palmerston* back to the FR for its restoration to be completed.

In 1990, the company became caught up in a great controversy over the future of the Welsh Highland Railway, suffering huge reputational damage as a result. A society had been formed with the restoration of that railway as its main objective in 1961, registering a limited company, Welsh Highland Light Railway (1964) Company Ltd, in 1964. Negotiations with the liquidator and then the

Official Receiver, custodian of the railway's assets as the Welsh Highland Railway (Light Railway) Company was still in liquidation, and the county council having made no material progress, in 1975 the 1964 Company bought the former Beddgelert Siding site at Porthmadog from British Rail to use as a base for restoring the railway in due course. The Beddgelert Siding Light Railway Order was made in 1980 and services started on a 2ft-gauge railway constructed on that property. Negotiations for access to the trackbed beyond the 1964 Company's Pen y Mount terminus and Pont Croesor had followed without success although planning permission had been obtained.

On 20 July 1987, however, it was announced that Gwynedd County Council and Cyngor Dosbarth Dwyfor, the district council, had agreed that the WHR trackbed should be in public ownership to guarantee its integrity, despite the county council being unwilling to commit to releasing land beyond Pont Croesor until the 1964 Company's viability was assured. The council had also rejected a scheme to reconstruct the original WHR company proposed by a group of former 1964 Company members under the banner of a company they had formed called Trackbed Consolidation Ltd.

Conway Castle and the complete push-pull train crossing the embankment. The loco was painted in push-pull livery in 1991. (Author)

The council had agreed to contribute £250 towards the cost of obtaining a Light Railway Order extending the 1964 Company's railway to Pont Croesor and to apply to purchase the WHR assets, substantially the trackbed, from the Official Receiver for £1. The LRO application had been made on 8 January 1988, which must explain the brief minute recorded by the FR directors on 5 February 1988: 'Letter from Welsh Highland: The GM was asked to reply saying that the Ffestiniog had not objected, this being the view of the board.' On 11 March, David Pollock was further instructed to say that not objecting should not be interpreted as support.

At some point during 1987, though, some FR employees had become concerned about the effect on their jobs if the restoration of the WHR was started from Porthmadog in competition with the FR with the backing of the local authority. The employees' concerns reached the directors, who agreed that the FR should submit its own (confidential) bid for the trackbed. In September 1988 Les Smith and David Pollock were instructed to

have confidential discussions with the council's chief executive to establish whether the council and the company could co-operate on the WHR, revealing its interest if the discussions proved promising.

It seems that they told the chief executive that if the company was successful, it was prepared to convey the trackbed to the council with covenants preventing it from being used for railway purposes. The discussions were obviously not promising, for on 29 November 1989, the directors minuted their agreement to counter the council's £1 bid with an offer of £16,000, noting that, 'It was considered desirable for the company to have control over and an interest in the development of that railway.'

However, when it seemed likely that the Official Receiver was to obtain court approval to sell the trackbed to the council imminently, in December

1989 John Routly and Pollock met the council's solicitor and secretary with a revised position, saying, *inter alia*, that if the company secured the trackbed, it expected to lease sections of it to the 1964 Company to develop as a railway and would not permit non-railway development. They also pointed out that the council had contributed to the FR's restoration and therefore had an interest in the Company's wellbeing.

When news of the company's actions became public in January 1990, there was widespread criticism, not all of it well-informed. Not only were 1964 Company members upset, but so were railway enthusiasts in general and a vocal minority of FR Society members. A time-served solicitor and old-school politician, John Routly's response was to say nothing, which made the situation worse. On 31 January, the directors decided to rely on a letter Routly had sent to the council as a policy statement and say nothing more. Later, it was said that the reason for the secrecy, an aspect which had upset many, was to prevent a bidding war. Members and supporters of the 1964 company mounted a

A gala held in 1990 saw a return visit by Hunslet 2-6-2T *Russell*, the arrangement still going ahead despite the locomotive's owners, Welsh Highland Light Railway (1964) Company, having recently discovered that the FR Company had taken an interest in the development of the WHR trackbed. The iron Cleminson (articulated) wagon is on display outside the goods shed.

campaign portraying themselves as David battling Goliath, to try and get the company to back down.

In the society magazine, the Company justified its interest on the basis that Gwynedd County Council had commissioned a study showing that there was room for two railways in Porthmadog; that anyone was free to bid for the trackbed; that the 1964 Company had accepted the need for a landlord, surely another railway company would be better than a local authority with other priorities; and the FR would be seen as complacent if it did not take an interest in the development of another railway on its doorstep. At first, the company insisted on vetting anything published on the subject in the society

Following an extensive mechanical overhaul completed in 1991, *Linda* was repainted midnight blue and fitted with a removable cab section on its tender. Soon afterwards, it was seen being prepared for service at Boston Lodge. (Author)

magazine, but came to accept the publication of letters objecting to the company's involvement as well as those supporting it.

Faced with the 1964 Company saying that it did not want the FR to be its landlord, sometime during 1990, though the decision was not formally recorded, the company decided that if it was successful in its bid for the trackbed it would restore the railway itself, the directors having realised that reconstructing and operating the WHR would expand the FR's business without increasing its overheads pro rata. Doing so, however, would depend on securing gifts and grants to pay for the capital work, avoiding the debt that had undermined the original railway. This account is perforce perfunctory.

The directors' unhappiness with the society magazine's editorial approach, which had been festering away since 1982, came to a head in 1990.

Editor Dan Wilson had acquired a reputation for writing editorials suspected of containing hidden meanings, which probably existed more in the reader's mind than in his, but the directors had made several attempts to control what was said. An alleged libel of Alan Pegler in an editorial gave them the opportunity they needed, with Pegler apparently threatening to resign his position of society president. Wilson resigned instead and was replaced by the author, the directors noting the outcome on 30 May.

On the railway, *Linda* was returned to service after a major overhaul carried out over the winter of 1990-1.

The automation of Minffordd level crossing was completed in October 1991. (Author)

Drivers who wanted it could make use of a removable aluminium cab made to be mounted on its tender.

The year 1991 ended with automation of the level crossing at Quarry Lane, Minffordd, otherwise known as Lottie's, after a former keeper. A level crossing order authorising the installation had been made on 13 June 1986 and effective since 1 May 1987. Although work had been started in 1988, it had been subject to interruption. The gates were finally removed in between trains on 28 October. Major Olver had inspected the site on 5 November and submitted his report on 13 January 1992. He was concerned that the order required the crossing to be actuated either by track circuits or treadles, but the railway had used rail circuits that

would not fail safe. He asked the company to consider the matter most seriously, to either install treadles to back-up the rail circuits or to change the rail circuits to track circuits, which he recognised would require considerable rewiring. Treadles were installed. Olver also seemed bemused that standard bilingual signs had been altered to give priority to the Welsh version. It had been intended to automate Penrhyn crossing at the same time, but the application was withdrawn in response to objections from residents.

CHAPTER 11

1991-1997: LEGAL AND LOTTERY SUCCESSES, AND NEW LOCOMOTIVES

The Welsh Highland Railway affair cast something of a shadow over the events of the 1990s, but the validity of the company's cause was eventually accepted by the majority. The High Court hearing of the Official Receiver's request to sell the WHR trackbed to Gwynedd County Council for £1, started on 11 November 1991 and lasted for four days. With its costs underwritten by a sponsor keen to see the WHR restored under FR control, the company applied to be heard with its proposal to reconstruct the 1922 company, and validate the transfer of shares and debentures acquired by Trackbed Consolidation Ltd, a group of former 1964 Company members, to prevent the sale of the assets to the county council and to authorise their sale to the FR.

In his judgment delivered on 20 December 1991, Mr Justice John Vinelott ruled that the application to register transfers and revive the 1922 company was 'wholly misconceived', but he went to say that the FR ought to have the opportunity of exploring other avenues in pursuit of its objective to restore the Welsh Highland Railway. There was nothing to stop the FR Trust, or some other supporter, from applying for a Light Railway Order to transfer the WHR undertaking to the FR, for example. The merits of restoring the railway would then be a matter for the Secretary of State for Transport, following an application for the powers required. He therefore dismissed the FR's application and stayed the official receiver's application to sell the assets to the county council in order to give the FR an opportunity to explore other avenues of acquiring the assets.

Whilst the judgment was seen as being hugely embarrassing and a slap in the face for the company in some quarters, it actually provided the key to the impasse that surrounded the future of the Welsh Highland Railway.

Another legal issue, that had its origins in the 1968 light railway order and the deviation, had been brought to a satisfactory conclusion on 4 March 1991, when the Secretary of State for Transport made the Ffestiniog Railway (Light Railway) (Abandonment) Order 1991, releasing the company from any obligation to maintain or operate 28 chains of the former route north of Dduallt Station. The 1968 order had required the land concerned to be conveyed to the adjacent landowner. Anyone who had seen the notice in the *London Gazette* on 12 February 1990 might have been quite shocked to read 'Application to abandon Ffestiniog Railway Company'.

An administrative change that arose from the Welsh Highland controversy was the purchase of an off-the-peg company named Bealaw (284) Limited by the trust. On 21 February 1991, it was renamed Ffestiniog Railway Holdings Ltd. This development had occurred because some objectors had complained that the company was acting *ultra vires*, beyond its powers, and had threatened to take legal action. At first, the directors were those of the FR Company and it only dealt with WHR business. In 1992 the company's travel business was sold to it for £96,000 and this eventually became the company's prime focus. Its profits are covenanted to the trust; for several years it provided booking office services to the company.

Traffic initiatives introduced in 1992 included shuttle services to Minffordd and evening excursions to Tan y Bwlch for passengers to be entertained by a jazz band. For five days in May

Funded by the InCa scheme, *David Lloyd George* was the fourth 'bogie engine' built at Boston Lodge, making its first appearance on passenger trains on 21 July 1992, when photographed running round at Porthmadog. The full extent of the platform canopy erected in 1987 is visible.

the shuttle service was operated in the afternoons, some using the push-pull set, the others offering steam haulage and vintage carriages. In order that it could stand in the platform at the same time as an 'ordinary' train, the fence separating the railway from the embankment footpath was removed and the platform extended. The £2.50 fare included a voucher giving a 50p reduction on the Blaenau Ffestiniog fare. The service was judged a success, with many passengers travelling on both services. The jazz trains ran on four evenings in July and August, and continue to feature in the railway's programme.

Locomotive fuel was changed during 1992, clean gas oil being substituted for waste oil, resulting in improved reliability. As a means of reducing costs, volunteers had been collecting waste oil for more than twenty years, but it had become inconsistent in quality and required excessive handling.

In his statement distributed to shareholders on 1 August 1992, John Routly announced that after forty years he and Les Smith had decided that it was

time to retire from the board. They were much older than their colleagues and tensions that existed within the board probably arose from personalities as much as any other issue. Les Smith, therefore, retired at the company AGM on 16 September 1992. A surveyor and valuer by profession, he had dealt with the company's property issues and had managed the light railway order applications. On 12 June 1993, he was appointed a member of the Order of the British Empire, (MBE) for services to the company, in the Queen's birthday honours. Michael Schumann replaced him as a director.

In operational matters, the Company accepted the society's recommendation that the locomotive built around the boiler at first intended for *Earl of*

Finished and painted during the 1992/3 winter, *David Lloyd George* ran for a few weeks in 1993 with its nameplates covered. It was named by local solicitor and politician, William George, nephew of the politician, at Tan y Bwlch on 16 April.

Merioneth should be named *David Lloyd George*, a name with significance locally and which resonated with many visitors, on 25 September 1991. The author was amongst those who spoke against it being named *Earl of Snowdon*, proposed to create an Earl class of locomotives. *Charles Spooner* was another name considered.

The boiler was made by Bloomfield Steel Construction, in Tipton, Staffordshire, and was tapered to strengthen the join between the barrels and the firebox, and overcome the weaknesses in the Hunslet boilers. It was also constructed to operate at 200psi instead of the 160psi of the older boilers and also had twice the amount of superheating. Welded tanks were fitted with false rivets to age the locomotive's appearance.

In temporary black livery and without its cab roof, *David Lloyd George* entered service on 22 July 1992, having made three trips to Blaenau Ffestiniog previously. It was finished over the winter and named by William George, the politician's nephew, in a ceremony at Tan y Bwlch on 16 April 1993. The fourth 'bogie engine' built by the company, it brought David Pollock's InCa programme to a satisfactory completion.

Pollock was not there to enjoy the fruits of his labours, though, for he had 'retired' on 31 July 1991. Responding to an economic downturn in 1990 and taking a pessimistic view of traffic prospects in 1991, he had put in place a reorganisation at the end of 1990 that included five posts being made redundant. In an explanation published in the society magazine, he paid tribute to those who had lost their jobs, describing the contributions they had made to the railway. He received five months' salary as severance pay. On 29 August the directors awarded him a 10 per cent salary increase backdated to 1 January 1990, so perhaps there was a feeling of guilt about the way he had been treated.

He had joined the company at a difficult time and had stabilised its finances; he once suggested to the author that he felt he had been misled about the company's financial health when he had been appointed. The railway had been run-down from years of neglect whilst attention had been devoted to completing the deviation and restoring services to Blaenau Ffestiniog. He smartened it up, improving facilities at Porthmadog, Tan y Bwlch and Blaenau Ffestiniog stations, and starting the move away from standard liveries on locomotives and rolling stock. His InCa scheme produced long-lasting benefits.

Although he admitted that he could not understand why anyone should volunteer, planning

Two 'traditional' Fairlie locomotives were seen together for the first time in many years during the May 1993 event that celebrated the centenary of *Linda* and *Blanche*. The colour and front end of *David Lloyd George* had been made deliberately different from *Merddin Emrys* to make them easily distinguishable, although loco crews find the longer smokebox grab handles on *Merddin Emrys* more comfortable to use when steam has been raised.

David Lloyd George passing the 1863 water tank as it nears Dduallt on 18 October 1999.
(John Hunt)

Sgt. Murphy was a Kerr, Stuart 'Haig' 0-6-0T built in 1918 and which had been owned by the Penrhyn slate quarries. Acquired by general manager Gordon Rushton, it was rebuilt as an 0-6-2T and brought to the railway in 1993. It was photographed at Tan y Bwlch during an evening excursion for the society board on 3 April.

for the new Minffordd Hostel was started under his regime, but Gordon Rushton, the society chairman, remembers difficulties dealing with him over the use of and recruitment of volunteers. His attempt to improve the efficiency of Boston Lodge by separating operations from maintenance and new works both administratively and physically, which also meant that the works were closed to volunteers at weekends, was short-lived. The staff, mostly, did not understand him as he was rather shy, so unlike Allan Garraway. He also believed in letting the managers manage, which they were not used to. He died on 29 September 2015, aged ninety.

Without advertising, Gordon Rushton, a marketing officer in British Rail's Sealink ferries division, was appointed to take over on 1 August. Originally a traffic volunteer, he had been elected to the society board in 1979 and replaced Gordon Caddy as chairman in 1986. On 20 October 1990, the trustees noted that a new philosophy in the way the railway was run had been adopted; in future it would be marketing led rather than product led. Peter Jordan, an accountant and travel agent, replaced Rushton as society chairman.

Rushton found parts of the railway to be rather cliquish. Being particularly keen to remove the

mystique that surrounded locomotive operations, he bought his own locomotive, Kerr, Stuart 'Haig' 0-6-0T *Sgt. Murphy*, which had worked on the Penrhyn system, to use on excursions and during events.

The Minffordd shuttle and the jazz trains, already mentioned, were amongst his innovations. He also initiated a series of events, the first of which, 'Hunslet 100', sub-titled 'a steam festival', celebrated the centenary of *Linda* and *Blanche* over three days, 1-3 May 1993. They were joined by their 1882-built 'brother' *Charles* from Penrhyn Castle Museum, as a static exhibit, and seven other quarry Hunslets. A grant enabled the event to be extended into the harbour with visits from a steam tug and a steam dredger. It was a great success and is still fondly remembered at the time of writing. First held in June 1993, the vintage weekend remains a popular feature of the timetable, albeit transferred to the autumn.

Out of service since 1989, *Blanche* had been subject to a volunteer-led overhaul completed just a few days before the event. Another volunteer team had finished *Palmerston* in time to participate, too, and *Sgt. Murphy* also made an appearance. Ex-Penrhyn Hunslet 0-4-0ST *Lilla*, which had been based at the Bala Lake Railway, never went home

The biggest event of 1993 was a gala celebrating the centenary of the Hunslet duo, *Linda* and *Blanche*, on 1-3 May. For a few minutes each day they were posed alongside their older sibling, *Charles*, which had been borrowed from the National Trust collection at Penrhyn Castle. Still retaining its Penrhyn gauge, *Charles* (left) was very restricted in its movements.

A new event added to the calendar in 1993 was the vintage weekend, promoting the railway's heritage, which proved extremely popular. Lined out in traditional manner, *Palmerston*, then newly restored, was one of the first attractions.

Prince with one of the early vintage weekend goods trains, emerging from the short tunnel. (John Hunt)

and in 1997 was purchased by the FR Trust with funds, £1,500, provided by a group established to support it on the FR.

The Society was dragged into the Welsh Highland Railway dispute by a special meeting called by twelve members who proposed two motions, that the society dissociate itself from the attempts to obtain possession or control of the WHR trackbed and that the Society called upon the company, trust and holdings company to refrain from further

attempts to acquire it. The meeting was held in advance of the society's general meeting held in Blaenau Ffestiniog on 2 May. In a statement published in the society magazine, society chairman Peter Jordan called for members to reject the

Merddin Emrys passes Dduallt Manor with a mixed train. (John Hunt)

Restored to its 1920s condition, the Simplex tractor is seen at Penrhyn recreating the delivery of flour to the nearby bakery.

1993 was really the year of the locomotive, although not described as such. *Palmerston*, still in private ownership, had returned to the railway in 1988 and was steamed for the first time on 14 February 1993. *Prince*, moving alongside, produced a sight not seen for more than fifty years, two England locos in steam.

Palmerston became the most travelled member of the FR fleet in 1994, when it visited the Chemin de Fer de Chanteraines in Paris in June.

motions, saying that they were inspired by 1964 Company members.

In his report of the meeting, society secretary David Gordon said that the overwhelming view of those present was that restoration of the WHR was a good idea, providing it was done without using FR money, putting the FR at risk or diluting the FR's volunteer effort. The resolutions were rejected by 1,164 to 90 and 1,172 to 77 respectively. What the sponsors appeared not to have understood was that even if their motions had been supported by the society, they would not have been binding on the company.

The Association of Railway Preservation Societies, of which the society was a member, also appeared not to understand the difference between the society and the company when it had allowed a censure motion against the society to be tabled in 1991; it was eventually suspended and not put to the vote.

Construction of the thirty-two-bed hostel at Minffordd, to replace ex-deviation portable buildings re-located there in 1978 as an overflow for Penrhyn Hostel, was started with a first-sod ceremony on 2 May 1992. The work was carried out by a mix of contractors and volunteer labour, working under the auspices of the parks and gardens department with funding from the society. In 1993, a £30,800 Wales Tourist Board grant contributed to its cost, and the construction of a new passenger diesel locomotive.

The next day, 3 May, a reception at Penrhyn station marked the completion of a major renovation of the Station that had started two years earlier. The station building was restored to match the appearance shown in the photograph taken by R. H. Bleasdale in 1887, including reinstatement of the chimney stacks. The goods shed and store also received attention, and the platform paving was restored and extended. The wagon turntable outside the goods shed was also reinstated without being connected to the running line. Some 180 guests, including neighbours whose houses overlooked the Station, were taken to Tan y Bwlch by special train for refreshments in the newly-extended café.

Expected reductions in the Conwy Valley line services, or even its closure, following rail privatisation, prompted the company to consider taking it over on a micro-franchise basis in May 1993. On 20 August, the *Cambrian News* reported that

joint marketing had led to a 63 per cent increase in 'through ticket' travellers using both railways, but this was expected to be lost if the standard-gauge service was reduced as expected. Despite the support of Gwynedd County Council for the venture, it proved impossible to have the branch line separated from the national network in the manner proposed.

Two B-B diesel locomotives built by C. H. Funkey & Co in 1957 were delivered from South Africa to Minffordd on 16 October 1993, the first locomotives bought for the Welsh Highland Railway. More than twice as powerful as any of the existing FR diesel locomotives, they had 350hp Cummins diesel engines that had seen very little use since being installed in 1984. As built, they were too big for the FR loading gauge. They cost £5,000 plus £6,000 shipping each.

Progress on the Welsh Highland Railway development came with the publication of notices of the applications for the Welsh Highland Railway (Transfer) Light Railway Order and the Caernarfon Light Railway Order in the *London Gazette* on 23 October and 23 December 1992 respectively. The former was in response to the suggestion that the WHR assets could be transferred by means of an application under the terms of the 1896 Light Railways Act; the application was made by the FR trust and the holdings company jointly. The latter was to extend the WHR over the trackbed of the former Carnarvonshire Railway branch from Dinas to the site of the former LNWR station in Caernarfon; this application was made by the holdings company.

Gwynedd County Council and the 1964 Company also made applications, notices of which were published on 18 December. The proposed Welsh Highland Railway (Gwynedd County Council) Light Railway Order would provide for the transfer of the assets to the council and empower it to lease the railway, or any part, to any person, whilst the Caernarfon Light Railway Order provided for any lessee to construct and maintain a railway 80m from the southern end of the tunnel under the town to Dinas. A public inquiry was held to assess the merits of the schemes, whether they were in the public interest and who should have the powers if they were, in November and December 1993.

Ashbury carriage No. 23, built for the North Wales Narrow Gauge Railways in 1894 and

Originally a Welsh Highland Railway Ashbury carriage, No. 23 was rebuilt in 1992 and turned out in WHR livery early in 1993, a photograph of it being used to promote the launch of the WHR Society.

transferred to the FR from the WHR in 1937, was overhauled in 1992 and turned out in WHR livery, complete with original WELSH HIGHLAND RAILWAY iron branding to promote the launch of the Welsh Highland Railway Society, in the spring of 1993. Whilst it added to the FR's fleet of vintage carriages in authentic liveries, the development was seen as being particularly provocative in some quarters. The WHRS was established by members of Trackbed Consolidation Ltd to support the FR's attempts to revive and restore the WHR.

The company's estate was increased in 1993, with the purchase of the Urdd (youth) building and land next to the station at Minffordd for £14,000. The building is used as a workshop for the parks and gardens department, and the land for car parking.

As announced the year before, FR Company chairman John Routly retired from the board at the company AGM on 19 May 1993. He had managed the change-of-control of the company for Alan Pegler and had been determined that it should be compensated for the land taken by the CEGB for the power station, and that the railway should be restored to Blaenau Ffestiniog. He had also played a large part in persuading public bodies that the railway should benefit from more than £1 million in grant aid to achieve this objective. Remaining as

chairman of the FR Trust, he was replaced by Mike Hart as company chairman and by George Nissen as a director. Nissen had been a member of the stock exchange from 1956 until 1992, and was the chairman of the Investment Management Regulatory Organisation and a publisher. His appointment followed an exploratory lunch on his interest in taking a directorship in a Victorian railway company with Sir William McAlpine.

Delivery of the three carriages built by Carnforth Railway Restoration & Engineering Services in 1991 had been followed by a claim for further payment, although concerns over quality had been reported to the directors in May 1990. The claim, and a counter-claim for £14,000, went to arbitration at the Institution of Mechanical Engineers in 1994, the company being awarded £8,000, the claimant paying the £1,800 arbitrator's fees, in May. The contribution of solicitor member Stephen Murfitt to the successful claim was acknowledged by the directors.

The public inquiry inspector's report and the ministerial decision on the Welsh Highland Railway light railway order applications were released on 20 July 1994. The inspector concluded that the reconstruction of the WHR was in the public interest, and that the orders should be made in favour of the council and the 1964 Company because the 1964

The 'All Our Yesterdays' event in 1995 was linked to the fiftieth anniversary of VE Day, and extended the railway's international relations with the visit of this unmodified Alco 2-6-2T from the Chemin de Fer de Froissey in northern France and other locos from France. The French machine is seen passing the FR's much-altered Alco, *Mountaineer*. A reciprocal visit was made the following year.

Company had a good level of support from the local authorities that increased the possibility of public funding, its Porthmadog site had advantages, the company would be dedicated to rebuilding the WHR, and therefore not distracted by other matters, and its democratic form of control would attract more volunteers.

The Secretary of State, however, rejected these arguments, saying that the inspector had placed too much weight to the role of the local authorities as facilitators of railway infrastructure schemes and too little on the benefits of placing responsibility for such matters entirely within the private sector. The council/1964 Company scheme would result in direct local authority involvement and result in contingent liabilities and risk being placed on local tax payers when, consistent with [Conservative] Government policy, they should be transferred to the

private sector. The transfer order was made on 14 March 1995. It only allowed for the transfer of the assets; reconstructing the WHR would be dependent on a successful application under the 1992 Transport & Works Act.

A project to build a replica of the last Lynton & Barnstaple Railway Manning, Wardle 2-6-2T *Lew* came under the wing of the trust and the railway in 1995; the directors had given it their approval on

Despite *Mountaineer* being painted in War Department livery 'for the event' it was not repainted for three years. It was seen at Tanygrisiau on 29 December 1995.

The Reverend W.V. Awdry, writer of the popular *'Thomas the Tank Engine'* stories, was an early member of the society so it was quite appropriate that 'Friends of Thomas' should be hosted by the railway. After a trial in 1995 they ran for several years before conditions attached by the rights holders became too onerous.

The fortieth anniversary of the first public train since the change of control in 1954 was celebrated in July 1995. Photographed with the Simplex and *Prince* were Eric Cooper, who drove the Simplex in 1955, Allan Garraway, Les Smith and Alan Pegler.

24 November 1994. It had been started by railway enthusiast James Evans at his home in Cornwall several years before, to satisfy his curiosity about what the LBR locomotives were like to operate. He had made or accumulated components, including the frames, of a locomotive that he named *Lyd*, valued at £30,000. On the FR, the project and its fund raising, which included several successful guest engine-driving programmes, were managed by Paul Lewin.

At Rhiw Goch, the signalling, which had been switched out for several years, was refurbished by a volunteer team and recommissioned on 12 April 1995, enabling the company to be more flexible in its timetabling, although at the expense of providing a (volunteer) signalman.

To explain their plans for the Welsh Highland Railway, the directors invited thirty-five members of Gwynedd County Council and other local authorities on its route to a reception at Tan y Bwlch Station on 21 July 1995. They were told that to build the railway between Caernarfon and Rhyd Ddu would cost £9.1 million and that an application had been made to the Millennium Commission for a 50 per cent grant. The railway was expected to be opened by 31 December 1999. A bilingual glossy brochure about the project was given to the guests

and distributed from a display set up in the castle square at Caernarfon, with *Blanche* as its focus, on 21-22 July.

On 22 July, the directors marked the fortieth anniversary of the first trains under the current regime with a reception at Porthmadog and a special train. Allan Garraway made his first visit to the railway since his retirement in 1983. The operation of the recreated first train was delayed by the carriages concerned being stabled in an inaccessible location. The occasion also marked the retirement of Mark Wright as company clerk; he was presented with a cut-glass decanter. The directors, having decided that they needed access to legal advice, had appointed their legal adviser Stephen Murfitt in his stead. Wright, a society member since the 1950s, was upset by his removal from office, accepting it with good grace, but not visiting the railway since.

The new passenger diesel locomotive was named *Criccieth Castle/Castell Criccieth* by William George on 29 September 1995. Mechanically similar to the permanent way department's *Harlech Castle*, it incorporated some components made by Baguley-Drewry Ltd for a cancelled export order and a 140hp Caterpillar diesel engine, the first time the FR had ever bought a new engine for an internal-combustion locomotive. The locomotive

Criccieth Castle was another grant-aided diesel locomotive. Built at Boston Lodge, it was specified to be capable of hauling trains of six carriages in push-pull mode. It was named by William George, seen here with director Hugh Eaves, on 29 September 1995.

was rated for six cars and was equipped for push-pull working.

News about the Millennium Commission application for Welsh Highland Railway funding was received on 2 October, with the announcement of a £4.3 million award. This was quite a coup, as the company did not have any authority to rebuild the WHR; rules were subsequently put in place that required any relevant permissions to be obtained before an application is submitted.

To facilitate the purchase of rail and other equipment from South Africa for the WHR during 1995, Michael Schumann lent the company £150,000. The other directors joined him in supporting the company in this way and in 1996 their loans totalled £753,000; subsequently most of the loans were converted into gifts. A new subsidiary of the company, Welsh Highland Light Railway Ltd, was registered to manage the project on 7 May 1996 and WHR expenditure was made by it.

A Government-funded strategic development scheme had been put in place to mitigate the effects of the closure of Trawsfynydd Nuclear Power Station in 1991. In 1995, the FR secured a £500,000 to fund a package designed to enable the company to expand its business at its inland terminus. Works included replacing the access ramp with steps,

constructing a pedestrian route from the car park to the platform, extending the canopy and installing a second platform at the station, providing a carriage shed at Glan y Pwll, and a signalled passing loop at Tanygrisiau. A permanent way mess carriage was also included in the package. By a remarkable dint of negotiation, the grant represented 100 per cent of the capital cost of the projects concerned.

Despite a 1 per cent increase of traffic in 1995, the company made an operating loss of £41,629; the overdraft had more than doubled to £229,036 as well. Analysis of expenses focused on the cost of employment, about half of the turnover at £750,000, and a projected budget shortfall of £70,000. General manager Gordon Rushton informed employees that pay cuts or redundancies were needed to achieve a 5 per cent reduction on the wages bill. Seven posts were identified for termination. Two, one from the permanent way department and one from the carriage workshops, were made redundant from 21 November; two contracts were not renewed; one employee had already left; a temporary employee was dismissed; and another employee was expected to retire in 1996.

The Liverpool office of the National Union of Rail, Maritime & Transport Workers circulated a press release linking the redundancies with projected profits

On 2 October 1995 the Millennium Commission announced that it would make a grant of £4.3 million to the company towards the restoration of the Welsh Highland Railway between Caernarfon and Rhyd Ddu. The commission's representative handed over the symbolic cardboard cheque to Mike Schumann, with Alan Pegler and Gordon Rushton in attendance.

Coincidentally, work to 'strengthen' the Britannia Bridge, which entailed demolishing the extension constructed by McAlpine in 1923 to carry junction railway No. 1 towards the Welsh Highland Railway, and replacing the entire deck, was started just before the Millennium Commission's grant for the WHR was announced. The new deck proved to be suitable for accommodating the Welsh Highland Railway track in due course on 3 November 1995.

David Lloyd George runs past the new Minffordd Hostel on 8 June 1996, a few weeks after a part of it had first been occupied by volunteers. The building's construction was carried out by a mix of contractors, employed staff and volunteers.

of £85,000 for 1996. It also claimed that the net loss of jobs was seven, two redundant, three from retirement and illness, and two temporary maintenance positions utilised the year before and not replaced. It also claimed that the company had refused a meeting and stated that the staff had voted in favour of industrial action, which the *Cambrian News*, reporting on 24 November, interpreted as a threat to strike.

The paper also observed that the company had received £450,000 from Cyngor Dosbarth Meirionnydd and £90,000 from Cyngor Dosbarth Dwyfor. Rushton replied that whilst full use was being made of the grants, there was no alternative to the redundancies in view of the efforts being made to generate an operating surplus. The Meirionnydd grant was designed to attract more traffic to Blaenau Ffestiniog and the Dwyfor grant, £30,000 a year for three years, was for marketing additional events.

Responding to the NURMTW release in a circular to staff on 22 November, Rushton explained that despite 10 per cent fewer visitors to Wales, the railway had managed a 1 per cent increase in traffic whilst other attractions had seen up to 15 per cent

reductions. He added that the union's request for an organiser to attend a consultation meeting had been approved, but the organiser had not attended. He concluded by observing that when NURMTW members had agreed to pursue a 5.1 per cent pay rise in September, their chairman, asked to prioritise posts or pay levels, had answered pay levels. The threat of action faded away.

The directors evidently felt that stronger action was required to stabilise the company and on 13 February considered the general manager's position. They noted that under Rushton's management, the appearance of the railway was considerably improved, that volunteer numbers were considerably increased, and that income had been maintained during a period of decline in North

Wales tourism, but were unable, for several reasons, to give him their support. On 16 February 1996, they announced that he would be replaced as general manager by Alan Heywood, the former traffic and commercial manager, who had been concentrating on developing the travel business since 1991.

Charged with maintaining a stable enterprise and matching the travel company's £39,000 profit, Heywood's strategy was responsible for the 'New railway boss puts brakes on gravy train' headline in the *Daily Post* on 7 May. He had reduced the staff discount on shop purchases, introduced a £100 minimum charge on special trains run to celebrate staff and volunteers' birthdays, and imposed diesel haulage on the Minffordd shuttles. He exceeded his target with a 1996 profit of £94,799, when traffic receipts exceeded the landmark figure of £1 million for the first time.

Local government reorganisation and the creation of Gwynedd Council as a unitary authority from 1 April 1996, affected the railway insofar as it absorbed Cyngor Dosbarth Dwyfor, the last area in Wales to impose Sunday closing on public houses under the terms of the Sunday Closing (Wales) Act 1881 and the Licensing Act 1964. The abolition of Dwyfor, which included Porthmadog, also removed the licensing restriction. For more than 30 years, Sunday trains had

been busy carrying residents who wished to quench their thirst without travelling out of the area.

As the new Minffordd Hostel approached completion – the first rooms were occupied in April 1996 and it was deemed complete in November – the society decided to fund a second phase, increasing its capacity by 50 per cent, which was completed in 1998.

The first of the Funkey diesel locomotives obtained for the WHR in 1993 was restored at Boston Lodge and completed in 1996. On 5 May, members of the 1964 Company were invited to travel on a train hauled by it across the embankment. This was a gesture aimed at improving relations between the companies, following the discovery that the 1964 Company had sought to make an adverse possession claim against a part of the Welsh Highland Railway trackbed near its property and had, without publicity, changed its name to Welsh Highland Railway Ltd, preventing the company from forming a new entity with that name. The loco was named *Castell Caernarfon* by Dafydd Wigley, the MP for Caernarfon, in Caernarfon on 20 August and then stored in Minffordd Yard.

Construction of a supermarket on the site of the intended Welsh Highland Railway station in Caernarfon, and Gwynedd County Council's plans

Two 350hp diesel locomotives had been imported from South Africa in October 1993. Built by C. H. Funkey Pty for the Port Elizabeth Cement Works in 1967, they had been re-engined in 1984 and taken out of service in 1986. Serviced at Boston Lodge, one of them retained its original profile and was stored at Minffordd awaiting accommodation on the Welsh Highland Railway.

The grant-aided carriage shed at Glan y Pwll under construction on 27 May 1996.

In advance of accommodation being available on the Welsh Highland Railway, the first two Garratts, Nos. 138 and 143, were delivered to Glan y Pwll in January 1997. A third, No. 140, is shown being reassembled there on 7 April.

In October 1996, *Linda* emerged from a volunteer-led overhaul in Penrhyn quarry condition, complete with sand bucket and small sand pots. The coal wagon concealed a tank containing fuel: 25 October 1996.

for diverting road traffic through the former rail tunnel under Castle Square, were responsible for shortening the intended Caernarfon Light Railway by 1,460m and changing its terminus. A notice to this effect was published in the *London Gazette* on 29 May 1996, saying that the company had requested the Secretary of State for Transport to alter the draft order.

At Blaenau Ffestiniog, the first visible sign of the strategic development scheme programme was the construction of the Glan y Pwll Carriage Shed, undertaken during 1996. In January 1997, it was used for the storage of the first two NGG16 Garratts, Nos. 138 and 143, obtained from South Africa for use on the Welsh Highland Railway. Donated by Michael Schumann and Hugh Eaves, they had received workshop attention before being exported, but were found to need more work to bring them up to UK and FR standards; No. 138's bogies were therefore dealt with at Boston Lodge and it was re-assembled

and commissioned at Glan y Pwll. No. 140 joined them on 7 April. The 'Festival of Steam' gala held on 3-5 May featured No. 138 in steam on the carriage shed siding giving visitors the chance to 'drive a Garratt' for £10; HM Railway Inspectorate subsequently rebuked the company for using the locomotive without approval.

When one of *Linda's* superheater elements had failed in 1995, and the ten-year boiler overhaul was due, the company decided that as the loco-motive was not immediately required, it would be put into store. A group of volunteers, therefore, undertook to raise the money needed for the boiler overhaul and to carry out a mechanical

On 7 April 1997, *Linda* moved No. 138's bogies from Minffordd to Boston Lodge for servicing.

overhaul. The boiler work, undertaken by a contractor, cost £24,000. The locomotive was returned to service in Penrhyn quarry livery, its first outing being a photographic train run for the volunteers who had worked on it on 25 October 1996, a coal wagon being adapted to carry an oil tank to make its appearance look more authentic. Intended to be temporary, the Penrhyn livery was later reapplied and lasted until 2004.

Welsh Highland Railway construction was started at Dinas on 15 January 1997. *Castell Caernarfon* had been moved from Minffordd a few days before, becoming the first motive power on the new railway. A £700,000 contract to design and build the railway between Dinas and Caernarfon, including re-locating the Lôn Eifion cycle track, was awarded to John Mowlem plc. Roland Doyle, who had led the team that completed the restoration of

Palmerston, and leader of the *Taliesin* project, was appointed general manager of Welsh Highland Light Railway Ltd.

On the FR, the platform at Blaenau Ffestiniog was extended towards Bala during 1997, enabling the installation of a foot crossing to the car park in October 1998 and the replacement of the ramp from the overbridge by stairs in 1999, developments that had required several years of negotiations with Railtrack to achieve. The booking office and shop were moved out of Isallt into new accommodation in the basement of the Queen's Hotel, accessible from the car park, in 1997. The location of Isallt was felt to be inconvenient and expensive at £2,500 a year.

At Blaenau Ffestiniog the overbridge ramp was replaced by steps in 1999. Two years' later *David Lloyd George* arrives, the site of the ramp visible in the tarmac.

On 10 October 1998 construction of the board crossing across the-then Railtrack tracks at Blaenau Ffestiniog was underway, the platform having already been extended to meet it. The FR's commercial operations had moved out of Isallt into the basement of the Queen's Hotel in March 1997.

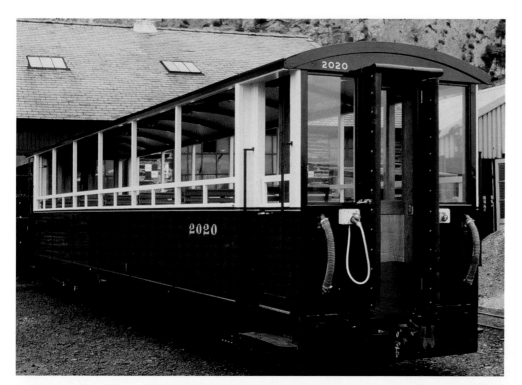

Seen at Boston Lodge on 30 July 1997, Welsh Highland Railway carriage No. 2020 had been delivered to Minffordd on 1 July. Ride tests were carried out with it before it was transported to Dinas in September.

Withdrawn in 1992, when cracks had been found in its firebox throatplates, *Earl of Merioneth* returned to service in 1997, its boiler repairred and with new, circular, smokeboxes. It also ran on *Merddin Emrys'* bogies for a time. It was photographed passing derelict cottages at Tanygrisiau.

The first carriage built for the Welsh Highland Railway had been delivered to Minffordd on 1 July 1997. Semi-open No. 2020, it had been intended to gain operating experience with it on the Minffordd shuttles, but approval to use it for the carriage of passengers was not received in time so it remained at Boston Lodge until it was required at Dinas in October.

A photocopier that caught fire in one of the Boston Lodge offices at lunchtime on 30 August 1997 caused severe smoke damage, but no injuries. Refurbishment took longer than anticipated when staff and contractors started reacting to some element in the smoke. All the partitions, ceilings and furniture were replaced, and the suite redecorated by the insurance company.

On 6 September 1997, the timetable was altered to avoid trains running during the funeral of Diana, Princess of Wales. A memorial service was held in the café at Porthmadog and the locomotives in service carried white wreaths.

The strategic development grant-funded permanent way mess carriage was completed in

The shell of the permanent way department mess carriage was delivered in May 1996, constructed by Bloomfield Steel Construction, the same company that had built *David Lloyd George's* boiler. Fitted out at Boston Lodge over two years, it received its first major service in 2016.

1997. At 40ft, it became the longest vehicle in the fleet, but narrower than normal to enable personnel to walk past it when stabled on embankments and to clear the sharper curves. In addition to seating and lockers it was equipped with heating, a kitchen, toilet, insulation and a drying cupboard.

On the board, Andy Savage stood down as the society's nominee on 12 June 1997 and was replaced by Mike Colville, the society's finance director, seconded from 21 August. After Hugh Eaves resigned in 1999, Colville became finance director.

On the Welsh Highland Railway, the contract arrangements with Mowlem delayed access to the Dinas-Caernarfon trackbed for tracklaying, so

services were not started until 13 October 1997, following a weekend of unadvertised trial running carrying local residents who paid a £1 fare. The few weeks of operating in 1997 produced a loss of £16,365 on turnover of £70,477. *Mountaineer*, still in 'temporary' wartime livery from the 1995 'All Our Yesterdays' gala, had been despatched to Dinas to backup Garratt No. 138, working the first steam-hauled test train on the railway on 4 October, and operating on days when the Garratt had its boiler washed out.

Concerned that it should be able to maintain effective oversight of the company whilst protecting the FR and having control of any company formed to operate the WHR, since 1994 the trust had been attempting to negotiate changes to its deed with the directors and the society. Neither party was enamoured of the proposals made; on 26 November 1997 the directors going so

On 29 June 1997, services were interrupted when a landslip was discovered at Pen Cefn, near Penrhyn. Volunteers and staff worked together to stabilise the site, enabling the railway to be re-opened with a 5mph speed restriction through the affected area the next day. A permanent repair was carried out in February 1998.

far as to write to the trust expressing their concerns and suggesting that John Routly should stand down as a trustee.

When the trustees met on 22 January 1998, 'Regret was expressed at both the lukewarm company reaction to the finalisation of the deed amendments and the negative comments on the interim agreement.' Routly was not present, but it was acknowledged that the final decision rested with him, and with Bill Broadbent, both of who were expected to have retired by the end of the year.

CHAPTER 12

1998-2003: TURNING AROUND, RUNNING TWO RAILWAYS

Whilst a decision on the Welsh Highland Railway Transport & Works Order application was awaited, attention was concentrated on the FR. The announcement of a £375,000 Heritage Lottery Fund grant to the trust on 28 October 1998 was a highlight. The award was for an extension to the carriage workshop and the restoration of the 1872-built bogie carriages, Nos. 15 and 16. Although it was made to the trust, the grant application was very much a society initiative. A registered charity since 29 August 1997, the society also contributed £125,000 in cash and volunteer labour to the project.

The carriages were stripped to their integral body frames, which had not been seen since they had been built in 1872, and their high-quality restoration was completed in 2001, No. 15 in an ornate Victorian livery: and No. 16 in the green livery of the 1920s and '30s. To comply with HLF rules, ownership of the carriages was transferred to a non-trading subsidiary of the company with directors appointed by the trust. This company had been registered by a trust officer for his own purposes in 1988; he gave it to the company and its name was changed to Ffestiniog Railway Heritage Ltd on 27 July 2001. It now exercises an oversight of the company's heritage affairs and its name was changed again, to Ffestiniog and Welsh Highland Railways Heritage Ltd, on 20 November 2013.

At the time the grant was made, the society was encouraged to expect to develop an ongoing relationship with the HLF for the restoration of other historic equipment and, ultimately, the development of a museum. However, a change in HLF

With support from the Heritage Lottery Fund, the new carriage restoration workshop had been started on 29 April 1999. It was connected to the carriage maintenance shed built with CEGB compensation money in 1975.

Vale of Ffestiniog, rebuilt from a South African Funkey to suit the FR loading gauge by Steve Coulson, entered service after a naming ceremony at Boston Lodge on 21 February 1998. It was photographed passing Penrhyn on 3 September 1999, when trains with lighter loadings were diesel worked.

management introduced changes in strategy that brought this vision to an end.

Commissioned in February 1998, *Vale of Ffestiniog* was the passenger diesel locomotive adapted from the second Funkey loco obtained from South Africa in 1993. A volunteer team had overhauled it and modified its superstructure to fit the FR's loading gauge, making it the largest diesel locomotive in the FR fleet, both literally and in terms of power output. National Power, whose subsidiary owned the power station at Tanygrisiau, had sponsored the project with a grant of £16,000. The locomotive had been styled and named to match the Class 59 locos then operated by the power company on the national network, and had been named at Boston Lodge on 21 February.

On 31 December 1998, two long-serving trustees, John Routly and Bill Broadbent, retired and were replaced by the Hon Sir William McAlpine Bt and Peter Jordan, the latter then a society director and the trust's auditor. They joined Robert Riddick, who had replaced P.J. Garland, appointed in 1973, in 1990; John Prideaux, a professional railwayman who had replaced founder Trevor Bailey, who had died in office on 16 September 1991; and Michael Schumann,

who had replaced the Hon Sir Osmond Williams Bt of Castell Deudraeth, appointed in 1979, in 1995. Prideaux became chairman. He had been a volunteer as a teenager, but had lost interest in the railway as it passed through its 'brutal era', concentrating on the deviation and restoration of services to Blaenau Ffestiniog. Hearing him tell how his experiences on the FR had fired his enthusiasm for railways had encouraged Alan Pegler to invite him to be a trustee.

Routly had effectively stood back some time before his final resignation, with Prideaux taking the chair at meetings and leading discussions with the company. The experience of the early 1990s led to the trust having three major concerns. The first was that the trust deed relied on Pegler to appoint trustees, and that this needed to be altered so that succession was not dependent on one person. The second was that the trust did not have effective oversight of the company despite owning a majority of all classes of shares. The trust did not see board papers, was not consulted on levels of debt, and, as all the directors stood for reappointment each year, had a very limited ability to manage succession. Trust powers seemed impressive but were essentially nuclear. The third issue was to find a better way to manage the

A busy scene on the erecting shop at Boston Lodge on 21 July 1998. From the left are new single Fairlie *Taliesin*, the frames of Lynton & Barnstaple Railway Manning, Wardle 2-6-2T *Lyd* and *Prince*.

railway's heritage, which was then split between the trust (ownership of some assets, the museum and archives) and the company. In practice both the trust and the company had many other priorities and practical management of heritage tended to be relatively low on the agenda.

The first of these issues could be agreed by the trust and Alan Pegler. The second was eventually resolved by a memorandum of understanding, and the third by the formation of Ffestiniog Railway Heritage Ltd as a subsidiary of the company whose directors were appointed by the trustees. It took time, and the further problems of the early 2000s, to develop the level of agreement that resolved these issues.

The amended trust deed was effective from 30 September 1998, mainly changing the way that trustees were appointed. The original deed gave the founder, Alan Pegler, the right of appointment and a trustee could remain in post as such as long as he wished. The new deed provided for five trustees with one trustee appointed each year, with one nominated by the society (after discussion with WHRS), one by the Company and

three by the existing trustees. Nominated candidates were then considered by an appointing body which comprised the trustees and the chairmen of the company and the society. Only if this body was in favour was a nominated candidate appointed as a trustee. Appointments would also be for five years, renewable. At the Charity Commission's recommendation, the new deed gave the trustees a general power to alter it, but not to alter the trust's objects.

A 20 per cent reduction in visitor numbers to Wales in 1998 was responsible for FR traffic revenue falling back to £976,071 and an operating loss of £16,726. An overdraft of £82,929, which had cost £4,327, and an interest-free loan of £100,000, had been required to balance the books. Although there had been no overdraft in 1997, in that year creditors were

The newly-built *Taliesin* made its first loaded run on 30 April 1999, a year before the target set by its sponsors. The sun had just risen by the time it had reached Tanygrisiau.

Taliesin with vintage stock at Dduallt tank curve on 9 November 1999. (John Hunt)

Fresh from the paint-shop on 7 April 1999, *Prince* is in light steam as the *Earl of Merioneth* passes. A pair of *James Spooner's* wheels lie on the ground.

owed £616,298, more than double the amount for 1996. The figure for 1998 fell slightly to £572,075. Two posts had been made redundant on 2 September.

Company treasurer since 1975 and a director from 1987, Hugh Eaves retired for personal reasons on 10 May 1999. On 10 February 2000 he was replaced by Ken Allen, who had replaced Peter Jordan as society chairman in 1997. Allen was to focus on business development and maximise profits.

There were two significant events in 1999. A year in advance of its target date for completion, single Fairlie *Taliesin* was launched at Porthmadog on 2 May, retired engineering director Bill Broadbent performing an unveiling ceremony in the company of project-founders Andy Savage and Gordon Rushton. Whilst the finishing touches were applied and it was being run in, it ran in black livery; repainted in Victorian style, it entered revenue service on 28 August 2000. Slightly larger than the original locomotive, effectively constructed at 13in to 1ft scale, use of the original locomotive's reversing lever

was felt to justify calling it a rebuild and worksplates indicating that were attached to the smokebox.

Boosted with the achievement of building a new locomotive with a large volunteer input, the society launched a £100,000 appeal to overhaul *Merddin Emrys*, with the objective of having it back in service before *David Lloyd George* was withdrawn from service for its ten-year overhaul in 2003. The loco had been withdrawn from service in 1996, when cracks had been found in the throatplates of its boiler, and its power bogies had been overhauled and placed under *Earl of Merioneth*. The society scheme included the provision of a second new

Merddin Emrys was withdrawn with cracks in its firebox throatplates in 1996. Following repairs, which included the installation of new stays, on 29 December 2001 its boiler was steam tested at Boston Lodge. One of the rivets required some additional caulking.

By 12 October 2002 the boiler cladding had been modified to introduce a taper and restore another element of the traditional Fairlie outline.

Prince and vintage stock at Tan y Bwlch on 5 October 2001. The train's passengers were in the café attending the company AGM.

bogies to accompany the spare started when *Taliesin*'s was made.

The positive news accompanying the launch of the new locomotive was in some senses eclipsed by the making of the Welsh Highland Railway Transport & Works Order on 30 June. The application had been made on 27 March 1997 and the associated public inquiry had lasted for twenty working days, plus two days of site visits, between 9 December 1997 and 28 January 1998. An interim decision in favour of making the order had been published on 7 April 1999 and the final decision on 28 June. In a marked similarity to the transfer order decision, the inspector's recommendation to refuse the application was overturned by the Secretary of State. In this instance, the [Labour] Government's policy in favour of developing public transport must have played a part in deciding that the railway's reinstatement was in the national interest, a test for allowing development in a national park.

Earlier, in July 1998, two days of the Snowdonia National Park Authority's local plan inquiry had been taken up with the authority's decision to

schedule the trackbed as a pedestrian and cycling route instead of a railway. On 21 January 1999, however, the inquiry inspector had reported, inter alia, that reinstatement was in the public interest and would not conflict with park purposes, recommending revising the policy to safeguard the trackbed in favour of the railway.

To wrap up the matter of the WHR order, the National Farmers' Union, lodged a request for a review of the decision to make it, in an attempt to have it overturned. The application was dismissed on 24 November 1999.

On the FR, an unusual train had been operated on three days in February and March 1999, when Welsh

Seen during its gauging trial over the FR, Welsh Highland Railway carriage No 2020 at Garnedd on 24 February 1999.

Highland open carriage No. 2020 returned to be gauged throughout the FR as far as practicable, to establish the location of fouling points for stock of its size. The train progressed at walking pace and, as expected, was unable to traverse the short tunnel, fouling at the eaves, but there were other locations, too, where it could not have passed in ordinary service.

At the cost of losing its museum accreditation, in 1999 the company adopted the inevitable strategy of allowing the space occupied by the museum to be taken over fully by the catering department, with the premises open into the evening. Railway ambience was maintained with the strategic use of appropriate items from the museum collection and by leaving *Princess* in situ. Under the name 'Spooner's', the outcome was a success, with takings substantially increased, and business attracted from residents and volunteers as well as passengers.

There was a downside however, in that it gave some residents in Britannia Terrace more opportunities to complain about the railway's activities. It might have been an overreaction to undertake not to run trains after 22.30, given that the company's statutes

placed no restrictions on its operation and late trains were not a regular feature of its timetable, but the gesture did not stop the complaints. A report in the *Daily Post* on 28 September 2006 quoted the-then general manager Paul Lewin as saying that they had started in 1997, one complainant making a considerable number of phone calls and objections to the licence. The paper referred to a letter that Lewin had sent in August 2006, saying that the company was considering its options to bring the complainant's unreasonable behaviour to an end, which appears to have had the desired effect.

Returning to 1999, it was established that some passengers were choosing the cheaper journey offered by the Minffordd shuttle when they might otherwise have paid for a full return, so the shuttle was withdrawn in favour of a twice-daily vintage train operating to Tan y Bwlch, but this variant was short-lived for the same reason.

An attempt to reduce Welsh Highland Railway operating costs saw *Blanche* transferred to Dinas on 13 May 1999, where it worked three-car trains on weekdays on off-peak days. Whilst this did reduce the amount of oil consumed, it was at the expense of increased maintenance, gradients as steep as 1 in 40 requiring the loco to be worked at the limit of its capability despite the lighter load. The same applied to *Mountaineer*, which returned to the WHR to replace *Blanche* in March 2000.

A development of the fund-raising 'guest driving' programme was introduced in 1999, the 'slate shunt' being described as 'a low-cost, low-mileage, high-season alternative', offering six hours shunting wagons in Minffordd Yard with *Lilla*. *Lilla* was joined in the trust's ownership by *Palmerston* in 2000, Mike Hart announcing at the society's AGM on 29 April that he had decided to donate his two-thirds share in the loco, adding that he thought it was inappropriate that such a historic loco should remain in private ownership.

The loss in 1998 became a £10,155 profit in 1999, despite an enormous effort made by both staff and volunteers, commented chairman Mike Hart in his report to shareholders, adding that the company must make a reasonable return each year to fund much-needed improvements.

Project Claptrack was an initiative to speed up the renewal of worn out, or clapped out, track. Since

re-opening to Blaenau Ffestiniog, track renewals had averaged one-eighth of a mile a year instead of the quarter mile required if it was to be completely renewed over the sixty-year life of the materials. Led by permanent staff with a large volunteer input, many of whom normally worked in other departments, it was started in January/February of 1999 and continued for several years. In the first two years, half-a-mile of ex-Penrhyn bull-head rail between Coed y Bleiddiau and Dduallt tank curve was replaced with South African 30kg/metre flat bottom rail in 18m lengths, the same material used on the Welsh Highland Railway, producing a significant improvement in the ride quality, eliminating the use of ex-British Railways sleepers from the main line and reducing the amount of 24ft rail in use. By 2001 1⅜ miles of South African rail had been installed.

Over the same period, attention had been paid to the views from the carriage windows by cutting back undergrowth although many of the problem areas were on property beyond the railway's boundaries.

Temporary changes to the track at Porthmadog were required in January 2000, to give the Environment Agency access to the seawards side of

On a crisp morning, Driver Paul Ingham marks the new year by moving to the fireman's side of *Earl of Merioneth* for the first train of 2000; Paul Lewin was the driver.

A forerunner of things to come. The environment agency's 2000 project to strengthen the Merioneth end of the embankment required access across the railway and construction of a stockpile of rock. This was the scene at Porthmadog on 1 February.

the embankment. Once a stockpile of stone had been hauled across, the track was reinstated. The stone was used to reinforce the embankment later in the year.

At Blaenau Ffestiniog, the signalling scheme was commissioned on 25 March. Largely undertaken by volunteers over five years, it was designed to permit trains to work into either of the platforms, one of the final pieces in the strategic development scheme package. The layout included a short siding called the 'Dorfil shunt' into which locos had to run to trigger the correct sequence for the signals whilst running round. The requirement to enter the siding, which increased the time taken to run-round, was not appreciated by crews or operators, but attempts to secure a staff instrument to increase flexibility had not been successful.

Welsh Highland Railway services were extended to Waunfawr on 7 August 2000, albeit without a run-round loop, nearly three months later than

planned largely because heavy rain the previous winter had delayed work on restoring the trackbed. With the loop complete, the official opening was performed by Dafydd Wigley, MP for Caernarfon and member of the National Assembly for Wales, on 15 September. The transfer of construction and then operation onto the historic route resulted in increases in volunteers for the former and passengers for the latter. Nearly 1,000 residents' railcards offering reduced fares had been sold locally before the official opening.

An attempt to adopt modern marketing techniques during 2000 was hindered by the discovery that someone, apparently objecting to the revival of the Welsh Highland Railway, had registered the domain name ffestiniograilway.co.uk to promote their objection, leading to the adoption of festrail.co.uk for the company's own purposes.

In 2000, profit was slightly increased to £16,008 although traffic revenue had declined by £54,464,

Almost framed by steam, on 25 March 2000, *Taliesin* was the first steam locomotive to enter the Dorfil shunt siding at Blaenau Ffestiniog after it was made operational.

the overdraft increased by £44,431 and money due to trade creditors increased by £34,813. The directors had been concerned about the state of the railway and its management earlier in the year, and a report compiled in June was considered on 11 September, when, after agreeing that Alan Heywood had been asked to do a difficult task, working for the company with loyalty and devotion for many years, the decision was taken that he should stand down as general manager from 1 October. Mike Hart made the announcement on 26 September. At the time the decision seemed rather sudden, the only explanation offered, in the society magazine, was that 'it was the right time of the year for the change to happen.'

Heywood was replaced by director Ken Allen taking the position of acting chief executive via his service company, tasked with managing the railway whilst developing the 2001 business plan and a long-term strategic plan with an appropriate organisational structure. A list of changes circulated to employees, volunteers and members in November included the development of 'Boston Lodge Engineering' to handle outside work, a clearer distinction between revenue and capital expenditure, the introduction of new purchasing and stock control systems, and the

cancellation of signalling schemes at Minffordd and Tanygrisiau, and further signalling-related work at Blaenau Ffestiniog.

At Minffordd, it had been intended to return the booking office to the operating department and restored to its original purpose for use during events, by moving the telephone equipment it contained to a new location in Minffordd Yard. A new building had been constructed in the Yard for the purpose. The Tanygrisiau installation was related to the 1995 strategic development scheme's crossing loop. It included construction of a vandal-proof signal box, which had been built, and was to incorporate McKenzie & Holland-style signals, the posts for which had been installed. The starting signals were subsequently sold and may be seen on the Isle of Man Steam Railway at Douglas. It appears that the schemes had become more complex and expensive than when first proposed, and that running costs had become an issue.

Leonard Heath Humphrys, who as a schoolboy had called the meeting held in Bristol in 1951 that started the FR's revival, died suddenly of a brain haemorrhage on 22 December 2000. A society director from 1954, he had been voted out of office in 1968. He was made a society vice-president in 1979

Over the years, accommodation for disabled passengers has been improved. Once the only vehicle capable of carrying a passenger in a wheelchair was the guard's van, which only had high-level windows. 18 July 2001.

The Blaenau Ffestiniog signalling system, including the Dorfil shunt, was taken out of use after carriage No. 105 was derailed when the points moved under it on 5 May 2001. The train, a special run to collect a railtour party, had been signalled into the second platform. It was not possible to establish the cause of the fault or to replicate it.

and a company patron in 1981. Later, having moved to Oswestry, he became a regular and popular volunteer with the parks and gardens department. His widow Monika maintains that connection with the railway.

The fiftieth anniversary of the meeting that he called was commemorated by a civic lunch on the SS *Great Britain* in Bristol docks on 8 September 2001. Arranged by the society's Bristol area group, fifty guests included Alan Pegler and Humphrys' widow and daughter. Four of those who had attended the meeting, including Allan Garraway, were also present.

The outbreak of foot and mouth disease in the spring of 2001 was responsible for restrictions being placed on access to the countryside in much of the UK. Despite the absence of outbreaks in Gwynedd, passenger numbers on both the FR and the Welsh Highland Railways were affected, and delayed the start of WHR construction beyond Waunfawr. An emergency timetable was introduced at the end of March and Tan y Bwlch and Tanygrisiau and the intermediate halts were closed. By Easter, however, 13-16 April, the situation was sufficiently clarified for the stations and halts to be reopened, and for the advertised timetable to be operated. A £45,000 compensation grant was paid by the Government the following year.

Notwithstanding the decision to end expenditure on the Blaenau Ffestiniog signalling scheme, a derailment on 5 May 2001 brought about the removal of most of what had already been installed. An empty stock train had been signalled into the 'new' platform when the trap point moved under it, derailing one carriage. An investigation failed to find the cause and the platform track was restricted to occasional use.

The final stages of Ken Allen's business plan and management structure was put in place in the autumn of 2001. He was appointed managing director, Clare Britton was commercial operations manager and Peter Randall was traffic and engineering operations manager. The former had worked for the company since 1992, the latter was a career railwayman who had first visited the railway at the age of six. He was also deputy managing director.

The pension scheme, founded on John Routly's initiative in 1974, was closed to new entrants on 31 October 2001 and two new schemes established on 1 November. Whilst not as beneficial to the employees affected, the outcome was a reduction in company outgoings.

Citing domestic and business reasons, Mike Hart stood down as chairman whilst remaining a director, on 5 October 2001. He had been spending

three days a week on company business since 1997. He also remained on the boards of the associated companies, Ffestiniog Railway Holdings Ltd and Welsh Highland Light Railway Ltd, relinquishing the position of chairman of them at the same time. He was replaced by George Nissen.

In his first report to shareholders, on 15 August 2002, Nissen noted that changes in accounting practices in dealing with depreciation was largely responsible for the loss of £23,722 in 2001; using the historic procedure, the company had made a profit of £89,005, a big improvement on the £1,244 profit in 2000.

By the date of the society's AGM on 4 May 2002, it was clear that there was great unhappiness around the railway. At first this had been attributed to the pace of change, but it soon became clear that there were more deep-seated issues. Despite his

Blanche and *Linda* depart from Tan y Bwlch on a frosty 1 January 2002.

The twentieth anniversary of the restoration of services to Blaenau Ffestiniog was commemorated when Lord Dafydd Elis-Thomas, for many years the local MP and then presiding officer of the National Assembly for Wales, unveiled a plaque at the station on 1 June 2002. To his right are Stuart MacFarlane, Mike Hart, Alan Tibbetts and Alan Pegler. To his left are Trish Doyle, Chris Richardson, Peter Dennis, Alan Heywood, Alan Skellern and Roger Schofield.

The connections to the national network were commemorated the next day, when Dean Finch, managing director railways of First Group, then the franchise operator of the Blaenau Ffestiniog branch from Llandudno Junction, unveiled a second plaque. He was photographed with traffic and engineering operations manager, Peter Randall.

experience as an enthusiastic volunteer, Ken Allen turned out to be abrasive in management and failing to consult where consultation was required. A special motion proposed by a group of members calling, briefly, for the society to urge the company to conduct its affairs with transparency, openness and honesty, was carried overwhelmingly, with no votes against and just two abstentions.

There were signs that the financial position was deteriorating, reports circulating in Porthmadog that bills were going unpaid, for one, but the number of full-time staff had nearly doubled over two years, cars were leased for the heads of departments; and the external accountant employed to oversee the finance department had been discharged. For obvious reasons, it took the directors a while to be convinced that there was a problem, but on 23 July they met to discuss the matter, saying they were disappointed that he had failed, with some exceptions, to re-establish good relations with his critics in the society; failed to report the financial position or the level of traffic and failed to achieve

Ken Allen on 15 June 2002. His appointment as managing director was terminated a few weeks later, on 25 July.

On 15 June 2002 the railway hosted the Queen's Jubilee Baton Relay, a precursor of the XVII Commonwealth Games held in Manchester. Ten-year-old Dilyth Haf Roberts carried the baton from Blaenau Ffestiniog to Porthmadog on a special train hauled by *David Lloyd George*. At Blaenau Ffestiniog she posed for photographs with driver Tony Williams.

the forecast profit. They decided to terminate his consultancy and invite Peter Randall to assume the duties of general manager.

The contract was terminated with immediate effect on 25 July 2002. Under pressure from the society, Allen had resigned as a director on 30 April and been replaced by Andrew Hayward as the society's representative on 10 July. Andy Savage had been appointed a director on that date, too.

It must be said that there are some positive elements to be attributed to Ken Allen's involvement with the company's management. He initiated the development of 'Boston Lodge engineering' and of Spooner's Bar whilst he was acting chief executive, both of which go from strength to strength; saved money by bringing the company's mobile phones into a single contract; and had a modern telephone exchange installed at Porthmadog, which enabled direct dialling to extensions, eliminating the need for all incoming calls to be handled by the booking office, or to go unanswered when it was unmanned. It should also be said that changes in the directorship and the personal situations of some board members had contributed to the lack of oversight of the company's affairs.

When they met on 15 August, the directors thought that the financial position was seriously short by reference to the budget and were concerned about the deteriorating cash flow. There was evidence of excessive expenditure caused by employment costs, but their knowledge of the current trading position was hampered by a lack of detailed financial information.

Malcolm High, finance director of Welsh Highland Light Railway Ltd, the WHR construction company, and a descendant of the clock winder George Westley, killed in the goods shed in a shunting accident in 1881, was appointed finance director in place of Mike Colville, who had also resigned on 30 April.

On 16 September, High reported that he had set himself six immediate tasks: to pay all staff; recruit finance staff; resolve VAT issues; produce a cash

The 2002 vintage weekend produced this spectacular line-up of 'traditional' FR motive power on 12 October. *Taliesin*, *Prince* and *David Lloyd George* are behind *Palmerston*. Two of them had not existed when the railway's revival had started in 1955 and one was believed to be a wreck.

forecast; produce a bank reconciliation and produce a reliable balance sheet. The first three had been achieved, the cash forecast, dependent on the bank reconciliation which would take two more weeks to complete, had been partially achieved, leaving only the balance sheet outstanding. The overdraft was likely to peak at £500,000 in May 2003. He had contacted the bank manager who was to visit the railway in October.

The question of redundancies was discussed, but the directors would not authorise any until the financial review and reconciliation had been completed, in the meantime asking Peter Randall to produce savings to enable the company to be cash positive and sustainable.

It took two months to establish the company's financial position, after which agreement was reached with the bank regarding the funds required to pay outstanding bills. The loss for the year was £300,315, up from £23,722 the year before, the overdraft was £386,924, up from £265,194, administrative expenses had risen to £621,675, compared with £395,397, and staff costs, including

social security and pensions, had increased to £1,058,920 from £920,344.

At the company AGM on 4 October 2002, chairman George Nissen addressed the situation, explaining that the finance officer had got out of her depth, the finance director was perhaps too sympathetic, and the chief executive presented an unjustifiable optimistic picture to the directors. The board had not performed as it should have done. He accepted responsibility for the situation and apologised.

Two days before, Nissen had announced the appointment of three non-statutory directors to strengthen the board and the establishment of a joint interest committee to improve the relationship with the society. The first non-statutory directors were

With Porthmadog as a backdrop, *Palmerston* crosses the embankment with vintage stock on 22 February 2003. Within ten years the view would be changed by the construction of the platform accommodating the Welsh Highland Railway.

Helen Waters, a volunteer and rail industry executive; Malcolm High, the new finance director; and Michael Whitehouse, son of P. B. Whitehouse, himself a former volunteer and member of temporary staff, a solicitor with experience in rail industry contracts and a director of Welsh Highland Light Railway Ltd.

Within a few months, fifteen employees had left and Nissen himself stood down on 13 February 2003. In any event, he said, when he accepted the position of chairman, he only wanted to do the job until a younger candidate could be found. Remaining on the board of the holdings company, he was replaced by Whitehouse. Strategies agreed between the latter and Prideaux covered the relationship between the company and trust, and the final phase of the Welsh Highland Railway construction, that it should be handled differently, with a new construction company responsible for implementing the FR board's decisions and policies.

In a circular to staff and volunteers in December 2002, Whitehouse had written of the need to 're-engineer the company, to make it fit as a twenty-first century tourist attraction', adding, 'The company must be profitable, cash positive, capable of being self-sustaining from a revenue standpoint and also able to contribute to its capital development; it needs to retain and develop its position in the top ten North Wales attractions. It should maximise the historical legacy of the FR, both as part of its tourist development and in its continuing wish to attract volunteer support. The FR family should develop a culture of openness in its dealings and finances, so as to facilitate a foundation of trust and harmony on which operations and developments can be based.'

One of those who left was Peter Randall, the general manager, whose employment ended on 20 December 2002; it was not minuted. Speaking to the author in 2015, Whitehouse said that it was obvious that the company was in a bad way, that hard decisions needed to be taken, particularly with regard to employment levels, and that Randall would find this difficult. Editorialising in the society magazine at the time, the author postulated that it was evidence that the directors were being pro-active; Randall told him that they were still not being active enough. He returned to the rail industry, maintaining his links with the railway, becoming a director of the Welsh Highland Railway Society, and leading the project to restore a South African NG15 2-8-2 for use on the WHR.

He was replaced on a temporary part-time basis by Paul Lewin, a locomotive volunteer since the age of fifteen and a former society director who had led the teams that built *Lyd*, overhauled *Linda* in 1994-5, and bought the Hunslet 0-4-0ST *Lilla* from Bernard Latham for the trust in 1993. He had just completed a review of the organisational structure at Boston Lodge. Until the new appointment was made, Helen Waters acted as *de facto* managing director and Nigel Burbidge, a loco volunteer and accountant and the company's auditor, was closely involved with the company's day-to-day operation. After a series of interviews, Lewin was appointed general manager with effect from 6 March 2003.

Photographed on 20 April 2003, Paul Lewin had been appointed general manager a few weeks earlier.

The lottery-supported restoration of carriages Nos. 15 and 16 proved inspirational to carrying out more authentic restoration work, the results starting to show in this view of heritage stock at Porthmadog on 2 October 2003.

The wagon fleet was also receiving attention and in 2003 it was possible to buy back most of the wagons sold to Maenofferen in 1962. This was the scene at Minffordd on 1 October 2003

After the company AGM held at Rhyd Ddu on 3 October 2003, the directors and officers posed for a photograph with Garratt No. 143. From left: Stephen Murfitt (clerk), George Nissen, Malcolm High, Helen Waters, Mike Hart, Michael Whitehouse, Andrew Hayward, Andy Savage and Mike Schumann, with Paul Lewin (general manager) in the cab.

Built at Boston Lodge, carriage No. 24 was a recreation of a North Wales Narrow Gauge Railways' Ashbury for service on the Welsh Highland Railway. On 23 August 2002, it was photographed at Minffordd awaiting transport to Dinas.

In 2003, the 140th anniversary of steam locomotives on the FR was marked by headboards carried on the locomotives on service trains. Thus adorned, *David Lloyd George* arrives at Minffordd on 13 April. The platform building was recreated by the Heritage Group in 2001-2, set further back than the 'small wooden cabin' criticised by Colonel Rich in 1872.

Speaking of the year's events to shareholders at the company's AGM on 3 October 2003, Whitehouse explained the financial problems by saying that money had been spent before it had been earned and non-productive administrative employment had increased considerably. Management was stuck in a 1980s time warp, he declared, it was necessary to develop imaginative thinking, reduce overheads, and debt and reinvent the railway. There was too much debt and it restricted choices. The leisure market, whilst growing, was more demanding. Investment should be focused on the pinch points to increase profits and make money. The comment about the company's management ethos attracted some complaints from staff when the author's report of the meeting was reprinted in the *Caernarfon & Denbigh Herald* a few weeks later.

Changes in the society leadership that occurred at the time Ken Allen's involvement with the company

was terminated in 2002 had been accompanied by a deterioration in its relationship with the company, the society's default position being one of distrust of the company and antipathy with regards to the Welsh Highland Railway. At its 2003 AGM, the society also failed to support the company's nomination for its representative on the society board. There were several resignations from the society board during this period, too.

On 22 November 2002, it had been announced that the Welshpool & Llanfair Light Railway had commissioned Boston Lodge Engineering to build a replica of one of the railway's 1902-built tramway-style Pickering composite carriages. The examination of the company's finances that had followed Ken Allen's departure had also established the true level of the costs of operating Boston Lodge, which revealed this carriage could not be built profitably for the contract price, requiring it to be renegotiated as a result.

Turned out in GWR livery as No. 6466, the carriage was delivered on 21 June 2004 and became an instant hit on the 2ft 6in-gauge railway. A donation to the WLLR from a former Boston Lodge volunteer funded the construction of a third-class carriage built in 2007 and the WLLR had the resources to order a second composite delivered in 2010, completing the recreation of the railway's original passenger train that had been scrapped by the GWR in 1936.

Construction of a new FR carriage started in 1998, No. 122, had been delayed when its design came into conflict with internal politics and the requirements of the Rail Vehicle Accessibility Regulations 1998, which had been implemented for the modern rail industry without any regard for the needs of narrow-gauge railways building new stock. No. 122, therefore, entered service only after the Rail Vehicle Accessibility (Ffestiniog Railway Company Vehicle Number 122) Exemption Order 2003 was made on 3 July 2003.

The order, effective from 31 July, exempted the company from fitting audible warning devices in the doorways, handrails on the interior of external doorways and a public address system, providing wheelchair spaces and authorised the width of priority seats for the disabled to be 430mm instead of 450mm, and allowed more force than permitted to operate door handles.

Steve Coulson, a volunteer who had moved to Porthmadog to be near to the railway, had designed and mostly built the carriage. Designed to make maximum use of the FR loading gauge, to increase the internal space and to make use of modern materials and techniques, it had diesel heating and double-glazed windows, features that became standard on future new carriages. Compliance with the regulations is the reason for the external doors being painted ivory, providing a contrast

with the remainder of the vehicle and making them identifiable for the partially sighted.

Funding for the carriage had come from travel company profits covenanted to the trust. Whitehouse then challenged that company to make sufficient profit to support the construction of one new carriage per year.

Whilst No. 122 has been a success, it remains a one-off, the Company deciding that future stock should have the more traditional appearance of that built in the 1960s. Subsequent new carriages did make provision for wheelchair access and retained the ivory doors.

John Routly, the solicitor who helped Alan Pegler to take over the company in 1954, and chairman of the directors and then company chairman until 1993, died on 4 March 2003, aged 88. Whilst he might have been a reluctant railway enthusiast, he became an enthusiast for the Ffestiniog Railway and played a crucial role in securing the grants required to complete the deviation and the restoration of services to Blaenau Ffestiniog.

Since Routly had retired as a director, the relationship between the company and the trust had deteriorated as each body sought to establish their roles in the absence of any definition of just what they should be. In the aftermath of the earlier problems, the trust developed the view that as the majority shareholder it should have an oversight of the company's management, whilst the company thought that the trust was interfering. In an attempt to clarify matters, a memorandum of understanding between the parties was brought into effect on 31 July 2003. It aimed to create a transparent relationship between the trust and the Company, setting out the framework within which the trust, as shareholder, expected the company to be managed, and an agreed basis on which the trust would exercise its rights as shareholder.

It declared that the general principles were that the trust had a duty to oversee the functioning of the company, with the aim of safeguarding the FR and its activities in the interests of all those concerned, and that the directors were charged with the management of the company. It called upon the company to conduct its business with a view to profit and, taking into account its heritage assets, endeavour to break even on an annual basis.

Carriage No. 122 was designed and mostly built by the late Steve Coulson. Then the largest carriage on the FR, it incorporated many innovative features. 17 August 2003.

It was also to produce a costed business plan of its proposals for development, operation and heritage management. In producing the plan, the company was to take into account the view of the trustees and consult with employees, and the FR and WHR Societies.

Capital expenditure in excess of £50,000 or not in the business plan was to be agreed with the trustees in advance, as should any intention to increase the aggregate level of indebtedness materially in excess of that proposed in the business plan. The trustees were also to be provided with copies of the annual reports and accounts of the company and its subsidiaries, and the agendas and minutes of board meetings. The company chairman, general manager or other appropriate officer was to report on the company's affairs to the trustees at their regular meetings.

Extension of Welsh Highland Railway services to Rhyd Ddu on 9 August 2003, preceded by a visit from HRH the Prince of Wales on 30 July, produced a big boost in traffic, generating an 80 per cent revenue increase by the year's end.

Reviewing the company's situation on 31 July, the trustees had noted that FR traffic was 8 per cent up on 2002 and trading had broken even up to June. 'The atmosphere on the line was much happier,' they thought. John Prideaux regretted the nature of the train provided for the royal visit, incomplete ballasting having required the use of lighter vintage stock with fewer seats, restricting the number of FR and WHR supporters invited. The trustees also thought that the company board required re-shaping and the impasse over society representation had to be broken.

For the year, the WHR's gross profit increased from £34,082 to £122,012, making a substantial contribution to the company's £169,799 profit. Boston Lodge Engineering contributed £321,000 of additional turnover. Sales outlets had not performed well, however, and a considerable amount of stock had to be written off.

CHAPTER 13

2004-2009: OUTSIDE CONTRACTS SUCCESSES

An exceedingly generous donation from a supporter, and a great deal of hard work by Mike Hart, preceded the announcement on 8 September 2004 that the Welsh Assembly Government would contribute £5 million towards the completion of the Welsh Highland Railway between Rhyd Ddu and Porthmadog. Named 'Phase 4', an appeal for £500,000 to bridge a funding gap launched at the same time succeeded in raising over £1 million, demonstrating a high level of public support for the project.

On the FR, one of the highlights of 2004 was a formal dinner held in the carriage workshop at Boston Lodge on 26 June to commemorate the fiftieth anniversary of the company's change of control. A special vintage train was routed via Tan y Bwlch, where canapés and champagne were served, before proceeding to the works, discharging its passengers at a temporary platform. Guests included Alan Pegler and Bill Broadbent.

The train included the replica of a Brown, Marshalls bogie 'curly roof' van of 1873-6 that had just been completed for use on the Victorian vintage train. It attracted many plaudits and was cited by journalist Handel Kardas as demonstrating that the revived FR had matured, in that it was able to commission and operate a carriage that had no

OPPOSITE: Heritage in action. *Prince* and the 1920s train on the 1854 road bridge at Tan y Bwlch on 22 February 2004.

Events marking the fiftieth anniversary of the change of control included a dress dinner held at Boston Lodge on 27 June 2004. Company chairman Michael Whitehouse (left) and trust chairman John Prideaux pose with Alan Pegler before joining the special train.

For many years a roof spar from van No. 3 was displayed in the museum as a reminder of something unique that had been lost. Thanks to a benefactor, in 2004 the distinctive features of No. 3 and its contemporaries reappeared in the carriage workshop with the construction of a new van to operate with the vintage train. Some parts salvaged from No. 3 were incorporated into it.

commercial remit. Whilst that was true at the time, the carriage has found a secure commercial role in the railway's vintage train operations.

The carriage works was also attracting some significant external work, in April having delivered two replica Darjeeling Himalayan Railway carriages ordered by former volunteer and society director Adrian Shooter. They were to accompany his DHR 'B' class 0-4-0STT No. 19B that he had then recently imported from the USA for operation on his private Beeches Light Railway in Oxfordshire. He had also ordered a replica of the 1901-built Sandy River & Rangeley Lakes Railway parlor car, arguably the most luxurious narrow-gauge carriage ever built. The BLR example was modified to fit the FR loading gauge and has an electric kitchen. It was delivered in March 2005, having made a run attached to an FR service train on 12 February.

For itself, the company had commissioned the carriage works to construct two new carriages that entered service in 2005. No. 102 was an observation saloon outwardly similar to Nos. 100 and 101 of 1965/1970, but was finished internally to a much higher standard that set a precedent for future construction and refurbishment; the interior was funded by society life members responding to an

appeal led by Alan Pegler. In operation it replaced No. 101, which was transferred to the Welsh Highland Railway from 2006 until 2009. No. 101 replaced No. 100, which had been transferred to the WHR in 2003. Renumbered No. 1000, from 2006 No. 100 was used as a mess car for WHR track gangs until it became unfit for use and was dismantled. No. 101 was rebuilt as a third-class observation car, re-entering service as No. 123 in 2011.

The second carriage was No. 107, which ran for the first time on 20 March 2005. A 1st/3rd vehicle built in the style of Nos. 104 and 106, new in 1964 and 1968 respectively; its body was built by a regular group of carriage workshop volunteers called 'Team X'. No. 106 had been extensively rebuilt in 2002.

A simplified system for controlling trains crossing at Tanygrisiau was introduced on 29 June 2004, using weighted points as used on the Welsh Highland Railway. The installation was inspected on 16 June. Unlike the other passing places on the railway, sighting requirements called for trains to cross on the left so the points are weighted for the left-hand road and trains trail through them when leaving. The tracks were swapped over on 10 June.

The signal box, never used for its intended purpose, houses the staff instrument that became

Boston Lodge has succeeded in attracting some significant contracts for outside customers. The original Sandy River & Rangeley Lakes Railway parlor car was built in 1901 to carry wealthy businessmen and their families from New York and Washington to the Rangeley Lakes, a popular up-market vacation area in Maine. Named *Rangeley*, it could accommodate twenty-eight passengers on payment of a $1 supplement. It is preserved in Portland, Maine. Former society director Adrian Shooter ordered *Carrabasset* as a replica, slightly reduced in size to fit the FR loading gauge, to accommodate diners visiting his private railway in Oxfordshire. On 13 February 2005 it was pulled out for his inspection.

Another order carried out for Adrian Shooter was the construction of two Darjeeling Himalayan Railway carriages to operate with his Sharp, Stewart 0-4-0STT 'B' class DHR locomotive. Delivered in 2004, they returned, with the loco, for gala operations in 2005, the ensemble being captured at Tanygrisiau on 23 April.

January 2005 and January 2006. More Polish rail was laid between Penrhediad and Plas Halt in 2007.

A lineside innovation for the benefit of passengers was made during 2004, with the creation of 'view windows' in four locations above Cei Mawr. Trainee tree surgeons from Moulton College, Northamptonshire, handled the required tree felling at three of the locations.

Malcolm High, the finance director, retired from the board on 19 August 2004 and was replaced by Nigel Burbidge. The directors paid tribute to the work High had done to resolve the company's financial problems since 2002 and gave him a free pass. He continued to supply support to the company.

Having accepted a position with the Rail Industry Investigation Board, Andy Savage resigned as a director, attending his last meeting on 15 October 2004 and being presented with a gift in recognition of his long service to the board.

There was great excitement at Boston Lodge on 3 September 2004, when the first Garratt, K1, was steamed onto the embankment. It had been transferred to the FR for its restoration to be

available after the management changed in 2003, and traditional FR circular-disc signals were the inspiration for the fixed distant and station stop boards, with key switches in the stop boards illuminating yellow starting signals mounted in them. An intermediate instrument was subsequently installed at Glan y Pwll.

Poland was the source of half a mile of new 30kg flat-bottom rail delivered in November 2004. It was installed between Hafod y Llyn and Penrhediad in

In October 2005 a half-mile of new S30 (60lb/yard) rail was delivered from the Huta Krowlewska Steel Mill in Poland. It had been ordered with 12 miles required for the Welsh Highland Railway, and another half-mile for the Welshpool & Llanfair Light Railway, to take advantage of the rate available for the total volume. It was laid between Penrhediad and Plas Halt.

The new boiler for the pioneer Garratt K1 was steam tested on 13 September 2002.

On 3 September 2004, K1 made its first moves in steam, running out onto the embankment at dusk. Its restoration was completed at the Welsh Highland Railway's Dinas depot.

Allan Garraway made what turned out to be his last visit to the railway in September 2004, the vintage weekend. He was captured chatting to one of his successors, Alan Heywood, at Porthmadog.

completed in 2001 and steamed for the first time on 22 August. It was transferred to Dinas, Welsh Highland Railway, by road on 2 October.

Signals and telegraphs volunteers working at Glan y Pwll designed and built, and had certified, a wagon-mounted cherry picker, enabling them to work safely at height whilst maintaining overhead cables and other lineside equipment. It entered service early in 2005. The same team went on to produce a wagon-mounted hydraulic crane that entered service in 2009. The FR Society funded both projects.

Celebrations commemorating the fiftieth anniversary of the railway's revival focused on the 'Ffestiniog Fifty' gala over the May Day holiday weekend, 30 April-2 May 2005, which included the operation of Adrian Shooter's Darjeeling Himalayan Railway train. The 1886-built double Fairlie *Livingston Thompson*, which had been returned to the railway from the National Railway Museum, York, featured in a line-up of Fairlie locomotives alongside

Merddin Emrys, Earl of Merioneth, David Lloyd George and *Taliesin*. It was returned to York in April 2006.

Merddin Emrys, which was in the throes of a ten-year overhaul that included the provision of two new society-funded power bogies, appeared with only one of the bogies operational and in a temporary black

The temporary return of *Livingston Thompson* from the National Railway Museum was one of the highlights for celebrations marking the fiftieth anniversary of the current regime in 2005. Counter-intuitively, a photo line-up was arranged with *Earl of Merioneth, David Lloyd George, Taliesin, Livingston Thompson* and *Merddin Emrys* for the afternoon of 30 April. Approaching the end of its protracted overhaul, *Merddin Emrys* was only working on one end.

Finding that the tanks made by John Summers & Sons for *Merddin Emrys* in 1959 were beyond repair, between Christmas and New Year 2003 a volunteer gang built two new sets of traditional-outline tanks, for *Merddin Emrys* and *Earl of Merioneth*, although the latter have yet to be used at the time of publication.

livery. Its new tanks had been funded by members of the railway's internet chat group and constructed by volunteers. Steamed with two working bogies on 27 May, it returned to service in Victorian livery during the vintage weekend held on 14-16 October. The company's strategy of using the bogie engines on its main trains was supported by having three of them in service for the first time in the current era.

Blanche was also returned to service in 2005, having been withdrawn in March 2003 when its boiler

certificate expired. A new boiler was made by Bartlett Engineering, based in Pembrokeshire, at a cost of £36,400. After testing in May, it was returned to service in June and ran 6,004 miles by the end of the year.

Spooner's 'boat' reappeared on the railway during 2005, in the form of a replica funded by a bequest from the company's late archivist, Michael Seymour. As no drawings existed, it was produced by scaling-up the single known illustration of the original vehicle and by taking advice from a boat-builder.

On 27 May 2005, *Merddin Emrys* was steamed for testing in this temporary black livery, still requiring the addition of some cosmetic features.

Converted to burn coal again over the winter of 2006-7, *Merddin Emrys* was seen at Boston Lodge on 25 May 2007.

The incomparable scene of a Ffestiniog Railway vintage train leaving Porthmadog before an admiring audience on 2 May 2010. On the left is the replica of the boat carriage with which C. E. Spooner entertained his friends and visitors from the 1860s until 1886. In use, it gravitates down the railway, stopping at Boston Lodge for the mast to be erected before sailing across the embankment if there is a suitable wind.

With the lease for the railway's booking office and shop in the Queen's Hotel, Blaenau Ffestiniog, due to expire in June 2005, the company decided not to renew it and to relocate the facilities to a container on the station platform. The remoteness of the hotel premises from the platform had not helped communications with passengers and did nothing to discourage vandalism which had sometimes occurred on the platform in between trains. The container had previously been used at the Welsh Highland Railway's Caernarfon Station.

Accommodation for Welsh Highland Railway trains in Porthmadog was considered by both the company and the trust during 2005. Referred to as a 'gateway' station', the company considered three sites. Firstly, alongside the-then proposed Porthmadog bypass, which had uncertainties regarding the availability of land and timing. Secondly, using the 1964 Company's property, which required more than the land available and difficulty was foreseen in obtaining agreement from the education authority, to release part of the Eifion Wyn School playing field. Thirdly, purchasing the-then vacant Co-op supermarket site close to the Britannia Bridge, which was on the market for £1.7 million, but would require about £3 million to acquire and develop. Grant aid and savings could provide £2 million, but a 25-year mortgage of £1 million would cost £80,000 a year to service and was beyond the company's financial capability, requiring a guarantee from the trust. Bids for the site rose to a level that the company could not afford and in February 2006 it

Palmerston and *Taliesin* passing through Tanygrisiau on 28 December 2005, both locomotives burning coal. Built to burn oil but convertible, *Taliesin* was on trial with coal following increases in the cost of oil.

Seen on 18 July 2006, the *Earl of Merioneth* had entered service burning coal on 27 May, having only burned oil since it was built in 1979. The work required included installing spark arresters, ashpans and dampers. It was also necessary to design systems for storing and handling coal.

Alan Pegler celebrated his eighty-fifth birthday with a trip on the train on 1 May 2006. Seen with the loco crews, he is holding the commemorative trowel given by Henry Archer to W.G. Oakeley in 1833.

accepted that the only realistic site for handling the traffic was at the existing Porthmadog Station.

Increasing oil prices, from £120,000 in 2003 to £140,000 in 2004 and rising, forced the Company to re-assess its locomotive fuel policy towards the end of 2005. The trust agreed to make a £25,000 grant, followed by a further £50,000 if trials were successful, for the 'fuel diversification project' on 12 October. Single Fairlie *Taliesin*, which had been built to be convertible in fuel, was converted to burn coal on a trial basis and found capable of maintaining the timetable, but refinement of grate and spark arrester design was desirable. *Earl of Merioneth* was converted in 2006. Cost savings in the range of 33-47 per cent had been predicted, but in practice 50-66 per cent was achieved. *Taliesin's* bunker was also extended to increase its capacity.

At first it was intended to maintain *Linda* and *Blanche* as oil burners, as they had benefited most

from conversion to oil and to maintain flexibility in fuel use, but by 2015 they had been converted, too, and all the oil-handling installations were removed.

The announcement that Alan Pegler, President, Ffestiniog Railway, had been awarded an OBE for services to railway heritage in the 2006 new year honours was warmly and widely welcomed. Despite a debilitating illness that weakened him, he remained a regular visitor to the railway. He received his award from HRH the *Prince* of Wales on 26 May.

Eileen Clayton was also nominated for an award, receiving an MBE for services to the railway in the 2006 birthday honours. Leading groups to improve

In the nineteenth century the railway installed a set of distinctive slate mileposts, probably intended, as well as complying with Board of Trade requirements, to assist semi-literate employees to tell where they were. Triangular posts indicate the distance to the nearest milepost, rectangular slabs showed the distance from Duffws and Portmadoc numerically. Some of them still remain in situ, others have been replaced by modern replicas, like this ¾ post at Trwyn-y-Garnedd.

the railway's appearance since the 1980s, developing gardens, maintaining buildings, building the Minffordd hostel and encouraging young volunteers, she had also become ill but maintained, and still maintains, an active engagement with these activities. She also received her award from HRH the Prince of Wales, on 7 December.

Demand for services by coach operators in January 2006, when track renewal at Penrhediad prevented access to the full length of the railway, led to the operation of services as far as Rhiw Goch or the Trwyn-y-Garnedd view window, passengers being accompanied by hosts providing a commentary. During the return journey a brief stop was made on the curve at Boston Lodge to view locomotives especially posed on the inspection pit.

The antipathy felt by some FR society members towards the Welsh Highland Railway was manifest in a special resolution proposed at the society's AGM on 29 April 2006. They sought to alter the memorandum of association to exclude the society from supporting any other railway or enterprise with which the company was, or might be in the future, associated. The society directors thought that this would be unhelpful as it would inhibit the society from having an input into any of the company's affairs that did not relate to the operation of the FR, and on which it might otherwise have an opinion. The motion was lost by 16 votes to 172 with four abstentions.

Shortly afterwards, on 20 July, the society chairman resigned, following his resignation with a two-page rant published in the society magazine, making unquantified comparisons with other railways and accusing the company directors of neglecting the railway in favour of the WHR, and bringing change to Porthmadog Station and Boston Lodge that would not be required without it. Of the seven letters published in the following issue, one

said that he was wrong, two explained why some of his claims were ill-founded and the others, in so many words, that he confirmed their prejudices.

A relic of the past had been donated to the railway in May 2006. The canopy that sheltered passengers at *'stesion fein'*, the narrow station opened to serve the LNWR terminus in 1881, had been sold to nearby Manod Football Club when it was derelict in the 1950s. Wishing to upgrade its facilities, the club offered it back to the railway. At the time of publication, no new use has been found for the material apart from some of the slates.

Some of them were used in the renewal of Rhiw Goch signal box, a volunteer-led project that was started later in 2006. To keep the box operational whilst it was improved, a new structure was designed to encase the old which was then demolished from the inside. The new building, designed to have the appearance of a nineteenth-century structure, was equipped with modern conveniences and complies with current insulation standards. One problem that had to be dealt with during the construction phase was the bats that had taken up residence in the old building. The £15,000 project was funded by an appeal supported by a sponsor. Alan Pegler cut a ribbon when the work was commissioned on 11 May 2007. In 2008 the project was runner-up in the National Railway Heritage Awards' Westinghouse Award for signalling schemes.

Observation carriage No. 100 was rebuilt without the guard's compartment in 2006, operating in

The Matisa tamper bought to aid track laying on the Welsh Highland Railway made its first moves at Boston Lodge on 1 May 2006. It had been regauged, equipped with chopper couplings and fitted with a roof to render it suitable for working outside.

partnership with service car No. 124 from 2007. This combination both increased the number of premium seats available for the booking office to sell and put the buffet facilities, toilet compartment and guard's compartment in a single vehicle, a strategy that was adopted on both the FR and the Welsh Highland Railway. No. 124, built on the underframe of 1981-built No. 121, was equipped with a generator to power-cooking equipment, fridge and freezer. The body of No. 121 had been in poor condition and was scrapped.

As the work on the service car was approaching completion, activity in the carriage workshop was ratcheted up a notch as three 13m-long carriages were started for the Welsh Highland Railway. One metre longer than the 1997-built WHR stock, the extra length provided space to improve wheelchair access. They were completed in May 2008.

Another task completed at Boston Lodge in 2006 was the regauging and adaptation of a metre-gauge Plasser KMX tamper for use, initially, on the Welsh Highland Railway. Built in 1995, it was the last item removed from a disused colliery in Lorraine, France, where it had been used underground, a function that explained its ability to be accommodated by the FR/WHR loading gauge. It had been delivered to Minffordd on 29 March 2005.

The deterioration in the relationship between the company and the trust had come to a head in February 2006. At a meeting of the trustees with the directors, John Prideaux had explained that he wished to ensure that there was no repetition of the perceived inadequate oversight of the company by the trust that had happened a few years before. He saw the trust's role as akin to that of a supervisory board, agreeing financial limits and general policy. The company was legally responsible for the conduct of its affairs. Although the memorandum was not binding as between the company and the trust as a shareholder, its terms, including the obligation to call an extraordinary meeting, could still be made binding in the form of conditions on which the trust provided grant funding to the company. The company was not, however, obliged to respond to a request for an emergency general meeting if the trustees thought one was necessary. Despite the trust holding a majority of the shares, extraordinary meetings can only be called by at least twenty shareholders holding at least 10 per cent of the company's capital.

Consultation with the trustees and directors on means to eliminate the friction gained unanimous support for Whitehouse's resignation. 'It was all very civilised' Prideaux told the author in 2015, a

Following a ten-year boiler service, *Earl of Merioneth* was lit up for the first time on 24 August 2007. Some wag had given the nameplates mauve lettering.

The stone that commemorated the 175th anniversary of the company's incorporation was made in the shape of the 1833 foundation stone.

view with which Whitehouse concurred when asked. On 4 August 2006, the directors were informed that the trust would nominate Prideaux to be a director in expectation that he would also be chairman. Whitehouse was asked to continue as a director, which he did for a further twelve months, when he was replaced by Stephen Murfitt, who retained his position as company clerk. Whitehouse continued as chairman of the holdings company.

At the AGM on 5 October 2006, Michael Schumann retired, whilst remaining a trustee, to be replaced by Prideaux as intended. Earlier in the year, society nominee Andrew Hayward had resigned for personal reasons and had been replaced by retired academic Richard Buxton.

An improvement in the company's relationship with the society followed further changes in the latter's leadership in 2007, although the issue of the company's nomination to the society board was not resolved and was eventually deemed to be unnecessary, the society's nominee to the company providing a two-way communications channel.

The key event of 2007, albeit a low-key one, was the celebration of the 175th anniversary of the company's incorporation at Tan y Bwlch on 22 May. The Lord Lieutenant of Gwynedd, Huw Morgan

Daniel, unveiled a slate plaque made in the style of the foundation stone laid nearby in 1833.

On 23 March 2007, *Prince* had participated in the launch of services on the Welsh Highland Railway between Pen y Mount and Traeth Mawr loop. This

A classic scene at Penrhyn that almost replicates R. H. Bleasdale's photograph of 1887. Seen 120 years later, such a sight would have been unimaginable in the 1950s. The buildings had been subject to a sympathetic restoration in 1991-2.

800m section had been constructed by Welsh Highland Railway Ltd members following an agreement made in 1997 and was operated by that company for two years. *Prince* had been one of two locomotives to inaugurate services on the original WHR in 1923, the other being *Princess*.

As well as the three WHR saloons mentioned earlier, the carriage workshop completed the overhaul of No. 19 and the construction of a replica 1868-Ashbury four-wheeled two-compartment carriage. The trust had funded the first whilst surplus monies from the *Taliesin* locomotive fund paid for the second, a volunteer project. Both were released to traffic after a test run on 19 May. For the Welshpool & Llanfair Light Railway, a second, third-class, saloon, Pickering carriage was built, delivered to Llanfair Caereinion on 17 August.

Completion of No. 19 brought to an end a trust-led scheme to create a Victorian train that had started in 2001 using donations made by John Prideaux. The vehicles concerned are listed in the table. Nos. 23 and 24 had been commissioned in 2001 when the

foot and mouth disease outbreak threated to close the railway, replacing routine maintenance with capital work and eliminating the risk of making personnel redundant. No. 24 had started as a scheme to restore No. 26 until it was found that No. 26 contained no original material. A lottery grant application for funds to support the restoration of Nos. 18 and 19 was rejected. They and No. 23 looked

No.	Maker	Date	Comments
23	Ashbury	2001	
24	Ashbury	2002	New vehicle
14	Bristol Wagon & Carriage Works	2002	Original bogies restored
18	Brown, Marshalls	2003	
Van No. 1	Brown, Marshalls	2004	New vehicle
No. 19	Brown, Marshalls	2006	

Boston Lodge, seen on 7 September 2006. A scheme to redevelop and modernise the site, whilst protecting the nineteenth-century structures, was started in 2016.

much better than they were and No. 18 cost more to restore than building a new vehicle.

Looking ahead to the completion of the Welsh Highland Railway, on 22 February 2008 the directors decided that it would not be sensible to attempt to widen the embankment and construct the new station in a single winter. In the meantime, a temporary connection could be made for the use of works trains. Apart from sponsors' and inspection trains, requests for special trains before the railway had been passed for passenger operations should be deferred, they decided, although photo charter trains could be run under restricted circumstances.

In March 2008, a six-month project to restore the 1863 locomotive shed at Boston Lodge to conservation criteria was started. Carried out by a specialist contractor, the work was done to the highest standards although the original clerestory and smoke vents were not restored. The scheme was funded by the trust, the society, Michael Schumann and Cadw, the Welsh heritage agency. The trust funding included legacies from Norman Gurley, once an employee, and Rodney Weaver, a volunteer. Like many of the other buildings at Boston Lodge, the shed is a listed structure. In 2009, the company was awarded the National Railway Heritage Awards' Network Rail Partnership Award for the restoration.

Along the line, derailment of a vintage train that occurred at Gysgfa, above Cae Mawr, on 3 May 2008 was subject to an investigation and report by the Department of Transport's rail accident investigation branch. The report, released in July 2009, explained that two vehicles of a vintage train had been derailed, none of the thirty-four passengers had been hurt, but the guard, one of three train crew, had sustained a minor injury. The immediate cause was identified as the failure of eight baseplates on the outer rail of a curve.

The track had been laid in in 1973, flat-bottom rail being fixed to jarrah sleepers with screws and clips. The clips had been replaced by pressed-steel baseplates and spring clips in 1993. Metallurgical examination revealed that the broken baseplates had failed at least three months earlier. During the four weeks that followed the incident, another seventy-one broken baseplates were found in six similar sites on the railway. In most cases, they had been broken because the sleepers had been weakened by fungal development on rotting leaves, leaving them unsupported.

Deficiencies in the railway's track inspection regimen that led to a failure to identify the broken baseplates during an inspection made on 8 March were also described. On that occasion, when the inspection had been carried out by rail, a lurch had been recorded as a rail joint requiring attention and the gauge was not checked.

The report concluded with five recommendations addressing casual and contributory factors leading

A derailment occurred at Gwsgfa on 3 May 2008. The next day the train concerned was still on site, blocked in by the permanent way train behind it.

to the derailment, establishing the number of consecutive defective baseplates that could lead to an unacceptable risk of derailment; develop techniques to detect baseplate deterioration; amend its track maintenance procedures; revise its system of track inspection and recording; and implement a change control procedure for standing instructions.

When the company had started using jarrah sleepers in 1969, they had a life expectancy of fifty years and there was no caveat about the damage that might be caused by rotting oak leaves. The sleepers at Gysgfa were 35-years-old. The pattern of baseplate used with flat-bottom rail was changed to cast steel, 700 sleepers were changed and a leaf blower was purchased.

An unusual commercial contract was undertaken in 2008, the installation of 18km of fibre-optic cable from Minffordd to Blaenau Ffestiniog for Network Rail, as a part of the national rail system's data network. Not only was the company paid for providing the facility and doing the work, it receives a handsome wayleave and is allowed to make use of the link for its own purposes, too.

At Boston Lodge in 2008, the carriage workshop turned out driving trailer/saloon No. 111 with a new interior that approached the standards applied to the other observation cars. No. 116, new in 1972, also received a new interior after its first-class compartment had been removed; its window frames were replaced with a different design and heating was installed, too. A service car was also built for use on the Welsh Highland Railway.

On 8 May, the main works steam tested a new boiler for the Hunslet 0-4-0ST *Lilla* and re-assembled it in time to be used on the spring bank holiday. The

Hunslet 0-4-0ST *Lilla* arrived on the railway as a visitor to the Hunslet 100 gala in 1993 and never left. In 1997 a group of admirers raised the money to buy it on behalf of the trust, forming a support group to maintain it. On 31 October 2004 it was seen at Tanygrisiau making a final run out for its supporters before its boiler certificate expired. The waiting shelter was built in 1996.

welded boiler was the first to be made in-house, receiving the number FRB1.

The onset of international recession during 2008 manifested itself by poor traffic figures, especially on the FR. In August, general manager Paul Lewin told *Steam Railway* magazine that traffic was lack-lustre, saying that it was also influenced by poor weather and Welsh Highland Railway construction works near the station at Porthmadog. The shareholders' report explained that traffic receipts on the FR fell by 7.9 per cent whilst WHR receipts increased by 1.7 per cent. The cost of fuel, the greatest expense after wages, exceeded its £200,000 budget by £18,000. The pension fund, which had been closed in 2001, was also putting pressure on the balance sheet, with a shortfall of £437,000 requiring £57,600 a year for ten years to eliminate.

In September, the directors took a pessimistic view of the company's prospects for 2009 and announced that nine posts would be made redundant by the end of the year; the holders of three other posts also left. Paul Lewin told the *Daily Post* that the economic downturn and rising fuel prices were responsible. FR traffic had fallen by 8 per cent in

Lilla's new boiler was the first to be built at Boston Lodge. It was funded by members of the locomotive's support group. 17 September 2006.

August and fuel had increased from 30p to 67p per litre over twelve months.

Most of the posts concerned were at Boston Lodge, where the completion of contract work, particularly the restoration of Garratt No. 87 and construction of new Welsh Highland Railway

carriages, was coming to an end with an associated fall in revenue. Started in 2006, the restoration of No. 87 for use on the Welsh Highland Railway had been sponsored by an enthusiast and had been the largest such project undertaken there.

Other measures taken included reducing the number of timetabled trains in 2009. A pension fund deficit had also come to light after the pension fund

To commemorate the completion of Welsh Highland Railway track laying, and the link up to the FR, a 'golden bolt' ceremony was held at Porthmadog on 28 February 2009. General manager Paul Lewin poses with the (brass) bolts and the 1833 trowel.

adviser had been changed in 2006. To eliminate it, the Cuneo painting that Alan Pegler had commissioned in 1964, and which the company had owned since 1971, was sold at Sotheby's on 23 October 2008, realising only £49,250 including the buyers' premium, although the auctioneers had expected that it would exceed their higher guide price of £60,000. Two company-owned houses were sold and ownership of two others was transferred to the fund.

The company's debt position, and hence its resilience to the recession, was helped by holders of £86,875 of the 1987 debentures waiving their right to repayment, many of them donating their investment to the trust. The first instalment of the debentures had been due for repayment during 2008.

Regarding the trust, Sir William McAlpine retired in 2008, and was replaced by Richard Broyd, a conservationist and hotelier.

Completion of Welsh Highland Railway track laying in 2009, and its connection to the FR, was marked by a 'golden bolt' ceremony, in which No. 87 participated, on 28 February. Dozens of volunteers joined a large crowd to watch as No. 87 made a symbolic crossing from the FR onto the Welsh Highland Railway using the point installed in the main line twelve months before to provide a temporary link until the Station was extended to accommodate WHR trains.

Seen on 12 March 2009, a temporary connection was made at Porthmadog to accommodate trains to and from the Welsh Highland Railway. It remained in use until the station was enlarged to accommodate trains from both railways simultaneously in 2014.

On 29 February 2009 'golden' bolts commemorating the connection of the Welsh Highland Railway to the FR were were installed by Paul Bradshaw (left) and Dafydd Thomas, the leaders of the track-laying gangs.

The first use of the connection to transfer stock to Dinas, WHR, by rail took place in darkness on 12 March, with a diesel-hauled train, including the new WHR Pullman observation carriage and a Romanian saloon. Designed to be distinctive and constructed to a high quality at Boston Lodge, the twenty-six-seat observation carriage is 14m long, the longest vehicle on either of the railways. The thirty-six-seat Romanian saloon had been built for use on 750mm (2ft 6in)-gauge railways in the Eastern bloc. It had been modified to suit the WHR loading gauge and regauged before delivery to Boston Lodge for internal fitting out.

The first steam transfer between the two railways occurred on 23 March, when No. 87 hauled carriage No. 2090 from Boston Lodge to Dinas. The carriage had been built as a brake/saloon with wheelchair-accessible doors in 1997. It had subsequently been

equipped with a buffet pantry, and over the winter it had been fitted with a toilet compartment and been repainted.

The track on the FR side of the bridge had actually been used on 22 November 2008, when a 762mm-gauge Chinese C2 0-8-0 had been unloaded from a road vehicle for delivery to Boston Lodge. Built in 1988, and possibly the last steam locomotive built for industrial use in the world, in January 2007 a group of volunteers had imported it from China with the intention of restoring it, agreeing with the company that they could use the facilities at Boston Lodge providing they supplied their own accommodation. A shed was built at the rear of the carriage works in 2009. The restoration, including regauging, is expected to take ten years. When it is completed the shed will be donated to the company.

Contract work at Boston Lodge during 2009 included the construction of a third Pickering carriage for the Welshpool & Llanfair Light Railway,

The first movement from the Welsh Highland Railway took place during the afternoon of 12 March 2009, when *Criccieth Castle* arrived from Dinas with carriage No. 111.

On 23 March 2009 the first steam transfer to the Welsh Highland Railway occurred, when Garratt No. 87 was moved to Dinas. The transition from 60lb rail to tram rail, via a short length of 75lb rail, is visible in the foreground.

Another new locomotive appeared on the railway in January 2007, a Chinese 762mm-gauge 'C2' 0-8-0, built in 1958. Its owners, a group of Boston Lodge volunteers, are restoring and regauging the loco in a shed they had built for the purpose.

delivered later in 2010, and the rebuilding of four carriage bogies for the 3ft-gauge Isle of Man Steam Railway. The bogies included the provision of new wheelsets that were fitted with Boston Lodge-designed roller-bearing axleboxes.

The Welshpool carriage was built alongside a thirty-five-seat saloon that was nominally a rebuild of the 1968-built buffet car No. 103 and which entered service on 11 February 2010. Given the same number, it had a new body constructed on a new underframe, panoramic double-glazed windows and recessed inward-opening doors, single at one end and double at the other to provide easy access for buggies and wheelchairs, insulation and heating, setting the standard for upgrading FR passenger accommodation. The recessed doors enabled it to have a body 39ft 1½in long and still clear the FR's sharper curves; except for No 122, stock built from the 1960s had 36ft bodies. The inward-opening doors did not need to be locked, unlike the outward-opening doors, which continued to be locked on the basis of Captain Tyler's recommendation. Described as a 'super saloon', it was funded by the society. The society also funded a similar vehicle, No. 121, which entered service in 2011.

In June 2009, the owner of a local company complained to the *Daily Post* that the non-payment of bills by the company's subsidiary, Welsh

Highland Railway Construction Ltd, had forced his company into receivership. The railway company, he continued, had received millions in grants, but had refused to pay him. WHRC disputed his claims.

The story led to a follow-up on 4 June, with the headline '£28m Welsh Highland Railway project delayed after running out of cash'. General manager Paul Lewin explained that although £28 million had been spent, and the track had been laid to Porthmadog, more money was needed to equip the level crossings at Pont Croesor, Snowdon Street and the Britannia Bridge. How much and how long it would take to complete the railway he was unable to say.

In fact, the poor results of 2008 and the gloomy outlook for 2009 resulted in the company having its most successful year since 1955, recording a record profit of £222,424. This was not only because of the cost-saving initiatives taken in 2008, but because Welsh Highland Railway revenue increased as it approached Porthmadog; services were extended to Beddgelert in April and through the Aberglaslyn Pass to Hafod y Llyn in May, generating a 65 per cent increase in bookings and more than doubling revenue, exceeding £1 million for the first time; FR bookings and revenue increased too, by 10 per cent and 14 per cent respectively.

CHAPTER 14

2010-2014: THE WELSH HIGHLAND RETURNS

Moving into the second decade of the twenty-first century, the company's confidence increased enormously. Not only was the restoration of the Welsh Highland Railway completed, but the naysayers of yore were confounded by the public's determination to travel its full length. The structural debt was eliminated and Boston Lodge's reputation for the quality of its output was secured by high-profile contracts successfully completed. Celebrations commemorated the company's 175th anniversary and the 150th anniversary of steam traction.

The first event to turn the spotlight on the company, though, was the visit of HM the Queen and HRH the Duke of Edinburgh to the WHR on 27 April 2010. Travelling in the new Pullman observation car from Caernarfon to Dinas, the royal couple might have remembered that they had travelled over the same formation in the royal train en route to the opening of the power station at Tanygrisiau in 1963. Before leaving Dinas by road, the Queen named the observation car *Glaslyn*.

The impact of the royal visit was followed on 30 October by the operation of the first passenger trains from Caernarfon to Porthmadog, run for sponsors and supporters. Despite being delayed by the actions of the disgruntled business owner at Pont Croesor, the first train was greeted by a crowd of hundreds as it crossed the Britannia Bridge and entered the station at Porthmadog.

With several awards having been made in respect to the WHR, the company built on the impetus

The first Garratt to reach Porthmadog from Caernarfon by rail. On 30 October 2010, sponsors and donors to the Welsh Highland Railway appeal travelled by two special trains over the complete length of the WHR for the first time, one group on the first train breaking out champagne as the train passed Snowdon Street.

At Minffordd on 21 July 2012, the Lynton & Barnstaple Railway Manning, Wardle 2-6-2T *Lyd* has become a regular performer on lighter trains. It has also visited the LBR in Devon.

generated to raise its profile. On 17-20 March the WHR observation car had been exhibited at the 'Best of Britain and Ireland 2010' travel trade exhibition at London's Olympia, and the display of equipment, usually locomotives, sometimes complete trains, at locations attracting visitors who might be encouraged to visit the railways, became a key part of its strategy.

The 2010 new year honours list announced on 31 December 2009 had included reference to the company and to Welsh Highland Railway Construction in the citation for an OBE awarded to Mike Hart for services to the rail industry. HRH the Prince of Wales presented the award on 19 November.

On the railway, carriage No. 114 had caught fire due to a gas leak whilst being prepared for service at Boston Lodge on 10 February 2010. Despite requiring the attendance of the fire service, the damage was relatively slight. The gas-fired heaters

were immediately withdrawn and, in due course, replaced by Eberspächer oil-fired heaters as used in commercial vehicles. No. 114 returned to service on 29 May.

The most significant locomotive development during 2010 was the completion of the Lynton & Barnstaple Railway Manning, Wardle 2-6-2T *Lyd*. It was launched at Beddgelert on 11 September and made a trip to Devon, making appearances in Barnstaple, on the Launceston Steam Railway, and the Lynton & Barnstaple Railway, immediately afterwards.

Dick Wollan, the chief executive from 1979 until 1983, died on 27 June 2010, aged eighty-seven. He

An established feature of the railway's operation since 1970 has been the operation of Santa trains, normally from Porthmadog to Tan y bwlch. In 2010 a service was operated from Blaenau Ffestiniog, seen near Tanygrisiau on 12 December.

had been determined that the company should be commercially viable and focussed on restoring services to Blaenau Ffestiniog, which was achieved before he retired.

Construction of the Porthmadog bypass caused the railway to be closed whilst an underbridge was built at Minffordd in January and February 2011. In substitution for the Trwyn y Garnedd 'sherry and mince pie' services, the company therefore operated trains between Porthmadog and Hafod y Llyn, the first time-tabled services over this part of the Welsh Highland Railway. FR seervices were resumed on 2 March.

The first revenue-earning trains over the entire length of the WHR, one return train from each end, ran during the half-term week that started on 19 February 2011. The event was signalled to a wider world by an editorial in the *Guardian* on 11 February. '… the journey will be spectacular and the achievement immense … politics overcome … it will be possible to make a 40-mile journey by narrow-gauge train … a step into the past, perhaps, but a charming one.' Some enthusiasts had complained when the timetable had been released, expecting an intensive service to be operated from the start.

In recognition of its significance, a premium fare was charged on the first day. Because of the limited layout at Porthmadog, WHR trains could not enter the Station when an FR train was present, or in the section between Porthmadog and Minffordd, and

2010-2014: THE WELSH HIGHLAND RETURNS • 297

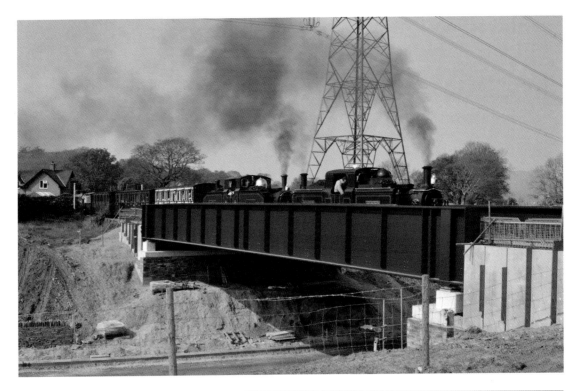

Merddin Emrys and *Earl of Merioneth* cross the Porthmadog bypass on the-then recently erected bridge at Minffordd on 21 April 2011. The two locomotives, both burning coal, were rostered to minimise the risk of fire during a spell of dry weather.

vice-versa. They also had to be shunted into and out of the Station by a second locomotive. The ground signal installed to control the connection was interlocked with the Britannia Bridge level crossing to ensure that it could not be activated unless the points were set to enable a WHR train to enter the Station.

The completion of the WHR between Rhyd Ddu and Porthmadog was marked on 20 April 2011, the FR's 175th anniversary. Record producer and railway enthusiast Pete Waterman unveiled a milestone that commemorated both the anniversary and the WHR, saying that the event demonstrated that 'enthusiasm does pay off … it is a testament to belief and enthusiasm … it really is magnificent'. He also pointed out that in connecting Blaenau Ffestiniog with Porthmadog and Caernarfon, the FR and WHR were significant in also connecting the three main Welsh-speaking centres of Gwynedd. The milestone, which indicates the direction and distance to Caernarfon and Blaenau Ffestiniog, was subsequently mounted on a plinth close to the junction between the two railways.

Later, at Pont Croesor, the president of the Welsh Assembly, Lord Dafydd Elis-Thomas, also commented on the links made by the FR and WHR, saying that his family was from Blaenau Ffestiniog, he had an office in Porthmadog and he had lived in

Two events were commemorated on 20 April 2011, the 175th anniversary of the railway's opening and the completion of the final phase of the Welsh Highland Railway. Record producer and railway enthusiast Pete Waterman, seen with John Prideaux, unveiled this milepost, which has been fixed in an appropriate place on the building.

Caernarfon. Saying that he spoke for the community, he continued 'you have rebuilt for us a monument to our industrial past …. That is very important for me because it is my own family history … Out of that grew a distinctive culture …, but also this distinctive view of society, and of people's comradeship together in hard times and in good times. That heritage now is being reinterpreted for a new generation and we are grateful to you for the vision that you bring to enrich that heritage.' Amongst the guests was Lord Dafydd Wigley, who as a local MP had supported the reinstatement of the WHR, and had opened the railway between Dinas and Waunfawr on August 7 2000. The next morning there was a queue of intending Welsh Highland Railway passengers waiting for the booking office to open.

However, the intention to run only a limited number of Welsh Highland trains to and from Porthmadog was reviewed in response to passenger demand to travel over the entire line and additional services were introduced from 19 July. The increased Welsh Highland traffic had a significant impact on operations at Porthmadog, with passengers arriving to catch the 9.30am departure responsible for the booking office, shop and café having to open at 8.30am instead of 9.00am. Breakfast was added to the café's offer, too. The outcome was another record profit, £292,823. The 1 per cent reduction in FR revenue was largely attributed to its closure whilst the bypass bridge had been built.

Lest there was any thought that the commencement of services over the full length of the WHR meant that the work was finished, in June shareholders and members of the FR and WHR societies were sent a twenty-page brochure entitled 'Ffestiniog & Welsh Highland Railways – a sustainable future', in which trust and company chairman John Prideaux addressed the developments that would make the railways sustainable.

To set the scene, he explained that whilst the headline achievement was the rebuilding of the Welsh Highland Railway in fifteen years, the FR had changed too, becoming more concerned about its heritage and improving its day-to-day passenger accommodation. On the WHR, only the track had been completed; it lacked facilities, particularly at stations, that make a complete railway. The business had grown from £1.45 million turnover in 1995 to more than £4 million in 2010.

The next challenge was to develop the railways in ways that made the most of their heritage and to turn the whole into a sustainable enterprise. An £8.6

million shopping list to achieve this included creating a second platform at Porthmadog; storage facilities at Boston Lodge, Minffordd and Dinas; restoration of historic buildings; powerful diesel locomotives; additional carriages; station buildings at Caernarfon and Blaenau Ffestiniog; and improved signalling on the WHR.

The FR Society responded with its own brochure, entitled 'The Development Strategy – a framework document', informing members how it would help achieve the company's aspirations with regard to its own core objectives.

A substantial bequest notified in 2009 was timely in enabling the trust to support the company in completing outstanding works on the Welsh Highland Railway and carrying out the works in Porthmadog Station. The deceased estate was handled quite efficiently and most of the bequest was received in 2011. This was not always the case, some estates taking several years to resolve.

These paragraphs only briefly touch on the work undertaken by the directors and the trustees to keep the construction companies funded and complete the WHR. Since construction was started in 1997, some very generous donations were made by individual donors, the Welsh Highland Railway Society, contributors to a track fund and contributors to the appeal determined to bring this remarkable project to a successful conclusion. There had been, however, a hiatus in 2000-3, when the company had struggled to obtain the match funding required to progress construction between Waunfawr and Rhyd Ddu, and had drawn heavily on the trust's uncommitted funds, taxing both parties.

The directors also had to devote a great deal of time on the Britannia Bridge level crossing since the rails had been laid in the road in June 2008, largely due to cyclists travelling from the Minffordd direction being unwilling to obey signs directing them to dismount to cross the track and then complaining when they fell off. One cyclist who fell off told a local newspaper that the rails had been in place for a month before he noticed them. Some local politicians also thought it appropriate to give their support to people who admitted ignoring the Highway Code, and in January 2010, North Wales Police threatened to bring charges of corporate manslaughter against the company if there was a

Linda and *Blanche*, both in the same livery for the first time since 1996, leave Tan y Bwlch on 23 July 2011.

fatal accident there, saying that no action had been taken to mitigate the risk.

The company pointed out that that the North Wales Trunk Roads Agency was responsible for installing mandatory signs, which it had not done, and asked why the police had not pursued the agency or taken action against those who ignored the Highway Code. A 'we told you so' letter from a member of the town council published the following week attracted others saying that the objections were illogical, one writer asking what was so special about the Britannia Bridge? In other places with tram lines cyclists coped, he said. It must also be said that in the event of a fatality any prosecuting decision would be taken by the Crown Prosecution Service, not a police inspector.

The level crossing order was made on 10 December 2010 and the directors determined to make every effort to ensure compliance with it, to protect the company and themselves from claims, although the local authority dragged its feet over allowing the crossing controls to be linked to the

nearby pedestrian crossing as required by the order. Closed-circuit television cameras were installed to observe the crossing and to secure an accurate record of any incident.

As for members of the public, they thought the sight of trains on the bridge was a huge attraction, a crowd gathering on most occasions that the crossing is used. At one point the question asked most often in the nearby tourist information office was, 'What time does the next train go across the bridge?'

Revision of the memorandum of understanding between the company and the trust was effective from 26 July 2010. Effectively restating provisions of the 2003 memorandum to take into account the completion of the WHR and to give better recognition of the parties' obligations under common law, the company and the trust agreed that the railways will be managed in accordance with the memorandum so far as it is consistent with the trust's obligations as a charity, and the company's under its Act of Parliament and other legislation. The appointment of non-statutory directors was also covered, and to the section on the conduct of the company's business was added a clause that no third party will be granted the right to operate trains over the railways, or any section of them, without the agreement of the company and the trustees.

The scope of an appeal that had been launched to raise funds with a bias towards the WHR in December 2010 was expanded to include more FR-focussed projects and linked to the sustainable railway objectives; by 1 May 2011 more than £450,000 had been raised. The organisers also commenced the operation of 'The Snowdonian', an annual excursion that covers both railways, as a fund-raising exercise.

Relationships with the national network were strengthened from 2011, when five groups of Network Rail permanent way apprentices spent a week each on track renewals as a part of the training in January and February. Staying in Minffordd Hostel, the apprentices' visit occurred annually until 2015.

In January 2011 the Heritage Lottery Fund awarded a development grant for a £500,000 project called Taith i'n Treftadaeth/Our Heritage Journey, designed to improve visitor experiences with initiatives to uncover, restore and interpret the railway's heritage. After two years of work and the withdrawal of Cadw, the Welsh heritage agency, the application was rejected.

An innovation started in 2011 was the publication of a magazine promoting the attributes of the railways. Named *TLC* and sub-titled 'in the top left corner of Wales' it had high design and production values, and was published annually for sale in the railways' shops and given away at events until 2016. It was a great success, although how many readers appreciate or understand the running gag of song titles in the headlines is not known.

Another innovation that saw the light of day in 2011 was a monobloc cylinder casting installed in *Taliesin*. Traditionally, Fairlie cylinders and steam chest comprised two castings bolted together, a point of weakness in practice, and used slide valves, which were less efficient than piston valves. Manufactured to steam at 200psi, *Taliesin's* boiler was also too competent for its mechanical components and induced excess wear.

In 2008, a team at Boston Lodge led by boilersmith Rob Yates had produced a design for a one-piece cylinder casting, incorporating piston valves, that could replace the existing cylinders in any of the bogie engines without changing their appearance. With *Taliesin* selected for trial purposes as it had only one power bogie, design work and patternmaking was funded by the residue of the *Taliesin* 2000 fund and the Society contributed £10,000 for the casting and machining. A test run with empty stock to Blaenau Ffestiniog on 13 October 2011 was deemed a success, with much less water being taken at Tan y Bwlch than would have been the case previously. With its working boiler pressure increased to 200psi, as designed, from 160psi, valve events adjusted and the addition of new lubricators, it was also found to be better at starting. Its haulage capacity was therefore increased to seven carriages.

Withdrawn from service with a leaking tube plate in 2004, *Linda* had become the subject of a volunteer-led overhaul and had returned to service in plain black livery on 26 April 2011. During the overhaul several original features were restored. On 4 June it made a guest appearance on the private Statfold Barn Railway in Staffordshire, afterwards being turned out in Penrhyn livery for a few weeks before being repainted in FR green livery, a scheme that resonates with those who knew the loco from 1963 onwards. *Blanche* was also repainted to match at the same time.

The additional work required to convert carriage-heating systems also allowed the interiors to be updated and seat spacing to be increased to provide more space for passengers. Nos. 112 and 117 were dealt with in this manner in 2011. No. 110, the former push-pull control trailer also received a refurbished interior when it had been taken in for body repairs later in 2010. Welsh Highland Railway carriage No. 2020, the open delivered in 1997, was adapted to operate as a service car, No. 2011, entering service in March 2011.

On 25 March 2011, former observation car No. 101 returned to service as third-class observation car No. 123. It had been turned around in order that it could be placed on the uphill end of FR trains, where its outlook would sometimes be restricted by the presence of non-corridor carriages, and made wheelchair accessible. No longer required as a first-class vehicle, but considered too good to be scrapped, the repairs and changes needed had been carried out by volunteers. It was the first FR carriage to be fitted with LED lighting.

The railway participated in the embankment's bicentenary celebrations on 17 September 2011, carrying a symbolic parcel of slate from Llechwedd by gravity train, and handing it over to the ghosts of Madocks and his agent, John Williams, to be conveyed to the harbourside.

A few weeks later, on 20 October 2011, the first visible sign of the 'sustainable railway' project came with the start of the thirty-month project to widen the embankment in order to make a second platform with run-round loop for the Welsh Highland Railway. Through its New Stations Improvement Programme, the Welsh Government contributed a grant of £600,000 to be matched by £343,000 in cash and £50,000 of volunteer input.

Prompted by the start of work in October 2011, a local councillor complained to the *Daily Post* that the company had no authority to start and was working on land that it did not own. Depending on information obtained from the transport department, he also claimed that the land was in the process of being transferred from the Welsh Government to

Gwynedd Council and called for work to stop until the council had agreed to it.

The Government's department of local government then asked if the company's claim to have the necessary rights made in the grant application was accurate, a development which threatened to delay grant payments. The rights were, of course, awarded in the 1999 Welsh Highland Railway Transport & Works Order, and notices to treat and enter had actually been served on the Government in 2004. Fortunately for the company's cash flow, the Government accepted that the work was properly authorised in January 2012. Sometime later it was established that the land concerned was actually owned by the Crown, which had also been served with notices in 2004. It seems that the transport department had not understood that it only owned the road and not the remainder of the embankment.

A keen price was negotiated for the widening contract because the contractor had been working on the Porthmadog bypass, opened earlier in October, and still had equipment and personnel in the town. Disruption was minimised by arranging for most of the work to be carried out during the closed season. Vehicular access to the work site and space for the essential site huts were created by removing one of

Commemorating the bicentenary of the Traeth Mawr embankment, over which the railway runs, the ghosts of W.A. Madocks (left) and his agent, John Williams, visited the railway to accept a symbolic cargo of slate carried on a gravity train on 17 September 2011.

The Harrogate Gas Works Peckett 0-6-0ST was owned by the company for thirty-two years and never restored or steamed. Now based at the private Statfold Barn Railway in Staffordshire, it made a return visit in 2012, operating shuttles between Blaenau Ffestiniog and Tanygrisiau. 5 May 2012.

the carriage sidings and constructing a haul road across the tracks. 25,000 tons of syenite was obtained from Minffordd Quarry, the widened structure being clad with rock-armour to protect it from the sea. This stage of the work was completed in March 2012, after which the new ground was allowed to settle.

To control the more complex layout, a signalling scheme was devised using a donated Westinghouse 'L' 12-lever miniature-power lever frame. It had been installed as part of a much larger installation at Darlington South Signal Box by the London & North Eastern Railway in 1937 and was owned by a signalling enthusiast.

Boosted by the increased revenues that accompanied the extension of Welsh Highland Railway operations to Porthmadog, in October 2013 the company announced a ten-year programme to upgrade the FR's main line, starting with the most heavily used turnouts at Porthmadog, Boston Lodge and Minffordd, and 3 miles of plain line. Four new turnouts were therefore installed at the water tower-end of Porthmadog Station in advance of the major works to realign the layout to accommodate the new platform and the WHR.

Two awards that followed completion of the Welsh Highland Railway were announced in October. The Heritage Railway Association's Peter Manisty Award is only awarded for projects of the highest quality; it ranked the WHR with London & Continental Railway's restored St Pancras Station and the A1 Steam Locomotive Trust's 'A1' class 4-6-2 No. 60163 *Tornado*. Transport journalist Christian Wolmar also nominated both the WHR and the FR for the *Oldie* magazine's 'railway of the year' award, recognising the achievement of the former and the heritage ambience of the latter.

After many years in store, the company's unique collection of historic archives was made accessible to the public at Gwynedd Council's Caernarfon Record Office in 2012. Access had become possible after Patricia Layzell Ward had spent several years in a voluntary capacity cataloguing some 50,000 documents ranging from the 1830s until the 1950s.

Alan Pegler, whose father had provided the funds that enabled the FR's revival, died on 18 March 2012, aged ninety-one. His last appearance in Wales had

The thirtieth anniversary of the restoration of services to Blaenau Ffestiniog was celebrated in 2012. On 5 May the timetable was arranged to provide for a simultaneous arrival with the Arriva Trains Wales service from Llandudno Junction.

been to attend the trust dinner on 5 October 2011. Since 1955, he had taken every opportunity to promote the FR and invariably wore a company tie or sweatshirt. Whilst he will always be primarily associated with the FR, he also supported the company's involvement with the Welsh Highland Railway, attending the Millennium Commission's £4.3 million WHR grant announcement at Porthmadog on 2 October 1995 to demonstrate his support, he told the author, for the-then controversial project. President of both the society and the company, both decided that he could not be replaced. More than £65,000 collected in his memory enabled the new Porthmadog signalling installation to be styled in the manner of the McKenzie & Holland equipment supplied to the company in the nineteenth century.

Whilst attention was being focused on the high-profile scheme to widen the platform at Porthmadog, along the line a start was made on restoring and reinstating the disc distant signals that were so

symbolic of the 'old' railway, a development that even extended to recovering or being given items that had been taken away in the past. To date they have been placed at Boston Lodge, Minffordd level crossing and Pen Cefn.

In the spring of 2012, the FR's fibre-optic network installation was completed. Built on the back of the Network Rail cable installed in 2008, it provided links to all stations and a new infrastructure office located in Minffordd Yard. The office provided modern facilities for all the 'outdoor' departments, replacing a motley collection of sheds and caravans.

Small train, big scenery. *Vale of Ffestiniog* in green livery heads for Porthmadog on the deviation line, which now blends into the landscape. The original formation is in the centre and the formation from the 1842 tunnel is on the right. 6 May 2005.

Hunslet 0-4-0ST *Hugh Napier*, built for the Penrhyn slate quarry in 1904, belongs to the National Trust at Penrhyn Castle. Completion of its restoration at Boston Lodge followed six years of negotiations.

On 11 May 2012 it arrived at Porthmadog for its relaunch with a former driver on the footplate.

A contract carried out at Boston Lodge in 2011-12 was the completion of the restoration of Penrhyn quarry Hunslet 0-4-0ST *Hugh Napier*, which included constructing a new boiler, for the National Trust. The loco, which had been at the trust's Penrhyn Castle industrial railway museum since 1966, had been the subject of a restoration plan that had stalled following the death of the employee carrying out the work. The work completed, it was launched with a special train from Porthmadog to Beddgelert on 11 May 2012, when *Hugh Napier* was assisted by the larger ex-Penrhyn locos, *Linda* and *Blanche*. With the company acting as the loco's custodian, it is used on special occasions, and taken to events to promote both the railway and the trust.

A second 'super-saloon', No. 121, also entered service on 11 May, replacing the 1981-built steel-bodied carriage with the same number withdrawn in 2005. Like its predecessor, No. 103, No. 121's construction was funded by the FR Society.

Whilst traffic in 2012 was affected by the London Olympics, the FR did benefit from the publicity surrounding the event by carrying the Olympic torch from Blaenau Ffestiniog to Porthmadog on 28 May. Torch-bearer Elin Owen travelled on a special train hauled by *David Lloyd George*, arriving at Porthmadog on the footplate. 150 children from Cefn Coch School in Penrhyndeudraeth joined the train at Minffordd and the headboard was afterwards presented to the School.

Despite the restricted accommodation at Porthmadog, in 2012 all Welsh Highland Railway services were terminated there, boosting the shop's profitability, but not the catering department's. An

Compare this August 2012 photograph with one on page 108 taken some forty years earlier

unusual working in the summer timetable was the operation of a late-afternoon working from Porthmadog to Beddgelert using an FR train that would otherwise have lain idle after returning from Blaenau Ffestiniog. Enthusiasts particularly enjoyed the opportunity of seeing the smaller locos operating through the Aberglaslyn Pass.

Work on altering the station layout at Porthmadog was resumed in October 2012, when the new wave wall, which comprised 270 1m pre-cast concrete blocks held together with a steel dowel anchored in adhesive, was built around the enlarged area. Construction of the relay room was started in December and the king points, the new junction between the FR and the Welsh Highland Railway, were installed in January 2013. The Blaenau Ffestiniog-end of the new island platform

was constructed before work was suspended for the 2013 season.

A project of some significance completed in the carriage workshop in November 2012 was the restoration of four-wheel Metropolitan Railway carriage No. 353 for the London Transport Museum. It had been built by Craven Brothers in Sheffield in 1892 and sold to the Weston, Clevedon & Portishead Railway in 1906. Withdrawn in 1940, it was used as a shed in Shrivenham, Wiltshire, whence it was obtained by the Museum in 1974. The contract to restore it to working order, motivated by the MR's then forthcoming 150th anniversary in January 2013,

Subsequently inspected by HM The Queen, four-wheel Metropolitan Railway carriage No. 353 was restored for the London Transport Museum, probably the most high-profile contract undertaken at Boston Lodge. On 16 November 2012 it was transported across the embankment on ambulance bogies on the first stage of its journey back to London.

had been started in December 2011. On 16 November 2012 it was transported across the embankment on ambulance bogies for loading onto road transport in Porthmadog and delivery to the Great Central Railway, Leicestershire, for testing.

Another outside contract had been completed in the carriage workshop in August 2012, the construction of a new body for Talyllyn Railway bogie carriage No. 21. Originally built in 1971, the saloon body was delivered unpainted, that part of the work being carried out by TR volunteers at Pendre Works.

Apart from the Olympics, traffic in 2012 was affected by the weather, chairman John Prideaux informing shareholders that it was one of the wettest years on record, and the poor economic climate. Welsh Highland traffic had been expected to fall by about 10 per cent, experience had shown that it always did the year after a new section of line had been opened. The parallel decline in FR traffic had been unexpected, however, which suggested visitors were making the most of a trip to Wales by travelling on both railways. Nevertheless, the company still made a profit of £156,409.

Perhaps more significant than the level of traffic and the profit was that during the year the company had succeeded in eliminating its long-term debt.

Mike Schumann had converted his loan to a gift and the overdraft had been substantially eliminated, although still required for short periods during the winter. The outstanding 1987 debentures had been reduced to £69,000 and this amount was cleared in 2013. Costs had also been contained by the operation of all timetabled trains by coal-fired locomotives.

Further changes to the trust deed were made on 5 October 2012. Copies were sent to the societies although details were not widely circulated until some six months later. The trust had been advised that it was entitled to change the deed and was not obliged to consult on the matter, and the Charity Commission's approval had been obtained. One of its objectives was to simplify the appointment of trustees, although the most obvious change was that the trust was renamed the Ffestiniog and Welsh Highland Railways Trust, *Ymddiriedolaeth Rheilffyrdd Ffestiniog ac Eryri* in Welsh, to emphasise that it was responsible for both railways and that it operated in a bilingual area of Wales; the Welsh version had been used informally since 2005.

The society's right to nominate a trustee, awarded in 1998, was diluted to the extent that it would in future be shared with the Welsh Highland Railway Society, a development that was not well received by some FR society members. The WHR Society

Commemoration of the 150th anniversary of steam locomotives on the FR in 2013 included the cosmetic restoration of *Princess* and its display at Paddington Station, London and Heuston Station, Dublin. It was photographed at the former on 1 March, St David's Day.

During the 'Steam 150' gala, 4-6 May 2013, an admiring audience watch as John Bell and Mark Gardner take *Merddin Emrys* on an excursion from Porthmadog to Rhyd Ddu on the Welsh Highland Railway.

chairman was also added to the trustee appointment committee, the other members comprising the chairmen of the FR Society and the company, the trustees and up to three former trustees.

Since Peter Jordan stood down in 2003, society-nominated trustees were Gareth Haulfryn Williams, a retired county archivist, Dewi Lewis, a local businessman, from 2007, and Dewi Wyn Roberts, a former high sheriff of Gwynedd, from 2011.

The year 2013 was one of celebration, for 150 years earlier the company had started on the road to international fame by adopting steam locomotives. In commemoration, *Princess* was extricated from

Spooner's and it, with *Prince*, was repainted in historic livery. *Welsh Pony* was made presentable, including being fitted with new brass spectacle frames paid for by donations, and was painted green, lined out in the same style as *Prince* and *Princess*.

For a time, *Princess* had the highest profile, five weeks on display at Paddington Station, London, from 24 February being followed by six weeks at

Another 2013 gala attraction was the operation of a Garratt-hauled train across the embankment to Boston Lodge Halt. Running late in the day, the sun appeared from behind Moel y Gest as it set, producing an unusual lighting effect.

Heuston Station, Dublin, reflecting both the locomotives' being built in London and the Irish capital that had paid for the railway's development.

The railway also benefitted greatly from the publicity attaching to Transport for London's celebration of the Metropolitan Railway's 150th anniversary and the operation of the carriage restored at Boston Lodge. *Prince* therefore visited London to participate in the London Transport Museum's Acton Depot open weekend on April 13/14. This, and other, promotional activity must have contributed to income on the FR being increased by 14 per cent and on the Welsh Highland Railway by 20 per cent by August. On some days, demand for the WHR at Porthmadog had been so great that would-be passengers were turned away; when spare FR stock was available, trains were increased to ten or eleven carriages.

Promotion on home ground was focussed on a gala event on 3-6 May and the vintage weekend in October. At the former, the delivery of *Princess* was re-enacted by mounting it on a wagon disguised as a road vehicle and recruiting members of Porthmadog

Rugby Club to pull it into the Station using the Welsh Highland Railway track across the Britannia Bridge. On arrival at the Station a theatrical troupe performed an entertaining item that put the arrival of steam locomotives in Porthmadog in 1863 into context. A popular feature of both events was the appearance of the four surviving original locomotives together.

As a prelude to the vintage weekend, on 11 October 2013 the Transport Trust honoured the company with the presentation of two plaques, English and Welsh, recognising its pioneering use of narrow gauge steam traction, articulated locomotives and bogie carriages in difficult terrain.

Earlier, on 9 February a new ticketing system had been introduced, supplanting the system introduced in 1985, nearly fifteen years since its replacement had first been mooted. The new tickets are produced on a laser printer and have coloured photographs pre-printed on the reverse. A new electronic-point-of-sale system was also introduced which, amongst other things, allowed the sales department's webshop to be enhanced; when

Welsh Pony, seen here in this cameo outside the old loco shed at Boston Lodge, also received a cosmetic restoration as a part of the Steam 150 celebrations. The shed had been restored during 2008, which involved removing the gable to renew the lintel. 4 May 2013.

trading had been difficult during 2012 webshop turnover was doubled.

A replica of the original footbridge at Tan y Bwlch was commissioned during the spring. Funded as a memorial by benefactors, it had been built with a concealed steel frame at Boston Lodge. The company's plans to remove the 1971 footbridge and improve pedestrian access to the platform were thwarted by objections.

During the year, the new signal box and associated relay room were constructed on the widened section of the embankment, with a useful contribution by students from Coleg Meirion Dwyfor at Dolgellau. In addition to making doors and window frames in college, they also slated the roofs, they and their tutors appreciating having the opportunity of working on a live building site.

At the company AGM on 11 October 2013, Paul Lewin, general manager since 2003, was appointed a non-statutory director. On the same date, Sam Miller was appointed the society's nominee director to replace Tony Catchpole who had died on 9 June; he had replaced Richard Buxton, who had retired in 2011.

The year 2013 produced another record profit, chairman John Prideaux later reported to shareholders, eclipsing 2011's result. In addition to noting that traffic had increased by 9 per cent on the FR and by 11 per cent on the Welsh Highland Railway, he pointed out that the company had been cautious in setting the number of train miles run when planning the timetables, producing excellent earnings per train mile.

As the conversion of locomotive fuel from oil to coal was approaching completion in 2014, with *Linda* and *Blanche* the last to be converted, although *Mountaineer*, out of service since 2006 and in store at

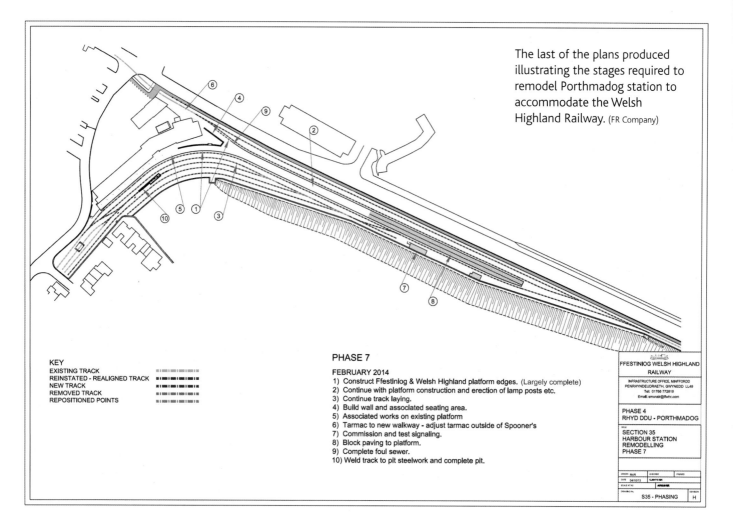

The last of the plans produced illustrating the stages required to remodel Porthmadog station to accommodate the Welsh Highland Railway. (FR Company)

KEY
EXISTING TRACK
REINSTATED - REALIGNED TRACK
NEW TRACK
REMOVED TRACK
REPOSITIONED POINTS

PHASE 7

FEBRUARY 2014
1) Construct Ffestiniog & Welsh Highland platform edges. (Largely complete)
2) Continue with platform construction and erection of lamp posts etc.
3) Continue track laying.
4) Build wall and associated seating area.
5) Associated works on existing platform
6) Tarmac to new walkway - adjust tarmac outside of Spooner's
7) Commission and test signalling.
8) Block paving to platform.
9) Complete foul sewer.
10) Weld track to pit steelwork and complete pit.

FFESTINIOG WELSH HIGHLAND RAILWAY

INFRASTRUCTURE OFFICE, MINFFORDD
PENRHYNDEUDRAETH, GWYNEDD LL49
Tel: 01766 772819
Email: smcnair@ffwhr.com

PHASE 4
RHYD DDU - PORTHMADOG

SECTION 35
HARBOUR STATION
REMODELLING
PHASE 7

S35 - PHASING

Glan y Pwll, remains a nominal oil burner until the resources are found for its restoration, the infrastructure that had supported oil was removed. A bogie oil-tank wagon found a new life as a water bowser for use in case of lineside fires. Coal handling at Boston Lodge had included a trial with a portable conveyor before settling on the use of adapted South African bogie wagons that could be machine loaded at Minffordd. A second wagon was positioned alongside the water tower at Porthmadog. The Garratts are fuelled by machine at Dinas.

A Bagnall 0-4-2T, the subject of a contract to repair its boiler and complete its restoration, was steamed across the embankment on 18 May 2013. However, its valve gear, which had been assembled by another contractor, failed during testing on the Welsh Highland Railway in July, requiring more work to be done. Named *Isaac*, painted green and lined out in November, the privately-owned locomotive is now based on the Lynton & Barnstaple Railway.

The major trackworks required to complete the reorganisation and extension of Porthmadog Station were carried out over the winter of 2013-4, with a break for Santa and new year trains. The Welsh Highland tracks were laid with lightly-used 75lb rail obtained from the Isle of Man Steam Railway in 2012. The strategic renewal of the points by the water tower had been undertaken in November 2013. The turnouts at Boston Lodge and Minffordd were dealt with in 2014/5.

Run alongside the track and platforms works from January 2014 was the radical refurbishment and modernisation of the café. The stainless steel counter installed in 1975 was removed, and the layout altered to suit current requirements and make more space for queueing customers.

After a concerted effort by contractors, employees and volunteers, the station enlargement, including

Four days before the station was closed to complete the remodelling, on 29 December 2013 *Blanche* and *Taliesin* left for Blaenau Ffestiniog on what became the WHR run-round loop. The FR main line was routed in front of the signal box. In the foreground are the foundations for one of three waiting shelters that might be erected on the platform at a later date. The photographer found a wagon-load of sleepers to be a convenient vantage point to record the scene. Morfa Lodge, the house from which James Spooner managed the railway's construction and its early operations, overlooks it from the flanks of Moel y Gest.

The new layout was brought into use on 22 March 2014, as scheduled. Before the first trains departed a photo opportunity was arranged, with the locomotives posed in the 'wrong' platforms.

A view of the changed layout on 25 May 2014. The space created by the realignment of the FR line has been used to create a beer garden with glazed wind breaks.

track, platforms and signalling, were completed, and tested where necessary, just in time for the scheduled start of services on 22 March 2014. With the spacious platforms reaching out onto the embankment, self-draining block paving, seating, period lighting and Snowdon in view at its southern end, the result is a most attractive promenade, a fine environment for joining and leaving trains or for just absorbing the atmosphere. The additional space created beside the goods shed, not only eliminated a pedestrian bottleneck but was sufficient to form an outdoor seating area sheltered by marine-grade glazing, to the café's commercial benefit.

After the signal box the most prominent feature of the installation was the signals, the home replicating the trident that had collapsed in 1967, although pressure on time had required the advanced starter and home signals to be commissioned as temporary colour lights, the permanent installations being activated in May and November respectively. Two of the posts had previously been erected at Tanygrisiau, part of the cancelled signalling scheme.

At 260m long, the FR platform was signalled to accommodate a short train whilst an ordinary train was in the platform. The 180m long WHR platform was signalled to permit departures in each direction and some FR trains were scheduled to use it. Each platform face had its own run-round loop, enabling the fully autonomous operation of both railways in the Station for the first time. Aware that the alterations would put the Station under increased scrutiny, the weekend before services started a major campaign of maintenance, cleaning and improvements was carried out on the building, with some eighty volunteers participating.

Before the first trains departed on 22 March 2014, the flexibility of the new layout was demonstrated by posing the locomotives alongside each other in the 'wrong' platforms. The official opening was on 22 May, when Edwina Hart, the Welsh Government's Minister for Business, Enterprise, Technology and Science, visited the railways. Her department had contributed £719,177 to the £1.22 million project through the national station improvement programme, financed by the European Union's regional development fund. In her speech, Ms Hart acknowledged the company's

David Lloyd George's boiler was given a ten-year service in 2013, receiving stainless steel smokeboxes and being converted to coal firing at the same time. 12 October 2013.

David Lloyd George also received two new power bogies fitted with monobloc piston-valve cylinders, one of them seen on 7 February 2014. Traditionally, the cylinders were separate items bolted together, and could work loose in use. The new design was produced in-house and a trial carried out from 2008 using *Taliesin* as a testbed was judged a success, enabling its boiler to be operated at its designed 200psi.

contribution to the local economy, both as an employer and by generating £25 million each year.

In December 2014, the signalling scheme won the National Railway Heritage Awards' Siemens signalling award, which was presented by Transport for London's commissioner, Sir Peter Hendy, in a ceremony in London, repeated in Porthmadog in May 2015.

To maintain momentum on the fundraising front, the appeal, which had raised over £2 million, became the diamond jubilee appeal, celebrating the sixtieth anniversary of the change of control. A twenty-page brochure with the sub-title 'let's finish the job' described how the works had been carried out at Porthmadog and explained the objectives for improving stations at Blaenau Ffestiniog, Beddgelert and Caernarfon; restoring heritage buildings; introducing electric token-block working on the Welsh Highland Railway; improving passenger accommodation on the FR, and facilities at Boston Lodge and Minffordd, with a target of raising £8.45 million over ten years. The appeals operated under the aegis of the trust, enabling it to benefit from the recovery of income tax paid by qualified donors; a sponsor contributed a further 10 per cent. Another £460,000 was raised within twelve months.

There were several developments on the locomotive front during 2014. In May, *David Lloyd*

George emerged from a two-year overhaul that had included converting it to burn coal and equipping it with two new piston-valve bogies as well as the routine boiler examination. The fuel conversion was the most complex carried out as the loco had been designed to burn oil from the outset. To make space for the ashpans, the well tanks on each side of the firebox were sacrificed, coal bunker space being reduced to increase water capacity in the side tanks. As built, it had second-hand bogies with a varied history that had little life left in them when the loco was withdrawn. The new bogies, with minor modifications to the design successfully trialled on

The new trident signal installed as a part of the new signalling scheme was commissioned later in the year. On 30 May 2014, fireman Matt Ellis keeps a wary eye on the photographer from the footplate of the newly-overhauled *David Lloyd George*. An intermediate measure whilst the loco was run-in, its light grey livery was a reference to *Taliesin's* appearance in 1956.

What better location could there be for preparing locomotives? *Mountaineer* was taken under the wing of a group of young volunteers who repainted it in 1998. Photographed on 15 May 2005, it was withdrawn in February 2006 to await an overhaul that might require a new boiler.

Taliesin, were financed by the society. As with *Taliesin, David Lloyd George* was also adjusted to enable its boiler to work at its designed 200psi.

In traffic, these changes were soon found to be well justified, with coal and water consumption reduced and the loco more powerful. It had also been fitted with traditional lamp brackets, enabling it to be run with replica heritage-style oil lamps. Commissioned by the Heritage Group, the lamps were actually battery powered with LEDs providing the illumination; *Prince* and *Palmerston* had already been equipped with similar lamps. Until it was repainted in 2015, *David Lloyd George* ran in a temporary 'works grey' livery.

Two very different locomotives appeared at Boston Lodge for contract work during 2014. The National Museum of Wales sent its replica of Trevithick's 1804 Penydarren locomotive, which is based at the National Waterfront Museum, Swansea, for its boiler to be serviced, and for repairs and modifications to be carried out. This was followed by the Talyllyn Railway's Fletcher, Jennings 0-4-2ST *Talyllyn* which had suffered a motion failure. The repairs were done, and the locomotive given a mechanical overhaul, too, before it was returned to Tywyn in time for the 150th anniversary of its delivery on 24 September.

Welsh Pony was the last 'restorable' locomotive of the pre-preservation era and the only 'large England' to survive. *Princess* and *Livingston Thompson* are preserved as historic relics, one as the last locomotive steamed in 1946, the other as an example of the railway's engineering achievements in its Victorian heyday. *Welsh Pony* had been withdrawn in 1938 and had spent some fifty years stored outside in a salty atmosphere. In 2010, general manager Paul Lewin asked for opinions on its future, should it be restored to working order, at the risk of losing some original material, or should it be left for display in some future museum, static and lifeless?

The consensus was that *Welsh Pony* should be restored and an announcement to that effect was made in 2013, with a target date for completion set as the locomotive's 150th anniversary in 2017. A conservation management plan report had recommended that restoration to the condition of its 1915 rebuild, as withdrawn in 1938, was the best option. Fund raising was taken under the wing of

the catering department and thousands of envelopes appealing for small change left in carriages raised around £30,000, a considerable sum. The society also contributed £42,000.

Considered by some to be 'unfinished business', restoration started with the dismantling of the locomotive on 4 May 2014, with an audience of visitors to the gala celebrating the sixtieth anniversary of the company's change-of-control. It was soon determined that if a working locomotive was to be produced, then new frames and cylinders would have to be added to the boiler in the list of components required. Repairs to the saddle tank were made using rivets found in the store at Boston Lodge. New cylinders were produced using a

Following a decision to restore *Welsh Pony* to working order, and some fund raising, a start was made on dismantling the loco. On 4 May 2014, Rob Coulson was seen burning bolts out inside the smokebox.

pattern previously used to make cylinders for *Prince* and *Palmerston*. They were on site, along with the new frames, by the end of the year.

Amongst the visits to other railways by locomotives that are a feature of modern operations, the most significant of 2014 occurred in September, when *Palmerston* hauled trains on the Vale of Rheidol Railway over two weekends, a reminder of the loans made by the FR early in the twentieth century.

The company's relationships with other railways extends as far as Australia and the 2ft 6in-gauge Puffing Billy Railway in Victoria, which is restoring and regauging NNG16 Garratt No. 129. During 2014, the FR supplied it with castings, including a chimney, for which it had patterns, and the PBR donated No. 129's old boiler for the cost of transport and sold some surplus tyres for a nominal sum.

During 2014, a start was made on the construction of a vacuum-braked permanent way

train for use on the FR. The restoration and modification of several ex-South African DZ bogie wagons was followed by the construction of a well wagon for the transportation of machines and large loads.

The directors having determined on a strategy of creating four eight-car trains, two for each railway, providing high-quality accommodation comparable on each line, an addition to the FR fleet, No. 119, was launched on 18 September 2014, paid for with a

In 2009 a start was made on upgrading the FR coaching stock, making new vehicles longer, slightly higher, with larger windows and improved access. The latest of the these, at the time of writing, was No. 119, funded by a bequest and seen at Dduallt on 18 September 2014, when it was launched. In service it replaced one of the steel-bodied carriages with the same number, built in 1980. The original No. 119 found a new home on the Golden Valley Railway in Derbyshire.

£100,000 bequest from Margaret Ritchie, a regular visitor to the railway. A development of the 2009 'super saloon' design with increased glazing, it replaced the 1980-built steel-bodied vehicle with the same number which could not be modified to meet twenty-first-century standards. By a streak of perversity both vehicles were to be found at Porthmadog for a few hours before the older one was withdrawn.

One of the highlights of the 2014 vintage weekend was the introduction into service of a replica four-wheeled brake van, one of the three used on passenger trains between 1865 and 1872. As no drawings existed, and they only appeared in a few photographs, it required some research to establish the techniques that were probably used when the original vehicles were built at Boston Lodge. Sponsored by the Heritage Group, the work was largely carried out by volunteers working in the carriage workshop. Coupled to a train of four-wheeled carriages, the van is much admired by visitors and passengers, but is something of an ordeal for the guards who are partially exposed to the elements.

Heritage Group sponsorship has produced several 'new' nineteenth-century vehicles, an open wagon and a 'port hole' Brown, Marshalls carriage in 2012, a second-generation quarrymen's carriage in 2013. The open Brown, Marshalls had had its canopy and aprons restored in 2010 and in 2014 former buffet car No. 12, originally an 1885 bogie van, was restored to its post-1963 appearance, albeit without the buffet counter and with improved access for wheelchair users. Former director Andy Savage sponsored the construction of a replica of Ashbury No. 21, on which work was started in 2014; the original vehicle had survived the closure period

A talking point by Tan y Bwlch water tower, with everyone appropriately dressed for the vintage weekend.
12 October 2014.

Gravity train operation has become an essential part of vintage weekends and other events. For the former it became *de rigueur* for the brakesmen (and women) to be appropriately dressed. On 12 October 2014 Cae Mawr is in the background as a train heads for Penrhyn.

Allan Garraway, the manager who led the railway's revival, died on 30 December 2014, aged eighty-eight, and trains that day carried a wreath. Thus adorned, *Prince* pilots *Taliesin* past the new trident signal.

with its timber underframe badly rotted and had been dismantled in 1962.

Following the restoration of the old Boston Lodge locomotive shed, in 2014 the company started to address the maintenance of its other heritage buildings, some of which had been neglected for a long time. Students from Coleg Meirion Dwyfor, who had already worked on the Porthmadog Signal Box, participated in the restoration of the former locomotive superintendent's office at Boston Lodge, which dates from the 1860s, reroofing it and restoring its chimney stack. Along the line, agreement was reached with the Landmark Trust concerning the restoration and use of Hovendon's cottage at Coed y Bleiddiau, which had been unoccupied for several years. It was immediately

re-roofed to prevent further deterioration and to enable the interior to dry out before restoration, estimated to cost £400,000, was started.

The year 2014 ended with a profit of £240,157. Whilst FR traffic had increased by 3 per cent (£45,255), that on the Welsh Highland Railway had reduced by 11 per cent (£127,289). Nevertheless, with traffic revenue on both railways close to £3 million, even allowing for inflation, the results would have been unimaginable for the pre-1954 directors.

POSTSCRIPT

Over the 94 years of Festiniog Railway history reviewed in this book the railway has been transformed. From being a struggling common carrier, it has become one of the major players in Welsh tourism, overcoming the setbacks caused by closure, abandonment, and confiscation of property by a powerful state-owned agency. The railway's history does not conveniently stop at the end of 2014 and there have been developments aplenty since, notably celebrations for the 150th anniversary of passenger services in May 2015 and the fiftieth anniversary of the start of constructing the deviation during the summer.

At Boston Lodge, construction of new FR-gauge carriages included a new observation carriage comparable to the Welsh Highland Railway's *Glaslyn*. Four steel-bodied carriages surplus to requirements because they could not be upgraded to current standards were sold to other railways as they were replaced by new vehicles. With the objective of removing the requirement for using FR carriages in WHR trains, construction of new WHR-gauge carriages also continued.

Anticipating the need to reboiler the 1979-built *Earl of Merioneth,* and realising that many of its structural components were worn out, the company decided instead to withdraw the loco, allocating its bogies to a new loco to be named *James Spooner*. A new boiler design has been approved for it that will also be used on *Merddin Emrys* in due course.

At Minffordd, the Heritage Group has funded the construction of a shed to house the railway's collection of over 200 historic wagons. A new work-shop and mess building, which also contains a pattern loft, was built with the benefit of a grant from the society. Both were erected in 2016. Restoration of the goods shed, including the reinstatement of its slate roof, was funded by Michael Schumann and carried out at the same time.

The first phase of works to improve facilities at Boston Lodge was started in 2016, with construction of a new access road, ground clearance and erection of a shed to house heritage carriages. Future works planned include the enlargement and renewal of the 1970s errecting shop and the construction of locomotive sheds, one large enough to house a Garratt, and a four-road carriage shed. These works, and others at Minffordd, were supported by the Golden Jubilee appeal, which had raised nearly £3 million by 2016.

Promotion, in the form of pop-up railways and displays, has continued, with *Princess* being displayed at London's King's Cross and *Britomart* running on temporary track through the Whitby & Pickering Railway's tunnel at Grosmont, Yorkshire, only used by horse-drawn trains in the past, being highlights.

Finally, for now, the start of the railway's revival was marked on 8 September 2016, when a blue plaque was unveiled on the building in Bristol where Leonard Heath Humphreys had held the meeting to discuss the railway's future 65 years before.

Completed in 2015, the railway's new Pullman observation car made its first public appearance at London's Paddington station, where it was seen by thousands of commuters and travellers. Its number commemorated the 150th anniversary of passenger services.

APPENDIX I

Summary of results 1921-2014 [Extracted from directors' reports to shareholders]

SUMMARY OF RESULTS 1921-1924

	1921	1922	1923	1924
Receipts	£30,357	£20,250	£17,274	£15,594
Expenditure	£31,964	£21,715	£19,298	£19,058
	£1,607	-£1,465	-£2,024	-£3,464
Passenger receipts	-	£8,387	£7,157	£5,362
Goods receipts	-	£9,576	£9,576	£9,616
Passengers	130,612	164,691	146,011	121,747
Merchandise (Tons)	2,028	2,388	2,665	2,361
Coal	3,171	2,481	2,573	2,787
Other minerals	65,827	51,400	66,699	64,106
	71,026	56,269	71,937	69,254
Passenger train mileage	43,502	58,341	51,307	50,191
Goods train mileage – steam	20,454	17,353	17,147	12,205
Goods train mileage – petrol	-	-	-	2,035
Shunting – steam	22,385	24,601	24,144	18,425
Shunting – petrol	-	-	-	9,205
	86,341	100,295	92,598	92,061

SUMMARY OF RESULTS 1925-1931

	1925	1926	1927	1928	1929	1930	1931
Receipts	£14,622	£14,502	£14,873	£14,328	£13,826	£10,764	£9,213
Expenditure	£13,254	£12,803	£13,602	£13,590	£12,683	£9,890	£8,177
	£1,368	£1,699	£1,271	£738	£1,143	£874	£1,036
Passenger receipts	£4,688	£3,503	£3,286	£2,737	£2,209	£1,249	£1,254
Goods receipts	£9,749	£10,816	£11,431	£11,423	£11,466	£9,374	£7,719
Passengers	208,006	153,676	150,364	140,867	118,159	74,057	58,165
Merchandise (Tons)	1,862	1,742	1,622	1,591	1,373	1,298	1,243
Coal	1,011	750	919	720	801	913	674
Other minerals	81,762	92,357	93,964	99,700	90,525	78,770	67,963
	84,635	94,849	96,505	102,011	92,699	80,981	69,880
Passenger train mileage	38,998	34,907	40,363	33,859	33,836	18,544	14,293
Goods train mileage - steam	9,743	12,341	14,856	11,995	8,146	12,919	13,023
Goods train mileage - petrol	1,392	-	(980)	2,913	3,383	2,479	1,835
Shunting – steam	15,483	26,073	29,307	19,139	17,167	17,108	15,942
Shunting – petrol	8,092			11,831	7,219	7,099	6,506
Engine miles	75,995	76,714	84,526	79,737	69,751	58,149	51,599

SUMMARY OF RESULTS 1932-1939

	1932	1933	1934	1935	1936	1937	1938	1939
Receipts £	8,036	9,735	11,742	10,830	9,136	8,624	8,544	7,527
Expenditure £	6,984	8,393	10,423	9,804	8,646	8,142	8,799	7,228
	1,052	**1,342**	**1,319**	**1,026**	**490**	**482**	**255**	**299**
Passenger receipts £	1,600	2,318	3,400	2,942	2,859	2,321	2,370	2,033
Goods receipts £	6,328	7,285	8,208	7,791	6,184	6,247	6,117	5,424
Passengers	50,364	65,854	78,001	70,473	65,395	59,300	59,088	46,475
Merchandise (Tons)	1,092	1,137	1,062	1,134	913	792	719	627
Other minerals	46,938	50,738	54,558	48,115	36,570	37,088	35,648	32,675
Coal	497	461	902	1,109	1,029	725	387	369
	48,527	52,336	56,522	49,358	38,512	38,605	36,754	32,675
Passenger train mileage	12,689	15,534	35,027	25,494	24,693	18,810	18,413	13,945
Goods train mileage - steam	9,455	10,154	11,369	12,260	10,980	10,615	12,189	11,100
Goods train mileage - petrol	2,517	1,864	733	2,483	2,057	1,393	1,536	1,365
Shunting – steam	9,792	11,262	13,309	9,971	9,055	8,676	8,239	7,770
Shunting – petrol	6,238	4,432	1,818	6,573	5,763	6,003	6,494	5,615
Engine miles	44,984	43,246	62,256	56,781	52,548	45,497	46,871	39,795

* Includes debenture interest   ** Includes Welsh Highland Railway rent

SUMMARY OF RESULTS 1943-1944

	1943	1944
Receipts	£2,755	£2,668
Expenditure	£3,419	£3,805
	-£664	**-£1,137**
Miscellaneous receipts	£300	£52
Net income	-£364	-£1,085
Balance brought forward	-£10,943	-£12,063
	-£11,307	-£13,148
Interest, rentals and fixed charges	£756	£744
Balance	-£12,063	-£13,892

The reports for 1940-2 appear to have been affected by a wartime paper salvage drive and surviving copies in the National Archives are incomplete

Produced in 1963, the silver Centenary of Steam medals entitled purchasers to travel on the first train to Blaenau Ffestiniog and free lifetime travel on the railway.

The first release of society buttonhole badges. Later issues had detail differences.

150th anniversary medals were produced in bronze, silver and gold.

SUMMARY OF RESULTS 1955-1962

	1955	1956	1957	1958	1959	1960	1961	1962
Passenger receipts	440	1,655	2,950	6,632	8,404	11,302	12,506	13,612
Miscellaneous sales (net)	262	262	489	814	929	1,326	1,271	1,305
Income	702	1,917	3,439	7,446	9,333	12,628	13,777	14,917
Current maintenance	752	880	1,104	1,520	2,108	2,782	2,782	3,095
Loco operating	221	320	559	1,200	1,470	1,629	2,243	2,289
Traffic expenses	190	338	365	618	580	720	998	1,367
General	819	967	1,020	1,238	1,237	1,548	2,319	2,271
	1,982	2,505	3,048	4,576	5,395	6,388	8,342	9,022
Gross operating profit	-1,208	-588	391	2,870	3,938	6,240	5,435	5,895
Restoration expenditure	1,505	1,759	2,210	3,040	4,216	4,981	5.563	6,191
	-2,785	-2,347	-1,819	-170	-278	-1,259	-128	-296
Other income	555	405	292	371	399	317	591	326
Profit/loss	-2,230	-1,942	-1,527	201	121	1,576	463	30
Gifts	-	1,918	1,414	1,370	2,083	1,500	1,504	1,603
Net revenue	-2,230	-24	-113	1,571	2,204	3,076	1,967	1,633
Passenger journeys	18,000	38,800	54,000	60,323	75,929	102,000	109,000	114,047
Miles open	1	2	3	7½	7½	7½	7½	7½
Locomotives	1	2	2	2	2	2	3	3-4
Bogie carriages	2	4	6	7	8	9	9	9
Other carriages	-	-	-	4	4	5	6	6
Seating capacity – 1st	-	12	34	34	34	46	46	51
Seating capacity – 3rd	80	156	187	307	363	419	435	429
FR Society members	569	831	1,077	1,346	1,630	1,925	2,096	2,300

SUMMARY OF RESULTS 1963-1970

	1963	1964	1965	1966	1967	1968	1969	1970
Traffic receipts	15,818	18,523	21,383	24,690	31,556	50,042	61,217	66,650
Shop/refreshments (net)	2,892	2,905	3,666	3,809	5,678	5,691	6,235	8,757
Income	18,710	21,428	25,049	28,499	37,234	55,733	67,452	75,407
Current maintenance	3,964	4,331	7,098	8,568	9,782	11,855	16,802	19,784
Loco operating	2,384	2,986	3,554	3,390	4,161	7,345	8,009	9,574
Traffic expenses	1,836	2,035	2,606	4,089	3,352	5,251	7,146	9,692
General	2,666	3,014	2,990	4,421	4,339	5,760	7,313	9,268
	10,850	12,366	16,248	20,468	21,634	30,211	39,270	48,318
Gross operating profit	7,860	9,062	8,801	8,031	15,600	25,522	28,182	27,089
Other income	78	933	597	915	-39	-82	63	-2,295
Profit	7,938	8,129	8,204	8,946	15,415	25,382	27,899	24,794
Deficit brought forward	14,530	10,747	11,280	10,839	10,462	6,725	6,802	17,899
Deferred maintenance	7,928	8,662	7,100	8,569	7,886	11,855	16,802	29,784
Transfers from share premium and general reserve accounts	3,773	-	-	-	-	-	-	-
Balance carried forward	-10,747	-11,280	-10,176	-10,462	-6,725	6,802	17,899	12,909
Gifts (cash and goods at nominal prices)	25,892	30,261	33,513	35,791	39,486	45,564	49,856	52,733
Estimated voluntary labour on capital account	70,000	80,000	90,000	90,000	90,000	90,000	90,000	90,000

SUMMARY OF RESULTS 1971-1977

	1971	1972	1973	1974	1975	1976	1977
Traffic receipts	86,335	94,431	112,270	133,592	184,156	192,464	244,366
Shop/refreshments (net)	11,262	15,612	16,109	18,570	22,017	22,843	28,535
Income	97,597	110,045	128,379	152,062	206,173	215,307	272,901
Payroll		[52,119]	67,532	73,314	92,403	111,703	133,100
Current maintenance	17,345	21,431	-	-	-	-	-
Fuel	-	-	[8,159]	17,453	15,815	16,037	24,200
Locomotive and rolling stock expenses	28,820	32,346	15,819	12,123	14,902	18,105	20,020
Permanent way and general maintenance		[15,643]	16,382	19,179	16,391	29,401	31,103
Traffic expenses	14,506	15,286	-	-	-	-	-
Administration	11,743	13,770	20,901	24,459	30,944	34,299	44,964
Miscellaneous receipts	-2,378	-2,443	7,307	10,307	6,678	16,235	-3,408
Profit	22,573	24,701	15,052	15,941	42,396	21,997	16,106
Balance brought forward	12,909	15,628	13,374	1,100	-19,825	437	-11,728
Surplus from sale of land							3,000
Restoration expenditure	19,855	26,888	27,326	36,866	22,134	34,162	18,954
Balance carried forward	15,627	13,374	1,100	-19,825	437	-11,728	-11,576
Gifts (cash and goods at nominal prices)	58,663	63,968	-	-	-	-	-
Gifts – FR Society	-	-	55,921	59,389	66,041	76,892	91,850
Gifts – others	-	-	2,536	8,720	14,338	15,697	19,889
Gifts – Wales Tourist board	-	-	5,462	11,455	63,266	-	-
Grants – Wales Tourist Board	-	-	-	-	-	94,191	160,806
Grants – Manpower Services Commission	-	-	-	-	-	18,746	104,806
Grants – Department of Trade & Industry	-	-	-	-	-	7,041	7,236
Estimated voluntary labour on capital account	90,000	90,000	-	-	-	-	-

Blaenau Ffestiniog in August 1966. The FR water tank remains in situ (left), the link line connecting to the GWR branch to serve Trawsfynydd, (lower left) had been completed two years earlier. Compare with the photograph on page 56.

SUMMARY OF RESULTS 1978-1984

	1978	1979	1980	1981	1982	1983	1984
Traffic receipts	348,572	398,363	454,989	450,610	502,679	501,564	500,197
Shop/refreshments (net)	25,684	33,784	36,650	32,284	18,750	32,752	42,087
Ticket agency receipts (net)	-	-	[13,281]	9,171	18,012	16,453	9,317
Income	374,256	432,152	491,639	492,065	539,441	550,769	551,601
Payroll	199,626	235,131	300,057	316,208	345,606	385,658	358,375
Fuel	27,823	34,060	45,084	44,101	55,576	56,535	48,997
Locomotive and rolling stock expenses	18,206	15,534	16,789	26,281	18,564	23,354	31,106
Permanent way and general maintenance	32,403	27,794	21,390	17,738	12,506	27,981	27,163
Administration	31,306	35,456	34,727	42,471	53,745	57,196	53,941
Utilities and road transport	15,257	13,708	17,036	21,728	26,217	27,521	24,327
Miscellaneous expenses	9,985	5,447	6,055	1,026	6,227	9,078	5,139
Miscellaneous receipts	-16,419	-23764	-18,907	-22,331	-18,312	-9,344	-13,284
Net profit/loss	23,431	41,253	31,594	181	2,688	-45,898	-4,450
Balance brought forward	-11,576	11,855	53,108	87,702	87,883	90,571	57,532
Surplus on sale of land/property	-	-	3,000	-	-	14,772	-
Loss/profit on sale of car	-	-	-	-	-	-2,557	1,469
Balance carried forward	11,855	53,108	87,702	87,883	90,571	57,532	63,451
Gifts – FR Society	113,750	113,750	113,900	170,581	190,144	210,544	226,894
Gifts – others	23,683	26,665	30,370	30,611	30,906	28,517	32,339
GRANTS							
Wales Tourist Board	194,843	205,196	205,196	212,166	311,016	318,085	-
Manpower Services Commission	134,852	139,368	152,039	159,561	185,394	-	-
Department of Trade & Industry	7,236	-	-	-	-	-	-
Department of Employment	6,240	-	-	-	-	-	-
Development Board for Rural Wales	-	42,517	75,010	-	-	-	-
European Economic Community	-	-	-	106,043	134,320	-	-
Others	-	13,476	13,476	28,977	43,392	41,516	47,892
CAPITAL EXPENDITURE							
Deviation	124,709	10,239	2,928	-	-	-	3,196
Locos and rolling stock	10,915	41,999	7,620	-153	10,301	-	10,874
Buildings and plant	6,742	7,838	12,597	761	8,542	-	5,240
Motor vehicles	-	6,500	-	-	-	6,500	5,697
Blaenau extension	-	5,272	112,708	106,904	145,556	395,024	-
Land and permanent way	-	13,024	-	-	39	2,320	2,535

SUMMARY OF RESULTS 1985-1991

	1985	1986	1987	1988	1989	1990	1991
Traffic receipts	539,315	557,829	591,134	679,099	763,072	780,538	817,155
Shop/refreshments (net)	45,559	40,771	50,324	54,930	62,683	63,388	56,523
Ticket agency receipts (net)	5,981	13,003	17,421	31,881	42,837	52,956	50,358
Income	590,855	611,603	658,879	765,910	868,592	896,882	924,036
Payroll	364,647	390,868	413,676	454,391	488,899	556,326	598,905
Fuel	51,950	38,864	39,762	33,246	33,217	35,066	32,094
Locomotive and rolling stock expenses	25,794	24,277	26,051	26,425	38,237	41,216	48,269
Permanent way and general maintenance	26,724	31,944	38,081	37,888	59,219	66,117	69,819
Administration	50,506	59,914	56,354	97,138	79,683	95,345	109,220
Utilities and road transport	26,597	31,270	33,593	33,706	34,232	49,708	44,758
Miscellaneous expenses	12,001	12,881	12,069	19,040	19,817	18,875	24,448
Depreciation on motor vehicles	-	-	-	-	-	-	5,740
Miscellaneous receipts	-19,734	288	1672	-16,805	4,107	19,829	3,094
Net profit/loss	13,479	21,813	40,965	59,665	137,710	61,111	22,752
Balance brought forward	63,450	76,929	100,242	141,207	200,872	336,405	397,516
Profit on sale of house	-	1,500	-	-	-	-	-
Profit on sale of locomotive	-	-	-	-	1,500	-	-
Loss on disposal of vehicles	-	-	-	-	-3,677	-	-5,572
Transfer to gifts and grants	-	-	-	-	-	-	-24,841
Gifts – FR Society	241,872	245,834	-	250,000	265,000	-	270,000
Gifts – others	134,372	174,641	-	-	-	-	-
Gifts – Festiniog Railway Trust	-	-	-	208,696	254,702	302,196	385,286
Gifts and grants	-	-	55,139	-	-	-	-
GRANTS							
Wales Tourist Board	319,297	375,370	400,136	-	418,218	464,531	476,135
Manpower Services Commission	185,394	186,094	186,519	-	-	-	-
Development Board for Rural Wales	-	-	-	82,010	101,210	-	-
European Economic Community	-	-	-	-	200,697	432,401	470,820
European Social Fund	-	-	-	-	-	-	24,841
CAPITAL EXPENDITURE							
Locos and rolling stock	34,080	47,773	58,001	-	137,633	184,288	144,686
Buildings and plant	13,951	36,695	30,292	-	88,538	213,851	37,085
Motor vehicles	-	952	-	-	4,923	-	8,631
Land and permanent way	32,487	20,631	21,897	-	30,871	43,564	73,193

SUMMARY OF RESULTS 1992-1997

	1992	1993	1994	1995	1996	1997
Traffic receipts	843,620	966,123	911,910	940,702	1,036,552	1,054,541
Shop/refreshments net	90,442	129,197	138,712	135,781	160,342	222,092
Miscellaneous	5,853	8,394	-	-	-	-
Revenue grant	3,344	-	-	16,636	36,195	52,507
Management charge FR Holdings Ltd	60,000	96,960	89,799	95,116	106,511	114,963
Payroll	616,929	700,606	688,183	727,701	751,800	771,797
Fuel	43,166	67,835	61,325	61,802	70,251	62,996
Locomotive and rolling stock expenses	37,441	44,637	35,430	53,861	45,551	83,214
Permanent way and general maintenance	60,920	63,016	44,538	46,613	47,772	54,544
Administration	121,795	169,429	148,650	146,110	176,902	225,530
Utilities and road transport	53,311	60,485	52,834	66,745	61,634	75,855
Miscellaneous expenses	27,648	23,273	30,060	69,435	32,367	57,615
Depreciation on motor vehicles	4,305	8,730	6,548	5261	3,196	2,989
Commission to Ffestiniog Travel	-	54,095	51,204	52,336	55,328	59,631
Employment case settlement	-	-	-	-	-	9,476
Operating profit/loss	37,744	8,568	21,649	-41,629	94,799	64,956
Overdraft	125,298 #	102,326	101,326	229,036	147,078	-
Net interest paid	6,266	3,982	9,697	13,950	7,770	7,519
Interest on 4 per cent debenture stock	3,111	2,982	2,653	3,126	2,015	3,620
Transfer to gifts and grants	3,344	-	-	-	-	-
Gifts – FR Society	275,000	280,000	340,000	385,000	395,000	401,000
Gifts – Ffestiniog Railway Trust and others	389,016	513,041	536,271	741,089	848,726	1,414,291
Transfer of WHR grant from Ffestiniog Holdings	-	-	-	212,906	212,906	212,906
GRANTS						
Wales Tourist Board	480,135	-	508,732	516,595	518,895	518,895
Manpower Services Commission	186,519	186,519	192,483	-	-	-
Development Board for Rural Wales	101,210	101,210	112,095	113,020	-	-
European Economic Community	648,193	712,250	862,074	879,984	952,495	1,669,254
Others	47,892	54,084	54,084	55,393	57,182	57,302
European Social Fund	28,185	-	-	-	-	-
Meirionydd District Council	-	-	-	62,436	259,191	259,191
Welsh Development Agency	-	-	-	-	-	190,845
Millennium Commission	-	-	-	-	-	1,303,918
Sustrans	-	-	-	-	-	33,000
National Power	-	-	-	-	-	16,000
CAPITAL EXPENDITURE						
Locos and rolling stock	84,936	103,189	145,014	107,314	152,643	143,141
Buildings and plant	77,592	70,427	155,422	170,964	96,576	119,503
Motor vehicles	-	22,005	-	-	-9,634	-
Land and permanent way	9,224	28,250	17,935	89,178	144,499	72,226
Welsh Highland Railway (net)	-	-	-	412,659	650,323	103,793

SUMMARY OF RESULTS 1998-2003

	1998	1999	2000	2001	2002	2003
Traffic receipts (FR)	976,071	981,998	927,534	987,616	1,069,119	1,053,764
Shop (net)	49,343	43,013	46,638	31,495	45,578	52,614
Refreshments (net)	31,429	45,709	64,504	43,714	116,691	43,766
Traffic receipts (WHR)	51,234	46,149	99,794	136,974	156,083	295,736
Shop (net)	1,449	4,110	6,948	14,368	4,626	6,772
Refreshments (net)	4,459	1,042	1,997	14,892	7,280	7,242
Revenue grants	47,438	49,374	22,485	50,571	10,000	11,246
Management charge WHR Light Railway Ltd	45,073	39,501	-	-	-	-
Management charge FR Holdings Ltd	128,045	129,719	141,431	99,293	-	-
Rents receivable	23,212	21,887	34,875	39,705	20,935	12,480
Consultancy fees	5,945	-	68,643	16,693	17,720	
Administration	394,609	416,863	446,587	395,397	621,675	644,418
Interest received	6,736	-	-			
Net interest paid	4,327	13,666	13,998	11,867	20,143	18,965
Interest on 4 per cent debenture stock	2,680	3,326	1,960	1,640	918	2,454
Overdraft	82,929	178,823	223,254	265,194	386,924	139,052
Gross profit/(loss)	128,441	203,529	(89,612)	278,213	290,452	794,733
Profit/(loss)	(16,455)	10,155	(105,499)	(23,722)	(300,315)	169,799
Payroll	861,993	853,450 *	962,637	920,344	1,058,920	1,084,527
Personnel (Full time/part time)	40/6	39/6	39/6	61/3	80/4	64/6
Commission paid to FR Holdings	58,042	57,704	48,989	-	-	-
Grants – Ffestiniog Railway Trust	290,738	586,503	1,014,937	1,207,510	-	-

* restated as £924,158 in 2000

The second train set at Portmadoc on 2 August 1960. Allan Garraway always had carriages shunted in numerical order, as shown. Van No 2, converted from a quarrymen's carriage in 1908, subsequently had its matchboard cladding restored.

SUMMARY OF RESULTS 2004-2009

	2004	2005	2006	2007	2008	2009
Traffic receipts (FR)	1,071,323	1,173,194	1,229,889	1,284,995	1,183,001	1,354,148
Shop (net)	42,752	52,432	49,518	13,028	34,112	41,782
Catering (net)	78,869	97,563	105,233	105,958	97,221	139,566
On-train catering (net)	51,176	45,894	44,651	36,688	35,430	34,703
Traffic receipts (WHR)	396,799	395,169	433,838	458,787	466,824	1,017,121
Shop (net)	11,292	10,226	11,818	13,028	11,826	14,356
On-train catering	26,583	20,274	20,833	19,746	20,880	35,923
Revenue grants	71,637	32,934	19,956	32,405	145,855	79,496
Rents receivable	13,404	19,746	25,966	33,003	66,491	26,559
Administration	659,053	714,719	737,907	795,279	963,531	924,449
Net interest paid	11,979	19,001	13,735	5,481	3,670	4,393
Interest on 4 per cent debenture stock	2,414	2,194	2,694	1,749	1,838	447
Overdraft	320,116	248,687	57,652	127,282	44,158	5,049
Gross profit/(loss)	686,411	736,128	845,391	874,295	791,569	1,045,658
Profit	108,734	59,561	149,186	128,133	38,459	222,424
Payroll	1,236,636	1,344,003	1,487,299	1,605,949	1,786,314	1,545,481
Personnel (full time/part time)	64/5	60/5	62/5	63/5	61/5	58/7

SUMMARY OF RESULTS 2010-2014

	2010	2011	2012	2013	2014
Traffic receipts (FR)	1,418,002	1,406,924	1,264,323	1,408,358	1,453,583
Shop (net)	31,743	44,772	85,328	78,691	73,358
Catering (net)	151,761	116,426	82,311	134,553	198,623
On-train catering (net)	50,252	44,526	96,157	117,081	73,291
Traffic receipts (WHR)	1,020,019	1,570,561	1,418,966	1,667,426	1,540,137
Shop (net)	13,363	16,612	+	+	+
On-train catering	30,724	63,236	+	+	+
Revenue grants	23,715	37,482	75,699	20,625	49,478
Rents receivable/sundry income	78,009	17,993	55,189	36,868	96,531
Administration	948,092	1,088,049	1,052,788	1,137,818	1,173,547
Net interest paid	4,281	2,128	990	345	493
Interest on 4 per cent debenture stock	400	610	594	(2,469)	-
Overdraft	13,627	3,619	7,782	2,133	5,334
Gross profit/(loss)	1,020,618	1,269,135	1,015,713	1,513,159	1,230,515
Profit	169,569	292,823	156,409	493,486	240,157
Payroll	1,780,080	2,014,832	2,171,678	2,221,479	2,268,943
Personnel (full time/part time/seasonal)	57/7	64/7	73/4	70/9	67/11/39

APPENDIX 2

Capital expenditure 1923-1929 [Extracted from directors' reports to shareholders]

1923	
Land, building and compensation	£536 16s
Construction of way and stations, engineering &c	£3,120
Legal and Parliamentary expenses	£400
Locomotive (Petrol tractor for shunting)	£376 13s 6d
Six coaching vehicles	£1,016 0s 9d
	£5,449 10s 3d

1924	
Land, building and compensation	£1,060 11s
Construction of way and stations, engineering &c	£1,478 17s 8d
	£2,539 8s 8d

1925	
Construction of way and stations, engineering &c	£226 17s 3d
Baldwin petrol locomotive	£248 13s 4d
Four 5-ton double-bogie goods wagons	£140
Three inspection trolleys	£13 10s
Repairing works and plant	£329 12s 2d
	£958 12s 9d

1926	
Construction of way and stations, engineering &c	£89 17s 9d
Baldwin petrol locomotive spares &c	£38 4s
Two wagon bodies	£35
Three inspection trolleys	£22 13s 7d
Repairing works and plant	£99 15s 2d
	£288 6s 2d

1927	
Construction of way and stations, engineering &c	£8 13s 11d
Locomotives	£166 2s 7d
Carriages	£23 12s 1d
Wagons	3s 5d
Repairing works and plant	£124 12s 11d
	£323 4s 11d

1928	
Construction of way and stations, engineering &c	£59 1s 8d
Carriages	£3
Repairing works and plant	£25
	£87 1s 8d

1929	
Construction of way and stations, engineering &c	£228 12s 8d
Locomotives	£12
Carriages	£150
Wagons	£74 6s
	£464 18s 8d

Mountaineer rolls past Whistling Curve on its way back to Portmadoc, circa 1970. By this time the loco has brass window frames fitted and has regained its own chimney. The last carriage in the train has been painted in the new cherry red livery.

APPENDIX 3

Levels of debt 1965-84 [Extracted from directors' reports to shareholders]

LEVELS OF DEBT 1965-1974										
	1965	**1966**	**1967**	**1968**	**1969**	**1970**	**1971**	**1972**	**1973**	**1974**
Mortgage	1,724	1,587	1,448	1,309	1,169	1,010	840	656	421	79
Overdraft No. 1					581	5,509	13,181	8,731	12,251	
Overdraft No. 2								1,946		
Sundry Creditors	2,761	11,488	8,386	10,933	9,948	6,428	6,711	3,442	7,896	36,317
	4,485	**13,075**	**9,834**	**12,242**	**11,698**	**12,947**	**20,732**	**14,775**	**20,568**	**36,396**

LEVELS OF DEBT 1975-1984										
	1975	**1976**	**1977**	**1978**	**1979**	**1980**	**1981**	**1982**	**1983**	**1984**
Sundry Creditors	49,272	97,192	85,222	84,234	72,040	68,725	64,937	48,927	36,311	46,197
Overdraft: National Westminster Bank	20,000	50,000	180,000	230,000	210,000	174,000	165,067	146,255	117,134	80,760
Interest bearing loans		4,295	3,740	3,241	2,656	57,545	20,560	21,000	3,000	3,000
Loan: FR Society	9,000	9,000	9,000	6,500	18,500	40,700	11,850	18.300	114,497	123,572
	78,272	**160,487**	**277,962**	**323,975**	**303,196**	**340,970**	**262,414**	**234,482**	**270,942**	**253,529**

Prince pulls away from Penrhyn during the 1960s. Paint on the paneling of carriage No 17 has been damaged by water getting into the timber.

APPENDIX 4

Passenger journeys/bookings 1956-2014

	PASSENGER JOURNEYS	BOOKINGS
1956	38,689	
1957	54,000	
1958	60,248	
1959	75,929	
1960	102,000	
1961	109,000	
1962	114,047	
1963	128,543	
1964	144,100	
1965	150,502	
1966	174,000	
1967	220,500	
1968	294,000	
1969	319,327	
1970	354,898	
1971	366,457	
1972	394,621	
1973	407,558	
1974	418,000	
1975	411,000	
1976	382,844	
1977	389,224	
1978	409,693	
1979	387,327	
1980	379,310	
1981	330,000	
1982	320,100	
1983	330,000	
1984	360,000	
1985	330,000	
1986	320,000	
1987	310,000	
1988	335,000	
1989	331,000	
1990	315,217	
1991	301,500	
1992	293,951	
1993	326,286	
1994	304,534	
1995	310,000	

	PASSENGER JOURNEYS	BOOKINGS
1996	327,598	
1997	313,677	
1998	285,293	
1999	264,822	
2000		131,031
2001		126,563
2002		127,073
2003		131,066
2004		136,104
2005		127,213
2006		128,547
2007		124,137
2008		117,714
2009		129,095
2010		129,049
2011		122,580
2012		102,825
2013		111,043
2014		116,600

Bookings represent over-the-counter sales, and exclude special events and sales via other train operators

APPENDIX 5

Non-statutory directors

Malcom High	2002-2005
Helen Waters	2002-2006
Michael Whitehouse	2002-2003
George Nissen	2003-2004
John Ewing	2004-2005
Chris Leah	2005 to date
Nigel Burbidge	2005-2006
Dafydd Gwyn	2006-2016
Paul Lewin	2013 to date

APPENDIX 6

Festiniog Railway Company Directors 1833-2014

	BIRTH-DEATH	TIME IN OFFICE	COMMENTS
Allen, K.A.	1948-	2000-2	Previously society chairman, acting chief executive 2000-1, managing director 2001-2
Archer, H.	1799-2 March 1863	1933-8	Nominated managing director by Act of Parliament
Bailey, H.T.S.	1920-16 September 1991	1954-66	
Ball, Air Vice Marshall Sir Ben	1912 - 24 January 1977	1974-7	
Bellamy, C.W.	1897-1963	1955-61	Secretary 1954-6, appointment as director not formally recorded
Bowton, R.	1860-March 1923	1907-1921	Quarry owner
Broadbent, W.B.	1924-8 June 2005	1954-1986	Society representative, chief executive 1977
Burbidge, N.F.	October 1957-	2006 to date	Previously auditor, finance director
Buxton, R.	April 1940-	2006-11	Society representative
Catchpole, A.G.	May 1949-2013	2011-3	Society representative
Colville, M.J.	May 1949-	1997-2002	Society representative, finance director from 1999
Cairnes, T.P.	1830-21 April 1894	1877-1894	Married to Sophia Gaussen
Carreg, E.		1835-8	Dublin
Cowper, H.A.	1871-12 August 1921	1904-1906	Dublin
Davies, C.E.	27 February 1904-9 November 1963	1931-1954	Solicitor, son of E.R. Davies, secretary from 1929
Davies, E.R.	1871-2 December 1934	1920-1934	Solicitor, chairman from 1931
Davies, N.R.	27th May 1910 - 3rd November 1989	1942-1954	Solicitor, son of E.R. Davies, assistant secretary from 1934.
Davies, W.C.	1880-1 January 1964	1934-1954	Solicitor, brother of E.R. Davies, chairman.
Durham, A.	1792-8 October 1876	1835-1876	Born Bombay, Irish family, Sir Joseph Huddart's brother in law
Eaves, C.H.	January 1943-	1987-1999	Financial secretary from 1973, treasurer from 1975
Elliott, J.	1871-	1904-1908	
Elliott, J.W.	1818-5 February 1907	1888-1905	Chairman 1893-1904
Felkin, H.M.	1837-7 May 1907	1899-1904	J. W. Elliott's son in law
Fiennes, G.F.T.-W.	1906-25 May 1985	1968-1973	
Gandon, J.		1838-46	Dublin
Garnock, Viscount (Earl of Lindsay)	9 February 1926-1 August 1989	1962-1989	
Gaussen, C.	1795-11 June 1887	1844-9, 1851-7, 1860-77	Will executed by T.P. Cairnes
Gibbs, G.		1847-56	Dublin
Greaves, J.W.	1807-12 February 1880	1944-8, 1850-7	Treasurer
Greaves, R.M.	1852-1942	1906-1921	Deputy chairman from 1907, chairman from 1908
Halpin, G.	1811-22 November 1891	1874-1888	
Hardy, F.N.	-1891	1884-1891	
Hardy, R.H.N.	1923-	1977-87	
Hart, M.C.	April 1951-	1989 to date	Chairman 1993-2001
Hayward, A.	February 1966-	2002-2006	
Huddart, C.H.C.	1848-24 August 1900	1887-1900	
Huddart, G.A.	1822-1 February 1885	1847-58, 1860-4, 1866-73	Joint managing director from 1868
Huddart, G.A.W.	1844-26 September 1908	1894-1908	Chairman from 1907
Huddart, G.W.O.	1879-December 1967	1908-1914	

	BIRTH-DEATH	TIME IN OFFICE	COMMENTS
Huddart, Sir Joseph	1767-1841	1835	Andrew Durham's brother in law
Jack, H.J.	9 October 1869-2 January 1946	1921-1925	Chairman 1921-4
Kerl, T.	1810-1902	1875-1887	Married to Emmeline Huddart, Sir Joseph's second daughter
Livingston, J.G.	1812-17 August 1902	1851-8, 1860-92	Chairman 1877-1892. Livingston Thompson's brother. Barrister. Retired to Westbury on Trym and Clifton. Changed his name from Thompson in 1863.
Macaulay, J.	1854-14 April 1919	1914-1919	
Mayne, F.		1835-	Dublin
Miller, S.G.	July 1976-	2013 to date	
Murfitt, S.E.	April 1949-	2007 to date	Clerk from 1995
Nicholls, E.H.R.	1895-24 April 1957	1924-5	
Nissen, G.M.	March 1930-	1993-2003	Chairman 2001-2003
Pegler, A.F.	1921-18 March 2012	1954-6	Chairman 1956-1972, president from 1972
Prideaux, J.D.C.A.	August 1944-	2006 to date	Chairman
Roberts, D.H.	1867-31 October 1943	1934-1943	
Robjent, F.P.	1859-12 January 1938	1908-1921	
Routly, E.J.	September 1914-4 March 2003	1954-1993	Chairman
Savage, A.J.	April 1952-	1986-1997, 2002-4	First period, society representative
Schumann, M.A.	January 1942-	1992-2006	
Smith, L.J.W.	November 1917-24 January 1997	1954-1992	
Spooner, S.	1795-16 May 1860	1850-8	Cousin of James Spooner
Stephens, Col H.F.	31 October 1868-23 October 1931	1924-1931	Chairman and managing director
Stewart, Sir John Henderson, Bt	26 November 1877-6 February 1924	1921-1924	
Thompson, J.G. – see Livingston, J. G.			
Thompson, L.	1811-19 September 1874	1835-1874	Dublin barrister and 'gentleman farmer', bought shares from Henry Archer, joint managing director from 1868.
Thompson, R.N.	1853-19 May 1907	1894-1907	Chairman. Livingston Thompson's youngest son.. Physician and surgeon, Dublin.
Vaughan, F.	1852-6 April 1922	1907-1921	Managing director
Westall, G.	1850-1930	1924-1930	
Westall, H.L.	1878-28 February 1942	1930-1942	
Whitehouse, C. M.	October 1952-	2003-7	Chairman 2003-2006

The blue plaque unveiled in Bristol on 8 September 2016, commemorating the 65th anniversary of the start of the Ffestiniog Railway's revival.

APPENDIX 7

Festiniog Railway Trust Trustees 1955-2015

	BIRTH-DEATH	TIME IN OFFICE	COMMENTS
Bailey, H.T.S.	1920-16 September 1991	1955-91	
Broadbent, W.B.	1924-8 June 2005	1961-98	Society nomination
Broyd, R.	October 1948-	2008 to date	
Garland, P.J.	22 April 1913-11 January 2005	1973-90	
Garraway, R.H.R.	1894-September 1972	1956-72	
Jordan, P.K.	September 1948-	1999-2003	Society nomination
Lewis, D.E.	June 1956-	2007-11	Society nomination
McAlpine, The Hon Sir W., Bt	January 1936-	1999-2008	
Prideaux, J.D.C.A.	August 1944-	1991 to date	Chairman from 1999
Riddick, R.J.G.	January 1951-	1990-2015	
Roberts, D.W.	March 1939-	2011 to date	Society nomination
Routly, E.J.	September 1914-4 March 2003	1955-98	Chairman
Rudgard, R.H.	4 September 1884-3 March 1958	1956-8	
Schumann, M.A.	January 1942-	1995-16	
Smith, M.L.	June 1948-	2015 to date	
Williams, G.H.	February 1944-	2003-07	Society nomination
Williams, Sir O., Bt	1914-2012	1979-95	

Until the new Porthmadog platform was commissioned in 2014, arriving Welsh Highland Railway trains pulled onto the embankment and were then pulled back into the station by a second locomotive. On 22 July 2011, *Vale of Ffestiniog* waits to perform the shunting duty.

APPENDIX 8

Deposited plans for 1923, 1968 and 1975 Light Railway Orders

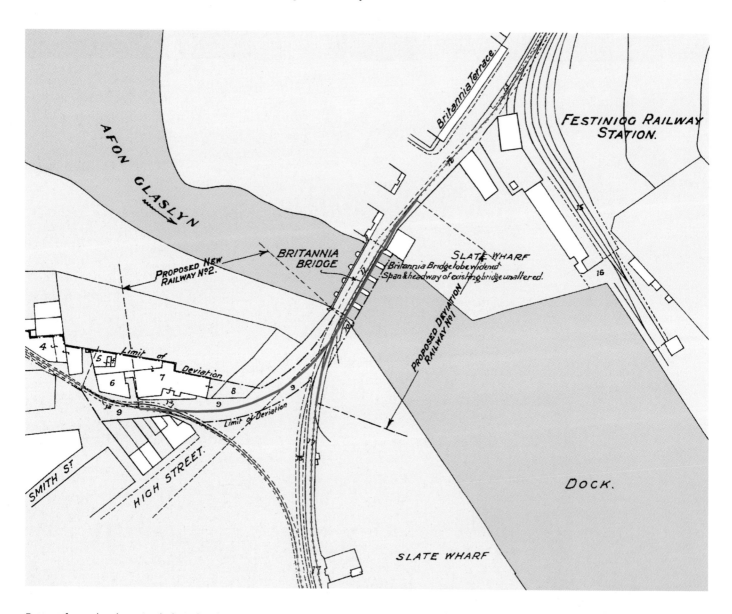

Extract from the deposited plans for the
1923 Light Railway Order.

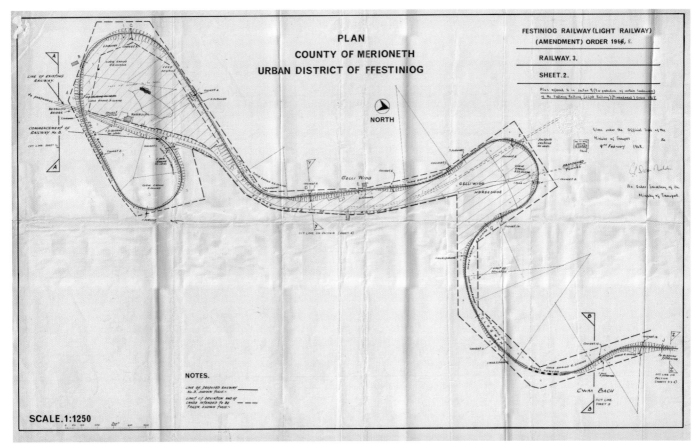

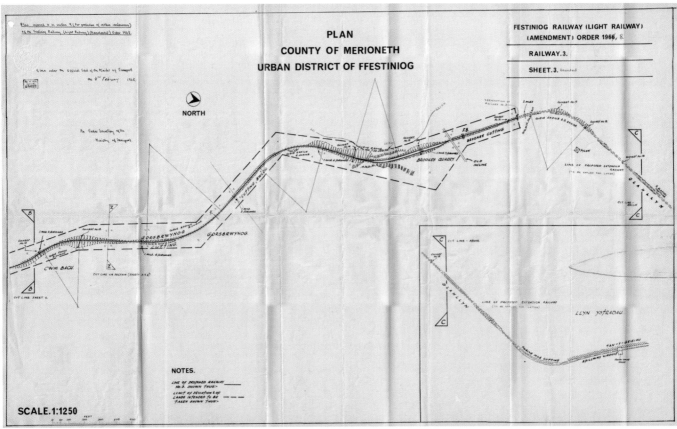

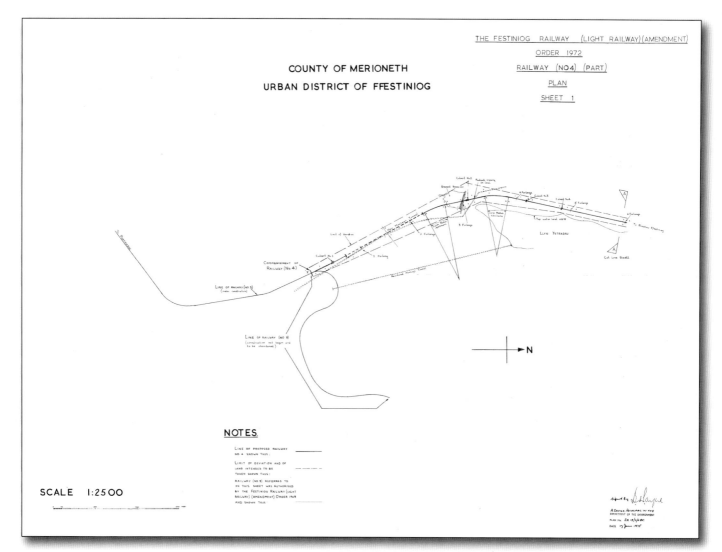

THE FESTINIOG RAILWAY (LIGHT RAILWAY) (AMENDMENT)

ORDER 1972

RAILWAY (NO4) (PART)

PLAN

SHEET 1

SCALE 1:2500

Seen shortly after public services started on 8 July 1977, Llyn Ystradau platform remained in use only until daily services ended in September.
(J.W.T. House)

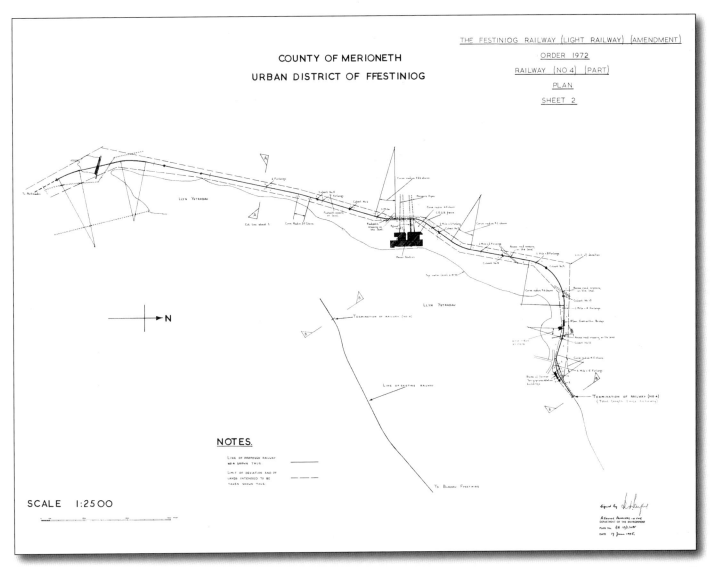

Prince and train pass over the power station summit in November 1980. Buffer car No 103 is sandwiched between two steel-bodied carriages built on ex-Isle of Man Railways underframes.

(J.W.T. House)

A classic view of Allan Garraway, then the general manager, at the controls of 'his' engine, *Linda*, at Whistling Curve during 1965.

Much drama is to be seen as *Welsh Pony* powers through the LNWR exchange station during the inter-war years. The chain of one of its sandpot covers has broken, the cover being lodged above the smokebox handrail. All being well, the loco will celebrate its 150th anniversary in steam.

BIBLIOGRAPHY

BOYD, J. I. C.; *The Festiniog Railway*; Oakwood Press, 1975 (2 vols)

BOYD, J. I. C.; *Narrow Gauge Railways in South Caernarvonshire*, Oakwood Press, 1988/9 (2 vols)

BRADLEY, V.J.; *Industrial Locomotives of North Wales*; Industrial Railway Society, 1992

ELLIS, C. HAMILTON & LEE, Charles E.; The Festiniog Railway; *Railway Magazine*, April 1936, July 1936, October 1936

GAIRNS, J.F.; *The Festiniog Railway of Today*; Railway Magazine, August 1924

HOLLINGSWORTH, Brian; *Ffestiniog Adventure*; David & Charles, 1981

JANES, Brian; The Grouping and the Festiniog; *Festiniog Railway Heritage Group Journal*, No. 83, Autumn 2005

JOHNSON, Peter; The Davies family and its railway interests; *Festiniog Railway Heritage Group Journal* No. 109, Spring 2012

JOHNSON, Peter; *An Illustrated History of the Festiniog Railway*; Oxford Publishing Co, 2007

JOHNSON, Peter; *An Illustrated History of the Welsh Highland Railway*; Ian Allan, 2002; 2nd Edition 2009

JOHNSON, Peter; *Festiniog Railway The Spooner era and after 1820-1920*; Pen & Sword Transport, 2017

JOHNSON, Peter; Henry Joseph Jack – a re-appraisal; *Festiniog Railway Heritage Group Journal* No 126, Summer, 2016

JOHNSON, Peter; *Immortal Rails – The story of the closure and revival of the Ffestiniog Railway 1939-1983* (2 vols); RailRomances, Vol 1 2004, Vol 2 2005

JOHNSON, Peter; In search of Sir John Henderson Stewart Bart; *Festiniog Railway Heritage Group Journal* No. 125, Spring 2016

JOHNSON, Peter; John Sylvester Hughes – in Spooner's shadow; unpublished article, 2016

ORGAN, John & KNIGHT, Martyn; *Locomotives and rolling stock of the Ffestiniog and Welsh Highland Railways – an illustrated stock list*; Festiniog Railway Company, revised 2011

RUSHTON, Gordon; *Welsh Highland Railway Renaissance*; Adlestrop Press, 2012

WHITEHOUSE, P. B.; *Festiniog Railway Revival*; Ian Allan, 1963

WINTON, John; *The Little Wonder - The Story of the Festiniog Railway*; Michael Joseph, revised edition, 1986

Built in 1886 and reaching the end of its operational life, *Earl of Merioneth* heads out along the dry-stone embankment at Gwyndy with a good load, circa 1968.

INDEX

Datblygiad Cyffrous ym Mlaenau Ffestiniog?

What's happening at Blaenau Ffestiniog?

Agor gorsaf newydd y Rheilffyrdd Prydeinig/Rheilffordd Ffestiniog
Opening of new joint British Rail/Ffestiniog Railway Station

Cynllun y cyfleusterau teithio newydd　　　　　　　　**Plan of new travel facilities**

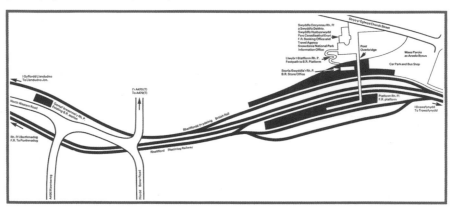

Disgwylir y bydd yn agor ym Mai 1982　　　　　　**Anticipated opening date May 1982**

Noddwyd cynllun Gorsaf Newydd Blaenau Ffestiniog ar y cyd gan Gyngor Sir Gwynedd a Chyngor Dosbarth Meirionnydd gyda chymorth gan Fwrdd Datblygu Cymru Wledig, Y Swyddfa Gymreig, Awdurdod Datblygu Cymru, Cyngor Tref Ffestiniog a Chymuned Economaidd Ewrop. Ar ôl ei hagor bydd yr orsaf newydd:
- yn cyfrannu'n helaeth at ffyniant y cylch yn y dyfodol;
- yn cyfrannu'n helaeth at ddatblygu twristiaeth yng Nghymru;
- yn gwireddu gobeithion Rheilffordd Ffestiniog;
- yn parhau'r berthynas glos rhwng y Rheilffyrdd Prydeinig, Cwmni Rheilffordd Ffestiniog a'r gymdogaeth.

Jointly sponsored by Gwynedd County Council and Cyngor Dosbarth Meirionnydd with the aid of the Development Board for Rural Wales, Welsh Office, Welsh Development Agency, Ffestiniog Town Council and the European Economic Community, the opening of the new Blaenau Ffestiniog station will:
- play a major role in the future prosperity of the area;
- greatly contribute to the development of tourism in Wales;
- see the aspirations of the Ffestiniog Railway realised;
- continue the long standing association British Rail, the Ffestiniog Railway and their partners have with the community.

Un o gyfres o ddatblygiadau ar Reilffyrdd Gogledd Cymru.
One of a series of developments which are part of a Rail Charter for North Wales.

 Rheilffordd Ffestiniog
Ffestiniog Railway

No 4　　　　　　　　　　　　　　　　　　　　　　　　　　NI626

A poster produced to explain the development at Blaenau Ffestiniog in 1982.

The Festiniog Railway
In the revival era

Gradient Diagram
(new route - post Deviation)

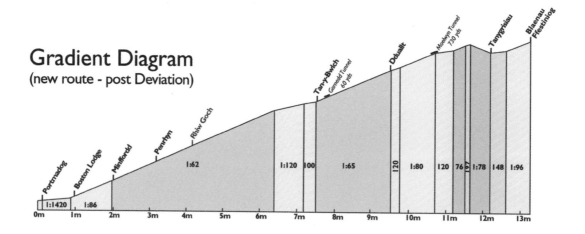

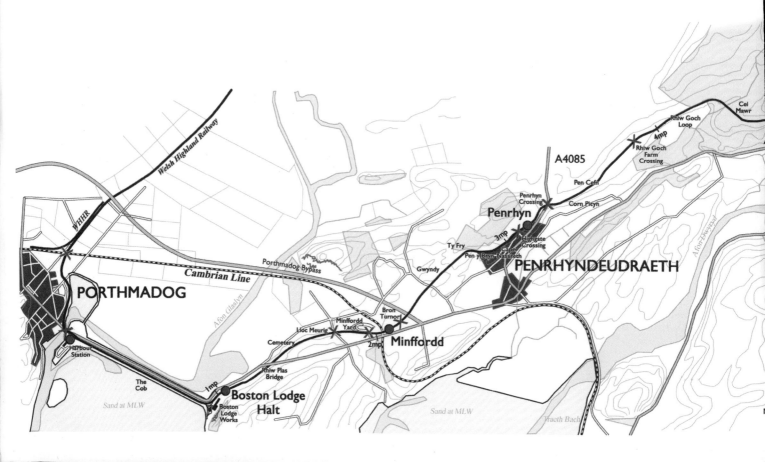